The Coinage of the Bombay Presidency

A study of the records of the EIC

By

Dr. Paul Stevens

Honorary Research Associate, Heberden Coin Room, Ashmolean Museum, Oxford University

Contents

Acknowledgements

My particular thanks go to Shailendra Bhandare for much advice and encouragement in the pursuit of knowledge about Indian numismatics and, specifically, for drawing most of the Persian legends.

Stan Goron, who has been a constant source of inspiration and help in my numismatic endeavours, read through the manuscript and corrected many errors.

Jan Lingen kindly provided the table of concordance between the AD, AH and RY dates as well as giving me many new ideas.

Preface

The purpose of the present book is to add much more information about the coins of the Bombay Presidency from the records of the East India Company, held in the British Library in London. Whilst Pridmore must have drawn on these records, he did not provide any references, which has meant that checking his sources has been very difficult. In addition there seem to be areas in the records that he overlooked.

The book has been structured into eleven chapters and each chapter into a summary followed by a detailed review of background information. There are extensive quotes from the records so that much of the work is the actual primary source material, and this is combined with information obtained from looking at the coins themselves. In some places the data has been interpreted to draw particular conclusions. Whether these are correct or not, is left to the reader to judge. It is also worth stating that the records have not been blindly copied, but the capitalisation and punctuation have sometimes been altered to enhance the meaning or clarity of the text. Some words, particularly Indian words, are difficult to read in the actual text itself and the meanings of some of these words require translation and I have tried to add this in the appropriate places. Because of the cursive script used in the records, it is entirely possible that I have made some mistakes in copying some of the words that are unfamiliar to me, and this may account for my inability to find them in dictionaries, particularly Hobson Jobson[1].

Photographs and Pictures

Since, in my view, the importance of illustrations is to reveal the features of the coins, and since actual-size photographs often do not show sufficient detail, all of the pictures are enlarged unless otherwise stated.

---

[1] Yule, Sir Henry, Hobson-Jobson: A glossary of colloquial Anglo-Indian words and phrases, and of kindred terms, etymological, historical, geographical and discursive. New ed. edited by William Crooke, B.A. London: J. Murray, 1903. Also at http://dsal.uchicago.edu/dictionaries/hobsonjobson/

The Arrival of the English in India[2]

Throughout the sixteenth century the English sought to emulate both the Portuguese with their monopoly of trade with the east, and the Spanish with their control of the gold and silver of South America. Initially they chose not to challenge directly these monopolies by force, but to find a new way to achieve a similar endpoint. Thus the century saw an extensive search for the North West Passage to the Indies and the "discovery" of Labrador and the colonisation of Virginia. The sixteenth century also saw the beginnings of the formation of companies holding monopolies of trade between England and certain other markets, and it was a company of this type, formed on 31st December 1600, that was granted a charter for the exclusive right to trade with the East Indies. The first two voyages did not go to India but to the islands of the East Indies, but the third expedition in 1607, was sent to explore the opportunities for trade in the Arabian Sea and specifically to call, *inter alia*, at Surat in Gujerat on the west coast of India. One of the ships of the small fleet of this third voyage, commanded by a captain Hawkins, eventually reached Surat on 28th August 1608.

However, they were not the first Englishmen to visit India. This achievement is attributed to a certain Mr. Stevens, who had joined a party of Portuguese to visit the famous Jesuit establishment in Goa during the 1570s. Hawkins, though, considered himself far more than a mere visitor, and styled himself 'the King of England's Embassador' and in this capacity he found himself faced with tremendous odds in trying to establish a factory at Surat. Not the least of these difficulties came from the Portuguese, who rightly recognised the danger to their monopoly, and twice tried to assassinate him before he finally determined to travel overland to the Moghul court at Agra and gain permission from the Emperor himself. However, although Hawkins managed to ingratiate himself with the Emperor Jahangir, his ambition to establish a trading post at Surat was eventually thwarted by a combination of the Portuguese Jesuits and Mukarrab Khan, the official in charge of the ports of Gujerat.

The English continued to try to establish themselves in Surat but, up until 1635, the Portuguese continued to challenge these attempts both by undermining the English representations to the local Indian Powers, and by directly engaging the English ships in pitched battle. Initially the English could only base themselves near to Surat at a place named Swalley Hole, but the twelfth voyage, commanded by Thomas Best, arrived at Surat in 1612 and finally succeeded in obtaining the necessary permission to establish a factory, possibly because the Moghuls were beginning to realise that the English were seriously capable of challenging Portuguese naval power. In 1635 the Portuguese and the English signed, in Goa, a treaty that gave the English access to Portuguese trading posts all around the Arabian Sea, including the posts along the west coast of India. One of the islands controlled

---

[2] Keay J (1991), The Honourable Company: A History of the English East India Company. HarperCollins

by the Portuguese was Bombay, and this island was ceded to Charles II as part of the dowry for his marriage to the Portuguese princess, Catherine of Braganza in 1661. Charles then leased Bombay to the East India Company in 1668.

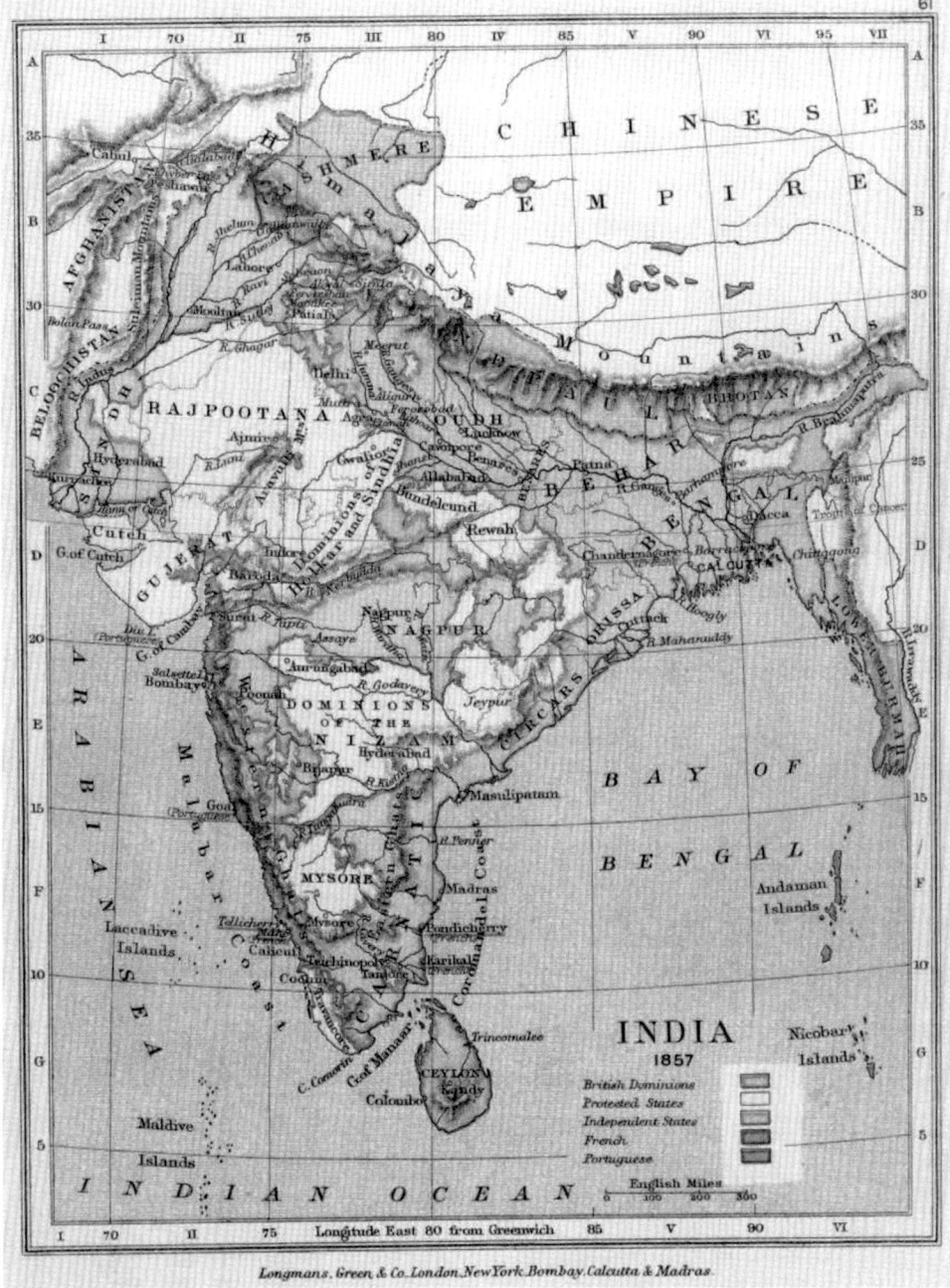

India 1857. Darker gray areas are parts of British India

The seat of government of the EIC did not transfer to Bombay, from Surat, until 2nd May 1687[3]. Up until that time, the English were obliged to have their bullion coined in the local mint at Surat and pay the appropriate charges (see Surat section).

By 1688 Bombay had expanded to a population of 60,000 and, having moved his headquaters to Bombay, Sir John Child took a very aggressive stance against allcomers. He began seizing Moghul shipping and by mid-1688 had fourteen 'prizes' lying in Bombay harbour. He then seized a fleet of barges belonging to Sidi Yakub and dismissed the idea that this would prompt a military reply from the Sidi. Consequently Bombay castle was completely unprepared for the arrival of the Sidi's army of 20,000 men, who landed unopposed on 14th February 1689. Bombay was besieged for the whole year until, in December, two factors were sent to seek terms. The Emperor demanded that all plundered goods and ships should be returned and an indemnity of 150,000 rupees should be paid. Furthermore he demanded that the Company should understand that they would have to obey his commands in the future and should not be forgetfull of this fact. John Child died during the negotiations, a fate that had befallen most of the English population of Bombay with only about 60 of the 700-800 people surviving. From this early beginning Bombay grew first into a major trading port and then into a Presidency covering large parts of western India.

---

[3] Keay J. (1991), The Honourable Company: A History of the English East India Company. HarperCollins

Bombay Fort 1803 (mint building shown with arrow)

Chapter 1 – Bombay Mint 1672 to 1717

Summary

The coinage of Bombay at the time of transfer from King Charles to the Company was Portuguese in nature and consisted of silver xerafins, copper pice, and tin bazaruccos, all of which were manufactured outside of Bombay itself. Sixteen bazarucco's went to one pice and 23¼ pice to one xerafin. In the books of the EIC the accounts continued to be kept in the old Portuguese way in xerafins (valued in the Company's books at 20 pence sterling), divided into 3 larins with each larin being reckoned at 80 reis (often spelt reas) and this continued for many years. However, most trade was carried out with the mainland and the coins in use there were gold mohurs and silver rupees, although other coins were also in use. Pridmore cites the use of a coin called a *Mahmudi* (with a sterling value of about one shilling), apparently issued by the Raja of Malher in Baglana, a place about 70 miles from Surat[4].

By 1672, the EIC had determined to issue coins from a mint in Bombay. Their plan was to issue gold, silver, copper and tin coins but no gold coins were ever produced. The copper and tin coins proved successful and continued to be issued, pretty much unchanged, throughout the period under review. However, the silver coins proved unsatisfactory because they were not widely accepted outside of Bombay Island, apparently because of their foreign appearance. In 1674 a suggestion was made to produce silver rupees in the name of Charles II but in the Moghul-style (i.e. with Persian writing). Although patterns were produced, the coin was not put into full-scale production. None of these coins is known to have survived. During the reign of James II, a few Moghul-style rupees seem to have been produced because a few of these survive and during the reign of William and Mary, in the 1690s, yet more Moghul-style rupees were minted, but the Emperor, Aurangzeb, forced the EIC to stop production. Thus the major coins produced during this period were copper and tin (though very few tin coins survive) while most silver coins are very rare.

Bombay Mint – 1668 to 1671

Bombay Island was given to Charles II in 1661 but was actually handed over by the Portuguese in 1665. In 1668 the island was leased to the EIC at a rent of £10 per annum.

Just before this happened, Henry Gary, the King's representative on the island, had suggested that a mint should be established. In 1668 he wrote[5]:

There is a very greate need for small money heere, if it agrees with your Lordships good liking that I may have procured a liberty to make and stampe a sort of copper and tinne money which is very requisite for these parts. They call it pice whereof 13¾ make a shilling: that of tin are called bazarookoes, whereof 16 goes for one pice. There being much cozenage

---

[4] Foster (1911). The English Factories in India 1634-1636. Clarendon Press, Oxford, p. 224.

[5] Henry Gary 1668. Quoted by Foster (1927). The English Factories in India 1668-1669. Clarendon Press, Oxford, p. 52.

used both in the one and the other. I shall therefore humbly recommend to your Lordship that a certaine quantity of copper bee sent hither in plates, such as the company use to send to Suratt. I doe assure your Lordship it will make some additions to His Majesties treasurie and revenue

However, Gary's attempt came to nothing because of the transfer of the island from the King to the EIC.

On 6th October 1668[6], a report to London included the statement:

"It would be expedient also to procure a stamp for copper and tinne for small money of exchange, which is much wanted on this island…"

This was followed a short time later with a request to coin gold, silver, copper and tin[7]:

"The next is a licence to coyne moneys that may pass currant upon the island, both silver gold and a small coyne of copper and tynne for exchange; which we designe shall somewhat agree with the present vallue, but not to be the same".

The Directors in London agreed to the proposal in a letter to Surat on 22nd February 1671[8] [9]:

"We doe thinck it convenient for us to have a coyne of our owne there (Bombay). We would have you therefore consider of such a coyne, soe as it bee not our King's Majesties or any stampe resembling the same, and of such sorts as will best suite with the traffique and exchange of the country, both in bigger and lesser speties. And if you shall find it necessary to have for change a small sort of copper coin, let it apeare to be what it is; but what you shall coyne of gold and silver, let it have an intrinsique value as to what it is stampt for, that it may be to our honnor and the begetting and preserving the esteeme thereof. But wee would not have you coyne any copper or other inferiour mettall before you coyne gold or silver, for to begin with that would be a disparagement to us."

Silver – 1672

Although there was an intention to start making coins at the beginning of 1672, a decision was made not to proceed at that time and the silver set aside for that purpose was disposed of[10]:

The [Ingott] of silver which was formerly ordered in Council to be employed in the mint to make money is ordered to be disposed of by reason there is as yet no conveniency for a mint to be settled.

---

[6] Pridmore p. 68.

[7] Pridmore p. 68.

[8] Fawcett Sir C. (1936). The English Factories in India Vol. 1 (The Western Presidency). Clarendon Press, Oxford, pp. 52-53. 1672.

[9] Foster W (1906), A Note on the First English Coinage at Bombay, Numismatic Chronicle, Fourth Series, Vol. IV, pp. 351-357.

[10] Bombay Factory Records, IOR G/3/1. 1672 p. 16. Meeting of Council 22nd January 1672.

At the time a Mr Richard Adams was in charge of the mint[11]:

Mr Richard Adams overseer of the mint having executed that office for above the space of one month past

In September of 1672 a decision was taken to use one chest of silver bullion for coining. No gold was available[12]:

The Company haveing ordered us to coine money for Bombay, and to begin with gold or silver, and haveing sent noe gold, wee have thought good to Keepe one chest of ingots to coine into money for the use of this island. The chest taken on shoar is No 109 wherein are 5 ingotts of silver, which as it increases our stock here wee shall be enabled to remit yet more money to you

Similar information was contained in a despatch to the Directors in London, dated the 7th October 1672, which refers to copper pice and silver coins[13]:

"Of the copper which we have taken ashoare… what we have not sold we intend to coyne into pice for the use of your island, which we hope will also turne you a proffit. Of the treasure sent on these shipps… the ingots we intend, God willing, to convert into a silver coyne of your owne, according to your order."

In November 1672, there was a reference to John Child being given charge of the mint and the entry goes on to say[14]:

"…which is to be erected in the East India House for coining pice and buzerooks until a convenient room in the Fort can be fitted for coining silver."

The Consultations of the 29th November record the names selected for the several denominations. The gold coin was to be called the Carolina; the silver coin the Anglina; the copper coin the Copperoon; and the tin coin the Tinny[15].

As far as the tin coins go, although called tinny by Aungier, they were more popularly known as buzerook or bujeruk, a name that originated with the Portuguese. Pridmore believed the name to be derived from BAZARRUCCO (=small money or bazaar money).

A report dated 21st December 1672 informed London of the establishment of a mint and forwarded specimens[16]:

---

[11] Bombay Factory Records, IOR G/3/1. 1672 p. 21 Meeting of Council 4th February 1672.

[12] Surat Consultations, IOR G/36/106. p. 136. Letter from Bombay to Surat, 28th September 1672.

[13] Foster W (1906), A Note on the First English Coinage at Bombay, Numismatic Chronicle, Fourth Series, Vol. IV, pp. 351-357.

[14] Fawcett Sir C. (1936). The English Factories in India Vol. 1 (The Western Presidency). Clarendon Press, Oxford, pp. 52-53. 1672.

[15] Fawcett Sir C. (1936). The English Factories in India Vol. 1 (The Western Presidency). Clarendon Press, Oxford, pp. 52-53. 1672.

[16] Foster W (1906), A Note on the First English Coinage at Bombay, Numismatic Chronicle, Fourth Series, Vol. IV, pp. 351-357.

"In pursuance of your order we began to erect a mint for silver, copper and tyn; and had reserved some barrs of silver and cruzadoes for that effect; but Mr Mathew Gray and your Councell of Surratt lamentably complayning of your great debt at interest, that your creditors demand eagerly for their money, which they had not to pay them (in regard your cloth and other goods would not sell), and earnestly desireing assistance from us to supply them what we could, we therefore after due consideration determined to send all our treasure away for Surratt towards the payment of your debts, reserveing onely just soe much as should begin the mint, in order to the carrying it on the more successfully next year. We have also begun the mint for copper and tynn. Which is of great and absolutely necessary use for your island. Wee began first with silver, having received noe gold of yours this year. We had often serious debate, and tooke the best advice we could of the banians, sheriffs and others that could direct us; and have concluded that the gold and silver coyne shall be exactly in weight and finenesse equall with the rupee of Surratt; the copper also equal with the pice of Surratt. The reason is because they will vend the more currantly in the neighbouring countrys of the Portuguese, Sevagee, and Decan, and in time probably pas as currantly in payments, which will be a notable accommodation to the trade of the island, if we can bring it soe about. As to the stampe, we have concluded that for the gold, silver and copper to be as followeth: On the one side the Honourable Company's arms, with this inscription within a circle incloseing the armes: Honorabilis Societas Anglicana Indiarum Orientalium, writ in short; on the other side, within the inward circle is engraven Moneta Bombayae Anglicani Regiminis Anno Septimo, and within the outward circle is inscribed the words: A Deo Pax et Incrementum.

The names of the coyne are thus: the gold is called Carolina, in remembrance of our Kings Majesty, and weighs [blank]: The silver is called Anglina, from the name of our nation, and weighs 11½ mas; the copper coyne is called Coperoon and weighs [blank] tolas 1.2 mass; the tin is called tinny. We designedly give the coynes English names, for in this and all things else we endeavour to ensure the people to and teach them the English tongue; and to disuse the Portuguese as much as we can, which will be a worke of long time, because these people have bin long accustomed thereunto.

Eleven tynnys make one copperoon; forty-eight copperoons make an Anglina; which is the currant rate at present between the rupee, pice and buzerook. This mint, when thoroughly settled, we hope will raise a considerable advance to the revenue…

We send your Honors tenne pieces of silver, tenne pieces of copper, and tenne of tinn for your satisfaccion, desireing that if you do not like the stampe, that you would please to signifie how you would have it altered, and we shall conforme accordingly."

Interestingly, Surat only sent 10 of each denomination to London although Bombay had asked that they should send twenty of each[17]:

We have sent you per Capt Anderson several [pieces] of our new coine money which ye Honble Company ordered us to make (Viz) thirty Anglinas, thirty copperoons & thirty tinnys, twenty of each whereof we desire you to send for England in two ships, ten in each ship. The remainder you may dispose of as you please among your friends…

From these extracts it is clear that although the Company's ships arrived at Bombay in September, they had brought out no gold, and most of the silver was used in Surat to repay loans taken out at high interest. Because of this, no gold was ever struck in the design of the Carolina described above and very few silver coins.

Pattern Anglina – 1672

Pattern Anglina 1672

In 1672 a trial or pattern coin with the Company's arms appears to have been produced, possibly submitted to the Company's President, Gerald Aungier (GA), and Council. The British Museum seems to have the only example of this and its exact status is uncertain.

Anglina & Half Anglina – 1672

The dating system used on these silver coins and the copper coins derives from the fact that Bombay was handed over to the English in February 1665 and the years were numbered from that time. Thus year seven – Ao7o (Anno Septimo) – was 1672[18].

---

[17] Surat Factory Records, IOR G/36/106. 1673 p. 54. Letter from Bombay dated 1st January 1673 (1672 in old terms).

[18] Parsons, H.A. The Bombay Pice Struck by the English East India Company during the reign of Charles II. BNJ 20 (1929/30) pp. 251-259.

Anglina 1672

Pridmore calculated that the total coinage would have amounted to about 9,700 anglinas, based on the estimated weight of the single chest of silver that was used for production and the assumption that no other coinages were undertaken.

Pridmore could not trace a reference to the issue of a half anglina for 1672. He states that the only known coin has the appearance of a much later striking, and further evidence is required to confirm its authenticity.

Anglina – Interlinking Cs – 1674

The Moghul Governor of Surat and the Portuguese both opposed the circulation of the 1672 anglinas. The Governor of Surat objected on the grounds that the coins were neither as fine, nor as heavy as the Moghul rupees and he would not, therefore, allow them to pass current. The official weight was approximately 171 grains troy although Pridmore recorded weights of actual specimens as slightly higher and nearly corresponding to the weight of the contemporary Surat rupee. It is more likely that the coins were not acceptable because of their foreign appearance rather than the weight and fineness, which were probably not really a problem. The Portuguese objected on the grounds that the inscription on the coins did not include a reference to the King or Queen of England.

Anglina, 1674

In response to that criticism, two new patterns were prepared in 1674. On one of these patterns, the reverse design bears the inter-linking C monogram referring to Charles and Catherine, King and Queen of Great Britain. There was a suggestion from President Aungier that the new coins should be named 'ingresses' (= English) rather than anglinas because this had become the more common name for the coins of the 1672 issue. This name does not seem to have stuck, at least in the records[19].

[.....] by a former consultation the stamp appointed to be made for the coyne to be minted on Bombay was ordered to have the Companys arms with their title on one side and on the other side within the circle Moneta Bombay Anglii Regiminis Anno 7o and without the words A Deo Pax et incrementum, and whereas by observation we have taken notice that the Portuguese our neighbours were not well afforded therewith because there was nothing in the stampe relating to the King or Queen [wheresofor] in regards that this island [...] for trade and provisions with the Portuguals country and [...] to let our money pass current in their country

That the coin to be made on this Island of Bombay be as follows:

On the one side the Companys arms with their title and on the other side two CC [...] with a crown over them and a cross upon the top of the crown. The two C representing the first two letters of the names of their Majesties and without the circle A Pax Deo et incrementum and that they be not called Anglinas as formerly but Ingresses in regards that word is much more common with all sorts of people than Anglinas

Moghul-Style Silver Coins in the name of Charles II

In July 1674, the Bombay Council again considered the coinage and suggested that a new pattern be prepared and sent to Surat[20]:

.....The President taking into consideration that it might be justly supposed that the new coyne lately ordered to be made will not pass in other [places], notwithstanding it is the full weight of a Surat rupee and of the same fineness of assay in regards it does not resemble the ordinary coins there, made a proposal to the Council for the making of another coin (Viz) to make the silver of the same fineness and weight and in the same form of a Surat rupee and on the one side to have stamped in the Persian characters Charles the second King of England etc and on the other side likewise in the same character Money of Bombay. Which proposal the President desired the Council to consider of seriously whether it might not give any disgust to the Moghuls or be of any prejudice to the Companys affairs.

Ordered that a stamp of the said coyne be made and that some [...] stamped [...] be sent up to the Deputy President and Council at Surat to have [....] and in regards it is an affair of weighty consideration to desire them seriously to consider whether it will be more hindrance or obstruction to the Company's trade in Surat by giving any disgust to the Moghull

The Surat Consultations of the 6th August 1674 record a discussion about the appropriateness of the use of Persian. The Council considered that the Company had as much right to use Persian, as had the Emperor and that he should have no cause for taking offence. They did suggest that the proposed inscription of 'Charles the

---

[19] Bombay Factory Records, IOR G/3/1. 1674 p. 49. Meeting of Council 12th June 1674.
[20] Bombay Factory Records, IOR G/3/1. 1674 p. 64. Meeting of Council 17th July 1674.

Second, King of England', might subject the Company to a writ of praemunire as having too close a reference to King's coin.

The Bombay Council considered Surat's response to the patterns in September 1674[21]:

Whereas formerly it was ordered that a new coyne should be made stamped on the one side in Persian characters, Charles the 2nd King of England etc, and on the other side, Money of Bombay, some [pieces?] of which coyne were stamped here and sent up to Surat to the Deputy President etc to have their [view] thereof, who have just advised the President that the [said?] title of His Majesty is too low and will not be esteemed in this country, whereupon the President proposed to the Council for the making of a coyne stamped on one side instead of Charles the 2nd King of England, Charles Shaw Inglestan and on the other side the same as before, which proposal was approved of referring the same to the Honble Company to have their orders concerning it before […] any further […] on […] the coyne and to advise the Deputy President and Council thereof in the meantime that we may know their opinions thereof

President Aungier was doubtful both about the King and the Emperor's views and referred the matter to London in a letter dated Bombay, 16th December 1674[22].

…We hoped you would have given us some positive instructions touching ye setting of a mint for gold and silver on Bombay, without which we cannot proceed. We have had several debates and arguments concerning another sort of stamp, under a Persian character, which we hope in time will pass as well as rupees and without loss or vattao [batta?] on ye maine, but it being an affair of noe mean concerne wee concluded to suspend our further proceeding & discourse thereon till we were strengthened with more sufficient power from you…

No further correspondence concerning this matter has been found and no examples of the patterns produced at Bombay have yet been identified.

Counterfeit Silver Coins – 1674

By 1674, counterfeit silver coins were beginning to appear and action was taken to try to prevent this[23]:

…and as false rupees had been discovered, a proclamation was issued, strictly forbidding the importation of any false coin or the counterfeiting of the Company's coin on pain of death

Silver – 1675

By 1675 there appears to have been a growing need to obtain money to pay the

---

[21] Bombay Factory Records, IOR G/3/1. 1674, p. 97. Meeting of Council 28th September 1674.
[22] Bombay Factory Records, IOR G/3/7. 1674, p. 11. Letter from Bombay to London, dated 16th December 1674.
[23] Bombay Consultaations. IOR G/3/1, pp. 25-26, 25th July, 1674.

garrison of the fort. The silver mint was therefore re-opened[24]:

"…A mint house had been built and the coinage of copper and tin continued"

On 13th November 1675 four chests of silver were taken to the mint and turned into coins[25]. These first coins were produced from dies made the previous year (1674) and, at least the first few produced, were probably therefore the interlinked Cs type. However, at the end of 1675 new patterns were prepared and more coins produced and the coins struck were probably of the later PAX DEO design (see below)[26].

"…On the arrival of the Unicorn, four chests of silver, worth Rs 40,000, were taken off her, but the bullion could not at once be converted into money and further bills for Rs 6,000 had to be drawn on Surat. Gifferd explained that they were so indebted to the Modi [House-Steward] that, without his help, he could not supply provisions for the island, and they were in great straights for money to pay the soldiers. Aungier asked him to avoid drawing any more bills, in view of the need for husbanding resources at Surat and of the arrival of a stock of silver. Financial exigencies thus forced the Council, with the approval of Aungier, to coin the bullion into rupees. A stamp made by the Modi in the previous year was first of all used for this but at the end of the year Giffard submitted two other patterns, saying he proposed to use one with PAX A DEO on it, pending the orders of the Surat Council, for the purpose of coining Rs 2,000 for the next garrison pay-day"

Two New Patterns Sent to Surat. Pax Deo Type

On 31st December 1675 three types of rupee were sent to Surat for the consideration of the council there. One of these was described as the 'old' type, which presumably referred to the interlocking Cs type, but the other two were new designs. Twelve of one and nine of another were sent to Surat[27].

Wee have sent up by Capt Norgrave 24 Rupees, 12 of one sort of a new stamp & 9 of ye other & 3 of ye old and desire to know which of the 3 you best approve of. That of ye PAX A DEO in ye middle is most likt here. That with MONITA BOMBAYS hath to many letters in it for ye middle which makes it not look so well as [they] think, we must be forced to coyne two thousand to pay our souldiers this pay day which we think to be that of PAX A DEO. If not approved of they are quickly called in & if carried off of ye Island, trouble will be saved…

---

[24] Fawcett Sir C. (1936). The English Factories in India Vol. 1 (The Western Presidency). Clarendon Press, Oxford, p. 129.

[25] Pridmore p. 105.

[26] Fawcett Sir C. (1936). The English Factories in India Vol. 1 (The Western Presidency). Clarendon Press, Oxford, p. 139. 1675

[27] Bombay Factory Records, IOR G/3/7. 1676, p. 4, Letter from Bombay to Surat, dated 31st December 1675

PAX DEO rupee

As can be seen, the Deputy Governor of Bombay stated that he intended to prepare 2,000 of the Pax Deo (although called PAX A DEO in the extract) type ready for the next garrison pay day.

In a letter from Surat to Bombay dated the 8th February 1676[28], President Aungier replied:

Multiplicity of business hath made us hitherto forget to write to you o[r] opinion about the coynes you sent us wee like well of the new stamp with PAX X DEO on one side and the Comp[as] armes on y[e] other side, but not with the Comp[as] mark

and would have you proceed in minting y[e] remaining silver of the same stamp, and the copper we would also have of the same stamp

From this it would seem that one type of new coins was the well-known PAX DEO rupee whilst the other had the PAX DEO design on one side with the Company's balemark on the other. No examples of this second pattern are known to have survived.

Folkes[29] (1763), discussed another coin but it does not seem to match the one described above. Folkes stated:

"…had again only the Company's arms on one side and Arabic or Indian characters on the other".

No such coin is known at present so it is possible that other patterns were also prepared at various times.

---

[28] Pridmore p. 105.
[29] Folkes M., (1763), Tables of English Silver and Gold Coins, p. 113.

The weight of the rupee was increased to one tola, (report dated 27th March 1677[30]) probably in response to the criticism of the Governor of Surat of the 1672 issue (see above).

Thus, the Pax Deo type rupee was approved for issue by President Aungier in February 1676 and possibly continued to be minted until about 1692, although the output must have been small because the coins are now very rare. Pridmore states that many varieties exist, although he did not record them. The comparative rarity of the coins makes the identification and recording of the varieties difficult but a start has been made in the recently published catalogue[31].

Half anglinas were also issued between 1676 and 1692. They appear to have been struck from anglina dies onto smaller flans. There is a possibility that they are anglinas cut down in size for collectors, but Pridmore considered from their appearance that they are genuine. The current author concurs with that view.

Rupee of Bombaim – 1677/78

In considering the style of the coins to be produced during the early part of the 1670s, the President and Council at Bombay had been concerned over their rights to issue coins in the name of the English king (see above). However, in London, Bombay was considered to be held as a sovereign territory of the King of England and was in fact considered to be part of 'the Manor of East Greenwich in the County of Kent' just outside London[32]. King Charles was asked to grant the necessary permission to issue coins in his name in Bombay, and did so on 5th October 1676[33]:

"…AND also of our farther especiall grace vertue knowledge and meere motion We doe by these presents for us our Heires and Successors give and graunt unto the said Governor and Company of Merchants of London Trading into the East Indies and their Successors full and free liberty power and Authority from tyme to tyme and at all tymes hereafter within the Port and Island of Bombay in the East Indies and the Precincts and Territoryes thereof and there unto belonging to Stampe and Coyne or Cause to bee stamped and Coyned moneys of Gold Silver Copper Tynne or Lead or in any mixt mettall Compounded or made up of them or any of them to bee Currant within the said Port and Island Fort and Townes and Precincts and Territories thereof. And also in all the Islands Ports Havens Cittys Creeks Townes and Places whatsoever within the East Indies Expressed mentioned or contayned in our severall Charters or Letters Patents herein before mentioned or either of them with such Impression and Inscription there upon to bee called or known by the Name or Names of Rupees Pices and Budgerookes."

---

[30] Pridmore p. 105.
[31] Stevens (2016). The Coins of the English East India Company. Spink.
[32] Keay J., (1991), The Honourable Company. Harper Collins.
[33] Pridmore pp. 105-106.

The rupee of Bombaim. London striking

Having legalised the situation, the officers of the Company in London went on to have a rupee coin designed, and patterns prepared (at the Royal mint?) and on 21st February 1677 the design was shown to the Court of Directors[34]:

"on one side is inscribed 'the rupee of Bombay', with two roses underneath, and, in the circle '1677, by authority of Charles the Second', and on the other side His Majesty's arms, and, in the circle 'King of Great Britain, France and Ireland.'"

The King approved the design.
A further entry dated 23rd January 1678 records[35]:

"The Surat Committee having desired Lord Berkeley to show the pattern of a stamp for rupees to be coined at Bombay to the King for his approbation, and to ascertain whether any inscription should be put at the edge of the said coins. His Lordship this day reports to the Court that His Majesty approves of the design for the rupee, but leaves it to the Company to decide whether any or what inscription should be put on the edge of the coin."

Having gained the approval of the king, the next step in the process was to get the coins into production in Bombay. Accordingly, on 20th March 1678[36], George Bowers was employed to make twenty or forty pair of stamps for coining rupees and to obtain engines, and other necessaries for coining rupees at Bombay. For all this he was paid £126. The Company also employed an expert coiner from the London mint, named John Morrice, to go out to Bombay to get production started. Two new factors named Annesley and Cooke, who were due go to Bombay at the same time, were also given some training.

Surat had been notified that the king had granted the right to strike coins in his name at Bombay on 17th March 1677[37]. They decided to abandon the use of the names for the coins agreed in 1672 (Carolina, Anglina, Copperoon and Tinny) and to stick

---

[34] Sainsbury E.B., (1938). A Calendar of the Court Minutes etc of the East India Company 1677-1679. p xii
[35] Pridmore p. 106.
[36] Pridmore p. 106.
[37] Pridmore p. 106.

to the more popular names then in use (Mohur, Rupee, Pice and Buzerook. See extract above).

All of these arrived at Bombay during the second half of 1678 and work began on the new coinage in October on a chest of silver delivered from Swalley Marine in Surat. However, the work soon ran into difficulties as seen from a report from President Oxinden to the directors[38]:

We have received the coining engine and stamps etc, there unto belonging and have made tryal thereof, but to our admiration (surprise) and sorrow cannot with all our skill and experiments make a clear impression therewith – the words proved blurred and imperfect, as well as the Royall Arms. All possible industry hath been used to find the reason of its deficiency without the desired effect. John Morrice to our great greife deceased within a weeke after his landing, being a person addicted to drink strong drink... Had it pleased God to have spared him, he would have set all things in their right postures but Annesley and Cooke know little thereof, so that we allmost despaire of bringing the coine to its due perfection. We suppose the fault to lye in the stamps, which in our opinion are too shallow cutt

and he asked for dies which were more deeply engraved[39].

Notwithstanding all our endeavours we cannot possibly make the mint that the Honble Company sent out, so serviceable as we desire and they expect, for besides the unhandiness of these people wee cannot make a clear impression with it but in that we will prove defective, whole words being imperfect & blurred as well as part of the Royal Arms

This was effectively the end of this attempt to strike English-designed coins using machinery at Bombay. The Company did send out further machinery and another expert named Robert Smithas in 1680-81[40], but his appointment as mint and assay master on a salary of £60 p.a., annoyed Surat because of the cost. Whether any coins were produced as a result of his arrival is not known, but by February 1682 he was employed as an armourer and was discharged and returned to England at the end of 1683[41].

Rupees, of the design described above, exist dated 1677 and 1678. The 1677 coins are well struck and show a clear impression. They were the patterns prepared in England for the Court of Directors and the King. The coins dated 1678 come in two standards of quality.

Those of high quality are very rare and are probably trial strikings prepared in England before the people and machinery were sent to India. Those of lower quality and only slightly less rare are probably those struck in Bombay late in 1678. It is very doubtful that any of these poor quality coins were put into circulation. They were

---

[38] Pridmore p. 107.

[39] Bombay Factory Records, IOR G/3/8. 1678, p. 59. Letter from Bombay to Surat Council dated 4th December 1678.

[40] Pridmore p. 107.

[41] Pridmore p. 107.

probably sent back to London to demonstrate the problems that were encountered in Bombay.

The rupee of Bombay. Bombay trials

It also seems likely that experiments were made in Bombay to produce a half rupee as well as a rupee denomination because a specimen of half the normal rupee weight has recently come to light. The production of a half rupee should not be unexpected given that halves of the PAX DEO type were produced.

New Mint Master Appointed – 1677

In 1677 Mr John Jessop was appointed to the position of mint master[42]:

Mr John Jessop being [enordered] a factour and there being great want of one to look after the mint, it was:
Ordered that ye charge of ye mint be committed to his care

However, his appointment did not last for long and he was replaced by a Mr Cooke

New Mint Regulations – 1679

In 1679 new mint regulations were adopted[43]:

"The question of improving the mint had been raised in the previous year and in February the Surat Council settled revised regulations for its administration. These laid down that there should be only one mint and that its employees should: 'work jointly in one place without distinction or division'. The proposed reduction of the rate at which the minters were paid was approved. Minting for private persons, which the Council had suspended, was allowed, but the charge for it was raised from one lari to one rupee a maund. Cooke was appointed to take charge of the mint in place of Jessop, who had taken an illicit commission from the coiners as a bribe for overlooking their misappropriation of 92 pounds of broken pieces of copper, worth Xs 300, which they sold to their profit. Such fragments were to be remelted and minted in future. Oxinden and his Council said the orders would be observed, but expressed the view that the charge of one rupee a maund for private minting was too

---

[42] Bombay Factory Records, IOR G/3/2. 1677, p. 12. Meeting of Council 19th October 1677.
[43] Fawcett Sir C. (1954). The English Factories in India Vol. III (Bombay, Surat and Malabar Coast). Clarendon Press, Oxford, pp. 26-27. 1679.

high and would result in stopping this source of revenue. The Surat Council, however, disagreed and confirmed their order on the point…

No coinage of silver is mentioned; and the mint stopped working during the troubles that ensued towards the end of the year."

Pattern Rupee – PAX DEO – 1687

PAX DEO rupee, 1687

Up until 1687, the President and Council of the Bombay Presidency had continued to reside at Surat, with Bombay being gradually developed as a factory. In 1687 the President and Council moved from Surat to Bombay, arriving there on the 2nd of May[44]. From that date, Bombay replaced Surat as the seat of Government for the Presidency.

The 1687 Pax Deo rupees may have been struck to commemorate this event.

Rupee James II

The production of the anglinas, copperoons and bujerooks addressed the needs of the island itself, but trade with the mainland continued to be problematic because the English silver coins were not accepted there. The Council at Bombay and the Court of Directors in London tried very hard to get permission from the Moghul Emperor to strike Moghul-style coins at Bombay. When this failed, it would appear that attempts were made to get the King of England to authorise the production of this type of coin, and in 1686 they did obtain letters patent that have been interpreted as giving them this power. However, Pridmore has argued convincingly that this was not in fact the case. He records that Bruce under the years 1686/87 remarks[45]:

"It having been a subject of fruitless negotiation for many years to obtain permission from the native powers to coin the country money, the Court, in this season, adopted the bolder measure of obtaining authority from the King to institute a mint for the express purpose".

---

[44] Pridmore p. 108.
[45] Bruce, Annals, Vol 2, years 1686/87.

Rupee in the name of James II

Pridmore cites a copy of the charter granting this authority and dated 12ᵗʰ April 1686[46]:

"…and further we do for us and our successors hereby give and grant unto the said Governour and Company their Successors and Assigns for ever full power licence and authority to Coin in their Fort any species of money usually Coined by the Princes of these Countries only and so as the Moneys to be coined by the said Company or their Order be agreeable to the Standards of the said Princes Mints both in weight and fineness. And that they do not make or coin any European Money or Coin whatsoever and that all money or Coins so to be coined as aforesaid and no otherwise shall be currant in any City Town port or place within the Limits of the same Charters or Letters patents."

Pridmore argued that this Charter merely sanctioned the Company to issue coins equal in weight and fineness to those of India, and did not authorise their imitation or forgery. He also cites a letter from the Court of Directors to the Madras Council showing that they, too, understood quite clearly the extent of the power now granted, for they specified that the coins to be struck should have an English design. However, as usual, he gives no reference to the source of this information. Nevertheless, he concludes that there is no evidence to support the assertion that the Company assumed it had obtained the right to copy native coins in their mints.

Whatever the reasons, attempts were made in Bombay to strike Moghul-style coins in the names of James II and then William & Mary, because rupees with the names of these monarchs exist. The use of the English monarch's name may have started in the reign of Charles II although no coins with his name have been found. The Emperor stamped on these attempts, and the production of this style of rupee was stopped in about 1697/98 (see below). The coins in the name of James II are extremely rare.

---

[46] Pridmore p. 107.

Rupee – William & Mary

Rupees are known in the names of William and Mary[47,48].

Moghul-style rupee in the name of William and Mary

Sharma has given a description of some of the events surrounding these rupees[49]. He informs us that during the second half of the seventeenth century, there was an increasing problem of piracy in the Indian Ocean and the Red Sea. Many of these pirates were English and they particularly preyed on ships returning from the Haj. A pirate named Henry Bridgeman (also known as Every) attacked and captured a ship called the Ganj-i-Sawai carrying a cargo of 6 lakhs of rupees and many people returning from the Haj. His capture of the ship and abuse of the people aboard, outraged the Indian princes on the western coast. A writer named Khafi Khan recorded:

"This loss was reported to Aurangzeb, and the newswriters of the port of Surat sent some rupees which the English had coined at Bombay, with a superscription containing the name of their impure King. Aurangzeb then ordered that the English factors who were residing at Surat for commerce should be seized. Orders were also given to Itimad Khan, superintendent of the Port of Surat, and Sisi Yakut Khan, to make preparations for besieging the fort of Bombay….

…After confinement of their factors, the English, by way of reprisal, seized upon every imperial officer, wherever they found one, on sea or on shore, and kept them all in confinement, So matters went on for a long time."

Some time later Khafi Khan became involved in negotiations about this matter and was invited to visit the English 'diwan' (presumably the Governor) in Bombay. Khan described the conversation that he had, particularly about the piratical attack on the ship in the Red Sea and to which he seems to have considered he received a rather devious answer. He then went on to the matter of the rupees and declared:

"What a manifest declaration of rebellion you have shown in coining rupees!"

---

[47] Goron, S, SCMB April 1985.

[48] Gupta, P. L., (1959), Journal of the Numismatic Society of India, 1959, part 2, pp. 174-5.

[49] Sharma S.R. (1934), Mughal Empire in India, parts 2 & 3 pp. 606-611.

The President replied:

"We have to send each year a large sum of money, the profits of our commerce, to our country, and the coins of the King of Hindustan are of short weight, and much debased; and in this island, in the course of buying and selling them, great disputes arise. Consequently we have placed our own names on the coins, and have made them current in our own jurisdiction."

From these events, it is clear that the English at Bombay had begun to strike rupees in the name of their own King in the 1690's. This must refer to the rupees struck in the name of William & Mary.

Rupees of Persian style with the names of William & Mary were struck in 1692, 1693 and 1694. This incurred the displeasure of the Moghul Emperor, Aurangzeb Alamgir, and in 1697/8 the Court issued a statement that the production of coins bearing Persian inscriptions should be discontinued[50].

There must be a possibility that coins exist for 1695 (and 1696?) because the following letter was sent from Bombay to Madras in 1695[51]:

We send you by conveighance 6 of the rupees we coin here desiring by the first conveighance you'll send us the same number of your coins. Also the charge of your mint and what you loose or gain on the invoice of your silver now coined, also what you are allowed percentage for coinage when you coin for other persons & how your rupees pass in the Moghul's country.

The following extract, written in 1698, seems to indicate that the local authorities in Bombay had stopped making coins of this description well before being ordered so to do by London[52]:

We having been at sundry times advised that the Moghul and his Ministers very strictly resented our coining rupees with Persian characters, esteeming it an [encroachment] on said King's prerogative and the President and Council having now as well as formerly wrote us to the same effect, we did write them that we had not coined any this last 18 months and that we would coin no more with such characters, and accordingly resolved that when we did coin any then it should be with ye lattin inscription with which rupees were formerly coined [........] and we also order new stamps should be made ready for ye purpose.

Thurston (1890, p. 24) records that the Company presuming to coin money drew down upon them, in the reign of William III, the high displeasure of the reigning Great Moghul, and Bruce (vol. 3, p. 226) records that in the 1697/98 season:

"as the Moghul had been offended by the Company's coins having Persian characters on them, the Court desired that, for a time, this might be discontinued."

---

[50] Pridmore p. 108

[51] Bombay Factory Records. IOR G/3/11. Book 2, no page numbers. Letter from Bombay to Madras dated 18th April 1695.

[52] Bombay Factory Records, IOR G/3/5. 29th June, 1698. Consultation

An extract from Bruce[53], cited by Pridmore, refers to a report written in the 1705-6 season:

"the Mogul had refused to allow us a mint to be established (at Surat) which had obliged them to form one in Bombay Castle to prevent the stoppage of the circulating coin."

As discussed above, the Bombay mint had been established in 1672, and had struck coins for several years. The extract above implies that by early in the eighteenth century minting activity had ceased and was then revived. This is confirmed by entries in the Bombay records of 1705 [54] authorising the production of tin bujerooks, copper pice and, most interestingly, countermarked foreign silver coins. Furthermore certain buildings were allocated to this task [55], implying that there were no buildings being used as a mint at the time and that coining must have been in abeyance for some time before 1705.

Pridmore refers to yet another petition sent to the Emperor in 1715 (see below)[56] requesting permission to strike the Moghul-style coins at the Bombay mint. In it is the following statement:

That on the island of Bombay belonging to the English, European siccaes are current.

This statement confirms that English style rupees (anglinas?) were still in circulation. What's more, an entry in the records for 1716[57] confirms that rupees were being struck in Bombay at that date, though of what type is unknown.

It was not until 1717 that the Company eventually obtained authority to strike coins of Moghul design but bearing the name of the Moghul Emperor. These are known as 'Munbai' or 'Mumbai' rupees (see next chapter).

Countermarked Foreign Coins – 1705

In 1705, the Bombay Council considered how they might make silver coin available for paying the officers and men of the garrison. They had not got authority to make rupees, and were not to get this until 1717, and presumably the silver coins struck in the 1670s-1690s were becoming scarce. William Aislabie was instructed to open chests of foreign silver coins and estimate the value of the various coins: [58]

And that Wm Aislabie and who else with him in the Treasury, open any chest or chests of coyn'd silver whether Spanish Dollars, French Crownes, Duccatoones or Ryx Dollars carefully casting up the full cost, true value and weight of each specie – to be stampt in figures upon every piece great or small the best method we can at present – effectually supplying a valuable incourageing Coin to Trade to be taken in all paym^ts if not defac't, till obtain

---

[53] Bruce, Annals Vol 3, p. 397.
[54] See under appropriate sections for more details.
[55] Bombay Public Consultations, 24th April 1705. IOR P/341/2 p. 174.
[56] Pridmore p. 111.
[57] Bombay Public Consultations, 5th January 1716. IOR P/341/4.
[58] Bombay Public Consultations, 5th April 1705. IOR P/341/2 p. 163.

authority coyning rupees, to be laid in Council before any stamp or issues be made by the Treasury.

Coins such as Spanish Dollars, French Crowns, Duccatoons, Ryx Dollars or lesser denominations were evaluated[59].

Wm Aislabie and who else with him in the treasury pursuant to a resolution of Coun^cl the 5th instant laying before Coun^cl the true value, Spanish dollars, French crowns, Duccattoons or Ryx Dollars cast up as invoyct out of Eng:- 73 [?] p ounce at 2 [?] 3[?] each rupee makes a dollar of 17½ [?] wt amount to 2 Ru 24 pi and 1 ounce troy 2 R 48 pi intended by said consultation to be proportionably stampt upon each of said species as appears more or less in weight, supplying the present payments till coinage of rupees can be obtained.

At the same meeting it was resolved to stamp the silver coins with their values in rupees and pice so that they could be issued from the treasury:

Resolved and unanimously agreed that Wm Aislabie Esq. and who else with him in the treasury, carefully have stampt one chest or more as the exigency of affairs may now or hereafter require, foreign bullion supplying paym^ts to the Garrison and otherwise, Spanish Dollars, French Crownes, Duccattoones or Ryx Dollars or lesser denomination of said coynes have stampt in English figures 2R 48p, true cost to be esteemed the value for one ounce of silver in said coynes and so in proport' more or less as each peece shall weigh. To be issued out of the treasury for all payments [Gen^tl] that shall be directed in Coun^cl whither to ye Garrison officers and soldiers &c:-

[W^th] said species so stampt if not deminisht in weight shall be rec^d in all payments made into the Public Treasury of this castle but not otherwise whereby the Comp^y will save not being carried into the Mogulls country 3½ p C^t custome from 40 to [90] days time rebate besides the loss as the coynes appears more or less in fineness will all amount to at least fourteen p. Cent

…what defects if any shall casually appear in the currency of said foreigne silver coin stampt 2R 48p p ounce till a stamp can be obtained coyning rupees to be continued as the said proffitt or loss may appear to ye Company wch the treasury is hereby monthly directed laying before the Gen^tl and Coun^cl wth the wet what silver coyn stampt and copper pice coyned as aforesaid.

Whether this instruction was ever put into practice, we do not know. No coins with the specified countermarks are currently known

Copperoons – 1672 to 1673

The design for the hammered copper coinage followed that of the silver and is described in Aungier's report of 1672 (see above). The first coins were struck in 1672, although the majority bearing this date were probably struck in 1673. The early coins

---

[59] Bombay Public Consultations, 24th April 1705. IOR P/341/2 p174

were comparatively well made and show most of the design, but later coins were very crudely struck and complete designs have not yet been fully established.

The official weight was 1 tola 2 mashas (approximately 210 troy grains)[60] and the dates, A°7° or A°9°, represent Anno 7 or Anno 9 = 1672 or 1674.

Copperoon 1672

Coinage of this type of copper pice continued until about 1692. Some of the coins of the first year are well struck and show the full impression but even during this year the quality began to decline and later issues, especially after 1674, fall to a very poor quality. The coins were struck on flans too small for the dies, so the designs are difficult to see and the dates are often missing.

A number of references to the striking of copper coins during the period up to 1677 have been located in the records. By 1673 pice were being exported from Bombay Island to such an extent that a customs charge was levied on this practice[61]:

Ordered that all Pice which are exported from this day off from the Island shall pay 5 per cent customs and whoever shall export any without paying the said duty, what pice soe taken shall be forfeited, one halfe thereof to the Honble Company and the other halfe to the customer and informer.

At the end December 1673, a thousand maunds of copper were coined into pice[62]:

…taken on shore
1000 Maunds Surat Copper for the mint…
…

Copperoons – 1674

The mint continued to produce copper coins profitably during 1674[63]:

The President takes notice what you write concerning supplying you with part of the copper, as to that he replies that he would willingly have done it but for our market here exceeds yours at least 3 or 4 rupees per maund for we mint all our copper here [....] all charges of mintage etc deducted amounts to above 21 Rups per maund, and the President is apt to think copper

---

[60] Pridmore p. 100. See also extract of 1672 above.
[61] Bombay Factory Records, IOR G/3/1. 1673 p. 27 Meeting of Council 7th March 1673
[62] Bombay Factory Records, IOR G/3/1. 1673 p. 1. Meeting of Council 6th December 1673
[63] Bombay Factory Records, IOR G/3/7. 1674, p. 27. Letter from Bombay to Surat, dated 23rd December 1674

at Surratt will not sell (in regard of the great quantity the Dutch have brought) above 18 rupees per maund. Besides we desire you to consider that there is coming in the Golden Fleece & Rainbow 1500 chests more of copper which we have taken all or most part of it on shoare here for the mint, for our pice do not only pass current in Sevagees country, but in all the portugals country…

As can be seen from the above extract, the copper coins were being used widely outside of Bombay itself.

Copper was obtained from various sources, not just England[64]:

…As for copper pice, the merchants have imported some from Surratt & have minted some copper brought from Surratt & from the Bantam ships, whereby the island hath been supplied with small change, but we hope we shall hereafter be better furnished with your own English [blank] & copper from ye South Seas which wil turne you some reasonable profit.

Copperoons – 1675

In January 1675 the Bombay Council reported to Surat that although some small profit could be made in the mint from coining gold and silver, copper could yield a much higher profit and they asked that they should be supplied with copper on a regular basis. Furthermore, Japan copper made more profit then European[65]:

…Ye mint for gold & silver also [when] well settled will turne to some advantage but wee cannot proceed therein without further positive order from you. Ye copper & tinn coin goes current in these parts but that of copper of far greater expense [than] ye tinn and it will be a constant addition to your revenue. If you please to give order that we be yearly supplied with Japan copper from Bantam where if it be cheap bought it will turne to a reasonable profit in your mint, but copper sent from Europe being very deare & chargeable to be cut into small bars, will not turne to account.

Copperoon 1675 (Aº9º). These later coins were very crudely struck

By March all of the available copper had been coined[66]:

---

[64] Bombay Factory Records, IOR G/3/7. 1674, p. 11. Letter from Bombay to London, dated 16th December 1674

[65] Bombay Factory Records, IOR G/3/7. 1675, p. 54. Letter from Bombay to Surat, dated 18th January 1675

[66] Bombay Factory Records, IOR G/3/7. 1675, p. 105. Letter from Bombay to Surat, dated 20th March 1675

Your Japan copper and tin taken on shore here out of your ships Falcon and Mary is all disposed of in your mint to good profit and if we had double the quantity it would yearly vend, for the copper and tinne made here doe pass current in all these places in soe much that if the Golden Fleece and Rainbow doe not arrive in May we shall be in great want of the said commodities for expense of your mint which in time wee doubt not will give a good addition to your revenues especially if the mint of gold and silver were settled as it ought to be. Touching which we expect your Honble further directions.

Presumably the copper arrived as planned because a large coinage of copper pice took place in May 1675[67]:

Ordered that Capt [Testick] deliver to the mint one hundred chests of copper to make pice and that all ye remainder of the copper be made into pice as soon as possible it can

In July an order was issued that labourers were to be paid six pice per day[68]:

That for the encouragement of strong and able labourers that are capable to be employed in merchants business to the number of 200, an order be issued out that they shall be paid six pice a day…

At the same meeting the problem of light-weight pice being produced by the mint workers was discussed and steps were to be taken to prosecute the offenders:

…Managee and Muckancheer, shroffs being employed in the Comps mint to make pice, a large quantity which they made was found to be soe light that they would not pass in the neighbouring parts, whereas they past very current before. Which cheat hath brought upon us much dishonour and the crime being of a very high nature it was thought convenient to take publique notice thereof and so:

Ordered that the Attorney General for the Comp should prosecute them by law at next sessions and that they receive condign punishment according to the merit of their crime

By the middle of 1675 problems were encountered because of the importation of pice from Surat. It was therefore ordered that Surat pice would no longer be allowed to pass current on the island[69]:

The Honble Comp having a great quantity of pice ready made on the Island and cannot put them off by reason of the great quantity of Surratt pice that are imported which supplys the Shroffs it is:

Ordered that noe Surratt pice shall pass on the Island

Half Copperoon – 1675

A half copperoon was reported by Wiggins[70] and is dated Ao Do (1675). This coin is

---

[67] Bombay Factory Records, IOR G/3/2. 1675, p. 75. Meeting of Council 24th May 1675
[68] Bombay Factory Records, IOR G/3/2. 1675, p. 103. Meeting of Council 19th July 1675
[69] Bombay Factory Records, IOR G/3/2. 1675, p. 113. Meeting of Council 23rd July 1675
[70] Wiggins (1984) SNC pp. 288-289.

identical to the copperoon but struck with a smaller die onto a smaller flan of lower weight (7.28g).

Copperoons – 1676

In January 1676, a letter from Surat to Bantam records[71]:

there is a great consumption of copper yearly at Bombay in the mint; our pice and other coin made there, passing in all parts of the Deccan….

In August 1676, Bombay informed Surat that they had retained 329 plates of copper for the mint from the ships arrived that season from Europe[72]:

We have taken on shore 329 copper plates which will be sufficient to keep your mint employed with [w…], there being loss in making ye plates into duganoos and therefore would not take to great a quantity of tinn. We have a great quantity by us

Copperoons – 1677

On 21st November[73], they instructed Bombay to remove what copper they required for the mint from a ship due from China. This vessel arrived at Bombay on 16th February 1677[74], and all the copper, amounting to 157 chests was taken ashore.

A letter from Bombay to London, dated the 19th March, contains the information that[75] copper:

"is very wellcome to us, wee haveing not a barr left to keep yor mint imployed."

On 21st October 1677[76], Bombay informed Surat of the sale of 1,000 mans of copper:

"we have remaining by us a great quantity of coin'. Reference was also made to a small parcel of Barbary copper in cakes, sent out that season by the Directors for trial into coin."

Swedish copper from Europe cost the Company £6-10-0 per cwt, whereas the Barbary copper cost £3-10-0. The result of the trial was notified to Surat in November 1677 [77], when they reported that most of it had been coined and that they had not found any visible difference between the two qualities, but there was a loss of about one third in melting it down.

Copper 1678

During 1678 the mint had severe problems obtaining copper although they did

---

[71] Pridmore p. 102.
[72] Bombay Factory Records, IOR G/3/7. 1676, p. 55. Letter from Bombay to Surat, dated 21st August 1676
[73] Pridmore p. 102.
[74] Pridmore p. 102.
[75] Pridmore p. 102.
[76] Pridmore p. 102.
[77] Pridmore p. 103.

manage to strike a certain number of coins[78]:

"In January 1678, the mint got 625 chests of bar copper from the ship, Advice, but Rolt ordered all the plate copper in hand to be sent to Surat and allowed none of the copper in the Company's frigate Tywan, which arrived early in February, to be landed. The Bombay Council said they were certain the mint would soon be in want of more copper, to the detriment of the Company, which made considerable gain by coining it; but they had to wait till the arrival of the Company's ships in August for a fresh supply. They were then limited to taking only as much as would just suffice to meet the requirements of the mint till the arrival of the China ships. The Surat council also objected to their having landed other copper for sale. In November, Oxinden reported that they had only a small quantity left and asked for orders as to the amount to be taken from the China ships."

Copper Coins – 1679

As predicted by Oxenden, the new regulations introduced in 1679 (see above) greatly reduced, if not stopped, the activities of the mint in 1679[79].

"..A protest by the minters that coining fragments of copper into pice would entail double the ordinary labour was ineffectual. The mint had plenty of copper available, as the Council took 367 chests of it from the Advice, which arrived from Amoy on 20th January. The coining of tin into buzerooks was specially recommended by the Company on account of tin being a home-production, but it is doubtful whether much was done during the year, as in August the Council reported that they had a quantity of it on hand, which they proposed to send to Surat for sale…"

Copperoons – 1680 to 1681

The shortage of copper continued throughout 1681. In March Bombay wrote to Surat[80]:

The copper that we had for the use of the mint is now almost spent. We do therefore desire that you would be pleased to supply us with 300 chests of Japan copper which is much fit for our use as plate and the charge of minting it much lesser, and if we have it not to keep a mint going, that we may have some sort of money to pay our soldiers…

On 7th September they wrote again[81]:

… we would have taken one hundred plates of copper out of the ships but on enquiring find that there is none on board. It was the great want we are in that was of […] have not any

---

[78] Fawcett Sir C. (1954). The English Factories in India Vol. III (Bombay, Surat and Malabar Coast). Clarendon Press, Oxford, pp. 17-19. 1678.

[79] Fawcett Sir C. (1954). The English Factories in India Vol. III (Bombay, Surat and Malabar Coast). Clarendon Press, Oxford, pp. 26-27. 1679.

[80] Bombay Factory Records. IOR g/3/9. Letter from Bombay to Surat, 25th March 1680.

[81] Bombay Factory Records. IOR g/3/9. Letter from Bombay to Surat, 7th September 1680

copper coin on the Island, but are forced to make use of bazarookes, which are not so current a coin nor so satisfactory as the other. Therefore pray supply us with copper as soon as possible, but in a little time it will prove a very great prejudice to the Honble Comp in payments, which we desire to prevent.

And on the 17th September[82]:

…we are in great want of copper…

It appears that the charge levied on people bringing copper to the mint for coinage was so high that no-one had brought any there for some time[83]:

We have often thought to have wrote you about the mint. The settlement made by your orders of 1 rupee per maund of copper for coinage is so large that since it has been, not any has been brought into the mint house to coyne as formerly, and indeed we have thoroughly examined and find it will not be to the advantage of any to coyne copper here, so that the Honble Compy loses by this what they formerly got; and the Island prejudices in the customs etc, which we humbly beg you will consider of and reduce it to the former duty of 1 la [larin?] per maund of copper, which in our judgement will be to the advantage of the Honble Company.

In November 1680 Bombay informed Surat of that a profit of 25 Xerafins could be made in coining copper[84]:

A maund Surat copper makes 1205 Duganees which passes here on the maine at 42 to the
Xerafin is ye money   *Xf 28 2*
Out of which is to be deducted:
The prime cost of a maund of copper will come […]   *Xf 1*
Duty to the Company for minting   *Xf 1 1*
Copper Smith's labour   *Xf 1 1*
                                                             Xf 3 2

                                                             Xf 25

By December 1680, the shortage of copper pice for paying the soldiers, who did not want to be paid in tin coins, forced the Bombay Council to make a decision to buy coins rather than make them[85]:

Having been for several months without copper, by reason thereof no copperoons hath been coined, so that for want thereof the soldiers have been paid in buzerooks at ye same rates, between which coins the difference being 3 Fedeas in a X[erafin] which is a loss to the soldiers and of which they have made complaint att [seberal?] payments, and we having in several letters advised the President and Council of the great want we were in of copper, and the great

---

[82] Bombay Factory Records. IOR g/3/9. Letter from Bombay to Surat, 17th September 1680.
[83] Bombay Factory Records. IOR g/3/9. Letter from Bombay to Surat, 25th October 1680.
[84] Bombay Factory Records. IOR g/3/9. Letter from Bombay to Surat, November 27th 1680.
[85] Bombay Factory Records, IOR G/3/2. 1680, p. 63. Meeting of Council 3rd December 1680.

prejudice the Honble Company would receive if we were not supplied, and none as yet being sent us, it was concluded to prevent any disturbance that might arise by paying the soldiers in Bazarookes that Copperoons should be bought at as cheape rate as possible in which though there will be a loss, yet not so considerable a loss as if they should once be paid all in silver or gold, they having been paif hitherto the one half of their pay in gold or silver att the bazarr rate which is twenty five Fadeas and the other half in copper att twenty one Fadeas, and therefoere should they once be paid their full pay in gold or silver at the rate above mentioned there would be noe likelihood of reducing itt againe as itt is now. Therefore it was unanimously concluded more to the Company's interest to buy Duoonees or Copperoons so long as they were procurable.

By October 1681, the Bombay Council appeared to be thoroughly fed up with the fact that Surat would not, or could not, send them copper for the mint and continued to insist that they charge too high a rate for coinage of copper[86]:

Upon writing about lowering the order of one rupee per maund to the Hon Company for coining copper, we have discoursed so largely in ours of the [benefits], that it's needless to say anything more here. You will there find what benefit the Honble Company may really get by coining copper. Formerly they had a greater gain because their soldier's pay was paid in dugganees at 30 to the Xerafin but now that is over, caused by their orders this year; and now 150 chests of copper will not be sufficient to supply our mint. Without the gains by coining it may persuade you to send a larger quantity.

Copperoons – 1692 to 1703[87]

A slight change to the design of the copper coins was introduced in about 1692, with a second coinage taking place in 1697 and another in 1703. The coins continued to be very poorly made[88].

Copperoon 1703 (3 retrograde)

---

[86] Bombay Factory Records. IOR g/3/9. Letter from Bombay to Surat, 12th October 1681.
[87] Pridmore p. 158.
[88] Bombay Factory Records, IOR G/3/5. 3rd February, 1697. Consultation.

There being a great quantity of copper on ye Island to be sold at 16 rupees per maund, which is a very low price, we did agree that about 46 [cwt?] should be bought on the Right Honble Company's account to be made into pice, by which they would be considerable gainers.

And in March 1697[89]:

The copper that was bought for account of our Rt Honble the master ye 3rd February last being made all into pice and there being 37 [cwt] more on this Island to be sold at 18 rupees per maund, it was agreed that it should be bought and immediately delivered ye mintmen to coyne to make into pice

In October 1703[90]:

…having ordered as much of her copper to be landed & sold here as was vendible immediately at Rs 16 per maund Surat & not […]. But ye price being not procurable, & there being at present very few pice on ye Island & it appearing by ye books that ye Company were considerable gainers by when last coined, It was agreed to take two hundred chests of said copper on shore to be coined into pice.

Single, Half and Quarter Pice – Stars Type – 1705 to 1716

Pridmore attributes certain coins to the period c1704-1716 on the basis of style and weight. From a stylistic viewpoint, the letters in the reverse inscription show the I's of AUSPICIO REGIS and ANGLIAE are barred. This is a feature of late issues of the copperoon type and was adopted to distinguish the letter I from the similar l used to represent the letter L. The weight of the stars pice, at approximately 210 grains, is the same as a copperoon pice. All of these features would suggest that this coinage is a continuation of the earlier issues (c1692-1703). In addition, the coins show the motto Auspicio Regis Et Senatus Angliae, which is taken from the new Company formed in 1698, thus giving the earliest possible date for the coins. The attribution of these coins to this period has now been confirmed from an entry in the records giving authority to make the coins on 24th April 1705[91]. This gives the weight at 33 pice to the pound avoirdupois (= 212 grains = 13.75 grams), and also mentions the production of quarter pice, none of which are known to have survived.

The coins are very crude, and many mis-spellings and bad letter-forms occur. The distinguishing feature is the presence of stars on each side of the orb and cross at the top of the crown

Pridmore examined a few specimens, and noted that the ending of the word ANGLIAE is peculiar. In place of the diphthong there occurs [w]. It is large and prominent. On some specimens the appearance is rather like a countermark, but it is a feature of the die. He suggested that the native engraver had to copy the diphthong

---

[89] Bombay Factory Records, IOR G/3/5. 26th March, 1697. Consultation.
[90] Bombay Factory Records, IOR G/3/5. 7th October, 1703. Consultation
[91] Bombay Public Consultations, 24th April 1705. IOR P/341/2, p. 174.

from script [ae] and because he was not accustomed to English letter forms, the [w] was the final result.

Pice. Stars Type

Stars each side of orb and cross

Letter 'w' at end of ANGLIw

Snartt[92] has attempted to determine the rarity of the various varieties of copperoon. He classified them by the dates found on them and came up with the following proposal:

A 7	R^2
A 8	R^2
A 9	N
A D	S
AnD	S
A D9r	R^3
1703	S

Tinny or Bujerook – 1672

The first type of bujerook introduced in 1672 is not described in the literature, although it is referred to by Aungier in his letter to London with which he enclosed specimens of tin coins (*inter alia*)[93].

Tinny (Bujerook) 1672

However, specimens exist with the numerals 1 over 72 on the reverse. The numerals 72 probably represent the date, [16]72 but the purpose of the 1 above the 72 is more

---

[92] Snartt SCMB (1977) pp. 391-394
[93] Pridmore pp. 101 & 103.

difficult to determine. Pridmore suggested that this refers to the fact that this was the 1st set as opposed to the 1675 issue (see below) which was the 2nd set. This seems somewhat unlikely since to designate something as the first of a series implies that it is known in advance that a second and subsequent set would be issued. It seems unlikely that this happened. Moreover there were other issues in 1673 so the 1675 issue was not the 'second' set except in the sense that it was 10% heavier than the earlier coins. A more likely explanation is that the numeral 1 indicate a denomination of 1 tinny or bujerook. The 1675 coins appear to have a numeral 2 over 75 and since they weigh about twice the 1672 coins, it seems likely that this indicated a denomination of 2 bujerooks. A coin weighing about 4 times the 1672 coin has come to light and seems to have the numeral 4 above the date, thus confirming the meaning of the numeral.

This first type of tinny, dated 1672, is exceedingly rare.

Bujerooks (Tinny) – 1673

By 1673 all of the tin had been coined and a request for more was made to Surat[94]:

That 500 Maunds of tinn be sent for from Surat for the use of the mint in regards all the tinn on the Island is already minted

More tin eventually arrived in December[95]:

…taken on shore…
2000 [maunds] tinn for the mint
…

Bujerooks – 1674

There was no tin available for making the coins by December 1674[96]:

… Of tin we have been totally in want for making of buzrooks…

Tinny or Bujerook – 1675

[94] Bombay Factory Records, IOR G/3/1. 1673 p. 114. Meeting of Council 26th November 1673
[95] Bombay Factory Records, IOR G/3/1. 1673 p. 1. Meeting of Council 6th December 1673
[96] Bombay Factory Records, IOR G/3/7. 1674, p. 11. Letter from Bombay to London, dated 16th December 1674

A letter dated 17th January 1676, from Surat to London, includes the following information about tin coins[97]:

"We herewith send you the several sorts of coins now minted on the island. Among the rest we desire you to take notice that in order to its greater consumption the tin coin is made 10 per cent more weighty than it used to be. It first went currently off till the envious Portuguese hindered its passage in their countries and transport to the main, abating the value very much. Now we hope it will be better esteemed, and if we could procure a large vent for it, it would consume a good quantity of tin yearly and make it worth Rs 22 the man to you."

Bujerooks – 1676

On 8th February 1676, President Aungier wrote to Bombay relative to the coinage. Concerning the tinny he remarked[98]:

"As to the Tinnys or Bugroocks wee like well the new stampe and weight, and hope now they will pass current, and desire to know how many"

This presumably refers to the coins made in 1675.

Bujerooks – 1677

In 1677, a decision was taken to call in the 'old' tinnys (i.e. those made before 1675) because they were lighter than the 'new', and were not acceptable to the general public[99]:

The bugerooks being light will not pass current in the adjacent places which is a very great loss to ye Commonality and cause of disaffection and there being now a quantity of new buggerooks made which are 10 per cent weighter, it was ordered:
That a proclamation be issued out to call in all the old buggerooks and ye time appointed for ye bringing it in be twenty days from the proclamation thereof in which time all those that bring in old buggerroks shall have them exchanged for new

and this seems to have been put into effect at the beginning of the following year[100]:

The old Buggrookes being called in and new sett out, that those brought in might not be imbezzled being in small parcels and also a small coine it was:
*   Ordered that the Warehousekeeper should melt downe all the old Buggrookes into blocks of Tynn that they be ready to dispose of if any merchant should offer to buy Tynn, none careing to buy them as they are*

The Bombay Consultations of 10th January 1677 (ie the beginning of 1678), record that the old bugerooks called in after the issue of a 'new set' (i.e. in 1675?) were ordered

---

[97] Pridmore p. 103.
[98] Pridmore p. 103.
[99] Bombay Factory Records, IOR G/3/2. 1677, p. 8. Meeting of Council 11th July 1677
[100] Bombay Factory Records, IOR G/3/2. 1677, p. 21. Meeting of Council 10th January 1677

to be melted into blocks for disposal to merchants. In August 1679, Bombay proposed sending a further quantity to Surat for sale.

Tinny (Bujerook) [16]77

Bujerooks – 1679

The new regulations introduced in 1679 (see above) recommended that tin bujerooks should be coined[101]:

"…The coining of tin into buzerooks was specially recommended by the Company on account of tin being a home-production, but it is doubtful whether much was done during the year, as in August the Council reported that they had a quantity of it on hand, which they proposed to send to Surat for sale…"

Bujerooks – 1694 to 1707

A tinny has been found dated 1694 (see Stevens' catalogue) and more tin coins were produced in 1705 but none have been discovered with this date[102]:

And that until the Court of Managers shall be advised sending out tin the product of England, there be purchased at least 20 Pecull Siam or [Mallian] tinn as soone as any offers for sale, supplying coinage of said budgerooks useful and beneficial to the inhabitants and poorer sort of this island [for] buying provisions and other things

and it is possible that some tinnys were produced in [17]02 because a coin exists that may bear this date although it is very worn and is more likely to be [16]77.

[17]02 or
[16]77?

---

[101] Fawcett Sir C. (1954). The English Factories in India Vol. III (Bombay, Surat and Malabar Coast). Clarendon Press, Oxford, pp. 26-27. 1679

[102] Bombay Public Consultations, IOR P/341/2 p. 174, 24th April 1705.

Bujerooks – 1716

From a source in the records of 1716[103] and the fact that tin coins exist with the date 1716, Pridmore concluded that the issue of tinnys recommenced in that year, leaving a gap of about forty years since the previous tinnys had been issued in 1675.

…Agreed that the warehousekeeper deliver forty B'bay maunds of tinn to the coppersmiths to make into Budgerooks.
That four chests of treasure be delivered the Goldsmiths for coinage into rupees for the supply of our treasury

However, as we have seen, tinnys were issued in the intervening years with the record entries presumably having been missed by Pridmore.

Even, Pridmore himself referred to a note made in the year 1710[104], which states that buzerooks passed at 14 to the pice. This would suggest that the coins were very much still in circulation in 1710, supporting the idea that other issues occurred between 1675 and 1717.

Tin Pice, 1717

In 1717 a decision was made to use surplus tin in the Government's warehouse, to produce tin 'ducannees'[105]:

The Gov[r] being out of Town ordered the Secretary to advise the Gent[ll] of the Council that for replenishing the Treasury which att present is very low and also to gett rid of Tinn in the Warehouse there being no vent for it, he would Coin it into Duccanees, with their consent the Secretary Gave Notice thereof to them this Day and they assenting the Presid[t] ordered that said Tinn be del[r]ed out for coining accordingly the Secretary to Prepare a Proclamation for the Ducanees passing Curr[t] on the Island which being Drawn out was this day Published.

Pice, 1717

The name ducanee, used in the extract above is apparently the colloquial name for the copperoon or pice. Pridmore believed that this was derived from do-kani i.e. a piece of two Kani, the Kani being the 1/64 of the mediaeval Delhi silver tanka. In later years the term dugani was applied in general to both copper and tin pice, but in 1677, it referred only to the copperoon. The name was still in use as late as 1825.

---

103 Bombay Public Consultations, Thursday 5th January 1716. IOR P/341/4.
104 Pridmore p. 111.
105 Bombay Public Consultations. IOR P/341/4, 23rd September 1717.

Mint and Mint Workers. 1672-1717

Of course, things did not always go smoothly and Bombay had difficulty recruiting and keeping experienced mint staff. A letter from Bombay to the Surat Council in September 1676, informed Surat that the chief coiner had run away[106]:

Our Chief Coyner is run away having stolen an other mans wife so [yet] we have nobody who knows how to coin. Please to send us down one other as last or we shall be put to great straights.

In November they again requested that a skilled workman be sent from Surat stating that those coiners left were really not capable of carrying out the necessary work[107].

... & most tedious coiners to make us money, [so] we again desire ye speedy finding a coiner.

This obviously did not happen because, in July 1677, Bombay sent another missive:

There is a coiner in Surat by name Ruttangee, who did promise ye late Presid^t to come to Bombay, & did engage to coin o^r Dugonys for 6½ Larys p.md., whereas we now pay....Lar wch will amo^t to considerable sum yearly if we are but supplied wth good quantities of Copper; & though he came to no agreem^t for coining of Rup^s & Bujerooks, yet he promised to make y^m 20 p. cent, cheaper y^n at present they are made; besides wee are given to understand he is a able workman, which will be of great benefit in making all ye mony of a true and equall weight, wch is very difficult to these coiners not being bred up to the trade

Muddam Kissingees son, by name Bagvandas can inform ye Hon^rs where he lives. Please hasten him hither wth all speed possible, we being in great want of coin.

In response to this, Govindji Madharji was sent to Bombay from Surat as chief coiner in August 1677[108].

Occasionally less reputable people were employed in the mint[109]:

We know not how Muddum came to be employed in ye Honble Company's mint but it seems he wound himself in like a snake...

Problems with finding workers for the mint continued into the 1690s. For instance on 3rd July 1694 a letter from Surat records:[110]

I have got two jurobs for the mint at Bombay and two Chucksees am in hopes of. They ask unreasonable considerations to go but I expect to bring them to more moderate terms and send them with what haste I can.

---

[106] Bombay Factory Records, IOR G/3/7. 1676, p. 60. Letter from Bombay to Surat, dated 22nd September 1676.

[107] Bombay Factory Records, IOR G/3/7. 1676, p. 65. Letter from Bombay to Surat, dated 1st November 1676.

[108] Fawcett Sir C. (1936). The English Factories in India Vol. 1 (The Western Presidency). Clarendon Press, Oxford, pp. 180-181. 1677.

[109] Bombay Factory Records, IOR G/3/8. 1679, p. 14 Letter from Bombay to Surat Council dated 10th March 1679.

[110] Bombay Factory Records. IOR G/3/20, Book 1, p. 21. Letter from Surat to Bombay, dated 3rd July 1694

On 10rd July of the same year[111]:

I have got 2 jurobs & one Chucksee for the mint but at such extravagant rates that I shall not entertain them 'till Your Excellency's answer. The Chocksee demands 300 rupees a year there. He can have 150 or 200. The jerabs demand 8 rupees a month when there is no business and 6 per mill on all they coin. In the [jankjall] they have 5 per mill. They want the charges [down] & liberty to return if they like not the place and all charges of fire etc in the mint is to be provided them.

The President obviously thought the mint workers were too expensive so he wrote to Cambay to try to get some cheaper labour[112]:

The workmen of the mint being so dear, the Pr wrote to Cambay to get four from thence and yesterday had an answer. Two Choksees at 20 rupees per month. Two jurabs are to be allowed their way charges to Bombay, their diet there at 6 rupees per month & 4½ per mill on all they coin. This being far cheaper then we can have them from Surat, Vittal Parracks hath wrote to the Cambay broker to send with all expedition to us.

And he seems to have been successful in this endeavour[113]:

This serves only to accompany two Choksees & two Jurobs from Cambay for your mint, which were procured with much difficulty. We refer for their wages to the enclosed list. We shall write to Your Excellency the needful by an express which will be a humbler conveyance.

However this seems to have caused problems[114]:

The Cambay broker is in a great deal of trouble from that Governor for sending the Choksees and Duraps to Bombay to coin in our mint and have forced him to give security for their return. He has sent two expresses to us. Inclosed is our broker's letter concerning this. However, we desire to be referred.

Having got the new men from Cambay it seems that they could not do any work because the man responsible for melting the metal had been discharged. Bombay informed Surat that the men would be returned[115]:

The mintmen altho' nice have had no satisfactory trial of them for want of the melting man you discharged, we have [di... in order ... return] hoping you will take the necessary care to receive of them what you shall think fit to be returned of the charges

---

[111] Bombay Factory Records. IOR G/3/20, Book 1, p. 29. Letter from Surat to Bombay, dated 10th July 1694

[112] Bombay Factory Records. IOR G/3/20, Book 2, p. 11. Letter from Surat to Bombay, dated 9th August 1694.

[113] Bombay Factory Records. IOR G/3/20, Book 3, p. 38. Letter from Surat to Bombay, dated 13th October 1694.

[114] Bombay Factory Records. IOR G/3/20, Book 3, p. 58. Letter from Surat to Bombay, dated 6th November 1694.

[115] Bombay Factory Records. IOR g/3/10. Letter from Gayer at Bombay to Samuel Annesley, dated 16th November 1694.

and Surat replied that they would try to ensure that the Company was charged as little as possible[116]:

We have not seen the mintmen as yet & shall endeavour the Rt Hon Co. be as little charged on their account as maybe. The Governor at Cambay has already [ffleeced?] our broker there about them.

In 1705 the mint was housed in some tiled sheds[117]:

Some of the Tiled shedds wth in the fort remote from the powder bastions to be made use of for said purpose [i.e. minting silver and copper coins] till a proper and conven^t place for such work can be made within the House of the Fort

---

[116] Bombay Factory Records. IOR G/3/20, Book 3, p. 75. Letter from Surat to Bombay, dated 26th November 1694.

[117] Bombay Public Consultations, IOR P/341/2 p174, 24th April 1705.

Chapter 2 – Bombay Mint 1717 to 1799 – Coins

Summary

In 1672 the English at Bombay had begun to strike silver coins in an English style but they soon found that these were not acceptable outside of the confines of Bombay Island. They quickly realised that they would have to strike coins in the style of the surrounding native silver coins, which was of course the Moghul-style, if they were to get them accepted in trade. Since Bombay was considered to be English sovereign territory, and the English king had given his permission for them to strike coins, they considered themselves within their rights to strike Moghul-style coins in the name of the English monarch. This they did, first in the name of James II and then William and Mary. However, as discussed in the previous chapter, the Moghul emperor was not happy with this and the English were forced to stop the practice in about 1697. This meant that they were forced to have their silver coined into rupees by the Governor of Surat, a practice that they found very slow and costly. Consequently they continued to try to get permission to strike Moghul-style coins in their mint at Bombay.

In 1717 they succeeded in this effort and Moghul-style rupees, often called 'Munbai rupees' were struck throughout the eighteenth century. However, it was only one of many types of rupee issued by different authorities in the region (e.g. Ahmadabad, Broach and Surat rupees). In particular, the Surat rupee competed with that of Bombay, and the Nawab of Surat found it convenient to debase his rupee by a few percent from time to time. This caused many problems for the Bombay authorities and these were not resolved until Bombay adopted the Surat standard in 1800 (see next chapter).

Gold coins were issued from time to time, usually struck in the style of the silver rupees, although some European-style gold coins were tried in the 1760s and 1770s. The mintages of these gold coins, where known, are very small and these coins are all extremely rare.

Copper coins were issued from time to time during the century but for most of the time, lower-value coins were produced in tin or tutenague (zinc), although by the 1770s forgery was such a problem that all these coins were called in and replaced by copper coins.

Permission to strike Moghul-style Coins

On 27th March 1713[118], the Directors in London instructed Bombay as follows:

"We expect you encourage our own mint at Bombay by coining rupees there of the same weight and fineness with those at Surat, or very near it. If you make them finer, we shall lose by it and therefore you must be very careful to prevent it. If coarser they

---

[118] Taken from Pridmore p. 110

will get an ill character and very likely if one or two per cent worse, they will be undervalued to three or four per cent. Therefore they should be the same; and though at first the shroffs may endeavour to decry them, yet in time the rupees will retrieve and afterwards preserve their reputation, as experience tells us those have which were coined at Madras."

This instruction appears to have been an attempt to get the Bombay authorities to strike coins in the Moghul-style or at least to the same weight and standard. By 1713 the authorities at Bombay already knew that they could not strike coins in this style without the permission of the emperor. They also knew that English-style rupees would not be accepted very widely outside of Bombay. So they were unable to comply with the instruction. However, it may have helped ensure that the matter of the Bombay coinage would be included for discussion by the embassy sent to the Moghul court in 1715, which resulted in the granting of the firman allowing coinage of Moghul-style coins in 1717.

This embassy was sent to the court of the emperor Farrukh-Siyar, and included yet another request to extend the coining rights of the Company in Bombay[119]:

"That on the island of Bombay belonging to the English, European siccaes are current, they request that, according to the custom of Madras, they may at Bombay coin siccaes."

This time the emperor acceded to the request and in an edict (firman) dated the 6th January 1717[120], the Company was granted the right to produce gold and silver coins in the name of the emperor and with the mint name Munbai (Bombay):

"On the island of Bombay let there be the glorious stamp on the siccaes coined there, passing them current as all other siccaes are throughout the Empire."

Pridmore also quotes another version from James Fraser[121]:

"And in the island of Bombay, belonging to the English where Portuguese Coins are Current, that according to the custom of Chinapattan, the fortunate coin may be struck."

The Bombay Council discussed the subject on 16th September 1717 and was particularly concerned about the title they should apply to the emperor. His standard title effectively recognised him as king of the world and, by default therefore, king of England. However, they agreed that the title was merely flattery rather than actual truth and that Madras had already adopted the practice and shown the way so they would not be sensible to miss such a profitable opportunity. It was agreed to strike coins in the Mughal style and see if they would be accepted[122]:

Our Rupees coined att Bombay being by said Phirmaund to Pass Currant in all the Mogulls

---

[119] Taken from Pridmore p. 111

[120] Pridmore p. 112.

[121] Fraser. The History of Nadir Shah, London, 1742, p. 46.

[122] Bombay Public Consultations, 16th September 1717. India Office Collections P/341/4.

Dominions in the Same Manner as those coined by his Gov' if Stampt with his Stamp brought on a Debate concerning the Title therein given him which Runne Thus

The Stampt
Made by Ye Grace
Of God on Gold and
Silver by Farruck Soor
Emperor of Ye Sea
And Land

The Stamp
Of Bombay, in
The fifth year of
Ye Happy Reign of
Ye Emperor

The Question being putt whether wee should condescend thereto, Since it Insinuates the Jurisdiction not only of this Island but the whole world to belong to him and thereby Derogates from the Hon' of our Nation as well as all others, after some time spent in the Debate tho' our Complying to Impress those Characters on our Coins may not be so much to the Credit of the English Nation & R' Honble Comp' as we desired or could wish; yett the following reasons being Offered were Unanimously approved.

First it has been the Practice of the Emperours of India to take upon them that Stile and Title, and whatever European Nation addresses him, must flatter that Prince therewith or Loose their Suit.

Secondly, the benefitt that is likely to accrue from the case in Dispute is very considerable.

Thirdly the Presidt and Councell att Fort St George have already shewn us the way in the Stamp of their Rupees, and Allumgeer Pagodas.

Fourthly and Lastly there is no other Prospect of procuring the Currency of our Rups so that rather than Loose this Advantigious Part of our Grant it is Unanimously Resolved that the Rupees we Coin for the future be Stampt with the words above mentioned, and that we Deferr Settling what shall be paid by private Persons for Coinage till wee do see that our Rupees do pass currently.

Rupee of Munbai, Farrukh Siyar RY 7

Regnal year 6 is currently the earliest known rupee with the mint name Munbai. Half rupees were also struck. Initially the Company used metal from its own resources as shown in the consultation of 16th September 1717 but, by about August 1719, they felt confident enough to accept bullion from other sources, presumably in order to increase the output from their mint. The mint must have quickly grown in size because a letter from Bombay to Surat dated 26th August 1719[123], asked for twenty moneyers to be sent for employment in the mint.

THE FORT CIRCA 1750 – after Grose

Diagram of Bombay c1750 showing position of the mint [124]

[123] Pridmore p. 112
[124] Tindall G, (1982). City of Gold. The Biography of Bombay. Temple Smith London.

Gold – 1717 to 1765

Not very many references to the production of gold coins have been found in the records of the eighteenth century, nor are many gold coins known to exist.

Pridmore (p.112) stated that a mohur of Shah Jahan is recorded although neither the regnal nor the hijri year is known. The whereabouts of this coin also is not known and there must be some doubt about its existance.

The Caldecott sale catalogue[125] described two mohurs in the name of Muhammad Shah (1719-1748), although the whereabouts of these coins is not known. A few extremely rare mohurs of Muhammad Shah have come onto the market in the last twenty years or so but this is the only indication of the production of these coins.

Mohur in the name of Muhammad Shah

Later in the century, in 1762, there is an indication that the mint was in the habit of producing gold coins[126]:

An examination of the treasure received by our Honble Master's ship Royal Captain from Gombroon being now laid before us, ordered that the Nadarees be delivered into the mint to be coined & the merchants offering to take the other coins at the following rates, the same are ordered to be issued to them as we want to realize them and cannot expect at present to dispose of them on better terms.

Nadir Shaw Gold Rupees	*at 13 Rs 4 An*
Venetians	*at 4 Rs 11 ½ @ 12* [not sure what this means]
Muhammad Shaw Rupees	*4 per cent discount*

Mohur 1765

In 1765 consideration was given to the production of a new type of gold coin[127]:

The great scarcity of silver which has prevailed for a considerable time past on the island, being attended with many inconveniences and a very great prejudice to the trade of the place, the establishing a gold currency has been thought of and the minters have delivered in a

---

[125] Caldecott sale 1912
[126] Bombay Public Consultations, IOR P/341/25, 1762. p. 264. 11th May 1762.
[127] Bombay Public Consultations, IOR P/341/28, 1765. p. 464. 30th July 1765.

calculate of one accordingly, the same is ordered to follow this consultation, and to be sent round to the several members for their inspection before next meeting.

Mohur 1765

The calculation is shown on page 470 of the records along with a number of footnotes amongst which are:

…4th As the making this intended coin is a new trial, we desire you will be pleased to order to be delivered to us 300 Venetians to know whether it will turn out agreeable to the above calculate or not, also to fix the exact weight of each piece.
5th That you will inform them in what manner they are to be stamped etc.
6th We offer, if the above calculate is not approved of, to make a gold coin that shall pass current for 15 rupees and to weigh 38 Vols* pure gold so that 100 Venetians full weight (after having been heated) shall deliver 30 gold coins amounting to rupees 450, and stand to all our own charges, and the coinage duty. We also propose to make this coin halves and quarters for the greater convenience of the inhabitants of this place.

However the price of gold was too high so the production of the coins was delayed[128]:

Agreeable to yesterday's resolution of Council, the calculate of gold coins was sent round to the several members for their inspection, when the majority concurring in thinking it better to await the arrival of the Mocha Ships, as gold will probably then be cheaper, the same was determined on.

November 1765 was considered the appropriate time for issuing the new coins[129]:

Resuming the consideration of the propriety of establishing a gold coin to pass current on the Island it is remarked that this seems the proper juncture for carrying the same into execution as gold is now very cheap.

Resolved therefore that a gold coin to contain exactly 38 vols of pure Venetian gold be established and to pass current for fifteen rupees, which the mint master is accordingly ordered

---

* Vols appears to be some measure of gold bullion
[128] Bombay Public Consultations, IOR P/341/28, 1765. p. 471. 31th July 1765.
[129] Bombay Public Consultations, IOR P/341/28, 1765. p. 651. 5th November 1765.

to make, also halves and quarters of the same with the Honble Company's arms on one side & Bombay with the year on the other.

That to the amount of 60,000 rupees to be made of this coin for the present as a trial & should it be found to answer more may be made hereafter & as from the present low price of gold the Honble Company will gain considerably by this coin it must at all times be changed at the Treasury whenever tendered for that purpose.

Thus, 4000 mohurs worth of the coins were made although some were halves and quarters so the exact numbers of each denomination is not known. A proclamation was issued in January 1766[130]:

This day a publication was issued signifying to the inhabitants the establishment of the gold coin and enjoining them to receive the same at the rate of fifteen rupees each and halves and quarters the same

By September 1766 counterfeit coins were being found although the exact type of the coins being forged is not specified and it could refer to counterfeit gold coins imported from surrounding areas[131]:

Some counterfeit gold coins having been lately circulated in the bazaar, it is resolved in order as much as possible to prevent their currency to issue a publication requiring all persons whatever possessed of gold rupees to deliver in the same to the Treasury within eight days that they may be shroffed and carefully inspected before they are issued out again.

Mohur 1770

In July 1770 Council considered issuing another type of gold coin[132]:

It being more advantageous to coin than sell the gold in the treasury, the President acquaints the Board that having heard, and being himself of opinion, that the stamp which the Bombay Gold Rupees coined in 1765, viz. that of the Honble Company's small seal on one side, is highly improper, as none but sovereigns have the right to affix any stamp on public coin, he proposes that those now to be coined should instead thereof bear the same inscription in Persian characters on one side as the silver rupees now do on both, and which their superior breadth will admit, the Honble Company's privilege of coining here being derived solely from the Moghul; and on the reverse the words 'BOMBAY 1770', similar to those of 1765, with the addition in figures of their current value. He would propose that these should in every respect bear the same stamp of each side as the silver, and which the gold formerly coined in this mint ever did, but those being much superior in the standard to them of 1765, the last being intended solely to preserve a currency on the island, he thinks the above distinction will not be improper to prevent the credit of our mint suffering if coined [at] the place. And further that as neither those at present current, nor those now proposed, can with any sort of propriety

---

130 Bombay Public Consultations, IOR P/341/29, 1766. p. 27. 8th January 1766.
131 Bombay Public Consultations, IOR P/341/29, 1766. p. 501. 2nd September 1766.
132 Bombay Public Consultations, IOR P/341/33, 1770. p. 330. 3rd July 1770.

be called gold rupees, from their differing so much in standard and value, he proposes they should in future bear the name 'BOMBAYS' and be stamped as follows, all which the Board concur in, and it is ordered to be carried into execution accordingly

1 side Persian characters,   Allumgueer Padshaw Gawsee 1183
Hegeyra and 9th of His Reigne

2 side English characters   BOMBAY
1770

————————

15 Rupees

The proposed Persian design on one side was based on the design of the existing rupee and Pridmore makes much of the fact that this was the chosen design, rather than taking the opportunity to change to the name of the reigning emperor, Shah Alam. He suggests that the Alamgir legend was used to avoid having to renegotiate with Shah Alam those agreements concerning coinage that had been obtained from Alamgir II. However, by 1770, the EIC had obtained so much power that it is difficult to see why the Bombay Council would still be concerned about this. It seems equally likely that the design was chosen simply because it was the existing rupee design and no further thought had gone in to the matter.

Mohur 1770

Moghul-Style Mohurs – 1774

In June 1774 gold coins were under consideration again[133]:

It having been determined that the treasure lately imported from Bussora, which we procured on account of our Honble Employers for bills on Bengal, should be coined in our mint & that the silver should be made into rupees of the present standard, it remains now to consider of what weight & fineness to make the gold rupees, which being taken under deliberation together with a letter from our Mint Master, as entered hereafter, shewing the gain arising by coining gold rupees of the present weight & standard, Resolved after a full discussion that the gold rupees be made of the same fineness as those at present current but that an addition of two Vol be made to the weight, that is that they be now made of 40 Vol weight instead of 38 [7dwt 1gr] & that they bear the same impression as the silver rupees, by which raising the

—————————————————

[133] Bombay Public Consultations, IOR P/341/40, 1774. p. 417. 15th June 1774.

real value (as they are to pass for 15 silver rupees as before) they will be current in the adjacent countries.

As the price of gold in this place is at present low, some profit will still arise by coining it into rupees of the weight & standard above resolved on, and it is agreed, in order to increase the currency of the place, to permit private persons to coin gold in the mint on their paying the customary duties of one & a half per cent.

The gold rupees now current must be called in in proper time & re-coined of the present weight standard. The deficiency in weight must be made good by the Company as they enjoyed the profit that was made on their being first coined.

Gold Rupees 1775

Further consideration was given to the issue of gold coins in 1775[134]:

As there is at present a want of silver currency in the Island, it is agreed in order to obviate the inconveniences resulting therefrom to coin gold to the amount of 60,000 rupees into pieces of the value of one silver rupee each, to be in fineness exactly equal to the gold rupees now current and of 3/15th part of the weight of a gold rupee

This extract seems to indicate an intention to strike gold coins weighing one fifth of a mohur with the same fineness as a full Mohur but with the value of a silver rupee. This does not make much sense since that amount of gold would have had a value of about three rupees. It seems likely that this is an error in the records and it should read '1/15th part of the weight of a gold rupee' not '3/15th'.

Use of Foreign Gold Coins

The Bombay merchants had taken to using foreign coins in their business dealings and this was discussed in 1786[135]:

Read a letter from sundry merchants of this place respecting the present mode of buying and selling Venetians as lately attempted to be introduced by the shroffs. On consideration of this letter and the proposal of the merchants appearing equitable & fair, a publication must be issued signifying that all shroffs, in buying and selling Venetians, are to weigh them by fifteen new Bombay rupees or a brass weight equal to fifteen tolas, which answer to fifty Venetians full weight and so in proportion for a greater or smaller number. They are accordingly directed from and after the 10th of next month to provide themselves with those weights to be stamped by the Mint Master and any shroffs acting in disobedience to this order, shall on conviction before a Magistrate be fined for the first offence, 50 Rs and for the second 100 Rs.
This resolution to be communicated to the Mint Master with directions to comply therewith so far as concerns himself.

---

[134] Bombay Public Consultations, IOR P/341/41, 1775. p. 291. 25th April 1775.
[135] Bombay Public Consultations, IOR P/342/5, 1786. 25th January 1786. p. 61.

Gold Coins 1790 to 1799

Counterfeit gold coins were discussed in 1791 and these were re-coined[136]:

…On 19th November last I delivered him for re-coinage 373 counterfeit gold mohurs & 60 2/3 gold mohurs which were cut in the treasury from a supposition of their being counterfeit but were found to be standard coin. On my daily report these are stated at Rs 6505 but as yet no part of this sum has been returned into the Treasury…

The mint master was asked to produce a report of the number of mohurs coined[137] and in June 1791, he duly provided the report[138]:

Agreeable to your order of the 18th instant, I have the honor to enclose an account from the Mint Undertaker of the re-coinage of the counterfeit gold mohurs delivered to the mint from the Treasury by which it appears the actual loss is one hundred and seventy five gold mohurs, as follows:

Gold mohurs counterfeit received from the Treasury   433.666
Ditto paid into the Treasury   258.666
Balance   175
Lost by burnage from the admixture of silver and other metals

Number of Gold Coins Produced from 1770 to 1799

In 1805 the mint master provided a report of the output of gold coins from the mint between 1770 and 1800[139]:

Statement of the Gold Coinage in the Bombay Mint from 20th December 1770 to 30th September 1804

Year of Account	Touch	Mohurs	Thirds of Mohurs	Single Rupees	Total Value in Rupees
1770/1	99	1968			29,520
1773/4	"	10,260			153,900
1774/5	"	15,563			233,445
1775/6	"	235			3,525
1778/9	"	3,000			45,000
1779/80	"	352			5,280

---

136 Bombay Public Consultations, IOR P/342/13, 1791. p. 233. Letter from the assistant to the treasurer to Government, dated 12th April 1791.

137 Bombay Public Consultations, IOR P/342/13, 1791. p. 453. Resolution 17th June 1791.

138 Bombay Public Consultations, IOR P/342/13, 1791. p. 480. Letter from the Acting Mint Master (Patrick Crawford Bruce) to Government, dated 25th June 1791.

139 Bombay Public Consultations. IOR P/343/22. p. 2197. Letter from William Crawford (mint master) to Government, dated 19th April 1805.

Year of Account	Touch	Mohurs	Thirds of Mohurs	Single Rupees	Total Value in Rupees
1781/82	99	3,336			50,040
1782/83	"	548			8,220
1783/84	"	14,498			217,470
1784/85	"	9,337			140,055
1785/86	"	1,178			17,670
1786/87	"	6,817			102,225
1787/88	"	4,789			71,835
1788/89	"	1,950			29,250
1791/92	"	6,532			97,980
1792/93	"	5,407			81,105
1794/95	"	18,635			279,525
1795/96	"	24,706			370,590
1796/97	"	6,218			93,270
1797/98	"	8,811			132,165
1798/99	"	28,967			434,505
1799/1800	"	3,009			45,135

Gold Standard

The gold standard was considered again in 1790[140]:

In reply to your letter of the 22nd instant communicating to me [from] the Honble Governor in Council his commands that I would inform him from the documents in my office what weight and fineness is the standard for gold rupees, I have to request that you will inform him that there are no records in the mint office prior to 10th August 1773, nor any subsequent orders of Government relative to the fineness of the gold rupee further that they should continue to be made of the same standard as previous to the 18th June 1774. What that standard was nowhere appears except in a letter from the Mint Master, Mr Church, to the President in Council dated the 16th May 1774, in which he says "one gold rupee weighs 7 dwt 1 grain or 38 Vols of the fineness of 24 Carats, which is Venetian standard". The Mint Undertaker confirms the gold rupee being of the same standard as the Venetian, but says the Venetian is only 99 touch, which answers to 23..76 [dwt], which fineness he has invariably followed in all the gold rupees coined by him since his first contract with the Honble Company in July 1778 and agreeable whereto he is ready to renew his contract. Under the 18th June 1774 the Honble the President and Council directed that the gold rupee should be made of the weight of exactly forty Vols or 7dwt 16⅔ grains, at which weight it has continued ever since.

---

[140] Bombay Public Consultations, IOR P/342/12, 1790. 26th February 1790. p. 163. Letter from the mint master (Edward Galley) to Government, dated 24th February 1790.

In 1801, the mint and assay masters discussed the gold standard that had been set during the previous century in response to criticism from a Mr Constable[141]:

…With respect to the gold mohur, the orders of government were equally accurate and in fixing its standard they were just and enlightened. Until 1774 the gold mohur weighed 7 dwts 1 grain and contained one part in [90] of alloy or it was of the fineness of a Venetian. In this regulation the value of gold in proportion to silver was over-rated and accordingly government in August 1774 called in the gold mohurs and fixed their standard and weight. The weight was that of a silver rupee or 178.31 grains and the standard that of a Venetian, as before. This regulation did very wisely determine the value of gold in proportion to silver as 14.9 to one. This is the regulation that subsisted until November last. There surely has never been a mint master nor a mint contractor who could, as Mr Constable thinks, be ignorant of those standards for silver and gold (see on this subject a letter to government from Mr [Galley] mint master in 1790). The mint contractors in their contracts are expressly bound to coin according to the existing regulations and have been perfectly acquainted with the established standards…

Rupee of Farrukh-Siyar

Rupee of Shah Jahan II

Rupee of Muhammad Shah

---

[141] Bombay Public Consultations. IOR P/342/49 p. 2751. Letter from the mint master (J.A. Grant) and the assay master (A. Scott) to government, dated 31st August 1801.

Silver Coins – Farrukh Siyar

The firman issued by the Emperor in 1717 allowed the striking of both gold and silver coins in his name. The Bombay Council agreed that the coins should carry the Emperor's name and the regnal year 5. Thus the first coins attributed to the British should bear this regnal year although none is currently known. Rhodes refers to Hussain[142] in attributing a coin of RY 2 to Bombay, but the mint name is not clear and it seems unlikely that this coin belongs to this mint. Likewise, Rhodes refers to Ahmad[143] in attributing a coin of Jahandar to the Bombay mint. Again this seems unlikely

Silver Coins – Shah Jahan II

In addition to rupees, half rupees appear to have been introduced during the short reign of Shah Jahan II. Pridmore found requests for supplies of half rupees in the Tellicherry factory records and drew the conclusion that the coins were minted to meet this demand rather than for use in Bombay itself.

Silver Coins – Muhammad Shah

The consultations of 23rd December 1738[144] gave the new weight of the Bombay rupee to be 7 dwt 10gr 314/1000 (=178.314 troy grains) and the fineness to be better than standard by 15 dwt.

This figure was arrived at after consideration of the assay results of the Bombay and Surat rupees and the results from imported silver coins:

the Bombay and Surat rupee weigh each dwt. VII gr. XI (=179 troy grains).

Bombay rupees had a fineness better than standard by 16 dwt and Surat rupees better than standard by 11 dwt. The fineness of the foreign coins was slightly less than standard.

A comparison between English and Bombay fineness standard is shown in the report of 1738:

STANDARD FOR SILVER

| | English | | Bombay | |
	oz	*dwts*	*oz*	*dwts*
Fine Silver	11	2	11	17
Alloy		18		3
	———		———	
Ounces	12	0	12	0

---

[142] Rhodes (1975) BNJ Vol 45 pp. 98-99. Refers to Hussain MK (1973) Catalogue of coins in the Central Museum, Nagpur, part II p. 95.

[143] Rhodes BNJ vol45 pp. 98-99. Refers to Numm Supp XIV, Art 324, 'Some rare Moghul coins in the State Museum, Hyderabad (Deccan)' by K M Ahmad.

[144] Bombay Public Consultations, IOR P/341/9, Saturday 23rd December 1738.

The weight and fineness of the rupee remained unaltered until 1748.

There are a number of possible explanations for the different marks found in the س on the reverse of these coins. The mint contractor was known as the darogah and Pridmore believed that the marks were those of the darogah. Thus the marks would indicate, not only the person responsible for the coins, but also, to later numismatists, the frequency that the contract changed hands. However, there is no incontrovertible evidence that this is the meaning of the mark and the mint contractor seemed to change much less frequently than the symbols (see later in this chapter). Perhaps these were marks of someone like a die engraver or some other person in the mint.

Rupee – Ahmad Shah (1748 to 1754)

Rupee of Ahmad Shah, RY 5

In 1738, the standard for the silver coins had been fixed at a weight of 7 dwt 10 gr 314/1000 (=178.314 troy grains) and the fineness to be better than standard by 15 dwt. The Consultation of the 25th March, 1748[145] made a slight adjustment to this:

The rupee to be an exact tola or dwt 7 and grains 11 and in fineness 14½ dwt better than English standard

Mitchiner (Non-Islamic & Colonial Series) attributes one-fifth rupee coins to Ahmad Shah, but these coins more likely belong to Muhammad Shah. The fifth rupees are dealt with in the chapter dealing with the Malabar Coast coins.

Rupee – Alamgir II (1754 to 1759) – Reverse: Bead above *julūs*

There appear to be two distinct varieties of Munbai rupees struck in the name of Alamgir II. The first of these was issued in 1753-54 with the regnal year Ahd (1) and hijri years 1167 or 1168. A distinctive feature is the presence of a bead above the first part of the word julus, instead of the usual *pesh*. A rupee of this type was sold as Ahd of Shah Alam II in the Wiggins sale (Baldwin (2001), sale 25 (Wiggins), lot 692), the mistake arising because the 'gir' of Alamgir was off the flan.

---

[145] Bombay Public Consultations, IOR P/341/15. 25th March 1748.

Rupee of Alamgir II AH 1167 RY 1 (ahd)

Bead above julus

pesh above julūs

Rupee – Alamgir II (1754 to 1759) – Reverse: *pesh* above *julūs*[146]

The second type of rupee issued in the name of Alamgir has the *pesh* above the first part of the word *julūs*.

Alamgir II was assassinated on 30th November 1759, at a time when the Company had just received the firman (dated 4th September 1759) granting them charge of the Castle and Tanka of Surat. The Bombay Council considered making a request to the new Emperor for the firman to be renewed and confirmed, but the council at Surat was very much against this approach:

Alamgir II rupee RY 3

We cannot consent by any means to your requesting our Honbᶫᵉ Masters Rights or Priveledges in Surat and their Phirmaunds & Hookums may be renewed or confirmed, as we deem them valid & because such a step would of course be a good plea for rendering them invalid on the demise of every King and every change of Government[147]

---

146 Pridmore p. 155.
147 Pridmore p. 113.

51

Pridmore believed that this statement of policy led to the adoption of the fixed regnal year on the Moghul-style coins of Alamgir II minted at both Bombay and Madras. Alamgir II died in 1759, in his sixth year, and Madras coins show Ry 6 as their fixed year after his death. For some unknown reason, Bombay adopted the 9th year. This continuance of the coins in the name of the dead emperor may have provided an argument for not bothering to renew the grant with the new emperor since the coins were not struck in his name.

Competition from Imported Silver Coins

As stated above, many different rupees were in circulation in the area of Bombay and many of these were of lower quality than those of the Bombay or Surat rupees. This provided an opportunity for the shroffs, buying the lower quality coins on the mainland at a large discount and importing them to Bombay. This was obviously not good for Bombay, and on 14th February 1729[148]:

The President acquaints the Board that he has been informed of late considerable quantity of old Punch'd rupees have been bro^t upon this island from the neighbouring places of a less weight and baser alloy than those of Surat & our own mint, which are paid away to the shroffs and shopkeepers at disco't and by them passed again at parr, to the great abuse of the publick & discouragement of trade in general. To prevent which in future he proposes the issuing out his proclamation forbidding and prohibiting all persons whatever to receive or pay any old Punch'd rupees except those coin'd here under penalty of forfeiting the same after 20th of this month, but that they bring them into the mint to be anew coined, which is agreed to

and again on the 3rd December 1733[149], action was taken to try to stop the practice[150]:

Whereas a considerable quantity of silver rupees of different coins and alloys are brought to this island from the inland provinces, of an inferior value to the standard of Bombay and Surat rupees and the same bought up by the shroffs and other people at an unreasonable discount and sometimes at par to the great prejudice and discouragement of trade in general and that this pernicious practice has been carried on with impunity notwithstanding a publication issued by order of this board under the date 14th February 1728/29 to prevent the evil tendency of which it is agreed that a publication be forthwith issued enforcing the observance of our former under the following penalty, namely that all persons whatever inhabitants of this island who have in their possession any number of rupees above ten of any other coin or alloy besides those of Surat and Bombay shall in ten days after the issuing of the said publication bring the said rupees to the Hon'ble Company's mint where due attendance shall be given to receive and exchange them for their real value discounting only one p. cent for their re-coinage and all persons not duly observing this publication shall forfeit all such sum or sums of foreign rupees as shall be found in their custody ten days after the issuing thereof, one third to be paid

---

[148] Bombay Public Consultations, IOR P/341/6, Friday 14th February 1729.
[149] Bombay Public Consultations, IOR P/341/7A, Monday 3rd December 1733.
[150] Bombay Public Consultations, IOR P/341/7A, Monday 3rd December 1733.

to the informer and two thirds to the Hon'ble Company, but all strangers who shall bring the foreign rupees hither and are not willing to exchange the same in the mint but desire to export them again shall in three days after their first arrival declare to the Custom master for the time being the quantity they desire to export and it is hereby expressly prohibited that any rupee but those of Surat and Bombay shall be tendered or received in payment as current coin under the same penalty to be incur'd by the tenderer or receiver.

Directed that a publication to the [tenure] of this resolution be immediately issued in English, Portuguese and Gentue languages, and that it be added that proper persons are appointed at the land pay office to exchange silver rupees for pice at the rate of eighty pice for a rupee.

Thenceforth, payment could only be made in coins of Bombay or Surat, anyone with more than ten rupees worth of coins other than those of Bombay or Surat was instructed to take the coins to the mint for exchange for local coins minus 1% for coinage charges.

Bombay Silver Coins Used in Bengal and Malabar

The Bombay mint produced coins not only for use further south in the area known as the Malabar Coast (see chapter 8) but also for Bengal, at least until the establishment of the Calcutta mint in 1757. The records of 1748 state[151]:

…Being in want of treasure for the Coast factories as also for the new Surat investment, and having no rupees in the treasury but such as have been chopt or puncht in several of the Country Governments, altho' they pass current in this place, but which will not pass either at Surat or Bengall without a considerable loss, nor on the Malabar Coast without a loss of at least six per cent, and as it is found that can be rectified by running thro' the fire and stamping anew, which can be done for about half per cent, the loss in weight by wear being found by first duly weighing them to be so inconsiderable as not to deserve notice, it is therefore agreed that all the chopt rupees in the [ ] Company's treasury be delivered into the mint for being so rectified.

and again in 1752[152]:

As we shall be in want of money for sending to the Coast and Bengall and having a number of old uncurrent rupees in the treasury – resolved that orders be issued to the mint undertaker for new stamping with the utmost expedition.

and 1754[153]:

Read a letter from Mr John Spencer, mint master, setting forth that there are several lacks of Bombay chopt rupees in the treasury which, though current here and in the countrys adjacent will not pass either on the Malabar Coast or in Bengall and therefore he proposes re-coining them, as the whole expense, allowing for the deficiency in weight will not exceed three quarters per cent. Which being taken into consideration, it is unanimously resolved for the reasons set

---

[151]Bombay Public Consultations, IOR P/341/16, p.75, March 10th 1748.

[152] Bombay Public Consultations, IOR P/341/18, p. 113, 10th March 1752.

[153] Bombay Public Consultations, IOR P/341/19, p. 111 16th April 1754.

forth in said letter, that the chopt rupees in the treasury be immediately issued to the mint in order to be re-coined.

Relationship between the Bombay and Surat Rupees

Half Rupee of Surat

By 1765, problems with the standard of Surat rupees were beginning to surface[154]:

Read a report assay of the rupee received per Royal Admiral from Surat as entered hereafter by which we are glad to perceive they are of a better standard than those before assayed.

In 1767 London was becoming concerned about the Nawab of Surat debasing his coinage[155]:

The Nabob's debasing the Surat rupees in their mint without consulting our servants was a very wrong step and we are pleased to see you obliged him to alter them to the former standard for, was he permitted to continue such measures, he might very soon enrich himself but it must be highly destructive to our affairs as well as to all the inhabitants of the place and to trade in general. In future if anything of this kind should happen he must be told that our orders are positive: that he should do no acts that are prejudicial to trade or the interests of the subjects. In any case whatever, this must appear so very reasonable to him considering our situation in that place that we make no doubt of his compliance.

London tried to keep control of the Surat mint and in 1768 sent a dispatch stating[156]:

In our letter of last season we gave some orders with regard to the management of the mint at Surat to which we expect due attention should be paid as we esteem this very essential for our interest and the trade of Bombay in particular.

However in 1771 the Surat rupees were not so good[157]:

Also a letter from the Mint Master, entered hereafter, enclosing a report of 42 Surat rupees by which it appears the rupees of Surat are about 2½ per cent worse than the Bombay standard.

In 1767 the Bombay shroffs were asked for their views on controlling the silver coins that were circulating in the island[158]:

---

[154] Bombay Public Consultations, IOR P/341/28, 1765. p. 651. 5th November 1765.
[155] Dispatches to Bombay. IOR E/4/997 (1761-1767) p. 1074. Dispatch dated 4th April 1767.
[156] Dispatches to Bombay. IOR E/4/998 (1768-1771) p. 99. Dispatch dated 25th March 1768.
[157] Bombay Public Consultations, IOR P/341/36, 1771. p. 1308. 17th December 1771.
[158] Bombay Public Consultations, IOR P/341/30, 1767. p. 301. 28th April 1767.

Great abuses having lately been experienced by the petty shroffs refusing to receive rupees in the Buzar, the principle merchants and shroffs were called upon to give their opinions what rupees should pass current, when they declared no objections should be made to any Bombay rupees whatever whether cracked, broken, chopped with holes or otherwise, provided that each rupee was within one Gunge of full weight (100 gunge making a rupee) nor to any Mamud Shaw and Amud Shaw Surat rupees whether broad ones cracked or are even chopped or with holes on the rim, provided they are not chopped or have holes on the facing and are full weight. The secretary is therefore directed to issue a publication enquiring that all such rupees as are mentioned above are received and do pass current at the full value of eighty pice per rupee.

In 1805 the mint and assay masters discussed the Bombay and Surat standards of the previous century[159]:

…Among other regulations which were at different periods entered into between the Government of Bombay and the Nabob of Surat, was that in the year 1768, when for the purpose of mutual accommodation, it was agreed that the rupee of the two Governments should circulate at Bombay and Surat on a footing of equality, the Nawab engaging to keep his coin of the same purity and value as ours.

This engagement he soon however violated and our circulation was in time engrossed by debased rupees of the Surat coinage, varying from 7 to 14 per cent below the standard of the Bombay rupees, all of which were withdrawn from circulation for the purpose of being re-coined in the Surat mint and returned here in a debased state.

We observe that frequent representations were made to the Nabob, particularly through the Chief and Council of Surat, for the purpose of inducing him to conform to the original agreement with the Government of Bombay but these remonstrances failed to produce the equalization on which that agreement between the two Governments was founded. Owing however to this repeated interference, the Nabob's coin in later years, acquired a character of greater regularity and tho' it contained near 8 per cent of alloy, had a preference throughout Guzerat as being the most pure and most regular of the coins current there, and indeed of any rupee on this side of India.

It requires to be noticed that the coinage of rupees of the old Bombay standard has been nearly discontinued for twenty five years past, during which time our circulation has been supplied with the debased Surat rupee, to which mint all bullion was in consequence drawn…

In April 1771 London informed Bombay that they approved of the measures that Bombay had taken to make the standard of the Surat and Bombay coins the same[160]:

The resolution you have taken to make the standard of Surat rupees the same as the standard of those coined at Bombay appears to us a very proper measure and may tend to put a stop to the currency of Broach rupees, the continuance of which will be highly prejudicial to the

---

[159] Bombay Public Consultations. IOR P/343/22. p. 2186. Letter from William Crawford (mint master) and Helenus Scott (assay Master) to Government, dated 19th April 1805

[160] Dispatches to Bombay. IOR E/4/998 (1768-1771) p. 1059. Dispatch dated 25th April 1771.

interest of the Company as well as that of private merchants and we hope your next advices will inform us that the state of your cash has enabled you to carry that measure into execution.

However, by June of the same year London was criticising Bombay for interfering in the activities of the Surat mint[161]:

The innovations you have made in the coinage of Surat & the duty to be levied thereon are of a nature too complicated to admit of our giving any precise orders thereon. By the present dispatch we must however here observe that the [discouragement] which you appear to have thrown in the way of our servants at Surat by the various regulations you have directed them to pursue in the business of their mint, have too obvious a tendency to the benefit of that of Bombay to give us any assurance that you have been wholly guided therein by the general good of the Company. It is therefore our pleasure that you no longer interfere in the coinage of Surat otherwise than by advice or such intimations as may conduce to the mutual interests of both settlements, and we, in an especial manner, direct that our President do in no wise attempt to regulate the business of Surat mint as the interests he may have in the effects of it renders it highly improper for his having any part therein, & therefore we enjoin you to revert to the old practice & leave our servants at Surat responsible to you for their conduct in respect to the coinage at that settlement.

Mint Master's Review of the Coinage 1767 to 1784

In 1784 Charles Ware Malet took over as mint master from Samuel Martin and, on taking office, he undertook a review of the mint during the preceding 17 years, i.e. from 1767[162]:

Mr Samual Martin, having delivered over to me charge of the mint agreeable to your commands of the 3rd instant, permit me gentlemen to lay before you a state of the department on my succeeding to the direction of it deduced for the purpose of greater perspicuity thro' a retrospect of 17 years.

The new mint master observed that in 1767 an official had been appointed to oversee the coinage of Surat. This appears to have been derived from regulations created by the Bombay Council but later agreed to by the Nawab:

On the 26th June 1767 the prejudicial effects of base coinage issuing from the Surat mint being experienced, regulations were formed by the Governor and Council of this Presidency to obviate the detriment arising therefrom to the trade and revenue of this Island. On the 28th July following, a Tankshaul Master was appointed to inspect the coinage of the Surat mint and enforce the rules made for its regulation and on the 1st October of the same year the Nabob of Surat consented that his rupee should be of the same standard as that of Bombay.

---

[161] Dispatches to Bombay. IOR E/4/998 (1768-1771) p. 1169-1170. Dispatch dated 12th June 1771.

[162] Bombay Public Consultations, IOR P/342/1, 1784. p. 242, 29th March 1784. Letter from the Mint Master (Charles Ware Malet) to Government, dated 28th March 1784.

However, Surat had very similar problems caused by the debasement of the Broach rupee and the Nawab proposed that the production of the Broach rupee should be stopped:

This point being effected, the Nabob, influenced probably by a consideration that as Surat and Bombay were the only places to which bullion was or still is imported in any quantity, which seems to give them a natural right to an exclusive coinage, and finding equal reason to complain of the baseness of the Broach rupee as Bombay has to criminate[163] the Surat mint, proposed a stoppage of its currency. This measure was not only approved by the Presidency under date 22nd July 1768, but the Surat Government was further directed to take such precautions as might entirely prevent the passage of bullion to Broach.

This approach seemed to work until 1771 when it was found that the Surat rupee had been debased by 2½ per cent and this rapidly got worse, partly because the office of tanksaul master had been abolished:

Under the influence of these regulations the Bombay Mint continued to flourish until the year 1771 when in December of that year it was found that abuses had again crept in to the Surat Mint & that its rupee was debased 2½ per cent. This debasement having been suffered to pass with impunity, has been increasing with a swift progress and the check on that mint having been removed by the abolition of the office of Tanksaul Master under the 3rd April 1776, it now appears from an essay made by my direction of six new rupees sent me by the Chief of Surat, that the Surat rupee is debased from the Bombay standard no less than 10.2.55 per cent as per report enclosed. The great disuse and discredit into which the Bombay Mint has fallen by so unequal a rivalship will be seen by the enclosed statement of its coinage from 1767 to 1783 whence its decline appears to have commenced from the 1771 being the period of the debasement of the Surat mint. In considering this statement it will be necessary to observe that tho' the replacing this mint on a respectable footing has been thought so important an object to induce the Governor and Council to deprive the Governor & Council of all revenue from it, by abolishing in the year 1781 every Government duty on coinage reserving only a charge if 1¾ per cent for the bare expense of the manager, yet that end neither has nor ever can be answered so long as the degeneracy of the Surat Mint holds forth advantage so superior to the bullion holder, and its base produce continues equally current in Bombay, with that of your mint.

Malet discussed the fact that, whilst it was highly desirable to maintain the standard of the silver coins, if other local polities debased their coins, then the Bombay coins would be taken out of circulation and re-coined at the lower standard:

The purity of the coins is deservedly an object of attention to a wise Government, but when by the neighbourhood of other independent states each claiming an equal right to coin, the pure specie of that one wise Government is exhausted and drawn into their mints to be

---

[163] i.e. incriminate

returned in baser state, and while in that base state it is equally well received and equally current with the pure coin of that one Government, I flatter myself Gentlemen you will agree, that if any specie is coined, and it cannot be much in a mint labouring under such difficulties, yet will the tenacious resolution of keeping up to standard purity answer no other end than of benefiting a more designing and a less scrupulous neighbour, since even the credit of a pure coinage vanishes when the instant a rupee appears, it is hurried away to receive a new form & a new quality.

He observed that the Nawab of Surat had cleverly managed the silver standard and mint charges so as to derive a greater revenue for his mint and thereby deprive that Bombay Presidency of the income:

Permit me Gentlemen further to observe that such a stagnation of the mint must greatly affect the circulation of specie in this Island and that it is probable the great inconveniencies of the want of specie now universally [complained] of would in some manner be remedied by an active coinage, whereas from the great disproportion in the standard of the two mints, the Bombay merchants and all others, are now forced to have recourse to Surat, so that while this Government is deprived of a branch of revenue, and its circulation, the Nabob has artfully improved both by increasing his mint charges in proportion to the debasement of the rupee only observing in those charges to keep within such bounds as may render the process of his mint cheaper than it would be for the bullion holder to refine his silver to the standard of the Bombay rupee

Following the mint master's letter, the Council discussed the debasement of the Surat rupee[164]:

The Board now resume the consideration of the letter from the Mint Master read the 29th March last, being desirous to ascertain the late debasement of the Surat coinage in the most public and unexceptional manner, directed that the Chief and Council [of Surat] have orders to take samples of twenty rupees each from the different coinages of the last five years, either from the Company's treasury, if any of that coinage be now there, or else from the most reputable shroffs immediately on receipt of our orders for that purpose. They must also procure samples of the present coinage from the Nabob's mint without giving him any previous notice. One half of each of the said samples must be sealed up with the Company's seal, and sent immediately to the Presidency. The other half to be essayed at Surat in such manner as the chief and Council may think will best answer the intention of the Board in ascertaining the actual state of the coinage. We would recommend that one half of the remaining samples be essayed in the Nabob's mint, and the other by some creditable goldsmith residing under the Company's protection. They must also be directed to procure and send hither the exact standard of the Surat mint as fixed at the time of its establishment under the Mogul Government. Also the standard and charges as fixed upon in the time of the Nabob Cooley Khan as referred to in the proceedings on that subject in the year 1767. The Chief and Council

---

[164] Bombay Public Consultations, IOR P/342/1, 1784. p. 371, 14th May 1784.

[of Surat] *must be directed to proceed in this business with the greatest secrecy, so that it may not be known at the Durbar 'til the samples are secured.*

Bombay and Surat Silver Coins in the 1790s

Further attempts were made to ensure that the Surat coins were kept up to standard in the early 1790s. For instance, the weight and fineness of silver coins was discussed in 1790 in a letter from the mint master[165]:

In reply to the commands of the Honble the President in Council communicated to me in your letter of yesterday, I have to request you will inform him that the Bombay rupees should weigh exactly 1 Tola or 7 dwts 10⅓ grains and in fineness should answer 14½ better than English standard or 591 [Rice] ..25 [dwt] of pure silver and 8 [Rice] 75 of alloy

In 1790, the assay of Surat rupees showed them to be superior to any that had previously been received[166]:

Having assayed the two parcels of muster rupees just received from Surat, I am to request you will inform the Honble the Governor in Council that they not only proved of a superior quality in point of silver to any lately received, but likewise exceeded in weight, the alloy on each tola of silver being on a medium of 31¾ Rice* and excess of weight about 5 Rice

and London approved of the steps taken by Bombay to regulate the fineness of the Surat rupees[167]:

Having perused the proceedings referred to in these paras, relative to the debased coinage of the Surat mint, we very much approve your endeavours to regulate the same, trusting that your next advices will acquaint us with their having proved effectual.

In 1791 London wrote to Bombay[168]:

The information in this para that the Chief of Surat has been successful in engaging the Nabob to restore the currency of the mint to its established fineness is pleasing to us and we rely on your promised endeavours for effectually checking any attempt to debase it in future.

From all these various entries it would appear that the Bombay authorities had quite a lot of control of the Surat mint even as early as the 1760s. The tone of the records suggest some direct involvement with the mint, although this is not explicitly stated and it may have been that Bombay could only control the Surat silver standard

---

* 'Rice' appears to be used as a measure of weight in a number of instances.

[165] Bombay Public Consultations, IOR P/342/12, 1790. 26th February 1790. p. 164. Letter from the mint master (Edward Galley) to Government, dated 25th February 1790.

[166] Bombay Public Consultations, IOR P/342/12, 1790. 22nd June 1790. p. 396. Letter from the mint master (Edward Galley) to Government, dated 18th June 1890.

[167] Dispatches to Bombay. IOR E/4/1006 (1789-90), p. 288-289. Dispatch dated 21st April 1790.

[168] Dispatches to Bombay. IOR E/4/1007 (1790-91), p. 516-517. Dispatch dated 4th May 1791.

through influencing the Nawab. However it is possible that an English mint master had been appointed at Surat in the late 1780s (see chapter 7, Surat mint).

Broach Rupees

Broach Rupee. Uncertain date

Broach rupees, produced by the Nawab of Broach, were also a problem and were discussed in 1772 in a dispatch sent to Bombay from London[169]:

It is not without surprize we find that after the prohibition of Broach rupees has so repeatedly been declared to have taken its rise from their being of a quality so base and so much adulterated that to receive them into the treasury at Surat would occasion great loss to the Company, we should now be informed that they prove by assay finer than Surat rupees. It is not less astonishing that the quantity of Surat rupees should have exceedingly diminished by export whilst they were inferior in fineness to others imported under great disadvantages. These are circumstances not accounted for in your consultations. We hope the late regulations proposed and acquiesced in by the Nabob will have the desired effect but under such difficulties as appear likely to occur, we cannot altogether decide on the propriety of the measure until its utility shall have been evidenced by effects.

The effect of the Broach rupees on the trade of Surat was discussed again in 1775 in another letter from London, where the inability of the local authorities to control the quality of the Surat rupee was also discussed[170]:

The detriment which Surat must have suffered by the business of the mint having been impeded for so long a time and by the continued alarm respecting the Broach coin, which formed the chief currency of the city, and also by the peculiar hardships laid upon the Gulf traders thereby, is so evident as to render it a matter of the greatest surprize how it could escape your observation. Your conduct in this affair has been very contradictory for we find that at the time you took it up, your professed intention was to settle the standard of the Surat rupee (which you represented as having been debased) at its proper original fineness but after near four years spent in adjusting the point, it was at last so ordered that the standard was further debased than that which you had complained of. The charges for the coinage were likewise increased and the bullion of course produced fewer rupees to its owner than before you interfered in the matter. If no alteration has been made in consequence of our

---

[169] Dispatches to Bombay. IOR E/4/999 (1771-1778) p. 281-282 (in red ink). Dispatch dated 1st April 1772.
[170] Dispatches to Bombay. IOR E/4/999 (1771-1778) p. 819-822 (in red ink). Dispatch dated 12th April 1775.

disapprobation of your conduct, signified in our letter of 12ᵗʰ June 1771, it is now our positive injunction that you immediately establish the former standard and charges of the Surat mint which were customary in the year 1767 before you interfered in the business, as we can view the alterations made in no other light than as calculated for the advantage of private persons.

The Effect of Mint Charges on the Silver Coinage

In order to keep silver bullion in Bombay and persuade the owners to have it coined in the mint, Council agreed to abolish the 2½ per cent mint charges in 1781:

The President acquaints the Board that there is a quantity of private silver on the Island brought by the Freight Ships from the gulf of Mocha & that it would be of the highest benefit to the place if such an advantage could be held out to the proprietors as would induce them to continue their bullion upon the Island & convert it into Bombay currency, otherwise that they will as usual export it to Surat & Broach where it will yield a larger return from the mints.

To accomplish this end the President proposes that the mint duties should be struck off, which amount to 2½ per cent & are divided as follows: one to the Honble Company, one to the President & ½ per cent to the mint master.

The accounts of the coinage duty for the last four years being sent for, it appears upon inspection of them that the sacrifice to be made by the Company is very trivial & the President declares that he doubts not the saving of 2½ per cent. If we concur in this proposed indulgence, which when made known to the inhabitants [&] merchants will induce them to carry their silver to our mint, which at any rate will have the general good effect of throwing a greater quantity of the best rupees into circulation.

This matter being taken into consideration, it is resolved for the reasons above set forth to strike off the coinage duty of 2½ per cent heretofore collected on all private gold & silver coined in the mint of which due notice must be given by Proclamation

Duty to Reduce Export of Silver from Bombay

In 1785, the mint undertaker suggested that a 5% customs duty should be levied on anyone exporting silver from Bombay so as to induce them to take their bullion to the mint for coining[171]:

The [Betrery] has arrived from Mocha and has brought treasure in Dollars and there are the other vessels expected from thence, which will also bring treasure. The Dollars by the [Betrery] are exporting to [Nof..] to be coined then into rupees, as the rupee of the coinage of that place is less in value than Bombay rupees in 25 per cent. Dollars are therefore carried thither in order to reap that advantage. This exportation of Dollars from this Island [tends] prejudicial to the mint of this place so much that even the expenses of keeping the mint house cannot be cleared. May it please Your Honor etc, it is an established rule at Surat that all merchants who import Dollars are obliged to give in a manifest into the Phoorza [i.e.Customs] office & the mint office and if afterwards found that the proprietors of the Dollars or other kinds of

---

[171] Bombay Public Consultations, IOR P/342/4, 1785. p. 975/979. 30ᵗʰ September 1785. Petition of Lolldass Goverdondass. mint undertaker at Bombay, read on 30ᵗʰ September 1785.

silver did not send their Dollars to be coined, they are charged five per cent customs on the amount of the Dollars they imported. This rule was established to prevent the Dollars being exported and thereby prevent a scarcity of cash. Your petitioner humbly conceives that if the same rule was adopted and ordered by Your Honor etc, to be observed here it will be attended with great convenience to the Publick in having plenty of cash in the place and it will also be a benefit to the Mint Officer of this place.

The Bombay Council did not immediately adopt this idea but in 1786 they did impose a 3% duty on the exportation of silver except, ironically, to Surat[172]:

Taking into consideration the very great scarcity of silver on the Island and the evil which arises from the exportation of all the silver brought to this place, particularly to Poonah, where a mint is kept in which they coin a debased rupee, whereby it becomes an object to private persons to carry off our Bombay rupees to re-coin; moreover, as this is the season when ships arrive with treasure from the [Gulph], it is resolved in order to put a stop to the above inconvenience as far as possible, that the resolutions of this Government of the 17th August 1770 be revived and that all bullion, silver, or silver coins exported from hence (except to Surat) be charged with a duty of 3 per cent, which must be made known by publication and the Bombay and Mahim Customs Masters must be directed to pay the strictest attention thereto.

Silver Output

The amount of silver coinage produced was only occasionally discussed by the Bombay council. In December 1727 an entry in the records stated that bullion coined that year amounted to about 686,123 rupees[173]:

…The President lays before the Board the mint masters acct of the Honble Company's bullion coin'd in the mint this present year ending the 18th instant amounting to rupees six hundred and eighty six thousand one hundred and twenty three, two quarters, fifty one Raes which is received into the treasury and on examination found to balance the acct of silver consigned this Presidency.

Records show silver being delivered into the mint during most months in 1749, 1750 and 1751 but do not state the amount. For instance[174], [175], [176]:

There being a quantity of chopt and uncurrent rupees in the treasury, which will not pass but at a great discount, and we shall shortly be in want of a sum of new money to send to the coast settlements – Ordered that they be new stampt in like manner as has been done the two preceding years, being the method by which the Hon Company sustains only a loss of little more than half per cent.

---

172 Bombay Public Consultations, IOR P/342/5, 1786. 7th July 1786. p. 594.
173 Bombay Public Consultations, IOR P/341/6, Friday 22nd December 1727.
174 Bombay Public Consultations, IOR P/341/17, p. 13, December 1749.
175 Bombay Public Consultations, IOR P/341/17, p. 47, January 1750.
176 Bombay Public Consultations, IOR P/341/18, p. 134, 2nd April 1751.

The mint output from 1767 to 1782/3 was given by Mr Malet, the mint master in 1784. This appears to show the value of silver coins produced but may include gold coins as well[177]:

	Rupee Value (rounded)
1767 to 1768	400,937
1768 to	619,618
1769	146,118
1770	764,860
1771	663,774
1772	425,946
1773	298,858
1774	442,172
1775	156,805
1776	576,227
1777	6,201
1778	124,004
1779	30,225
1780	11,016
1781	75,155
1782 to 1783	190,103

In 1810 the mint master produced a report showing the mint output from 1780 to 1800[178]:

…I have the honor to report that on a retrospect of the last thirty years, the Bombay mint does not appear to have ever ceased working altogether except during the short period of one year (the official year 1794/5) and that the native establishment were not then deprived of their stipends.

Previously to the year 1800 the mint was in a very inefficient state and the coinage was small compared to what it has since been…

…For the further satisfaction of the Honble the Governor in Council I annex a statement exhibiting the annual extent of the operations of the mint for the last 30 years, viz 1780/1 to 1809/10.

---

[177] Bombay Public Consultations, IOR P/342/1, 1784. p. 242, 29th March 1784. Letter from the mint master (Charles Ware Malet) to Government, dated 28th March 1784.

[178] Bombay Public Consultations. IOR P/344/36. p. 430. Letter from the mint master (GC Osborne) to Government, dated 31st December 1810.

Date	Total Output			Calculated approx. silver output (Rs value)
	Rupees	Annas	Reas	
1st May 1780/1	16,030	2	81	25,000
1781/2	75,155	1	17	
1782/3	240,146		17	25,000
1783/4	10,311	0	73	
1784/5	252,182	1	01	100,000
1785/6	145,391	0	52	50,000
1786/7	29,072	1	52	
1787/8	130,923	0	0	60,000
1788/9	74,950	2	54	44,000
1789/90	161,935	1	57	Insufficient information
1790/1	105,251	0	04	Insufficient information
1791/2	209,979	2	44	110,000
1792/3	97,987	2	0	15,000
1793/4	86,097	2	80	Insufficient information
1794/5	0			0
1795/6	279,532	2	36	0
1796/7	370,596	0	75	0
1797/8	93,284	2	87	0
1798/9	132,168	2	62	0
1799/1800	434,508	3	0	0

This statement presumably includes both gold and silver. The output of gold was given separately in a different report (shown above under the discussion of the gold coinage) and by subtracting one from another it is possible to estimate the silver output, which is shown in the right hand column above. The annual outputs shown in the two tables do not match exactly so some of the years have been merged and there are figures missing in some years. Despite this, it seems fairly clear that the mint was producing silver coins up until the early 1790s although Prinsep[179] stated that the coinage of silver in the Bombay mint was suspended for 20 years during this period. Pridmore believed that Prinsep may have copied Milburn[180] in making this statement but it is clearly not true given the information shown in the table above.

Source of Silver

Silver bullion was either imported into Bombay by the ships of the EIC and then delivered to the mint for coinage, or was obtained in trade by local merchants who might then deliver it to the mint and have it coined at a charge. The silver came in various guises and there are a number of entries in the records revealing the different

[179] Princep (1834), Useful Tables p. 19.
[180] Pridmore p. 123.

sorts of silver coins that might be delivered to the mint. In 1724 the mint master discussed various coins that had been presented at the mint[181]:

The mint master, his account of coinage of the Hon'ble Company's silver last month where in chest No. 629 it appears that the bag No 2515 said to be Pillar Dollars is found to contain the following species [W^gt]

	lb.	Oz.
Pillar Dollars	*49*	*1*
& Mexico	*1*	*7*
German Crowns	*16*	*10*
French Crowns	*5*	*2*
	lb.	*Oz*
	72	*8*

which being a mixture of coins of baser alloy occasions a loss to the Hon'ble Company of Rupees thirty one quarter ninety four Raes & a half.
Resolved to give our Hon'ble Masters Acco't thereof in our next advices'

In 1768 a letter from the mint master includes a list of the different silver coins and the prices paid by the mint undertaker. The list is as follows[182]:

English Crowns
French ditto
German or Hungarian ditto (coined before 1750)
New ditto (coined since 1750)
Old Piller Dollars (coined before 1726)
New ditto (coined since 1726)
Old Mexico ditto (coined before 1726)
New ditto (coined since 1726)
New Phillip (the round, new milled ditto)
Telatas and Piccasters
Lyon Dollars
Rezeens
Pistereens
Goa Pardoes
Nadarees fine
Ducatoons
Rose Dollars
Mamoodys
New Abassees

---

181 Bombay Public Consultations, IOR P/341/5, Friday 19th June 1724.
182 Bombay Public Consultations, IOR P/341/31, 1768. p. 445. 26th July 1768.

Old ditto
Crusadoes
Rix Dollars

Private persons were also allowed to bring silver from England to Bombay. In 1790 several individuals are recorded as having been allowed to take various amounts of gold and silver to India, mainly in south American dollars[183, 184]:

We have permitted Mr Francis Wm Pemberton to take with him to Bombay the value of £10,000 in Dollars or Portugal gold coins. The silver to be consigned to you and to be coined into rupees.
Mr James Morley has also permission to take with him to your Presidency the value of £26,000 in Spanish Dollars on the same terms and conditions.

We have permitted Mr George [Loribind] to remit to Mr James Stevens at Bombay, Dollars to the amount of about £600 on the terms and conditions mentioned in the 2nd paragraph of this letter.
Messrs Alburn & Carstairs have likewise our permission to remit to Bombay the amount of £4000 in New Mexico Dollars on the same terms.

Assays

There are a number of entries referring to the methods of ensuring the quality of the coins produced in the mint at Bombay. An order from the Directors dated 5th February 1741[185], required:

For our satisfaction the assay master must report to you in writing that he hath duly assayed every parcel of rupees and acquaint you whether or not they come up to the standard in fineness and weight. He must enter the same upon Consultation, and, as is the custom at Fort St. George, one of the Council must draw five rupees promiscuously out of each months coinage, and seal them up immediately with his own seal, which must be transmitted to us in the packet.

This order was obviously based on an earlier instruction because an entry in the records confirms that the rupees were selected[186] and sent to Madras following instructions given on 6th February 1740.
Bombay complied with the instructions from London[187]:

Comformable to our Honble Masters directions in their letter of 6th February 1640, Mr. Dudley has promiscuously taken five rupees out of the money coined this month which he

---

[183] Dispatches to Bombay. IOR E/4/1006 (1789-90), p. 187. Dispatch dated 21st April 1790.
[184] Dispatches to Bombay. IOR E/4/1006 (1789-90), p. 265. Dispatch dated 21st April 1790.
[185] Letters to Bombay, 5th February 1741. India Office Collections. Cited from Pridmore p. 118.
[186] Bombay Public Consultations, Friday 16th October 1741. India Office Collections P/341/12.
[187] Bombay Public Consultations, IOR P/341/12, Friday 16th October 1741.

now delivers in, sealed with his own seal. Directed that the same be accordingly enclosed in the Fort St George Packett.

A Mr Davis was in Bombay as the assay master in May 1741 because a record exists of him being asked to provide a report to the Bombay Council specifying the standard for rupees and also how to make them more quickly[188].

Counterfeiting

Forgery was a constant problem. In 1775 fake gold rupees (which probably meant coins of Mohur weight at this time) were discovered in circulation and steps were taken to find the culprit[189]:

There being several counterfeit gold rupees now circulating on the Island, it is agreed to offer a reward of one thousand rupees to any person or persons who will make discovery of the persons concerning them, so that offenders may be brought to justice.

And in December of the same year several people were accused, found guilty and punished for forging silver rupees[190]:

Mr Draper lays before the Board some depositions he has taken in consequence of an information made before him against a Parsee Priest and two goldsmiths for counterfeiting silver rupees, and the circumstances appearing strong against them, Resolved that they be flogged at the pillory put upon the works for six months & then turned off the island & their effects confiscated. The Sepoy who made the discovery to have a reward of three hundred rupees.

In 1789, the mint contractor discovered some gold coins that turned out to be gold plated forgeries with a silver core[191]:

That as he was passing through the Buzar the day before yesterday, he saw Bicardass and Jevandass, two shroffs, disputing with each other. That on enquiring the cause, he found that the former had just received one hundred gold mohurs from the latter, and that he was challenging six of them as uncurrent. That, suspecting the rupees were false, he, on his return home, sent his servant for Jevandass, desiring him to bring with him the six rupees in dispute. That, finding them not to be the coinage of the Honble Company's mint, he, in presence of Jevandass, immediately cut in pieces two of the rupees and found that each of them contained a plate of silver in the centre. That on his asking Jevandass where he got the rupees, he answered he had received them in the course of business but could not tell from whom. Jevandass has lately arrived from Radalpore, a place near Bhwanagar and opened a shop here. The rupees are worth about ten rupees each.

---

[188] Bombay Public Consultations, Friday 15th May 1741. India Office Collections P/341/12.
[189] Bombay Public Consultations, IOR P/341/41, 1775. p. 619. 12th December 1775.
[190] Bombay Public Consultations, IOR P/341/41, 1775. p. 628. 22nd December 1775.
[191] Bombay Public Consultations, IOR P/342/11, 1789. 4th December 1789. p. 838. The information of Loldass, the Honble Company's mint contractor.

In consequence of the above information, we think it necessary that the shroff on whom the debased gold rupees were found should be taken before the sitting Magistrate for examination, in order that a discovery may be made if possible by what means he became possessed of the rupees in accusation.

Copper Coins – 1728

Double pice 1728

Between about 1716 and 1728 no copper coins appear to have been produced and the need for small change was met by tin coins. In 1728, a large shipment of copper coins had been received from Persia, and a decision was made to reintroduce copper coins[192]. The coins were to be issued at 72 to the rupee and 20½ rupees to the Surat maund of copper[193]:

The President observes to the Board that thro' out tinn duccanees being made currant in the Portuguese country there has been lately a considerable decrease in the bank gains on the monthly exchange of them, but as a conveniency will hereby offer of getting rid of a good quantity of those ducannees & more so, by lowering still their value, whereby we may introduce their passing currant the copper Goz we have rece'd from Persia at seventy two to the rupee, which will be more than equivalent to answer for the loss that will accrue by lowering the value of the former, as the said Goz will yield about thirty per cent profit. Besides that we may expect on them the like gain by exchange as was before made by the other.

Which being agreed to as the President shall find most convenient. It is ordered that the warehousekeeper issues out to the bank what copper shall be thought necessary for that use to be stampt anew at twenty rupees and half per Surat maund.

Three denominations appear to have been struck in 1728 – a double, single and half pice. Occasionally, on the larger pieces, traces of an earlier design can be observed and the weights between specimens of similar sizes are very erratic. Goron[194] has identified the underlying coin on a pice dated 1733 as a Persian fulus or goz, and it seems likely that, based on the observations above, the larger coins, at least, were struck directly onto the goz coins. The copper coins imported from Persia were not always used for coinage. For instance, In July 1742, a consignment of copper goz was received from Persia, but as copper was still in short supply, it was sold as metal at public auction. It had been intended when the consignment was ordered, to re-coin

---

[192] Bombay Public Consultations, IOR P/341/6, Friday 9th August 1728.
[193] Bombay Public Consultations. IOR P/341/6, Friday 9th August 1728.
[194] Goron, S, (1997), ONS 154, p. 22

them into Bombay pice, but the Council considered this would serve no useful purpose as they would soon have been drained away to the mainland[195]

A new style of tin coin had been issued beginning in 1717 (see later) and the design of the copper coins followed this. This design, together with the weight, distinguishes the coins from earlier issues. The presence of G and R on each side of the orb at the top of the crown, instead of stars, is often a feature that can be seen. The decoration around the top of the crown is also a distinctive feature on the double and single pice of this type. This is a number of beads as opposed to the loops on the previous issue. Some half pice show beads and some show loops[196] so this cannot be used to identify which issue this lower denomination belongs to.

Because the dies are too large for the flans, the date is often not visible, particularly on the smaller denomination coins. A pice with the date 1728 has been confirmed since Pridmore's original listing[197].

Copper Coins – 1733

In 1733 the rate of exchange between the copper pice and the silver rupee was fixed at 80 pice per rupee. This was the official exchange rate but the actual rate in the bazar would have fluctuated depending on the availability of the coins. Prior to this, in 1728, the rate had been 72 pice to each rupee[198]:

In obedience to the 39th para of our Honble Masters' commands last received by the Mary, that for the future the officers, soldiers and sailors in the military and marine shall be paid as their covenanted servants in silver. Directed that the land and marine paymasters do accordingly pay them in silver or pice, at the rate of eighty pice for one silver rupee and that there may be no objection to this exchange, it is agreed that for the future eighty pice shall be received into the Honble Company's treasury, the custom House cash, the warehouse and the general stores, as a rupee.

Directed that a publication be issued to this purpose that all inhabitants may be apprized thereof, to take place from the first of April.

Copper Coins – 1738

In 1738 a private merchant had obviously bought some copper from the Company and planned to have it coined at the mint. He first had a small quantity coined in order to ascertain the charges. In the end, the Bombay Council decided against allowing him to have the remainder coined at Bombay as it might undermine the activities of the Surat mint[199]:

---

[195] Bombay Public Consultations, IOR P.341/12, Thursday 30th July 1741.
[196] Personal communication from Thompson.
[197] Stevens P.J.E., SCMB Sept 1985 p. 279.
[198] Bombay Public Consultations, IOR P/341/7A, Friday 30th March 1733.
[199] Bombay Public Consultations, IOR P/341/9, Saturday 23rd December 1738.

The purchaser of the Honble Company's copper having been allowed to coin ten maunds in order to ascertain the mint charges & to know how much more he could afford to give the Honble Company for permission to coin a quantity. The President acquaints the Board that the mint undertakers had delivered him on account coinage of ten maunds whereby the charges appear to be rupees three per maund as follows:

	Rupees
Waste in melting or running the copper into small bars, two seers per maund	*1,0,00*
Earthen fire places and pots	*0,0,50*
Workmanship per maund	*1,0,50*
Cutting stamps and stamping	*0,0,60*
Charcoal, three baskets used to one maund of copper, at five baskets per rupee	*0,2,40*
Charges per maund	*3,0,00*

The purchaser being then called in and asked what he is willing to give (besides paying the charge for the liberty of coinage) he makes an offer of one rupee per Surat maund, which, the Board refusing, he at length offers one rupee and half per Surat maund, declaring it to be the most he can give.

The Board debating thereupon it is observed that our giving permission for coining said copper here would occasion some trouble and dispute with the Surat Governor as it would be depriving him of so much of his revenue, besides that we have not people enough here nor would others care to come without being certain of a constant employ. We therefore don't think proper to grant the permission requested but agreed that we represent the case to the Honble Company that if they think it worthwhile to hazard a dispute with the Surat Governor (which we believe would only be for one year) for the profit they may reap by coining the copper here they may give us our orders accordingly; and we must observe we are informed a considerable quantity even seven or eight thousand maunds per annum may be sold and coined here if they are pleased to give permission…

A possible candidate for this trial coinage has been discussed and is shown on the next page[200], although a more recent example that has come to light shows a possible regnal year of 10, which would equate to 1728/29, instead of 1738. Perhaps a similar event occurred at the earlier date. This coin was first published in 2002 in the Newsletter of IIRNS where the regnal year was read as a possible 16 but 10 now seems more likely.[201]

---

[200] Stevens PJE, (2014), JONS 220, pp. 41-42
[201] Sanjay Sahadev, IIRNS Newsline Issue 34, April 2002, p.6

Copper dam possibly struck as a trial in 1728 or 1738

Copper Coins – 1748 & 1749

On 23rd February 1748[202] the Bombay Council discussed the copper coinage and considered that if they could produce a high quality die then a new copper coinage would not be counterfeited like the old coins were. They happened to have received a large quantity of copper from Persia and calculated that turning this into pice would yield a profit of over 19 per cent.

The calculation showed a pice weighing c90 troy grains at 80 pice to the rupee. No copper coins are known dated 1748. It could be that the project was abandoned because the management of the mint changed at about this time[203].

Council discussed the shortage of copper pice on 13th June 1749[204] and instructed the Warehousekeeper to deliver 75 maunds of copper to the mint. Pice dated 1749 do exist, so this coinage presumably went ahead.

Copper Coins 1751

In 1751 a request to have copper coined in the mint was agreed to[205]:

The President acquaints the Board that some people are very desirous of coining copper pice, stamping them in our mint. As this will increase the Honble Company's revenue and be a means of raising the price of copper (which is now a falling commodity) considerably, as that which comes from Europe is chiefly used for this purpose, it is assented to.

No coins dated 1751 are known so perhaps this did not happen or the coins were dated 1749.

Copper Coins – Balemark Type – 1773

By 1773, the zinc pice were causing problems (see below) and a decision was taken to issue a new copper coinage[206]:

---

[202] Bombay Public Consultations. IOR P/341/15, 23rd February 1748.

[203] Bombay Public Consultations. IOR P/341/15, 25th March, 1748.

[204] Bombay Public Consultations IOR P/341/16, 13th June 1749.

[205] Bombay Public Consultations, IOR P/341/18, p. 440, 29th October 1751.

[206] Bombay Public Consultations, IOR P/341/39, 1773. pp. 682.5th October 1773.

...But as we are convinced that the only effectual means of putting a stop to all those complaints regarding pice, is to call in those made of Tutenague [i.e. zinc], and to coin such a quantity of copper pice as will be sufficient for the currency of the place.

Resolved that to the amount of 20,000 rupees of copper be coined into pice as soon as possible, a proportionable quantity of which must be in halves and quarters, and when the same are ready to be issued, the toothenague pice coined by the Company will be called in and all others rendered uncurrent.

Double pice 1773

In October 1773 a proclamation was created announcing a new copper coinage[207], although it was not actually issued until November[208]:

by beat of drum all over this town and fixed in the necessary languages at the usual places. It was also made publick at the same time at Mahim and other places:

Whereas it has been represented to the Honble the President and Council that inconveniences do arise to the trade of this place and particularly to the lower sort of people because pice are not freely accepted in payments made into the Honble Company's Treasury, the Honble President and Council aforesaid, in order effectually to put a stop thereto do hereby declare that from henceforth so far as one half of the amount of all sums paid into the Treasury will be accepted in pice, if desired, provided always that the pice so tendered be of the Honble Company's, but as there are many pice now on the Island that have been coined surreptitiously, which are easily distinguished from those coined by the Honble Company, it is therefore further declared that proper persons are ordered to attend at the Treasury for examining all pice that are offered in payment, and should any be found not of the Company's coinage, orders are given for their being [directly] cut in two, and they shall be forfeit to the Company.

By November 1773, between ten and twelve thousand rupees worth of pice had been coined[209]:

As the amount of from ten to twelve thousand rupees of the copper pice are now coined. Resolved that they be issued from the Treasury on the first of the ensuing month of December.

---

[207] Bombay Public Consultations, IOR P/341/39, 1773. pp. 694. 6th October 1773. A Proclamation.

[208] Bombay Public Consultations, IOR P/341/39, 1773. pp. 849. 30th November 1773.

[209] Bombay Public Consultations, IOR P/341/39, 1773. pp. 839. 26th November 1773.

Against that time that a proclamation must be prepared noticing that the same are to pass current and declaring all toothenague pice uncurrent from that time. All Toothenague pice that are of the Company's coinage and may be brought into their Treasury on or before the 31st of the ensuing month of December will be received on their account and we shall hereafter determine how to dispose of them.

Described by Pridmore as a 'wretched issue', these coins are crudely designed and poorly struck.

Copper Coins – 1775

Pridmore did not find archival references to coins with later dates and considered that they might be forgeries. However, further entries have now been found and it seems likely that coins were struck in several later years. For instance, a further coinage took place in 1775[210]:

Ordered as it is represented that there is a want of copper pice on the Island, that copper to the amount of 20,000 rupees be issued from the warehouse to the mint where it must be coined as soon as possible.

Copper Coins – 1783/4

It is possible that a further issue took place in 1783 because a double pice exists and appears to show this date:

Double pice 1783

However, no archival reference has been found to confirm the striking of copper coins in 1783. In 1784 an entry in the records states[211]:

The President also acquaints the Board that there is a great want of small currency in the place, and proposes that a quantity of copper be immediately coined. Ordered that 100 maunds of plate and the same quantity of Japan copper be delivered to the minters and that directions be given to the Mint Master to have it coined into single pice of 100 to the rupee of the usual weight. He must further have directions to keep a separate account of the produce and charges of coinage of each [sortment]

---

[210] Bombay Public Consultations, IOR P/341/41, 1775. p. 265, 14th April 1775.
[211] Bombay Public Consultations, IOR P/342/2, 1784. p. 862, 9th November 1784.

By 1785, it appeared that too many pice had been produced[212]:

Read two petitions from the Tobacco and Arrack Farmers representing the great loss they daily sustain by the very high value or exchange there is at present in the Buzar of pice into silver rupees, desiring such relief as the Board may think proper. These petitions are ordered to be entered after this consultation.

On consideration of these petitions, we have to observe that the exigencies of Government during the late war have at times obliged us to coin copper pice, which after the conclusion of peace and the restoration of our several acquisitions, have returned to Bombay. By a reference to an account (laid before us by the President) of the copper pice coined of this place within the last ten years, it appears it has amounted to Surat Maunds 6067..35 seer..15 Pice and may be valued at Rupees 199,570..-..33, a sum more than double what is required for the currency of this Island, Salsette and Caranja; and as we are desirous to remedy the evil complained of, which is now become a burthen insupportable to the laborious and poorer class of the inhabitants, from the great loss they suffer when obliged to change pice into silver rupees, It is resolved to adopt the following manners which appear but calculated to remove the grievance and [mend it] with the smallest possible loss to the Company Viz:

That the assistant to the treasurer be directed to purchase as many pice as will amount to two thousand maunds (being a third of the quantity now in circulation) at the present market price, which it is proposed shall be defaced and sold as lump copper.

Pice 1784

Pice – Countermarked – 1788

No records have been traced to explain the reason for the production of copper coins with the BOMB countermark in 1788. Pridmore suggested a possible answer. On 3rd April 1788 Tellicherry had asked Bombay to send more pice[213]:

"There being a great scarcity of Pice in our Buzar. We are to request your Honor &c will furnish us with that Coin to the Amount of ten thousand Rupees in the first Consignment of Treasure you shall be pleased to make us."

---

[212] Bombay Public Consultations, IOR P/342/4, 1785. p. 1136. 28th October 1785.
[213] Pridmore p. 124.

Countermarked pice, 1788

Bombay sent pice to the value of rupees 3537,,2,,50, and this may have drained the Treasury of its stock of pice[214]

Pridmore states that the Bombay mint appeared to have been at a standstill in 1788, although we now know that this was not the case, and that the production of the countermarked coins may have been a simple way of meeting the demands of Tellicherry. Another possible explanation, if they were used in Tellicherry, is that the Bombay authorities could not meet Tellicherry's demands for copper coin, so the Tellicherry authorities took it upon themselves to produce these countermarked coins. In December 1788 a letter from the Tellicherry factory in reply to a request for details of the coins that passed current there[215], states:

As to Copper coins – Bombay Pice are the only of that metal that pass.

---

[214] *Ibid.*
[215] *Ibid*

Tin Coins

In 1724 the number of tin pice that had been produced was found to be too high for the needs of Bombay and it was decided that a number of them should be turned back into bars and sold. Presumably these would have been the coins dated 1717[216]:

The President represents to the Board that there is about forty thousand rupees of tin pice on the island that he finds twenty thousand sufficient to answer the occasions thereon so that there remains continually in the treasury from fifteen to twenty thousand dead stock & therefore offers it as his opinion for the interest of our Hon'ble masters that it be run down into bars convenient for sale.

Which being debated and considered that the rate at which the pice is now current is about sixteen rupees the maund Surat, the running of them will be [asuming tho'] no real loss to our Hon'ble employers and whereas that commodity in all probability will be at a higher rate the next season than it has been for some years past, it is the unanimous opinion of the Board that such a quantity of said pice as shall be found unnecessary, be run down into proper bars for sale which is hereby directed to be done accordingly.

Another entry reads[217]:

The President observes to the Board that thro' our tinn duccanees being made currant in the Portuguese country, there has been lately a considerable decrease in the Bank gain in the monthly exchange of them, but as a conveniency will hereby offer of getting rid of a good quantity of those Docanees & more so by lowering still their value.

Tutenague (Zinc) Coins – 1741 to 1743

Double pice 1741

By 1741 there was a shortage of copper coins and a decision was taken to produce new pice made of tutenague (zinc)[218]:

The present scarcity of copper on the place having induced the people of the neighbouring countries to convey away the tin pice made of that metal, it is proposed to coin a parcel of tutenague ones to be of such weight as to reserve a profit to our Honble Masters of twenty per

---

[216] Bombay Public Consultations. IOR P/341/5, Friday 22nd May 1724.
[217] Bombay Public Consultations. IOR P/341/6, Friday 9th July 1728.
[218] Bombay Public Consultations. IOR P/341/12, Saturday 7th February 1741.

cent. Which is agreed to and ordered that the mint master do out of hand coin to the amount of two hundred rupees

Accordingly, in June 1741 tutengue (zinc) was purchaced for the purpose[219]:

In consequence of the order passed for coining tutenague pice the 7th February last, the President had purchased from [Rupjee Dunjee] two hundred twenty seven Surat maunds and twenty six seer at seven rupees and a half per md which amounted to rupees seventeen hundred and seven, one quarter and 88 raes, and produced rupees two thousand two hundred seven and an half, from the same person, another parcel of five hundred Surat maund at six rupees and ten annas per maund; But as these were not sufficient for the current service of the place, he had promised a further quantity of five hundred Surat maunds at the like rate from the [Cursettjee] which being the cheapest rates that commodity could be purchased upon. The Board approved thereof the account. Produce of the last parcels cannot now be ascertained as the mint people have not as yet coined the same.

By October 1741 the coins had been produced and were found to be very profitable[220]:

An account [of the] coinage of the several parcels of tutenague into pice being presented, we have the satisfaction to observe a neat gain of rupees 3841.1.57 accrued to our Honble Masters in this transaction.

Further quantities were minted in 1742 and 1743. The weight of this new pice was to be such as would return a profit of 20 per cent to the Company and certainly the 1741 coinages were profitable[221].

Counterfeit Tutenague (Zinc) Coins to be handed in – 1748

In February 1748 the public were to be given fifteen days to bring any counterfeit coins to the treasury where they would be exchanged for the value of their metal, after that they would be confiscated. The proclamation was issued on 29th February 1748[222]:

It being found there are false pice made of tutenague to a considerable extent on this island which are daily passed in payment to the prejudice of the inhabitants in Genl but more particularly of the poorer sort, resolved that a publication be made requiring all persons who may be possessed of such pice to bring them to the Ho Company's mint within fifteen days where it is agreed that they will be taken on the Honble Company's account according to the value of the mettle such false pice are composed and be paid for out of the treasury accordingly. But any person or persons shall after the expiration of these fifteen days, attempt to pass such false pice in payment or be found possessed of any such, the same will be forfeited, one half to the informer and the other half as this Board shall think reasonable to dispose of.

---

[219] Bombay Public Consultations. IOR P/341/12, June 1741.
[220] Bombay Public Consultations. IOR P/341/12, Thursday 8th October 1741.
[221] Bombay Public Consultations, IOR P/341/12, Thursday 8th October 1741.
[222] Bombay Public Consultations. IOR P/341/15, 23rd February 1748.

It being considered on this occasion that pice made of copper from a good die which can be cut in a neat manner by an European here would be less liable to counterfeit by these country people than the pice that have been heretofore coined on this Island, it is agreed that two hundred and twenty Surat maunds of the old copper received per Drake Ketch be accordingly delivered to the mint for being coined into pice, valuing it at about rupees twenty eight one quarter, sixty four reas (28.1.64) per Surat maund, which, exclusive of the charge of coinage, will yield a profit of Rs 29.136 per cent to the honble Company as appears by the following calculation…

The proclamation was issued on 29th February 1748[223] :

This day was issued in the usual manner the publication concerning false pice comformable to our resolution in consultation the 23rd instant.

Pridmore identified some of the 1741 tin coins that appear cruder than usual, and also seem to contain a high proportion of lead. These may be the counterfeits referred to above.

Tutenague (Zinc) Coins – 1754

In 1754 a further coinage of zinc coins took place[224]:

Double pice, no date

Read, a letter from Mr John Spencer, mint master, setting forth that the island is in great want of pice but that the present very high price of copper would make them turn out to the disadvantage of the Honble Company were they to be made of that article. That Toothenague is now cheaper than it has been for many years past and that 1000 or 1500 Surat maunds will supply the necessity of the place.

Resolved that this quantity be purchased on the most reasonable terms, and as we are persuaded that it will be for the Honble Company's advantage to make it on their own account, allowing the minters something for their trouble, directed that order be issued to the mint master accordingly.

No coins with this date are known so these may be the undated type shown above.

---

[223] Bombay Public Consultations. IOR P/341/15, Tuesday 29th February 1748.
[224] Bombay Public Consultations, IOR P/341/19, p. 61 19th February 1754.

Half and Quarter Tutenague (Zinc) Pice – 1757

Half pice with value written in numerals

In 1757 the mint master was ordered to produce half and quarter pice. Whether these were of copper or zinc is not clear, but zinc seems the more likely at this time[225]:

The poorer sort of our inhabitants complaining of the want of small money. Agreed that the Mint Master be ordered to get the value of ten thousand (10,000) rupees coined into half and quarter (1/2 & 1/4) pice

Two types of tin half pice and one type of quarter pice exist. One type of the half pice has the value written in numerals as does the quarter pice. The other type of half pice does not state the value and has a design similar to the undated double and single pice. Whether all of these should be attributed to this issue or the halves should be separated into two separate issues is not clear from the above extract. However, the great difference in the styles of the two half pice types, suggests that these were two separate issues. Since the above extract refers to halves and quarters, a reasonable inference would be that those zinc half and quarter pice of the same type belong to this issue of 1757. The other type of half pice matches the undated double pice and single pice much more closely and was probably issued with those coins in 1754.

zinc half pice. Wt = 10.23g

Tutenague (Zinc) Pice – 1769

A further coinage took place in 1769[226]:

---

[225] Bombay Public Consultations, IOR P/341/21, 1757 p. 249.
[226] Bombay Public Consultations, IOR P/341/32, 1769. p. 569. 5th July 1769.

There being a great scarcity of pice on the Island, Ordered that Tuthenague to the amount of twenty thousand (20,000) rupees to be purchased and coined into pice at its present price of eight (8) rupees per Surat maund.

Like the 1754 issue, no coins dated 1769 are known, so these might also be the undated type shown above.

Tutenague (Zinc) Pice – 1771

More zinc was bought in 1771[227]:

An offer being made us of Tuthanague to the amount of Rs 30,000 at 7/4 per maund for bills on Europe, it is agreed the same be accepted as it will be a means of assisting us with so much currency & the Company gain about 15 per cent in coining the same into pice.

Double pice 1771

By 1772 a problem arose with the high amount charged when changing zinc pice into rupees and steps were taken to control this[228]:

On this head. Read a letter from the Military Paymaster in respect to the exchange on pice, which is daily rising, enclosing one to him from the Brigadier General on the subject, & requesting the directions of the Board. As the exchange of silver and vice versa was limited by a publication in the year 1757 to half a pice per rupee which if duly observed will effectually put a stop to the evil complained of. It is therefore resolved that it be republished & the most punctual observance of it required under proper penalties.

Tutenague (Zinc) Pice – 1773 – Coinage stopped

However, the following year the problem still persisted and a decision was taken to reduce the value of the pice from 80 per rupee to 100. Furthermore it was decided to stop the production of zinc pice and to revert to copper[229]:

Notwithstanding the publication that was issued last year limiting the exchange to be taken on tutenague pice into silver to half a pice in a rupee which before then was very high and

---

[227] Bombay Public Consultations, IOR P/341/34, 1771. p. 176. 19th March 1771.
[228] Bombay Public Consultations, IOR P/341/38, 1772. pp. 845. 6th October 1772.
[229] Bombay Public Consultations, IOR P/341/39, 1773. pp. 663. 21st September 1773.

much complained of, yet the same has proved totally ineffectual, as the exchange is actually higher than before being about ten per cent on exchanging pice into silver, which is a great loss and detriment to the soldiers, sepoys and labourers who are chiefly paid in pice, as well as to the poor in general. The means for putting a stop thereto are therefore taken into consideration, when it is answered that from the very low price toothanague has been for some time past and from the vast quantity of pice upon the island we have reason to conclude that great numbers must be made on the other side and brought over hither. It is therefore resolved for putting a stop at present to the many inconveniences attending the same that a proclamation be issued tomorrow crying down the value of pice from 80 to 100 for every rupee commencing from the moment it is published, but as even then toothenague may be made into pice to great advantage by persons on the other side [not sure if this means on the mainland or on the other side of the Gulf of Cambay?], *as we suppose has been hitherto practiced, it is further resolved and agreed that all pice that may be coined in future shall be of copper and one hundred to a rupee, and that they be of such a weight as just to answer the value of copper, with the expense, and from henceforward no Toothenague pice will be coined in our mint.*

By October of 1773 the zinc coins would not pass current in the bazaar and it was agreed that the treasury would accept half of any payment due in zinc pice. However, the zinc coins had been extensively forged and a decision was taken to issue a large number of copper pice and to call in all the zinc pice[230]:

Great numbers of complaints are daily made that toothenague pice do not pass current in the Bazar, since our proclamation reducing them in value, which upon consideration we are of opinion may in a great measure be owing to pice not being received from all persons in payments made into our treasury. It is therefore agreed in order to remedy the many inconveniences complained of, that from henceforward in all sums tendered at the Treasury, one half will be accepted in pice, if desired, provided the pice so tendered be of the Company's Coinage. But as we are convinced from the vast quantity of Pice on the Island that great numbers must have been coined surreptitiously, which must have turned out to the great advantage of those who have coined them, toothenague for a long time past having been at a very low price and we understand that these surreptitious pice are easily distinguishable from those of the Company, it is resolved, in order to put a stop to this pernicious and unlawful practice of coining pice as well as to remedy evil [subsisting] by the quantity that has been already coined, that all pice presented for payment at the Treasury of the surreptitious coinage shall be instantly cut in two and forfeited to the Company for which purpose the necessary minters and shroffs must attend at the Treasury, who shall be answerable for the receipt of any not coined by the Company, and the assistant to the Treasurer must always be present in the Treasury that no favour or affection may be shewn to anyone.

---

[230] Bombay Public Consultations, IOR P/341/39, 1773. p. 682, 5th October 1773.

But as we are convinced that the only effectual means of putting a stop to all those complaints regarding pice, is to call in those made of Tutenague, and to coin such a quantity of copper pice as will be sufficient for the currency of the place.

This extract states that the counterfeit pice can be easily distinguished from the real thing but unfortunately gives no information about how. There is no obvious distinction amongst the surviving coins known to the author, so perhaps all the false ones were disposed of. There is one lead specimen that is so obviously different (because it is so heavy) that it is hard to imagine that it could have passed as genuine.

Disposing of the Tutenague (Zinc) Coins

In 1774, all the zinc coins that had been called in were to be sold[231]:

As we are now in immediate want of money, not only for our current expenses but also to discharge the bills drawn from Onere [presumably a place], which are now due, Resolved that all the toothnague pice which have been called in and are now in the Treasury, be sold at public outcry for the most they will fetch, the outcry to be made by Messrs Fletcher & Garden who are now approved a committee for that purpose & the amount to be paid as the pice are taken away.

But nobody attended the sale[232]:

The Committee appointed to sell the Tuthnague pice called into the Treasury, report that they met for that purpose on the day appointed, but that notwithstanding due notice was given of the intended sale no purchasers whatever attended. Ordered that they fix on another day for the sale, when they must endeavour to dispose of it.

and the Bombay Council was informed that it was not possible to get a reasonable price for the zinc[233]:

The Committee appointed to sell the Tuthenague pice that had been called into the Treasury, report to the Board that they again met to endeavour to dispose of them but that no person would be induced to offer more for them than three rupees & ten annas per Surat maund, which being so very low, they did not think themselves authorised to sell them at such a rate. The great scarcity of money was assigned as the reason for this very low offer.

By 1775 the price of zinc had risen and another attempt was made to sell the coins[234]:

As the price of Tuthnague is now something higher than it has been for a considerable time past it is therefore agreed again to try at public outcry the large quantity if pice now laying in the Treasury. Messieurs Fletcher and Ashburner are appointed a committee for the disposal of it & the Secretary is ordered to give due notice accordingly.

---

[231] Bombay Public Consultations, IOR P/341/40, 1774. p. 277. 1st April 1774.

[232] Bombay Public Consultations, IOR P/341/40, 1774. p. 298. 13th April 1774.

[233] Bombay Public Consultations, IOR P/341/40, 1774. p. 345. 3rd May 1774.

[234] Bombay Public Consultations, IOR P/341/41, 1775. p. 406. 5th August 1775.

This time the sale succeeded[235]:

The Committee appointed to make sale of the Tuthnague pice report to the Board by letter as entered hereafter that they have sold the whole quantity of Tuthnague pice in the Treasury, at four rupees and fifty reas per Surat maund & for ready money.

---

[235] Bombay Public Consultations, IOR P/341/41, 1775. p. 435. 15th August 1775.

Chapter 3 – Bombay Mint 1717 to 1799 – Mint Operations

Summary

During the eighteenth century the mint was run by outsourcing the operation to a contractor who had to provide security against loss of bullion, fraud etc. This chapter pulls together the various events around these contracts together with the people and places involved in the work.

Mint Operations – 1724

In 1724, Gunsett, a goldsmith from Goa, suggested that he could run the mint for the Bombay authorities at a lower price than the existing mint farmer, who was named Ragusett[236]:

The President informed the Board that one Gunsett a native of Goa and Goldsmith who lately came hither offering to work up the Company's silver fifty per chest more to their advantage then the present undertaker (Ragusett) does it, he had directed a chest of Pillar Dollars to be delivered to each of them to be worked up in the mint under the inspection of Mr Thomas Yeomans the mint master from whose acc^ot of the produce of each now laid before us – there actually appears fourteen rupees two quarters & sixty Raes from that worked up by the Goa Goldsmith than from Ragusett, Mr Yeomans farther relates thereof as follows.

Honble Sir

In obedience to your Honours commands I delivered to Gunsett, goldsmith one chest Pillar Dollars [W^t] two Hundred & Ninety Pounds Eight ounces that I received by your Hon^rs orders from the Hon'ble Companys treasury & had it carefully coined in the mint & likewise delivered one chest of Pillar Dollars to Ragoosett goldsmith [Wt] two hundred & ninety pounds eight ounces that were coined in the mint at the same time. The former produced rupees (when the lead, copper and slag were saved and brought to account) eight thousand seven hundred fifty six one quarter & forty Raes, from which deduct for sundry charges rupees one hundred and four (rupees) three quarters and it leaves neat rupees eight thousand six hundred fifty one, three quarters & forty Raes and as this Gunsett doth make appear by the Accot herewith delivered your Hon^r a greater produce than Ragoosett, the Honble Company's former worker in this employ & I make the calculate from that which is the most profit to my Hon'ble masters and is [xxxx].

	Rups	qrs	R
For each hundred ounces of Pillar Dollars	248	18	
Each hundred ounces of Mexico Dollars	245	3	32½
Each hundred ounces of Duccatoons	250	3	
Each hundred ounces of French crowns	245		87

---

[236] Bombay Public Consultations. IOR P/341/5, Friday 19th June 1724.

Tis well known to your Honour that Ragoosett Goldsmith has for some years coined the Hon'ble Company's foreign silver & hath paid into their treasury for each hundred ounces of duccatoons Rupees two hundred and forty nine two quarters forty eight raes and a half, ditto Pillar Dollars rupees two hundred and forty six two quarters and fifty raes, ditto Mexico Dollars rupees two hundred forty four three quarters & fifteen raes and a half, ditto French crowns rupees two hundred forty four & seventy one raes & is a difference in each per cent Duccatoons forty five decimals, in Mexico Dollars four hundred and twenty four, in Pillar Dollars fifty seven in French crowns four hundred twenty four – which is humbly presented to your Honour

etc

etc

Ragusett and Gunsett were then called into the meeting, whereupon Ragusett accused Gunsett of cheating in the test. The board asked Gunsett what security he could provide and when he was unable to produce any on the spot, they gave him seven days to provide it.

Ragusett & Gunsett being then called in and interegated whereon Ragusett accused the other of using some unfair practice which in some measure he seems to prove on him, by Mr Yeomans allowing thereof, that in his lead which holds the silver there was about double the quantity when separated as there ought to be & could be no otherwise as they averr but by throwing in some silver unobserved by them amongst his charcoal – to this Gunsett had little more to reply then that they should then have detected him.

Ragoosett being ordered to withdraw the Goa Goldsmith was required to inform the Board what security he could give for a post of so much trust, replys he will give security for whatever we would entrust him with, which the President informs the Board he had promised him for five months past but had not yet brought any tho' he had sometimes offered those who when called for had refused it.

The Board therefore gives him to this day se'enight for bringing his security for our acceptance & then he withdrew.

The mint master, Yeomans, expressed the view that Gunsett would not be up to the job and if Ragusett could lower his prices, he should be selected to continue the work.

Mr Thomas Yeomans being further asked his opinion of this person declares he does not think him equal to the office & will be very much confused in working up different sorts of silver which he has already experienced in some lately come from Persia wherein he did show himself much at a loss and adds that when we are in haste for coining of our silver on the arrival of our ships he will not be able to give that dispatch that Ragoosett has done, recommending therefore if Ragoosett can be brought to give the price for the several species as per his calculate, from the produce of the chest of silver worked up by the Goa Goldsmith that he be continued in the employ.

Ragusett claimed he could not lower his prices but, like Gunsett, was given seven days for his final answer.

Ragoosett is again called in and the President bid him remember that when he gave him the business from Mr Yeomans he did engage him to make the silver yield the utmost to the Hon'ble Company at the same time telling him that he did not desire otherwise but to leave him a moderate sufficiency for his trouble which he himself allowed twenty five rupees per chest was enough whereas it now appeared that he has gained more then sixty. He makes excuse of lowering his workmen's wages by degrees and buying his other necessaries much cheaper than formerly, but that he has at times mett with a great many [bass] Dollars among the Mexico which he has constantly made good and consequently his profits are far less than we esteem them.

Being then told he is an old servant tho' herein we have found tardy we were nevertheless willing to continue him in the business provided he would pay in according to the calculate made from the produce of the chest of silver worked up by the Goa Goldsmith to which replying that he could not do it without a great loss accruing to himself the Board insisted thereon and gave him 'till this day se'enight to give his final answer, he thereupon withdrew and the Board adjourned.

Gunsett the Goa goldsmith was not able to provide sufficient security against fraud and a decision was taken to re-employ Ragusett provided he agreed to produce the number of rupees from the given silver bullion coins as that produced by Gunsett[237]:

The competitors for the coining of the Hon'ble Companys silver attending pursuant to our resolution on Friday last, Gunsett the Goa Goldsmith is called upon to produce his security who naming Ponda Sinay – He is thereupon called in and interrogated if he would be security for this person's faithful discharge of the trust, to which he replies he is so far willing as to make a tryal of twenty five chests of silver and according as he finds he complys in coining of them he will continue to engage for him for more, that is, he will see the Ball[ac] of the same paid into the treasury that the Hon'ble Company be no loosers but as to any other frauds that business may be liable to, he has not to say which Mr Yeomans the Mint Master must look after.

The which taking into consideration that this persons having charge of our mint altho' under the inspection of Mr Thomas Yeomans 'tis possible he may unknown to him coin private silver of baser alloy & thereby bring discredit upon it, & if detected thereof is he of any substance to make [reparation] nor can he find security to be liable for any such fraud.

The board is therefore of the opinion that if Ragusett can be brought to give according to the calculate from what the silver produced by Gunsett that the [business] be continued in him. He being thereupon called in does at last agree rather than loose the same to give as follows:

---

[237] Bombay Public Consultations, IOR P/341/5, Friday 26th June 1724.

			Rs	qrs	rs
'For 100	ounces of	Pillar Dollars	248	0	18
100	do	Mexico	245	3	32 ½
100	do	Duccatoons	250	3	0
100	do	French Crowns	245	1	11
100	do	Old Sevil Dollars	249	0	61
100	do	Crusadoes	244	0	68
100	do	Peru	230	1	31
100	do	Lion Dollars	198	0	86
100	do	German Crowns	232	2	17

& in proportion for any other silver but requests if he shall hereafter make appeal to this Board that thro' any accident he cannot be able to pay in at the above prices that then we will relieve him according as we find reasonable.

And the President informing the Board that he had one hundred & twenty eight rupees surplus on three chests of treasure coined by Gunsett it is agreed that it be returned to him as a reward…

Mint Operations – 1738

In 1738 the Bombay council discussed the operation of the mint and the amount of silver that would be produced by the mint undertakers. The mint undertakers were called in and told that they could continue in the job provided they delivered the new coins from the mint within thirty days of receiving the bullion. If the amount to be coined was more than eight chests, then more time would be allowed[238]:

…The said mint undertakers attending are called in and promises not only to keep up to the due fineness of the rupees they coin (of fifteen pennyweights at least better than standard) but also to pay the amount of the silver delivered them to coin in thirty days time, unless the quantity be too large, when they must be allowed a proportionable number of days reckoning that the most they can coin in one month is eight chests of silver. They are also ordered to clear off the amount of their bond immediately; which they promise to comply with as fast as they can. When representing their great loss and praying us to consider the same, they are told that farther than giving up the interest we cannot relieve them but that we will recommend their case to our Honble Masters favourable consideration. When the mint undertakers withdrew…

There was then a long petition from Muckundsett Padamsett & Luxamonsett Ragousett about how they lost money over this and they would not be able to continue the operation under the present agreement. Various assays from the assay master, William Davies, supported their petition:

---

[238] Bombay Public Consultations, IOR P/341/9, Saturday 23rd December 1738.

The answer of Muckensett Padamsett & Luckmansett Ragousett, undertakers of the mint of Bombay to the remarks on the new Bombay coinage dated London 30th December 1737 received by the Nassau the 5th September 1738. By them humbly presented to the Honble John Horne Esq. President & Governor [of] Council of Bombay.

A Bombay rupee was formerly reckoned to weigh seven pennyweights ten grains & one fifth but by experiment often & accurately made, we are now convinced that they do actually weigh one with another full seven pennyweights ten grains three hundred and fourteen decimals which is nearest to the Surat standard of thirty [xx] & fifty six decimals or a Bombay Tola. Mr Davis the assay master in his assay reports made [hither] last month says they came out upon an average of six or seven different weighings of several different numbers, seven pennyweights ten grains & three fifths & that he found them in fineness fifteen pennyweights better than English standard which is only fourteen grains two fifths less then they ought to be, a difference so inconsiderable that the best assay masters in England cannot we conceive always ascertain it. And if Mr Edlines assays vary one pennyweight from the Tower assays as we observe they do in one place, & half a pennyweight in others, it is not to be expected but that we country goldsmiths (who are destitute of the proper instruments & materials to work with) should err one pennyweight more, & indeed the best of us here do not scruple to own that we cannot prevent a difference happening sometimes of a quarter per cent either way in the fineness of our rupees because in melting a large quantity of silver together (as we must do in coining) an extraordinary heat of fire too long continued under the furnace with a greater weight of lead to refine it than what is absolutely necessary, will occasion some loss, which cannot always be prevented and if it may at any time have happened that rupees have been issued out of the mint baser or less in weight than what we are obliged to coin (which we presume cannot be laid to our charge, no complaint having ever been made of it by those amongst whom they have been dispersed) the publick suffer by such a piece of knavery & not the Honble Company as the remarks would endeavour to make it appear. But as there is now an assay master kept here at the Honble Company's charge he will be able to prevent any fraud or abuse of that kind & we are very desirous that he should overlook and inspect us as narrowly & often as he pleases.

The species of foreign silver chiefly brought into our mint for the Honble Company are Mexico & Pillar Dollars the quantity of other sorts being very inconsiderable & of these only we perceive assays have been made at the Tower. The Mexico is there said to come out by four trials of different sorts in an average two pennyweights six hundred and twenty five decimals worse than standard, & the Pillar dated in the year 1728 is found to be exactly English Standard & that dated 1729 a half pennyweight better than standard English. Now for the readier calculation & because our rupees standard is (according to this country way of reckoning) 99 touch, that is to say 99/100 parts of fine silver or 1/100 part alloy – we shall bring the Mexico Dollars to the like touch & those being 2 dwt 625 dec worse than English Standard will be found equal to touch 91 .. 4. Then if 100 ozs (or Tolas 269 .. 188 dec allowing 7d 10grs 314dec to the tola) of Mexico or 91 .. 4 touch silver be refined until it is reduced into rupee silver of 99 touch

The weight remaining will be	248 ,, 515
Deduct the mint charges & loss by waste @ two per cent	4 ,, 97
	243 ,, 545
We deliver for 100 ozs new Mexico	243 ,, 57
Loss to us the undertakers in every 100 ozs	.025

Pillar dollars being found in the year 1728 to be just English standard or 92.5 touch, one hundred ounces of that specie by the same rules being reduced into rupee touch

The weight remaining will be	251 ,, 514
Deduct 2 per cent as above	5 ,, 03
We deliver for old Pillar Dollars to the year 1728	246 ,, 484
Because we esteem them better than English Standard	247 ,, 3475
Loss to us if they are not better than standard	.8635

So that unless the new Mexico Dollars which are by far the most material species proper to be taken notice of do actually come up to the touch or fineness above mentioned we the undertakers must demonstrably suffer and we are so far from thinking we reap any advantages by our own agreement that we are not only willing but desirous of quitting the employment…

Finally they discussed the number of rupees that would be produced from various types of bullion coin and the new terms of the contract:

…And the new undertakers being accordingly called in were made acquainted therewith who asserting to the same the terms of the contract to be entered into with them was explained to them as follows:

That the present rates of silver be allowed and which as contained in the consultations the 26th June 1724 are as follows:

			Rs	qrs	rs
'For 100	*ounces of*	*Pillar Dollars*	248	0	18
100	*do*	*Mexico*	245	3	32 ½
100	*do*	*Duccatoons*	250	3	0
100	*do*	*French Crowns*	245	1	11
100	*do*	*Old Sevil Dollars*	249	0	61
100	*do*	*Crusadoes*	244	0	68
100	*do*	*Peru*	230	1	31
100	*do*	*Lion Dollars*	198	0	86
100	*do*	*German Crowns*	232	2	17

And all other sorts of silver to be adjusted agreeable to their real value.

That they have always in store woodashes, charcoal, tamarine, earthen utensils etc sufficient to dispatch the coinage of twelve lack of rupees & if the mint business stops for want of any of these articles, they shall forfeit such a sum as the Governor and Council shall direct provided they are not impeded by a warr and other unavoidable actions [unread words].

The rupee to be an exact Tola in weight or 7 dwt. 11 gra. and in fineness 14½ dwt. Better than English standard.

As the mint can employ [x] workmen they shall procure and be assisted to procure this number and when completed they shall be obliged to keep them in constant pay and not discharge them [as] the present practice & if its proved they do, they shall be subject to such penalty as the Governor and Council may judge necessary to inflict.

The managers and their assistants be obliged to give constant attendance at the mint unless prevented by sickness during the time that silver dwells there or forfeit their contract.

That there may be no sweeps in the mint, they shall upon first coinage deliver in a calculate of what they find will remain in a lack of rupees or a less sum, & if on a trial its found just, to agree a time for payment which if they exceed, interest to be allowed by them.

New Assay Master – 1741

In 1741 a Mr William Davis, who has been mentioned above, had arrived from England as assay master to the Bombay mint[239]:

Mr William Davis who was [sent out in quality] of Assay Master by our Honble Masters having hitherto delayed any report of his trials for refining silver notwithstanding, the several utensils by him required from England have been received by the Royal Guardian. The secretary is directed to remind him of this particular and that we expect satisfactory account of the progress made in ascertaining the precise standard for rupees and making them in a speedier manner than our people have hitherto found out.

In October 1741, Mr. Davis proposed that a stamping mill and air furnaces should be constructed to help reduce the costs of producing coins. He was asked to determine the cost of such a mill but more importantly was asked if he could produce silver coins more advantageously than the present minters, to which he replied that he could not[240]:

Read a letter (as entered hereafter) from Mr. William Davis, Assay Master, in answer to our queries in consultation of 8th August, which not being yet esteemed fully clear, the consideration thereof is deferred 'till another time. But the mill proposed to be erected we will endeavour to get done when we are apprized of the expense, which must be calculated. Mr. Davis being then called in, the following question was put to him Vizt can you by any methods you can devise coin the Company's silver to more advantage than the present minters do, and will you undertake the same? He declares that he can do no more than he has already. Nor will he undertake the coinage, or does he know anyone that will.

Mint Contractor Owed Money – 1735 to 1741

By 1741, the mint contractor was still owed money, which he had petitioned for

---

[239] Bombay Public Consultations, IOR P/341/12, Friday 15th May 1741.
[240] Bombay Public Consultations, IOR P/341/12, Friday 16th October 1741.

several years previously, and he sent in a new petition for payment[241]:

The humble petition of Muckansett Padamsett & Luckmanset Ragousett Undertakers to the mint.

That whereas your petitioners in the month of June 1735 did set forth to the then President John Horne' Esq. Etc etc – They still hadn't been paid and the decision was deferred to sometime later so that Mr Davis the Assay Master could examine the accounts.

The petition was discussed but no decision was taken and the matter of the mint contractors was discussed and deferred to a future occasion[242]:

There are letters from Mr Davis the assay master and a letter from George Dudley, one time mint master, who warned that no one other than the complainants could undertake the coinage.

Council again considered the mint contractor's petition in August 1741 but felt that they needed to direct specific questions to the assay master. These are listed[243]:

Council the 30th ultimo having perused the several papers given in by the mint undertakers, as also the Assay Master's remarks, are of the opinion that they are spun out to considerable length yet they are not conclusive to the points in dispute and therefore it will be necessary for him to give an explicit plain answer to, to which we may the better be enabled to come to an equitable determination, which the secretary is ordered to do by letter, and to the following purport

1. *what is the real difference between the new and old Mexico dollars.*
2. *Supposing that the new are worse than the old, whether the difference demanded by the mint undertakers in their account now sent to you under 30th June 1735 ought to be paid them, or what part thereof. That is admitting the quantity of new Mexico [etc] as therein specified had been delivered to them.*
3. *That as the mint undertakers do pretend the allowance given them for waste of one per cent and charges of coinage one per cent more, does not answer, you must again examine by a farther tryal in melting a chest how the same will turn out according to the methods which the minters pursue.*
4. *You are moreover to make experiments in your own way if possible how the like quantity of silver will turn out; and if practicable bring the minters into the use of your own method, provided it should render the coinage more advantageous to the Company.*
5. *You are to point out whatever may prove serviceable in regard to the coinage in any respect, knowing first whether the minters can or will execute any proposals you shall make; remembering that amusing us with what cannot be reduced to practice will answer no end.*
6. *Advise what value you do imagine will remain in the sweeps on the experiment you make of a chest of money as directed under the 3rd head.*

---

241 Bombay Public Consultations, IOR P/341/12, [Friday 5th?] May 1741.
242 Bombay Public Consultations, IOR P/341/12, Thursday 30th July 1741.
243 Bombay Public Consultations, IOR P/341/12, p. 362, Friday 7th August 1741.

No further information on this subject has been found but it would appear that the incumbent contractors continued for a few more years.

New Mint Contractors – 1748

By 1748 the mint contractors were being accused of not running the mint very effectively and new contractors were selected[244]:

The present undertakers of the mint continuing their base practice of having a large sum constantly in the sweeps to the Honble Company's detriment, and from indolence or incapacity are not able to coin the silver brought hither unless assisted from the treasury or by the merchants with large transfer bills which by good fortune happened last year, else the mint had been brought to discredit. It is therefore proposed to give the management to Ransorett Luckmansett, Ragousett Bhensett, Ransorrett Isimbucksett of fair characters and capable of the business, who have also a set of able assistants, but as these, nor no other goldsmiths in Bombay can give the necessary security the following regulations will obviate the difficulty by leaving them no power to defraud the Honble Company or the merchants.

The Mint Master to have an Englishman as his deputy, who will be constantly in the mint when no silver can be carried in or out without his knowledge. This person to be paid by the President and the Mint Master…

… As there will be no sweeps & they obliged to keep a number of workmen in pay that theretofore the Honble Company allows them to have lead from their stores at the same rate as the former mint undertakers which is six rupees per pucca maund, and they deliver a calculate of what a lack of rupees may require and must be done after the first coinage.

In a consultation of the 25th March 1748[245] Council expressed its concern with the way that the mint had been managed and chose three goldsmiths as new managers. However, they were unable to find the necessary security and new regulations for governing the mint were issued. The Mint Master was to have a deputy who was to check the movement of silver in and out of the mint, with the movements signed for by the Mint Master as well as his deputy; the mint was to have two locks with the keys held by different people; the bullion and dies were to be removed to the fort at night; and finally, the Mint Master was to ensure that rupees were regularly assayed and their fineness checked.

However, more similar problems arose in 1753 and new contractors were chosen[246]:

Mr John Spencer, mint master, presents a letter to the Board setting forth the incapacity & inattention of the present undertakers, which if not timely remedied may be not only very prejudicial to the Honble Company's revenue, but productive of a great loss of trade to the Island by diverting the large quantity of silver that annually comes hither, to other channels.

---

[244] Bombay Public Consultations, IOR P/341/15, 25th March 1748.
[245] Bombay Public Consultations, 25th March 1748. IOR P/341/15.
[246] Bombay Public Consultations, IOR P/341/19, p. 241 25th July 1753.

Which, being taken into consideration and recourse had to the Consultations of the 25th March 1748, it appears that the principle view in admitting the present undertakers was to prevent a large balance remaining under the denomination of sweeps, which they engaged to perform, but it appears by the above letter that they have been so far from complying with their agreement, that the balance of sweeps is now Rups 101,382 – 57, which with the frequent complaints of the Honble Company of late years, of the weight and standard of the rupees, it is resolved that the present undertakers be removed and Rangajee Ramsett & Kensowjee Rumsett, offering proposals more advantageous to the Honble Company & [those] concerned in the mint than any hitherto offered, and being satisfied they they are persons of sufficient capital and experience in this branch of business, it is resolved to accept their proposals, and as the Mint Master represents that Ransot Luckmonsett, one of the present managers, to be a person who has a great influence over the under-workmen, resolved that he be likewise admitted and directed the Secretary draw out a contract accordingly.

London's View of Mint Operations – 1756 to 1758

London was in complete agreement with the actions taken by the Bombay authorities[247]:

It was high time to have done with your undertakers for the mint as from yours and Mr Spencer's representations it appears we might have been great sufferers not only by the great balance due from them under the denomination of sweeps but by their debasement of the coin which must in consequence have been a prejudice to our revenue and the trade of the Island in general. We hope you have taken care to recover the before-mentioned balance which we find amounted to upwards of Rs 100,000 and we expect you will carefully look after the new undertakers in such a manner that the reputation of the mint may be kept up entirely to our satisfaction as likewise to that of the proprietors of silver on a private account.

We now transmit you for your information our accountant's remarks on the several musters of rupees received from you the last season, every parcel of which you will observe falls considerably short of the standard fineness. Whether any of them were coined by the new contractors we are not informed. If they were, they ought to be most strictly looked after to prevent all future attempts for debasing the coinage.

However, by 1758 London was still not happy with the way the mint was run and made recommendations about the management and suggesting that the sons of one of the previous mint contractors should be given jobs[248]:

The late mint undertakers were dismissed in 1753 and the reasons you assigned were that the silver was debased and large sums continued in the sweeps. Upon a retrospection we do not see the present managers or rather manager, have done much better. The silver by our several lower reports is still short of fineness, and as large, or larger, sums of money continued in the sweeps. You joined we observe one of the late managers as an unexceptionable person with

---

[247] Dispatches to Bombay. IOR E/4/996 (1753-1761) p. 237-239. Dispatch dated 11th February 1756.
[248] Dispatches to Bombay. IOR E/4/996 (1753-1761) p. 654-655. Dispatch dated 5th July 1758.

those new contractors, but centered the sole power with Ramsett. We do not see the equity or utility of this measure, for surely a person bound to us in so large a trust, ought, for his own sake and ours to have the power of aiding and controlling, nor can we approve that so important a branch should at any time be under the sole direction of one person were he less exceptionable than the present. We do therefore direct that you do so far vary this contract as to fix Ransor Lucmonset in an equal share in the management and advantages and, as his family in conjunction with Pudumset's, have held the mint for near fifty years, it is but reasonable his name should stand first in the contract. Should any demur arise on the part of Ramset Gumbazet to so reasonable a regulation (which we do not apprehend) and he should decline this business, you are in his stead to join with Ransor Lucmonset one or two capable and unexceptionable persons upon the like terms and conditions as the mint is now held and we are under no apprehensions that you'll be at any loss because this business is too advantageous & creditable to want many competitors, and we expect you'll have a watchful eye upon the conduct of those who either undertake or continue the management.

The sons of Savajee Daramset merit our compassion. Their father did us signal service in raising our several revenues, particularly those of tobacco and arrack, and in many other respects a useful subject. We do not condemn your dismissing them from the mint, we are satisfied you acted upon very just motives and perhaps their youth and inexperience might have led them into errors, but as their characters are unexceptionable and the distress of this once opulent family call upon us for relief, if you can consistently restore them, they giving sufficient security for their conduct as well as their trust (which we are told they will be able to do) it will receive our approbation, and we accordingly recommend the same to you for your consideration.

New Mint Contract Drawn up – 1759

Bombay responded by making some changes to the contract[249]:

Ramgajee Ramsett, one of the managers of the mint, being called before us & made acquainted with our Honble Master's late comments regarding the contract, declares his readiness to continue in the management, agreeable thereto, the secretary is therefore directed to alter the contract accordingly by giving Ramsor Luckmonsett an equal share of the management and advantages and placing his name first, who attending, is also informed of this regulation in his favour, and we understanding that Rangajee Ramsett is possessed of a penalty bond whereby Ramsor Luckmansett engaged to relinquish all his advantages accruing from the mint in consideration of an annual allowance of seven hundred (700) rupees, Rangajee Ramsett is ordered (and accordingly agrees) to deliver it up to the secretary in order for its being cancelled. They are then both informed of our Honble Masters complaints regarding the silver being short in fineness and a large sum being continued in the sweeps and on being strictly ordered to prevent the like in future, they promise to faithfully comply therewith and to have the sweeps now remaining clear by the last of July next.

---

[249] Bombay Public Consultations, IOR P/341/22, 1759. p. 317.

A draft of the contract was read and approved and the new contract drawn up[250]:

Read a foul (sic) draft of the contract with Ransar Luckmonsett, Rangojee Ramsett and Kensowjee Ramsett for undertaking the management of the mint agreeable to our Honble Masters late commands, which being approved ordered to be fair transcribed in order for its being executed.

However, London was not happy that Bombay had not appointed the sons of the previous mint contractors and became more insistent that this should be done[251]:

In 1758 we recommended to your notice the families of Lucmonset and Savajee Daramset who were dismissed from the mint in 1753 and we did this from motives of humanity and good policy as their parents had been very useful subjects. In answer to this we notice that you had readmitted Lucmonset but continue to exclude the sons of Savajee. The chief charge against Savajee and Lucmonset in depriving them of the mint was their keeping large balances in their hands, but as the admission of Ramset Gumbaset has rather increased the evil and as Ramset bears a very different character and can have no pretensions to our favour, we order that upon receipt of this letter he be entirely removed and that the mint be given wholly to Lucmonset and Savajee's sons, each a moiety upon the terms and conditions it's now held, Lucmonset to be first named and as Vetuldas Kessewdass has offered himself for their security, we deem it sufficient.

New Mint Contractors – 1761 to 1766

In 1761 the mint contractors were removed from their position and new ones appointed[252]:

Rangajee & Kensowjee Ramset to be removed from their business as undertakers to the mint & Ranoor Luckmonseth jointly with Visoramsett and Mucondsett Savajee to be fixed therein on Vittuldass Kesondass being security for the two latter, agreeable to our Hon Masters commands, but Rangajee Ramsett etc, present undertakers, must be allowed a reasonable time or clearing their sweeps.

In 1766 two brothers of one of the mint contractors, who had died, applied to take on his share of the mint[253]:

Read a petition from two of the brothers of Ransor Luckmonsett, one of the Mint Undertakers deceased, desiring that his share of the mint may be transferred to them, which is agreed to.

In 1766, the person providing security for the mint contractors died and new security had to be found[254]:

---

[250] Bombay Public Consultations, IOR P/341/22, 1759. p. 326.
[251] Dispatches to Bombay. IOR E/4/996 (1753-1761) p. 902-903. Dispatch dated 25th April 1760.
[252] Bombay Public Consultations, IOR P/341/24, 1761 p. 161.
[253] Bombay Public Consultations, IOR P/341/29, 1766. p. 252. 14th April 1766.
[254] Bombay Public Consultations, IOR P/341/29, 1766. p. 336. 17th June 1766.

Wittuldass Kelsondass who was security for the due performance of the Mint Undertaker's contract, being dead, they have been called upon for another security in his stead, and have offered his nephew until the return of the widow & to mortgage their estates, which it is agreed to accept.

New Mint Contractors – 1767

In 1767 the Bombay Council found that the mint contractors were not paying enough for the silver that they coined in the mint and a decision was taken to offer the contract to the sons of the previous mint contractors, as desired by London[255]:

The President acquaints the Board that there is reason to believe the prices given for silver by the present mint undertakers are much too low, a reputable Banian, well versed in the business, having offered to give three (3) rupees per hundred ounces more on new German crowns (in which the greatest part of the silver now imported is brought) and one (1) rupee per hundred ounces on all other silver.

Resolved, as our Honble Masters in their commands of 25th April 1760 seem to intend that the present Mint Undertakers should have the preference, that it be offered to them at our next meeting on these terms, and if they do not chuse to accept them, that it be given to the person who has offered them as it will make a very material difference to the trade of this place by encouraging all Merchants to coin their money here in preference to carrying it elsewhere, which money will all circulate in the place and will not only increase our Honble Masters' coinage duty but the customs also by increased sale of goods.

However they refused the contract and it went to a shroff called variously Bucon Surdass or Bhocondass Sordass[256]:

The Mint Undertakers now attending agreeable to our resolution last council are informed of the terms which had been offered for carrying on the business of the mint and asked if they chuse to accept of it upon the same, which though repeated pressed to as well as jointly as separately, and assured of our inclination to give them the preference agreeable to the Honble Company's orders, and told that in the event it would in all probability be rather an advantage to them than otherwise, by the increased quantity of silver which would be brought to the place, they unanimously decline, in consequence of which the merchant who offered the terms mentioned in last consultation by name, Bucon Surdass Shroff is called in and asked what security he will give for the due performance of his contract, when he declares he cannot immediately give a general security as the shroffs and others may not chuse to become his sureties, merely that they may not appear to be in any shape instrumental in depriving the present undertakers of their employment, but that in a few days after being established, he will give ample security and in the meantime will give sufficient security for any sum he may receive to coin. Resolved therefore that he be entrusted with the management of the mint and an order be issued to the Mint Master accordingly. We are still further induced to this

---

[255] Bombay Public Consultations, IOR P/341/30, 1767. p. 422. 30th June 1767.
[256] Bombay Public Consultations, IOR P/341/30, 1767. p. 424. 2nd July 1767.

measure by Ransor Luckmonsett and Muccond Savajee, two of the late undertakers being both dead, the one a man of substance and the other a man of capacity and by the present undertakers being deprived of their security by the death of Wittledass Kelsondass. They must be however allowed till the end of this month to clear any sweeps there may be, though from the small quantity of silver lately coined we do not suppose there are any.

By the following year Bhucondass Sordass found that he had offered terms that were too generous to the Company and he wanted to reduce the price[257]:

Read, a letter as entered hereafter, from the Mint Master representing that Bhocondass Sordass, the present Mint Undertaker, having suffered greatly from the prices he engaged to, and did give last year for all silver delivered into the mint to be coined, he hopes we will take his case into consideration and accepted of two rupees and one half per one hundred ounces of German crowns, and half a rupee per one hundred ounces of all other silver, more than was given by the former managers, and which is half a rupee per hundred ounces or nearly ninety reas per one hundred rupees less than he gave last season, which being taken into account accordingly, it is observed that our Honble Masters seem desirous of giving the former managers Sivajee's and Luckmonsett's sons the preference to all others, and it therefore becomes our duty to apprize them of these offers, and give them the option of accepting the management of the mint upon the same terms They are therefore now sent for and offered the management accordingly, but which they unanimously decline, declaring they cannot possibly support themselves and families upon the advantages they should derive from it at that rate. Resolved therefore, as no one will undertake it upon better terms, that those now offered by Bhocondass Sordass be accepted, to commence the 1st of next month and continue till the 31st day of December 1770.

London agreed with the appointment of Bhocondass Sordass to the position of mint contractor[258]:

Your giving the mint contract at the Presidency to Bucon Surdass who made the highest offer and after the present contractors had refused to accept it on his terms, is, for the reasons given in the 76 and 77 paragraphs of your letter of the 23rd December 1767, approved and we are pleased to find the coinage duty has increased this year but we expect you will keep a watchful eye on the contractor that he keeps up the credit of the mint and gives sufficient security for all the bullion he is entrusted with.

They confirmed this in another dispatch dated 6th April 1769[259]:

As the sons of Savajee and Lucmonsett declined contracting for the management of the mint, and as better terms could not be procured than those offered by Bhocandass Sordass, who had been a sufferer by his former contract, we approve you continuing the mint in his hands for

---

[257] Bombay Public Consultations, IOR P/341/31, 1768. p. 443. 26th July 1768.

[258] Dispatches to Bombay. IOR E/4/998 (1768-1771) p. 400-401. Dispatch dated 31st March 1769.

[259] Dispatches to Bombay. IOR E/4/998 (1768-1771) p. 743. Dispatch dated 6th April 1770.

the time stipulated, and the terms on which you have settled the contract with him and Rama Sinay Lollecur who, as you inform us, is a man of substance and security for performance of such contract.

Death of the Mint Contractor – 1769

By the time that London had communicated their agreement to the new mint contractor, he had died and a decision had been made to allow his sons to run the business in the interim, as had been requested by London[260]:

Read likewise a letter from the Mint Master advising of the death of the late Mint Undertaker. Ordered the Mint Master to settle his accounts and recover whatever balance may appear due, that publications be issued advising proposal for a new contract will be received on the 28th of this month. In the interim the business must be carried on by the sons of the late contractor.

This was formalised soon afterwards in April 1771[261]:

The sons of the late Mint Undertaker offering to carry on the business on the same terms as their father & to give the like security, it is agreed to as no other offers have been made us in consequence of the publick notice we gave for that purpose, but a clause must be added, that provided they do not deliver the money coined within 20 days after the receipt of the bullion, they must pay interest thereon, which they on their part accept, & at the same time offering to pay 4000 rupees within seven days out of the remains of the sweeps, & the then remaining balance by 31st July next, which we also agree to.

New Mint Contract – 1773

The mint contract was due for renewal in March 1773 and applications for the job were solicited[262]:

The Contract for carrying on the mint business expiring the 2nd of the ensuing month, Ordered that the Secretary issues public notices that we will receive proposals for a new contract.

Only two applications were received and, as there was little difference between the two, the then current holders of the position were re-appointed[263]:

Opened two proposals for undertaking the business of the mint, delivered in consequence of the notice that was [issued]. The proposal of the present contractor is the same as the terms of their last contract, and in the other there is no material difference. It is therefore agreed that the contract be renewed to the present undertakers, against whom we have never had any complaints, provided they give the security they did before.

---

[260] Bombay Public Consultations, IOR P/341/34, 1771. pp. 86 & 88. 11th February 1771.

[261] Bombay Public Consultations, IOR P/341/34, 1771. p. 231. 2nd April 1771.

[262] Bombay Public Consultations, IOR P/341/39, 1773. pp. 231. 29th March 1773.

[263] Bombay Public Consultations, IOR P/341/39, 1773. pp. 264. 6th April 1773.

New Mint Contract – 1774

In May 1774 the contract again came up for renewal[264]:

The contract for carrying on the business of the mint being expired, ordered that notices be issued that we will receive proposals for a new contract within 14 days from this date

but this time only one proposal was received and this was from the then current contractors[265]:

Opened a proposal for carrying on the business of the mint, being the only one that has been delivered in consequence of the notices that were affixed, which proposal is found to be from the undertakers of last year, & the conditions they propose the same except that they desire it may be for three years certain instead of one, which particular however, it is agreed not to comply with, but that their proposal be accepted for one year only as usual & the secretary is ordered to execute a contract accordingly.

As can be seen, the mint contractors had became tired of the process of having to apply to renew their contract every year and asked that the term should be extend to three years when it became due in May 1774 but this was rejected[266]:

Your Honor etc having been pleased to affix notices for anyone to deliver in their sealed proposals for carrying on the business of the mint, we are willing to undertake the same on the conditions of the last contract, only requesting you will be pleased to extend the term thereof to three instead of one year.

The contract was renewed and the annual renewal process continued.

The contractors put in another proposal in 1775[267]:

Opened a proposal (being the only one that has been delivered) for carrying on the business of the mint and is from the present undertakers, offering to conduct it for the ensuing year on the same terms and conditions as before. Agreed that their proposal be accepted and they must accordingly execute the usual contract…

New Mint Contract – 1776 to 1790

Entries in the records show the contract being renewed in 1776[268], 1778[269], 1779[270] and

---

[264] Bombay Public Consultations, IOR P/341/40, 1774. p. 344. 3rd May 1774.

[265] Bombay Public Consultations, IOR P/341/40, 1774. p. 354. 17th May 1774.

[266] Bombay Public Consultations, IOR P/341/40, 1774. p. 357. 17th May 1774. Letter from Balmuckoondass Buckondass and Goverdondass Buckondass, dated 10th May 1774.

[267] Bombay Public Consultations, IOR P/341/41, 1775. p. 240. 28th March 1774.

[268] Bombay Public Consultations, IOR P/341/42, 1776. p. 151. 16th March 1776.
Bombay Public Consultations, IOR P/341/42, 1776. p. 162. 26th March 1776.

[269] Bombay Public Consultations, IOR P/341/45, 1778. p. 121. 14th March 1778.
Bombay Public Consultations, IOR P/341/45, 1778. p. 185. 22nd April 1778.

[270] Bombay Public Consultations, IOR P/341/46, 1779. p. 415. 4th August 1779.
Bombay Public Consultations, IOR P/341/46, 1779. p. 425. 18th August 1779.

1782[271] and in 1790 a problem arose because the person providing security for the contractors had died[272]:

Rama [Sinoy Lottiwur], who was security for the Mint Contractors, Balmacondass Goverdandass Bookandass and Loldass Goverdandass, having died the 31st ultimo, I conceive it my duty to inform you of the same. At the same time permit me to submit to you the propriety of immediately calling on the contractors above mentioned to renew their contract and find fresh securities.

Resolution

In consequence of the above intimation, the Mint contractors must be called upon to renew their contract.

A new person was found to provide the necessary security but this had to be checked by the Company's solicitor[273]:

The Mint Master acquaints the Board that the Contractors have tendered Baboo Sinvy and Ram Sinvy as their securities in the event of Government renewing their contract.

Ordered that the Solicitor report to us what property the above mentioned persons may be possessed of and are willing to make over by mortgage, when we shall judge of its sufficient

The new contract was drawn up in February 1790[274]:

The Company's Solicitor lays before the Board the final draft of an engagement for the Mint Contractor to execute, which is approved, but as we observe the former contract have fixed no standard for the fineness of the gold coinage, a matter we think it highly proper should be inserted, the Mint Master must be called upon to inform us what orders are extant in the mint on that head and by what standard gold and silver coins have been hitherto regulated.

Argument between Mint Master and Mint Contractors – 1793

In 1793 an argument arose between the mint master and the mint undertakers[275]:

As the contract with Lolldass Goverdundass and Manordass Goverdundass the mint undertakers is now expired, I take the liberty to mention the same to you and likewise to acquaint you they stand indebted on balance as per account current accompanying amounting, with interest to the 1st instant, to Rupees 24,402..2..37

On demanding this balance from the contractors they allege a claim on account the quality of the dollars which were delivered them for coining in the year 1790 from the Treasury, and by which they were very heavy sufferers, but acknowledging with much gratitude your goodness

---

[271] Bombay Public Consultations, IOR P/341/49, 1782. p. 635. 18th November 1782.
Bombay Public Consultations, IOR P/341/49, 1782. p. 799. 28th December 1782. Letter from Goverdundass Bascandass & Lolldass Goverdundass dated 26th November 1782.

[272] Bombay Public Consultations, IOR P/342/12, 1790. 22nd January 1790. p. 80.

[273] Bombay Public Consultations, IOR P/342/12, 1790. 2nd February 1790. p. 102.

[274] Bombay Public Consultations, IOR P/342/12, 1790. 19th February 1790. p. 135.

[275] Bombay Public Consultations, IOR P/342/15, 1793. p. 507. Letter from the acting mint master (P. Crawford Bruce) to Government, dated 10th May 1793.

in consenting to withdraw the suit formerly instituted against them, and wishing to avoid every dispute on this account, he has requested I would entreat the favour in his behalf to have the matter either submitted to arbitration, or to be investigated in such other manner as may appear proper to you

Resolution

He must be informed that we have agreed to give up to the mint undertakers the interest on their account, but they are to be called on immediately to pay the balance due on the 1ˢᵗ May 1792.

The mint master was told to recover the money from the person providing the security to the mint contractor[276]:

The Acting Mint Master must be directed to call upon the securities of the Mint Contractor for the balance due from him and in case of a non compliance to report the same immediately.

Which he did[277]:

In consequence of your orders of the 12ᵗʰ instant, I have called on Ramdass Manondass, the security for the late Mint Undertaker, Lolldass Govundunass, to pay the balance due from him by the account which I had the honor to lay before you, and he has given me an accepted draft payable in four months on Gopauldass Manordass, the Shroff, for the sum of Rupees 22,362-..-22, being the amount to be recovered from him agreeable to your orders to me under 25ᵗʰ May last. If the mode of payment is acceptable to Your Honble Board, I will then keep the draft and give Lolldass Goverdondass a discharge.

Reply

He must be directed to observe the established usage of his office

He is at liberty to accept the draft and give Lolldass Goverdondass his discharge

In the same letter he gave an interesting insight into the way that the mint operated:

Agreeable to the directions which I have been favoured with from the Secretary of Government to specify the regulations of the mint office and what are the terms on which people are allowed to coin, I beg leave to mention that there are no particular regulations in the Mint Office respecting the coinage because, the business being done by contract, the Contractor is at every expense for the coinage. When any person wishes to coin either silver or gold bullion he makes application to the Mint Master and as there is no particular restriction of Government against the coinage of silver, the Mint Master immediately gives direction to the Mint Undertakers to receive the silver bullion and to coin into rupees in the mode described in his contract with Government, but for coining gold, the Mint Master is to make application to the Honble the Governor specifying the person who has made application to him and the number of Tolas of gold he wishes to have coined, and must receive the permission of the Honble the Governor

---

[276] Bombay Public Consultations, IOR P/342/16, 1793. p. 645. July 1793.

[277] Bombay Public Consultations, IOR P/342/16, 1793. p. 728. Letter from the acting mint master (P. Crawford Bruce) to Government, dated 18ᵗʰ July 1793.

previous to his giving any directions to the Mint Undertakers, and to prevent any improper conduct in the Mint Undertakers, there is an Assay Man who receives a monthly pay of four rupees from the Company and who attends all meltings of gold or silver to take care that it is equal to standard and it is likewise the business and duty of the Mint Master to attend the meltings and to be careful that the Assayer makes a proper examination.

The Mint Undertaker has an allowance for burnage, wastage etc, on Gold one val for each Tola, and he is obliged by the terms of his contract to deliver the whole money whether silver or gold, in twenty one days, and for whatever part may be detained beyond that time, he pays an interest to the Proprietor.

New Mint Contract – 1793

When the contract was due for renewal in 1793 the mint master was asked what charges were imposed for coining and who received the benefit. He informed them of the rates that used to be charged but reminded them that the charges had been dropped in 1781 and that nothing was charged since that time[278]:

In obedience to your orders I beg leave to acquaint you that the former regulations respecting the coinage was a duty of 2½ per cent on silver and 1½ per cent on Gold collected on all bullion coined in the mint and which was divided as follows:

On silver	*1 per cent to the Company*
	1 per cent to the Honble the Governor
	½ per cent to the Mint Master
	2½ per cent
On Gold	*½ per cent to the Company*
	½ per cent to the Honble the Governor
	½ per cent to the Mint Master
	1½ per cent

But under the 21st October 1781 this duty was struck off by order of the Honble the Governor and Council and a proclamation was issued to that effect, and since that date there has been no coinage duty collected from individuals and the Mint Contractor has always coined both gold and silver according to the terms and restrictions of his contract with Government.

Agreed that we advertise to receive sealed proposals on Friday 28th instant from any person willing to contract for carrying on the business of the mint at Bombay from the 1st July next ensuing to the 30th April 1796

The same mint contractors had been running the mint for several years on an annual contract but the contract was to be extended to three years, as had been requested nearly twenty years before, and new applicants were considered[279]:

---

[278] Bombay Public Consultations, IOR P/342/15, 1793. p. 573. Letter from the acting mint master (P. Crawford Bruce) to Government, dated 22nd June 1793.
[279] Bombay Public Consultations, IOR P/342/15, 1793. p. 590. 28th June 1793.

Opened four proposals for contracting to carry on the business of the mint at Bombay from 1ˢᵗ July next to the 30ᵗʰ April 1796 when that of Curson Veddadhur being the most eligible, agreed that it be accepted upon his finding two responsible persons to be security for one lack of rupees.

[all the applications are fully reported here in the records. One from the old mint contractor].

However, on further consideration, Curson Veddadhur was not considered suitable and another candidate was selected[280]:

On enquiry into the character of Curson Veddadhur we find he is not a man of sufficient respectability to be entrusted with an undertaking of such importance & as the proposals of Narrondass Tulsidass are more advantageous than any of the others, agreed that they be accepted on his finding two responsible persons to be security for one lack of rupees.

A complete copy of the 1793 contract exists in the records[281].

New Mint Contract – 1796

The contract was put out to tender again in 1796 and proposals were received from various people[282]:

Opened Mint Proposals from the following persons:
Mr Miguel de Lima Souza
Ramchunder Madowsett
Lalla Nagidass for Chooney Loll
Pestonjee Eduljei
Agreed that these proposals be referred to the mint master and he be desired to prepare and send in a comparative statement showing which may be the most advantageous for the Honble Company and the Public to accept

However, no further entries have been found about who eventually got the contract.

Minting Method – 1794

Thurston gives an interesting contemporary account of the method used to mint coins in the Bombay Mint in 1794[283]:

Tippoo, from his coins being regularly stricken and milled, must have a regular die, which is an apparatus unknown in other parts of India. In Bombay there is no mechanical process either for ascertaining the value of the piece, or of giving it the impression. The manner is as follows: the metal is brought to the mint in bars the size of the little finger, where a number of

---

[280] Bombay Public Consultations, IOR P/342/15, 1793. p. 603. 2ⁿᵈ July 1793.

[281] Bombay Public Consultations, IOR P/342/23, 1796. p. 1015-1021. Letter from the mint master (Wm Simpson) to Government, dated 19ᵗʰ April 1796.

[282] Bombay Public Consultations, IOR P/342/23, 1796. p. 1358. 31ˢᵗ May 1796.

[283] Lieutenant Moor (1794), Narrative of Little's Detachment, App. Note ii, pp. 499, 500. From: Thurston E., (1890), History of the coinage of the territories of the East India Company in the Indian Peninsula. Government Press, Madras.

persons seated on the ground provided with scales and weights, a hammer, and an instrument between a chissel and a punch: before each man's birth is fixed a stone by way of an anvil. The bars are cut into pieces, by guess, and if, on weighing, any deficiency is found, a little particle is punched into the intended rupee; if too heavy, a piece is cut off, and so until the exact quantity remains. These pieces are then taken to a second person, whose whole apparatus consists of a hammer and stone anvil, and he batters them into something of a round shape, about seven-eighths of an inch diameter, and one-eighth thick; when they are ready for the impression. The die is composed of two pieces, one inserted firmly into the ground, and the other, about eight inches long, is held in the right hand of the operator, who squatting on his heels (the posture in which all mechanics and artists work; the posture, indeed, in which everything is done in India, for if a man has a dram given him, he finds it convenient to squat upon his heels to drink it), fills his left hand with the intended coins, which he with inconceivable quickness slips upon the fixed die with his thumb and middle finger, with his forefinger as dextrously removing them when his assistant, a second man with a mall, has given it the impression, which he does as rapidly as he can raise, and strike with the mall on the die held in the right hand of the coiner. The diameter of the die is about an inch and a half, inscribed with the Great Moghul's names, titles, date of the Hejra, his reign, &c., but as the coins are not so large, they do not, consequently, receive all, nor the same impression. The rupee is then sent to the treasury, ready for currency, as no milling, or any further process is thought necessary.

This process is very similar to that used at Calcutta at about this time and described in the Bengal book[284].

In 1796, Dr Helenus Scott was appointed to the committee examining the coinage. He would later become the assay master and play an important role in reforming the coinage of Bombay (see next chapter)[285]:

Dr Helenus Scott appointed a member of the Committee for reporting on the current coins

Mint Buildings

The mint buildings continued to require attention and there are several entries in the records discussing this. For instance in 1789 the roofs need repairs[286]:

I have examined the different roofs belonging to the Mint House which are much decayed and agreeable to your directions have drawn out an estimate of the expense which will be incurred by making them new. The estimate is for Bations which, although attended with a greater present expense than Boondy Bundles, yet are in the end much less expensive for they last a number of years longer and save the great charge for repairs which roofs covered with Boondy Bundles constantly require. I have made an allowance for the old materials. I suppose about a

---

[284] Stevens PJE, (2012), The Coins of the Bengal Presidency, AH Baldwin & Sons Ltd, p. 16

[285] Bombay Public Consultations, IOR P/342/23, 1796. p. 1371. 2nd June 1796.

[286] Bombay Public Consultations, IOR P/342/11, 1789. 2nd October 1789. p. 648. Letter from the Clerk of Works (J Stewart) to Government, dated 26th September 1789.

third of the rafters may be used again and all the tiles, making a deduction of one fifth for breakage.

<u>*Resolution*</u>

As the necessity of repairing the mint is evinced by the representation before us, ordered that it be carried into execution. Care be enjoined that the estimate be not exceeded.

Mint Security

The security of the mint was discussed at various times and very precise instructions were issued. In 1748, for instance an entry reads[287]:

…The Mint to be secured with two locks , one key to be kept by the managers, the other by the Mint Master and never to be opened or shut but when he or his deputy are present.

All bullion to be carried every evening from the mint to the fort and deposited in a chest under the joint charge of the Mint Master and managers.

The dies in like manner to be carried there every night. All receipts of silver into the mint and payments from thence to be reported as usual to the Mint Master and also undersigned by his deputy.

And that the rupees may be kept up to their due fineness it will be the Mint Masters care that the rupees are frequently assayed.

As these methods duly observed will certainly prevent embezzlements which answers the intent of any security that can be given, the Board unanimously agrees thereto.

---

[287] Bombay Public Consultations, IOR P/341/15, 25th March 1748.

Chapter 4 – Bombay Mint 1800 to c1830 – Coins

Summary

In 1800 a decision was made to adopt the Surat standard for the Bombay silver coins. This was adjusted slightly in 1824 to fit in with the proposed standardisation throughout the EIC possessions in India.

Gold coins of the same design as the silver were issued in three denominations: single mohur, panchia (third of a mohur or five rupees) and one fifteenth of a mohur (one rupee).

Crude copper coins were issued in quite large numbers on and off until 1829.

All the coins were struck by hand although attempts were made to build machinery locally (see chapter 6).

Introduction of Surat-Style Coins at Bombay

During the first half of the year 1800, the mint continued to operate in the way that it had throughout the eighteenth century. For instance In March 1800 a request was made to strike gold coins[288]:

That your petition[er] begs leave to request your Honble Boards permission to coin about twelve thousand tollas Venetian gold into mohurs in the Honble Company's mint, therefore humbly begs your Honble Board will be pleased to order the mint master for the same

and this was authorised. However, in August 1800 the mint master, William Simpson, was ordered to make dies for the production of Surat-style rupees in the Bombay mint[289]:

I have been favoured with your letter of the 8th instant and copy of a petition from [Hullysing Dongursey] praying to be allowed to coin silver rupees in this mint of the same standard as the Surat coinage, in reply to which I beg you will inform the Honble the Governor in Council that they can be made in every respect similar to them whenever he may be pleased to give me orders to have stamps cut, bearing the impression of the Surat rupees at present in currency.

It was agreed that the coinage should go ahead and the mint master was instructed to prepare the necessary dies.

In September 1800 the mint master asked about the amount of commission that he should charge for coining Surat rupees[290]:

I take the liberty of submitting extract of a letter received from Mr De Souza dated 8th instant on the subject of your orders of 5th instant relative to the commission to be collected for the

---

[288] Bombay Public Consultations. IOR P/342/41, p. 634. Petiton from Candass Bullackedass dated 19th March 1800.

[289] Bombay Public Consultations. IOR P/342/43, p. 1658. Letter from the mint master at Bombay (William Simpson), dated 12th August 1800.

[290] Bombay Public Consultations. IOR P/342/43, p. 1768. Letter from Bombay mint master (William Simpson), dated 9th September 1800.

Honble Company, from merchants coining rupees of the Surat standard in the mint, on which I beg leave to solicit your further directions as soon as may be convenient.

This was accompanied by a letter from the consignor of the silver saying, essentially, that if he had to pay the commission he would have to take his bullion elsewhere[291]:

I have received your note and much obliged to you by the order you have sent to receive my dollars and to coin them into Surat rupees, but I understand the Board have ordered to collect 2½ per cent commission, therefore it is necessary for me to know what number of rupees I am to get for 100 Spanish dollars clear of the commission and all other charges. I understood that we were to get 219.1.50, just the same as at Surat. If so I shall send about 200,000 dollars, but if the commission is to be deducted from the above sum, I shall only get 213.3.97 for every hundred dollars, which will not answer as I can dispose of my dollars in the bazar for 215 rupees.

It is impossible that the proprietor of the dollars can subject himself to such an expense if they are to get no more than Surat rupees 219.1.50 per hundred dollars. The commission was at one time considered so heavy a tax that Mr Hornby, when Governor, after examining into the business and by way of encouraging merchants to send their dollars into the mint, struck off the commission, but such have been the high price of dollars since, that for upwards of 16 or 17 years nobody has sent any to be coined. The present measure of coining Surat rupees is very wise as it will prevent the exportation of dollars and increase the currency of silver in the place, but there should be no commission to bring it upon a level with the price in the bazar.

It was agreed that no charges should be made on this occasion:

On the above representation it was resolved on the 11th instant that the Company's fee on the coinage should not, under these circumstances setforth, be exacted.

In November 1800, Smith, Forbes & Co. applied to the Bombay Council for permission to have gold and silver bullion coined. They were informed that they could apply directly to the mint master[292]:

In reply to the above application, Messrs Smith Forbes & Co are to be advised that they need only apply to the mint master from whom they will receive the requisite permission to coin their gold and silver provided they conform to the regulations of the mint at present in force respecting the standard of the coins & all other points.

In November 1800, Dr Helenus Scott, the Bombay assay master, undertook a detailed review of the Surat style coins that had been produced in the Bombay mint. The new Bombay Surat rupees contained about 8% alloy but the amount of alloy in the coins

---

[291] Bombay Public Consultations. IOR P/342/43, p. 1769. Extract of a letter from Mr Miguel De Souza, dated 8th September 1800.

[292] Bombay Public Consultations. IOR P/342/44, p.2233. Letter from Smith Forbes & Co to Bombay government, dated 7th November 1800.

produced at Surat (presumably the Nawab's mint) was not known and had varied over the years[293]:

By your desire I visited the mint and I took from the hands of different workmen 4 rupees still unfinished. It appears from assays that these rupees contained 8.3 per cent of alloy or each rupee had 64.15 grains of pure silver. I do not know the present regulation of the Surat mint for fineness but none of the Surat rupees formerly examined by me were one per cent superior to these Bombay rupees.

By the report of the mint master of Bombay for many years past it will be seen that the Surat standard has frequently varied as it appears at present to be between 7-8 per cent. It would be right to ascertain from Surat the exact fineness now established there that precisely the same degree may be fixed on here. The allowance for the variation to which the mint is always subject may then be determined. From what I have said it will appear to you that there is little variation here at present from the established fineness of 8 per cent.

Surat style rupee copied at Bombay

Scott then went on the compare the Bombay and Surat rupees:

Four rupees coined in Bombay taken from four different bags in the treasury weighed as follows:

	grains
No. 1	179
No. 2	179.3
No. 3	179.11
No. 4	178.8

Two rupees coined at Surat also taken from others in the treasury weighed:

	grains
No. 1	179
No. 2	179.1

---

[293] Bombay Public Consultations. IOR P/342/44, p.2282. Letter from Bombay assay master (Scott) to government, dated 12th November 1800.

From this it appears that both of those kinds of rupees are heavier than the standard weight which is 178.31 grains.

In order to compare together the weight of Surat and Bombay rupees, Mr Simpson and myself took indifferently from a number of each as follows:

Thirteen Bombay rupees were put in one scale of a balance & thirteen Surat ditto in the other

Trial 1, Bombay rupees weighed more by 5′ (the ′ indicates some unit which is not specified)

Trial 2, ditto

Trial 3, ditto

Fifteen of each were then put in the scales

Trial 4	Bombay rupees weighed more by	5′
Trial 5	ditto	4′
Trial 6	ditto	4′
Trial 7	ditto	4′
Trial 8	ditto	4′
Trial 9	ditto	5′
Trial 10	ditto	5′

I have heard one or two people suppose that the present Bombay coinage was much inferior to that of Surat and this has arisen from two circumstances: first the alloy of the present Bombay coinage is entirely of copper which gives a yellowishness to the rupees to which they are unaccustomed. Secondly, the Bombay rupees are at present not so well made as those of Surat, which the workmen tell me is for want of proper anvils but I suppose is in some degree also from want of experience.

He suggested that the rupees made at the Bombay mint should have the word Bombay (I assume he meant the word Munbai in Persian characters) on them:

I think it would be proper to [incise] the word Bombay on the coinage of this place.

Every government may make when it pleases some difference in the standard of its coin, nor could this be attended with any inconvenience or deception to the public, as all the rupees in circulation are Surat rupees tho' called Bombay rupees. It surely would be satisfactory to both mints to have their rupees thus distinguished.

His opinion was that the small differences he had found between the coins produced at Bombay and Surat should not cause any great problems:

Upon the whole I hope it will appear from what I have said that such a difference as I have mentioned not [exceeding] one per cent on the value of the rupee of Surat and Bombay should [create] no kind of complaint amongst the shroffs. The Surat rupee has often undergone much more material variations without being the subject of either observation or complaint. That the mints should be put on a footing of perfect equality is but fair and proper & the same regulations of all kinds should be established for both.

As a result of this report, on 14th November 1800, Mr Grant was appointed mint master and Dr Scott, assay master:

The Board taking into consideration the state of the coinage above mentioned and the necessity of establishing a full and effectual contract over the mint, are of opinion, without meaning in the smallest degree to derogate from the merits of Mr Simpson [in] whose conduct on the contrary has been perfectly satisfactory to Government, that the business of this department may be more effectually conducted and contracted by a person permanently resident on the spot than one whose public avocations necessarily require his chief attendance at a distance from it. With this view solely the Governor in Council is pleased to relieve Mr Simpson from the charge of this department and to rest it in Mr J.A. Grant as mint master with Doctor Helenus Scott as assay master, an appointment which appears to have become essentially necessary for the better regulation of the coinage of this Presidency and for which Mr Scott's knowledge in this particular branch eminently qualifies him.

They were instructed to produce rupees of a standard slightly higher than those produced at Surat and the alloy added was to be lead, rather than copper:

In communicating these appointments to the parties they are to be additionally advised that it is the Governor in Council's order that all silver presented in future or until further orders at the mint is to be coined into rupees with an admixture of [x½] per cent only of alloy whereby it is presented that the standard of the coinage in this mint will be rather higher than even the very best Surat rupee now in circulation.

The alloy is also to consist of lead instead of copper whereby a greater similarity will be preserved in the colour and appearance of the respective coins.

The first job of the new mint and assay masters was to produce another report on the mint and a little later in November 1800, this was duly presented to the Bombay Council. In comparing the Bombay and Surat mints they observed that both had been run by contractors, a system that they considered to be wrong[294]:

…We have attentively read the very distinct report of the Surat mint master, which you transmitted to us on the 19th instant. It appears to us that both mints have been conducted, but with some circumstances of difference, by contractors, who receive the bullion from the public and return in exchange a certain number of rupees. It is evident to us that this system is altogether wrong, and that the intervention of contractors of this sort is unnecessary. They are people who do not contribute to the expense of the coinage but who come in for a share of advantage for doing nothing. What is worse, they get an advantage that the public cannot calculate, which, again, is increased by any degree of debasement of the coin.

---

[294] Bombay Public Consultations. IOR P/342/46, p. 205. Letter from the mint and assay masters, dated 28th November 1800.

They then went on to calculate how many Surat rupees should be coined from a certain number of Spanish dollars and compared this to the number actually returned by the mint contractor:

...From this then it is evident that 100 dollars contain 37,402.56 grains of pure silver.

As the Surat rupee contains 7.97 parts of alloy, the whole rupee weighing 179 grains contains 164.73 grains of pure silver, and if by this number we divide 37,402.56, the number of grains of pure silver in 100 dollars, we shall have the number of Surat rupees that 100 dollars ought to produce which is Surat rupees 227..26.

We observe that the Bombay mint contractor has agreed to deliver to Mr DeSouza 219 rupees for 100 dollars, but the Surat mint delivers only 214¾ per 100 dollars.

It will be evident from what we have said that the profit in both cases is considerable and that it falls unaccounted for into the pockets of the contractors. It is to be feared that in bullion, and with coins, the value of which are less understood, that this abuse is still more considerable. There ought to be no secrets in the transactions of a mint. Every man should receive the whole number of rupees that his silver produces after the deduction of such a public duty as government may choose to impose.

They proposed that the system should be changed:

...business of the coinage be put under the direction of a native, who shall agree to accept of a fixed salary, or rather of a certain percentage every thousand rupees that he coins. From this sum he should pay the artists employed in the different operations of refining, cutting the rupees, stamping them etc. By Mr Church's [mint master at Surat at this time] report we observe that these duties are executed at Surat for 15 rupees per mille, which seems to be very reasonable.

Next they discussed how to maintain the fineness of the coins at Surat and Bombay:

...On this subject we can suggest nothing more effectual than the Bengal Regulation which orders occasional visits to be made to the mint, and at unexpected times, when pieces are to be taken from the hands of the men at work, and assayed. There appears to be no principle in human nature but this constant fear of detection by which we shall be able to preserve the purity of the coin.

With regard to the standard of the rupees to be coined, you have already determined that they be made of the Surat standard, which 91.03 parts in 100 of fine silver.

The weight of the rupee caused them a little more trouble:

In respect of the weight of the rupee of Surat, we labour under some difficulties. We observe that the Bombay government fixed the weight of the Bombay rupee by consultation, December 1738 at 7 dwts, 10 grains 314/1000, that is at 178.314, and this regulation still continues in force. When we got possession of Surat, it was understood that our rupees and the rupee of Surat, should in all respects be equal. We observe that the Surat rupees are now coined of a greater weight than this Bombay rupee of 178.314 grains. On enquiry at the mint here we are assured that the rupees of Surat and Bombay have always been of the same weight, having both of them one tola, or 40 valls.

They determined that the weight of existing rupees was 179 grains and suggested that this should be adopted:

On weighing some of the rupees both of Surat and of the late coinage here, with accurate troy weights, we find them at a medium fully equal to 179 grains each, and as such, at present, until the matter can be more accurately determined, they may be considered. We do not know how the Bombay and Surat standard weight came to differ from the other Moghul mints, which is 179 2/3. In Stevens's guide the Surat rupee is rated at 179.51219 grains, but the weights of India have never attained any great degree of accuracy.

It would be desirable that each mint should be furnished with, at least, one set of accurate weights and scales from England, that we might have some determinate standard to refer to; for every place in India has its own method of calculating and none of them appears to be sufficiently exact.

They went on to discuss the gold coinage firstly investigating the Bengal coinage:

With regard to gold it has now become absolutely necessary that some new regulations should be adopted here. It has been found to be requisite to all governments who employ both a gold and silver coinage, to adjust in the coins the respective values of those metals, by the value they respectively bear to each other in the market. A little latitude seems to be admissible without inconveniency, but this must not extend far. In June 1766 the Bengal gold mohur weighed 179.66 grains, was of the fineness of 20 carots and it passed for 14 silver sicca rupees. The gold was here over-rated, for it bore the proportion to the silver of 16.45 to one. It was found absolutely necessary after great loss to the Company, to remedy this and in March 1769 it was ordered that the Bengal gold mohur should weigh 190.773 grains, be 23 carats 3¾ grains fine and pass for 16 rupees. In this coinage the value of gold to silver was nearly as 14.8 to one. By regulation 35, anno 1793, we see that some further alteration has been made in the gold mohur of Bengal, both with respect to purity and weight, for the 19 sun gold mohur is now fixed at 190.894 grains and contains ¾ of a grain in 100 of alloy. It is ordered to pass for 16 nineteen sun sicca rupees, and the pure gold to the pure silver as 14.85 to one.

The Bombay mint and assay masters proposed that the new gold Mohur should be the same weight as the rupee (i.e. 179 grains) and be of the same fineness:

…As the Surat standard of fineness and weight is now adopted at Bombay for our silver coinage, it is indispensably necessary to adjust the gold rupee to it. We have seen that gold was, in the last coinage, and is still in the market very nearly to silver, as one to 15. We would propose therefore that this proportion be adhered to, and that the gold mohur shall in future be of the same weight as the silver rupee, or 179 grains troy, that it shall contain like the silver rupee 164.73 parts of pure metal, and 14.27 parts of alloy. This gold mohur should pass for 15 rupees and it may be desirable to coin thirds of it in preference to halves or quarters. We

cannot help thinking that this regulation will be altogether more simple and more convenient for arithmetic than the Bengal method, which makes one gold mohur equal to 16 rupees.

We shall find much more difficulty in preserving here the true standard of fineness of the gold than of the silver coin. The natives are acquainted with no method besides the touch of determining the value of gold, a practice that is liable to the greatest deceptions, being merely a guess from colour, and any colour may be perfectly imitated by the base metals.

They discussed the mint establishment:

There has been a small establishment only paid by the Company, on account of the mint, at the following monthly rates:

1 [Purvoe] [=writer]	*25.1.33*
1 ditto	*8*
1 assay master	*4*
4 Sepoys	*16*
	53.1.33

Of course, these were the people paid directly by the Company. Most of the employees worked for the mint contractor so the seven people mentioned above did not form the entire establishment. Indeed, they would have been only a tiny part of the total number of people employed.

In 1805 the mint and assay masters discussed the coinage that had been introduced in 1800 and their letter provides a nice summary[295]:

…The Surat rupee which had so long occupied our circulation was allowed to remain in it and Government authorized the coinage of rupees of that standard in the Bombay mint, the gold mohur was therefore adjusted to the silver rupee on principle of perfect equity.

The new gold mohur being ordered to be coined with the Surat stamp was to weigh one silver rupee, to have the same alloy and to pass for 15 rupees, thereby making one grain of gold represent 15 of silver. This is a proportion sanctioned by the relative value of the metals in our bazar and nearly so by the regulation of 1774, as well as by the coinage of Bengal. Our proportion of alloy is within a mere fraction of what enters into the gold and silver coins of Great Britain, and the value put on the metals is nearly a meanterm between that of Bengal and Great Britain, nor does it differ much from that of any European nation.

X-Ray Fluorescence Analysis of Surat Rupees

The analysis was conducted using a Tracer III XD machine kindly leant by the manufacturers, the Bruker Organisation. The elemental content of each coin was

---

[295] Bombay Public Consultations. IOR P/343/22, p. 2186. Letter from William Crawford (mint master) and Helenus Scott (assay master) to government, dated 19th April 1805.

measured twice, once on each side, except for the plated forgery where three measurements were taken.

The results show very clearly that all of the coins examined contained about 91% silver except for the two coins known to be forgeries. The contemporary assays already discussed, showed about 8% alloy and the silver content was finally fixed at 91.03% (see p. 112), so these figures align reasonably closely. The plated forgery showed widely differing results as might be expected since the coin appears to be mostly copper with a coating of silver that probably varies in thickness in different places. The copper forgery contained only about 20% silver (see section on counterfeit silver coins later in the chapter (pp.137-138).

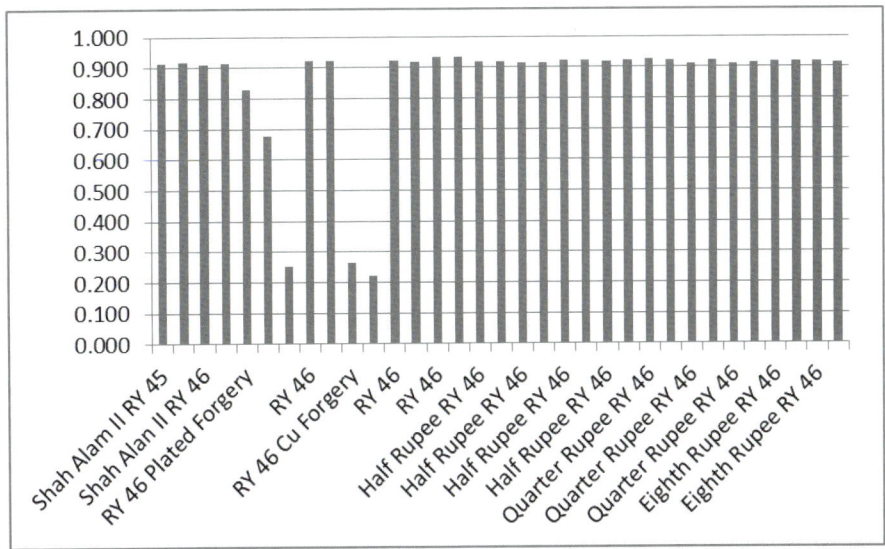

Coin design

Gold Mohur

The silver and gold coins conform to a design with the standard Persian legend of Shah Alam II (*sikka mubārak bādshāh ghazi shāh alām* = The auspicious coin of the victorious Emperor Shāh Alām) on the obverse and the mint name and regnal year on the reverse (*zarb surat sanah 46 julūs maimanat mānūs* = Struck at Surat in the 46th year of tranquil prosperity). The regnal year is generally considered to be fixed at 46 and this has caused much debate over the years. It is clear from the extracts quoted above that the Bombay mint started striking Surat-style coins in August or September 1800. This would have been regnal year 43 (started 30th August 1800). Regnal year 46 did not begin until 29th July 1803. It seems likely that the engravers would have copied coins issued from the Surat mint and Pridmore believed that a mistake was made by the mint master at Surat, Mr Church, because he had only been appointed to the position in July 1800[296]. In fact, it seems possible that Mr Church had been running the mint at Surat since 1789 (see chapter 9, Surat mint) and would therefore have been producing correctly-dated coins for a number of years. Even if his appointment did not occur until 1800, the actual manufacture of coins continued to be handled by a mint contractor and his staff, who must have been producing coins at Surat for several years and would immediately have spotted the incorrect date. Surat-style coins dated RY 44 and 45 have recently come to light so it is possible that coins date RY 43 will also appear at some time in the future. The output of silver coins during the first couple of years seems to have been very small (see below) so it is possible that these coins are quite rare. Most coins produced during these first few years seem to have been gold (see below) but no gold coins dated RY 43, 44 or 45 are known to the present author so this explanation is still not entirely satisfactory. Indeed the coins dated RY 44 and 45 may even be copies produced elsewhere (e.g. in a separate mint operated by the Nawab of Surat or in Bhaunagar, see Surat mint, chapter 9). The choice of RY 46 therefore remains a mystery.

Rupee RY 44

Rupee RY 45

---

[296] Pridmore p. 126. This entry in the IOR has not been found.

Gold Coins – 1801

In April 1801 the Bombay authorities persuaded the mint contractor to accept changes to the terms of his contract and to produce gold panchias or thirds of a mohur[297]:

…It was at the same time ordered in pursuance of the recommendation contained in the last paragraph of the above letter that for the convenience of the public the coinage of thirds of a gold mohur be authorized.

This was confirmed in October 1801 when the mint and assay masters agreed that gold denominations of 1 rupee and 5 rupees should be issued[298]:

…We agree with Mr Halliday that the issuing of gold pieces of the value of one and of five rupees will afford a considerable convenience to the inhabitants of this island although it may not in all respects answer the purposes of a silver coin.

We find that a few gold mohurs have been occasionally sent to the northward by the shroffs, but the number of those were really very insignificant as they are received as bullion not as coin…

As a result, an experimental issues of gold panchias and gold rupees was authorised:

…On the last of the above recorded letters it is resolved that the mint master be authorised by way of experiment to coin gold pieces of the value of 5 and 1 rupee to the amount of a lac of each description when, if they be found to answer the purpose intended, this amount may be increased.

Gold Standard raised – 1802

Gold Mohur with 1802 (not clear) on panel on obverse and leopard's head on reverse

In February 1802 the standard of the gold coins was raised by 2%[299]:

---

[297] Bombay Public Consultations. IOR P/342/47, p. 1009. Letter from the mint and assay masters, April 1801.
[298] Bombay Public Consultations. IOR P/342/49, p. 2760. Letter from the mint master (J.A. Grant) and the assay master (A. Scott) to government, dated 30th October 1801.
[299] Bombay Public Consultations. IOR P/342/54, p. 1471. Letter from PA Grant, mint master at Bombay to Bombay Board, dated 24th June 1802.

...PS In addition to the reference made to the Assay Master's memoir as per concluding paragraph of the above letter, it is necessary that I should remark that in pursuance of the orders of Government of 5th of February last, founded in Doctor Scott's previous suggestions, the gold coins in the mint have since that period been raised two per cent or from 92 to 94 touch so as to contain in 100 parts no more than 6 of alloy. All the gold coin of this improved standard is distinguished by the insertion in small characters on the stamp of the present year, 1802.

This increase in the standard does not appear to have been continued because in 1805 the mint master stated that the mohurs contained 8% alloy[300].

Source of Gold Bullion

The gold used to strike coins came from many different sources. For instance, gold coins were brought from Egypt in September 1802[301]:

According to your orders of the 21st instant we have enquired concerning the coins brought from Egypt by Assistant Surgeons Colquhoun & Grisdale. They consist entirely of gold gubbers [not sure what these are]. Their present value in the bazar is rupees 4.2.62 per gubber. Gold is at present scarce and uncommonly dear or they would not be worth so much. These gentlemen inform us that they received them at the rate of 4.3.53 per gubber, which makes a difference against them at the present bazar rate of 91 reas each gubber. If the Company allow them however the rate at which they received them there will still a gain arise on coining them in the mint, as they are above 98 touch

The mint was authorised to accept the coins. Gold continued to be offered to the mint for coinage. Mr Forbes offered 155,000 rupees worth in January 1803[302]:

Mr Forbes has offered to the mint for sale 6927 tolas of gold at 100 touch and 3240 at 98 touch, which we have assayed. For the whole of this (one touch with another) he demands rupees 15¼ per tola which amount to rupees 155,046.3

 This is at the rate of 15.1.39 for a tola of pure gold and rupees 15. . 16 for a tola of gold 98 touch...

Mr Forbes' offer was accepted. More was offered in February 1803[303]:

Syed Tuckey has offered to the mint for sale 1500 tolas of gold of 98 touch, which we have assayed, He demands rupees 15. .16 per tola which amounts to rupees 22,560. This tender

---

[300] Bombay Public Consultations. IOR P/342/49, p. 2671. Letter from Mr Halliday (superintendent of police) to government, dated 20th October 1801.

[301] Bombay Public Consultations. IOR P/342/56, p. 3033. Letter from Mr Le Messurier & Mr Scott to Bombay Council, dated 24th September 1802.

[302] Bombay Public Consultations. IOR P/343/3, p. 372. Letter from Le Messurier & Scott to Bombay Board, dated 18th January 1803.

[303] Bombay Public Consultations. IOR P/343/3, p. 664. Letter from Le Messurier & Scott to Bombay Board, dated 12th February 1803.

being exactly upon the same terms as Mr Forbes, which considering the state of the market is an advantageous offer, by which the Company will clear more than their duty of 3 per cent…

This offer was also accepted and in March[304]:

Gopaldass Manordass has offered to the mint for sale a quantity of gold bullion of 100 touch and some of 98 touch for which he demands, one touch with another, rupees 15.1…

and June[305]:

Messrs Bruce Fawcett & Co has offered to the mint for sale about 1500 tolas of gold of 96½ touch at the rate of rupees 14.3.23 for the tola, which price is on the same terms with our former purchases...

In November another 1500 tolas was offered[306]:

We are offered about 1500 tolas of gold by Swabjee Muncherjee of 98 touch @ Rs 15.7 annas per tola and it is likely that we may get about 1000 tolas more from other persons at the same rate. This offer is one anna under the present bazar rate and after paying the mintage will leave a profit to the Company of about 1¾ per cent.

and again in December 1803[307]:

The mint and assay masters were, on the 20th instant [i.e. 20 December 1803], ordered to receive such gold bullion as Forbes & Co might send to the mint for coinage on account of the Honble Company to be settled for at the fair market price which they were desired to ascertain and report.

This continued in 1805[308]:

Candass Boolakedass offers gold to the mint at 15 rupees and 3 annas of 98 touch. This is the rate at which we purchased the last gold we bought and is not unreasonable considering the state of the market. He has about 4000 tolas for sale. We beg to be favoured with the orders of the Honble the Governor in Council on this subject.

Gold bullion could also be obtained from other places. For instance in December 1810 there was a discussion about getting gold from Poona[309]:

---

[304] Bombay Public Consultations. IOR P/343/4, p. 1055. Letter from Le Messurier & Scott to Bombay Board, dated 25th March 1803.

[305] Bombay Public Consultations. IOR P/343/5, p. 2125. Letter from Le Messurier & Scott to Bombay Board, dated 6th June 1803.

[306] Bombay Public Consultations. IOR P/343/9, p. 4467. Letter from Crawford & Scott to Bombay Board, dated 23rd November 1803.

[307] Bombay Public Consultations. IOR P/343/9, p. 4845. Resolution.

[308] Bombay Public Consultations. IOR P/343/23, p. 3207. Letter from Charles Watkins (mint master) and H Scott to government, dated 1st June 1805.

[309] Bombay Public Consultations. IOR P/343/52, p. 10981. Letter from the mint master (Charles Watkins) to government, dated 23rd December 1807.

We have the honor to inform you that gold could be procured from Poonah and other parts of the interior at the rate of rupees 15..2..25 per tola of 98 touch, which would enable Government to derive a profit of 1¼ per cent after coinage. As no gold, we understand, is expected to be imported from China this season, we humbly submit to the Honble Board whether it would not be advisable to accept the bullion at that rate during the present stagnation of coinage business until the high price of gold be reduced in the market. We are assured that the quantity thus procurable would be equal to about tolas 100,000 or rupees 1,500,000

Assays of Gold Coins

Assays were carried out to check the weight and standard of the gold coins. For instance, in 1807, a number of gold coins were suspected of being inadequate but in fact proved to be up to standard[310]:

I received an hour ago your letter of this date accompanied with the gold mohurs for assay. It fortunately happened that Mr Watkins was with me in the mint when I got those gold mohurs. I instantly shewed them to our mint contractor who acknowledged that every one of them was of his coinage. I next and without [letting] them for an instant out of our sight weighed them with a very accurate balance and I found that the weight of them all was correct. It now only remained to determine the standard and for this purpose I had for the sake of expedition recourse to the touch stone. I was soon convinced as well as several other people about me, that the standard was right, or at least very nearly. I cannot pretend to judge in this way within a fraction of one per cent but from experience I know very nearly the truth. I should here have rested satisfied that all was sufficiently correct for the general purposes of a coinage But I was desirous of having the opinion of experienced judges. Mr Watkins and I therefore went to the pay office and then to the treasury where, without saying a word with regard to our motives we begged of the Honble Company's shroffs at both places to examine them. They tried them both with the touchstone and then weighed them in thir scales and they at both places declared them that they were (as they ought to be) 92 touch and full weight.

Nothing further remains but to subject the gold mohurs in question to chemycal analysis by which the smallest fractions of a touch may be determined but this will require time and indeed in the present case appears to me perfectly unnecessary.

Those gold mohurs beyond all doubt came as near in all respects to the standard fixed by Government as our mint can ever attain. I am happy to add that Mr Watkins will be happy to confirm what I have said and I doubt not the head shroffs of the pay office and treasury will do the same.

Speed of Conversion of Gold Bullion into Coins

The speed at which gold bullion could be converted into coins was clearly a source of pride for the mint master. The bullion that had been delivered to the mint on 6th

---

[310] Bombay Public Consultations. IOR P/343/45, p. 3117. Letter from H Scott (assay master) to government, read at a meeting on 8th May 1807.

June 1803 by Messrs Bruce Fawcett & Co had all been coined within a few days. On 13th June the mint master reported[311]:

In obedience to the verbal authority I received from you on Wednesday last at the Government House, to accept the offer of gold bullion made by Messrs Bruce Fawcett & Co, on their terms, payment in cash, I have the satisfaction to inform you that the whole quantity being 1500 tolas 14 val has been coined to the standard of 92 touch, and the amount purchased accordingly paid into the hands of Messrs Bruce Fawcett and Co, which came to rupees 22,216-1-12. After paying the expenses of coinage it yields a profit to the Honble Company of rupees 1007-2-40, which has this day been paid into the Honble Company's treasury.

This pride in the speed of work was also demonstrated by this letter of 1810[312]:

…This requisition on the mint was made under the idea that the bullion committee would begin their examination and delivery to the mint office from Monday 3rd December.

The Honble Board must be aware that an unexpected delay took place in the operations of the committee so that the mint could not begin its work until the 12th of this month. This delay will not however occasion any disappointment to the views of Government because, not only have the 6 lacs requested by Government been coined, but a surplus of two lacs of rupees…

Exchange Rate of Gold for Silver

As has already been discussed, the official exchange rate was fifteen silver rupees for one gold mohur and this seems to have held good in and around Bombay. However the Bombay gold coins did not only pass current around Bombay itself but were also used further south on the Malabar Coast, despite the fact that this area was then part of the Madras Presidency. Here, the rate of exchange of the gold mohur for the silver rupee, varied from place to place. For instance, in 1806 a letter to the governor stated[313]:

In reply to your letter which we received yesterday, we beg that you will be pleased to inform the Honble the Governor in Council that the Bombay gold mohur passes for 14 rupees of the present currency at Mangalore by order of the Madras Government. This is the sole cause of its depreciation at that place for that is the rate at which payments made in it were ordered to be received into that treasury. The same is the case at Goa and from the same cause. At Tellicherry on the contrary, as appears by Mr Torins table of coins, it passes for 15 rupees so that it is a matter of speculation and advantage for individuals to collect gold mohurs at Mangalore and send them to Tellicherry and other parts.

---

[311] Bombay Public Consultations. IOR P/343/5, p. 2202. Letter from Le Messurier to Bombay Board, dated 13th June 1803.

[312] Bombay Public Consultations. IOR P/344/36, p. 13. Letter from the mint master (GC Osborne) to government, dated 28th December 1810.

[313] Bombay Public Consultations. IOR P/343/24, p. 3558. Letter from Charles Watkins (mint master) and H Scott to government, dated 17th June 1805.

We may just observe to you that a gold mohur of the present currency contains 164.74 grains of pure gold and a rupee of the present currency precisely the same of silver. If therefore 14 rupees are exchanged for one gold mohur it is evident that 14 parts of silver are exchanged for one of gold, which is not the value of the gold in Malabar nor anywhere else in India...

At Anjengo the gold mohurs produced at Bombay after 1800 were valued too highly. In 1805 the mint master discussed this problem[314]:

In reply to your secretary's letter of the 24th instant desiring to know "if the relative proportionate value between the new and old gold mohur of Bombay be preserved at Anjengo" we beg to inform you that they have at that station given too high a value to the new gold mohur. They estimate it in proportion to the old as 99 to 105 which is as 94- -3 to 100. As the new gold mohur contains 8 per cent of alloy and as the old gold mohur was pure gold, it is evident that they should be estimated as 92 to 100...

Shortage of Silver Rupees – 1801

In October 1801, the superintendent of Police reported on his investigation into the shortage of silver rupees in Bombay[315]:

In consequence of your orders communicated to me thro' Mr Grant three days ago, I have called the pice shroffs before me in order to ascertain from them the reason of the scarcity of silver rupees in circulation and have received from them the following account.

That very few silver rupees have been coined lately in the mint. That those persons who have any silver rupees such as the grain merchants, the cloth merchants, etc, demand 1½ and 1¼ per cent.

Besides this the great shroffs purchase up what silver they can and send it to the northward and whenever any of the rupees which are coined at Surat come into circulation here the great shroffs purchase them up and send them back to Surat to discharge bills drawn by them there, the exchange being at present in favour of Surat 1½ per cent. Formerly when gold mohurs were of a superior quality then bills of exchange were paid in that coin but since they have been reduced they do not go for more than the quality of the gold and therefore a certain loss to the merchants. The shroffs are [of] opinion that if one rupee pieces & five rupee pieces of gold were coined in numbers that the evils would be considerably if not entirely remedied...

In August 1801, the mint and assay master discussed the report on the coinage produced by Mr Constable[316]:

...We are not ignorant of the difficulty of keeping a sufficient quantity of silver in circulation of this place and this arises from very different causes than the purity of our rupee, its

---

314 Bombay Public Consultations. IOR P/343/24, p. 3862. Letter from Charles Watkins (mint master) and H Scott to government, dated 1st July 1805.

315 Bombay Public Consultations. IOR P/342/49, p. 2671. Letter from Mr Halliday (superintendent of police) to government, dated 20th October 1801.

316 Bombay Public Consultations. IOR P/342/49, p. 2751. Letter from the mint master (J.A. Grant) and the assay master (A. Scott) to government, dated 31st August 1801.

perfections or its imperfections. It arises from the great purchases that our merchants make of cotton or of goods in the Guzarat, or the Northern Countries. The amount of the purchase of cotton alone may be estimated at 60 lacs of rupees a year. Our merchants who purchase it get bills from the Bombay shroffs on Surat and other ports to the amount they require. Our shroffs repay those northern shroffs by accepting bills on Bombay for the purchase of goods at this place or by sending them silver. As the value of the goods that are carried from hence is but small in proportion to what are brought from Guzarat, the Bombay shroffs are obliged to send great sums in silver to make up the difference, as gold does not circulate as a coin in those northern countries. It is therefore evident that our silver must be carried away. This state of trade makes bills much more frequently in demand on Surat and the northward than on Bombay, and hence too the reason is apparent, why the rate of exchange is commonly two per cent or more against Bombay.

They considered the possibility that the silver coins should be debased further, perhaps even as much as 50% but this was rejected:

It has been supposed that by putting in a great quantity of alloy in our silver, for instance one half, we should keep it to ourselves. It is probable that we should, but we suppose that government will never be disposed to try such an experiment. The alloy of our silver has been fixed at 8 per cent, which is nearly that of Great Britain. From considering that state of the coinage of the neighbouring mints such an alloy seems to be not exceptionable. No objection has yet been made to it and as every change of the standard of the coin is attended with many inconveniences, we trust that this regulation will long remain.

On 30th October 1801 the mint and assay masters reported:[317]

…We have no doubt but that the silver rupees issued monthly to the troops are carried away in several ways. Many of them are paid to shopkeepers & are thence carried to the shroffs, and a good many also are sent to the Mahratta country monthly by the sepoys who have left their families behind them…

Silver – Alloy used and Secret Marks on the Rupees – 1806

In 1806 the matter of the alloy added to silver was discussed. The mint and assay masters started by stating that they would find difficulty in producing rupees in Bombay that could not be distinguished by the shroffs. However they noted that the Surat shroffs, whilst they acknowledged that the Bombay rupees were not inferior to those of Surat, nevertheless were raising various dubious objections about the quality of the Bombay coins[318]:

---

[317] Bombay Public Consultations. IOR P/342/49, p. 2760. Letter from the mint master (J.A. Grant) and the assay master (A. Scott) to government, dated 30th October 1801.

[318] Bombay Public Consultations. IOR P/343/36, p. 4984. Letter from Charles Watkins (mint master) and Helenus Scott (assay master) to government, dated 19th September 1806.

In reply to your letter of the 16th instant, be pleased to inform the Honble the Governor in Council that we shall find some difficulties in coining silver rupees in this mint so like those of Surat that the shroffs shall not be able to distinguish them. We are at the same time pleased to see that the shroffs of Surat are obliged to acknowledge that the Bombay rupees are of the full value of those of Surat & that they are driven in support of a profitable trade to bring forward a number of petty and insignificant objections. The reasoning of Mr Crow on this subject appears to us to be perfectly conclusive. He is well aware that their ostensible, are very different from their real, reasons.

Next they discussed the different colours of the Bombay and Surat rupees. This arose because of the different alloys used, lead at Surat and a mixture of lead and copper at Bombay:

The Surat shroffs say that there is some difference to be observed in the colour of the Bombay and Surat rupees. This is true & it arises from the circumstance that at Surat the whole of the alloy is lead, at Bombay one half of the alloy is lead and the other half copper. We were aware long ago that it might be better to remove this small difference of appearance but the workmen here cannot make rupees with an alloy wholly of lead. They are apt to crack under the hammer, nor can it be avoided but by long experience. What is the advantage of an alloy of lead above that of copper we cannot conceive. We believe that Surat is almost the only mint in the world where an alloy of lead is in use. In all the mints of Europe, in those of Poona, Baroda, Broach & everywhere else, we believe, in India, a copper alloy is preferred. It is not the kind of alloy but the quantity of it that alters the value of rupees. We therefore beg leave to suggest to Government that as a little difference of colour seems to be so essential to the shroffs of Surat, that the Surat mint be ordered to use an alloy of copper instead of lead or an alloy of one half copper and one half lead. In either case the Bombay mint can do the same. There seems to us a further reason for making the Surat mint use a copper alloy for we see by the Surat mint master's letter to Government of the 21st ultimo that he says that this leaden alloy is one of the causes of the smaller return of silver at Surat from the mint than at Bombay...

There also appeared to be a tiny difference in one of the letters on the coins and a dot in the inscription, thus enabling the shroffs to discount the rupees struck in Bombay:

The second difference in appearance between the Surat and Bombay rupees as mentioned by the shroffs of Surat is some difference in a letter and a point of the inscription on the coin. We believe that this may also be the case but why it should induce a shroff at Surat to reject, or rather to force a discount on a Bombay rupee, we cannot understand. They cannot deny that they are of the same values, that they know them both & know that they emanate from the same authority. By their own confession it is not the people who observe any difference, or hold any doubt. It is themselves alone who raise the difficulty that they may subject the holder of a legal coin to loss & fraud.

To correct this last difference the mint and assay masters suggested that a set of dies be sent from Surat and copied at Bombay:

In order as far as possible to remedy this second objection we beg that Government will order from Surat a set of dies which we shall imitate with as much care as possible. If the difference of the workman's hand shall still appear, we see no other recourse but that of ordering a number of dies from Surat altho' (for reasons that we shall not now detail) that would be attended with much inconvenience. Even then we may not wholly elude the vigilance of the shroffs.

Surat was instructed to use copper as the alloy but this seems to have been before the mint master at Bombay had been asked what alloy was used at Bombay[319]:

We have the honor to acknowledge the receipt of Mr Secretary Wardens' letter…informing us that the mint master at Surat had been desired to adopt a copper alloy there in future. We conclude, in consequence, that it is of course your intention that the same kind of alloy should be adopted in this mint.

However the Bombay Council wanted Surat to use whatever Bombay used:

The mint and assay master were on the 10th instant informed that it was the intention of Government to introduce at Surat an alloy in the coinage similar in all respects to the materials used for it at the mint of Bombay. The mint master was therefore called on to specify what that was, whether copper or lead and if both, in what proportions of each, to the end that a correspondent mixture might be used at Surat

The Bombay assay master stated that they used a mixture of copper and lead, so the instructions to Surat had to be changed[320]:

…we beg leave to inform you that the alloy used in this mint is composed of equal parts of copper & lead.

We request to be favoured with any directions you may think necessary regarding any alteration therein and remain etc

and this was sent to Surat.

The above discussion is interesting from the point of view of the secret marks found on the silver (and gold) coins. It appears that up until 1806, at least, the Surat and Bombay rupees were meant to be indistinguishable, although a lack of co-ordination between the two mints had meant that the shroffs could tell the difference. It therefore seems very unlikely that the Bombay mint would have deliberately added any mark to make the difference more obvious. Pridmore attributes a star mark above the second *h* of *shāh* to the period 1800-1824. This needs to be revised to at least 1806-1824.

---

[319] Bombay Public Consultations. IOR P/343/41, p. 250. Letter from Charles Watkins (mint master) to government, dated 9th January 1807.

[320] Bombay Public Consultations. IOR P/343/41, p. 288. Letter from Charles Watkins (mint master) to government, dated 13th January 1807.

It is also interesting to note the difference in the alloy used in the early rupees. Bombay had originally been told to use lead as the alloy (see above) but they apparently chose to use a mixture of copper and lead because they had found that the coins cracked if they used lead alone. XRF analysis of a few examples of these coins did not reveal any significant difference in the alloy used but only a very small number of coins was available for study. A much larger investigation might prove worthwhile in identifying coins minted at Surat and may help in understanding the secret marks found on the coins.

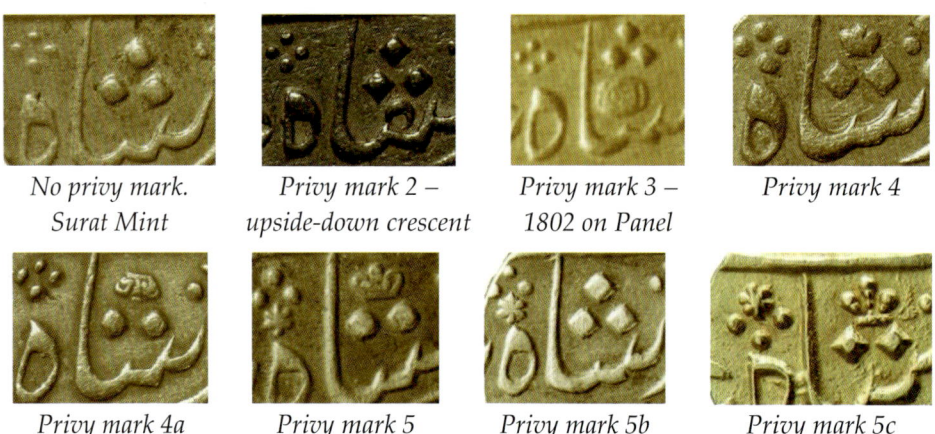

No privy mark. *Surat Mint*	*Privy mark 2 –* *upside-down crescent*	*Privy mark 3 –* *1802 on Panel*	*Privy mark 4*
Privy mark 4a	*Privy mark 5*	*Privy mark 5b*	*Privy mark 5c*

Some of the secret marks found on gold and silver coins

There is also the matter of the shroffs noticing the difference in the letter and the "point" (presumably one of the dots) on the coins. This comment provides an opportunity for more research.

Silver Fractions – 1810

It would seem that prior to 1810, the mint did not strike any fractions of rupees because a letter of that date requests the mint master to consider striking smaller silver coins[321]:

Ordered that the mint master to be called on to report what is the lowest silver and gold coin now stamped at the mint, and whether he be aware of any and what objection to even quarter and eighths of silver rupees, or four and two anna pieces such as would probably prove very convenient in the local circulation.

The mint master replied that he saw no problem with striking halves and quarters but was told not to do this until after a batch of gold bullion had been processed[322]:

---

[321] Bombay Public Consultations. IOR P/344/33, p. 7604. Minute of the Board, dated 30th November 1810.

[322] Bombay Public Consultations. IOR P/344/33, p. 7873. Letter from the mint master (Osborne) to government, dated 30th November 1810.

... I am opinion that the silver rupee may be coined in sub divisions of halves and quarters without inconvenience.

Ordered Mr Osborne be informed that ... the subdivisions or those proposed by Mr Osborne for the silver rupees need not be entered on till the grand object of coining 10 lacs of value in gold mohurs be effected.

Silver Rupees struck at Calcutta – 1823

In 1823, the new silver coin produced at Calcutta caused some questions to be raised by the Madras Government[323]:

A new coin having recently come into circulation [at] Canara and the shroffs there representing it to be a rupee current at Bombay, though it is different from all of the coins of the Bombay mint that have heretofore appeared, the principle Collector of the province has applied for instructions as to whether he should receive it in payment of revenue.

I am in consequence directed by the Honble the Governor in Council to transmit to you the accompanying specimen of the coin in question, and to request both that this Govt may be informed whether it is a rupee of the Bombay currency and also, in order to save time, that a direct communication of the same information may be made to the principle Collector.

If the coin is of the Bombay currency it will of course be received at Canara and held available for remittance back to Bombay.

The coin was sent to the sub-treasurer at Bombay for identification[324]. They were informed that the coin came from a batch produced for Bombay at Calcutta and that more of the same had just arrived[325]:

...I request you will have the goodness to inform the Right Honble the Governor in Council that the rupee in question belongs to the consignment of five lacs of Bombay rupees coined in the mint of Calcutta, and sent into circulation under the Government advertisement published in the courier of the 17th April last.

Another consignment of twenty-five lacs of Bombay rupees coined at Calcutta, having been likewise lately received, at this office, which will probably find their way to the provinces of Malabar and Canara. I beg to enclose a specimen of these coins for the purposes of being forwarded to the Government of Fort St George for eventual transmission to the Collectors on this coast as being (with the first consignment) received and issued at the General and Subordinate Treasuries under this Government at the same rate and value as the silver currency struck in the mint at this Presidency.

---

[323] Bombay Consultations. IOR P/411/41, 1823, p. 78. Letter from Madras government to Bombay government dated 25th November 1823.

[324] Bombay Consultations. IOR P/411/41, 1823, p. 79. Letter from Bombay government to Bombay sub-treasurer dated 9th December 1823.

[325] Bombay Consultations. IOR P/411/41, 1823, p. 79. Letter from sub-treasurer to Bombay government dated 10th December 1823.

The same question arose at Surat[326]:

I am directed by the Honble the Governor in Council to acknowledge the receipt of your letter dated the 22nd April last and to inform you that both the coins that have found their way to Surat bearing the inscription of Zirbe Soort and Zirbe Moombay are Bombay rupees coined at the mint of Calcutta and of the same value, and that there are no Farruckabad at present in this island.

A few of each of these coins will be forwarded to you.

The poor quality of the coins produced at Calcutta was discussed in some detail by the Calcutta mint master[327]:

The chief subject of the second letter of the Assay Master of the Bombay mint, is the impression on the coin. This was, no doubt, very defective. It appears that in the absence of any better guide, a Bombay rupee was formerly procured from the bazar, and the precise impression on it exactly copied. The blanks were, however, cut with a larger face and consequently the letters of the impressions were spread out beyond their original scale in order to cover a broader surface. This is what Mr Noton objects to. It will be easily obviated now we have correct and full impressions of the die. It does not appear that any objection is made to the size of the rupees as long as the same proportion is observed in the inscription. By a very inconsiderable alteration in this respect it will be possible to introduce the whole inscription into the rupee coined here, the superiority of which over the rude and imperfect coin of Bombay and the uncouth coin lately prepared in Calcutta [can] not be [denied]. I have the pleasure to submit a Bombay coin, one of the last Calcutta coinage, and one of the coinage contemplated for the future…

…The rejection of so large a number of rupees as 11,000 on account of their being plugged is certainly discreditable to the care exercised in their fabrication. They ought unquestionably never to have been sent out of the mint and in future due attention will be paid to the prevention of such issue.

Calcutta's first attempt to produce rupees for Bombay

326 Bombay Consultations. IOR P/411/42, 1824, p. 62. Letter from government to Surat Collector, dated 19th May 1824.

327 Bombay Consultations. IOR P/411/41, 1823, p. 47. Letter from Calcutta government to Bombay government dated 30th July 1823. Also Letter from the acting mint master at Calcutta (H H Wilson) to the Calcutta mint committee, dated 15th July 1823

The second attempt to produce rupees for Bombay at Calcutta

New Standard for the Silver Rupee – 1824

In June 1818 the Calcutta Government wrote to Bombay discussing the standardisation of the rupee between Madras and Bombay[328]:

…The measure of equalising the standard of the currency throughout British India, appears calculated to promote essentially a public convenience.

The great superiority in value of the Calcutta Sicca Rupees, [to those] of Fort St George and Bombay appears to offer the most serious obstacles to the adoption of any arrangement such as that which has been prepared by the Honble the Court of Directors for equalising the value of the currencies.

Adverting however to the trifling difference in the intrinsic value of the coins of Bombay and Madras and to their near approach in respect of standard, the Vice President in Council conceives that they might with considerable advantage be entirely assimilated.

The Vice President in Council begs leave therefore to suggest to the consideration of the Right Honble the Governor in Council at Bombay, the expediency of increasing the weight both of the rupee and gold mohur of Bombay to 180 grains, and of adopting the standard prescribed by the Honble Court and already adopted at Fort St George, Viz: 165 grains fine metal and 15 grains alloy.

The small increase in intrinsic value [which] will result from this operation would not appear likely to attend with any practical inconvenience, but the Right Honble the Governor in Council will be himself the best judge of the propriety of the measure, and will of course view this communication only as suggesting it for his consideration.

But nothing seems to have been done about this until September 1824, when the mint committee was asked to take immediate measures to coin the rupee at Madras standard, and to give their opinion on a general reform of the currency[329]. The mint

---

[328] Bombay Consultations. IOR P/411/38, p. 183. Letter from Calcutta to the Bombay, dated 12th June 1818.

[329] Bombay Consultations. IOR P/411/42, 1824, p. 76. Letter from government to the mint committee, dated 15th September 1824.

committee replied very quickly[330]:

We have the honor to acknowledge the receipt of your letter… desiring us to take immediate steps for the coinage of a new rupee of the Madras standard, at this mint, and further requiring us to offer an opinion on the measures to be adopted for a general reform of our currency.

With regard to the first point, the only step that seems to be absolutely necessary is the issue of a proclamation on the part of Government, announcing the alteration in the standard of our mint and declaring the new rupee current at par with the old. But we think it would be also advisable for the Government to relinquish as suggested in the 3rd paragraph of our letter of the 31st March last, such a portion of the mint duty as shall be equal to the difference of intrinsic value or about one fifth of one per cent, in order to prevent those who may bring bullion to the mint for coinage, from suffering by the change. This will be trifling with respect to silver and there seems no probability, to judge from present appearances, of any gold being coined for a considerable time to come…

…In conclusion we have only further to submit the draft of a proclamation of our mint standard to be issued if approved in a Courier Extraordinary and repeated in the regular paper both in the English and native languages.

The new standard was announced to the public in October 1824[331]:

The Honble the Governor in Council having been pleased to direct a new rupee of the following weight and standard to be struck at the Bombay mint Viz:

Troy Grains	*180 grains*
Pure silver	*165 grains*
Alloy	*15 grains*
Touch or parts of pure silver	*91 2/3*
Alloy	*8 1/3*

Is likewise pleased to declare the new Bombay rupee and its subdivisions current from and after the 15th instant at par with the present Bombay rupee and its subdivisions, within the territories subordinate to this Presidency and, as such, receivable wherever the present Bombay rupee and its subdivisions are current as a legal tender in all public and private transactions.

Rupee, 1825-c1830

---

[330] Bombay Consultations. IOR P/411/42, 1824, p. 80. Letter from the mint committee to government, dated 27th September 1824.

[331] Bombay Consultations. IOR P/411/42, 1824, p. 84. Advertisement, dated 6th October 1824.

Farrukhabad Rupee – 1824

Farrukhabad rupee

In 1824 the Farrukhabad rupee was declared current in the Bombay Presidency, although it was never struck there. How they managed to measure the weight to three places of decimals remains a mystery[332]:

…In reply we request you will have the goodness to represent to the Honble the Governor in Council that there appears to us not the smallest objection to the Farruckabad rupee being declared current at par with the Bombay rupee throughout the territories subordinate to this Presidency…

Proclamation

The Farruckabad rupee being of the following weight and standard

Weight	*180.234 troy grains*
Silver	*165.215 troy grains*
Alloy	*15.019 troy grains*

Touch or parts of pure silver per cent	*91 2/3*
Alloy	*8 1/3*

The Honble the Governor in Council is pleased to declare current until further orders, at par with the Bombay rupee, within the territories subordinate to this Presidency and as such receivable wherever the Bombay rupee is current, as legal tender in all public and private transactions.

Other Rupees Produced in the Region

The assay master was sometimes asked to examine coins from other mints to determine their value. For instance in 1807 he was sent coins from various areas[333]:

We also received the various coins as per your list from the districts of Salsette, Baroach and Kaira. Accompanying we have the honor to report on their different values as far as it is

---

[332] Bombay Consultations. IOR P/411/42, 1824, p. 40. Letter from the mint committee to government, dated 31st March 1824.

[333] Bombay Public Consultations. IOR P/343/45, p. 3373. Letter from the mint master and H Scott (assay master) to government, dated 18th May 1807.

possible to do so with any degree of accuracy in such a subject. The Cambay mints are in general so inaccurate in their coinage that the coins of the same denomination differ from each other at times several per cent in purity as well as weight. This is remarkably the case with regard to the mints of Broach, Cambay and Ahmadabad so that even a large specimen will hardly afford the means of forming a general value with much accuracy...

Coins from Baroda were examined in 1810[334]:

...The coins transmitted by Mr Rowles consist of 3 parcels containing five Rs each Viz: No. 2 denominated Maturer or Walkersoy rupees; No. 3 denominated Assasoy or Petland rupees.

On a careful assay of the above rupees there does not appear to be any material difference in their relative value, and on comparing that value with the assay of the new Baroda rupees transmitted to me by the acting resident, directly from the mint, agreeably to the orders of your Honble Board, being the coinage of the months of May and July of 1809, it will appear that the information of Mr Rowles respecting the intrinsic value of the new Baroda coinage is perfectly correct and that consequently there does not appear sufficient ground, as far as my information goes, to justify that Government in circulating it at the advanced premium of 3 per cent.

The following table exhibits the value of the different coins in question, computed from the weight and quantity of alloy contained in each. No 4 is the assay of new Baroda rupees transmitted to me by the acting resident for that purpose

	Weight (grains)	Alloy (per cent)
No. 1 New Baroda Rupee	177.4	11.9
No 2 Walkersoy	177.4	11.5
No 3 Petlander	176.8	11.8
No 4 Baroda rupees sent for assay	177.4	12
Average	177.2	11.18

From the foregoing table the greatest difference in the weight of these rupees does not excede half a grain which may arise from the length of time the coin may have been in circulation, and the greatest difference in point of purity does not exceed ½ per cent and that in only one instance. The others may be considered for all the purposes of coins, to be exactly of the same value.

According to the reports transmitted to me monthly by the Acting Resident of Baroda, there does not appear to have been any coinage in that mint from 1ˢᵗ May 1809, excepting the two months to which I have alluded Viz: May and July 1809.

Stewart, the Bombay assay master, went on to state his opinion that the numerous different coins circulating in Gujerat should be replaced by the Surat rupee:

---

[334] Bombay Public Consultations. IOR P/344/26, p. 3311. Letter from the assay master (R Stewart) to government, dated 18th April 1810.

The above remarks appear to answer generally, the different paragraphs of Mr Rowles letter. I have only to add further that I entirely agree in opinion with that gentleman, of substituting, for the numerous coins now in circulation throughout the Honble Company's districts in Gujarat and wherever else it can be done, one uniform coin, and there can be no doubt the best will be the Surat or Bombay rupee which are exactly the same…

Source of Silver for Minting

Much of the silver bullion sent to the mint was in the form of South American dollars. For instance, in September 1806, 62,682 dollars were sent to the mint for coining[335]:

The mint master was on the 5th instant directed to receive from the sub-treasurer the sum of 62,682 dollars now in the treasury for the purpose of being coined with the least practicable delay on the grounds of a recommendation from the accountant general.

More silver bullion was sent for coining in 1808[336]:

Although indents for coinage to the amount of nearly four lacs and an half were drawn upon the mint between the 12th and 16th ultimo it appears that there is not actually two lacs forthcoming as the contractor has just been given to understand (on applying to the merchants for more bullion and dollars, the balance in hand being very trifling) that they have none. The amount including this days issues will be Rs 148,500 returned to them since the 4th ultimo or on average upward of rupees 7000 per diem. As, in consequence of this disappointment, the workmen will be thrown out of employment in a day or two, I beg leave Honble sir to recommend that the bullion and dollars lately purchased on account of the Honble Company be sent to the mint to keep them employed now so many are collected together

The dollars had become so trusted that they were accepted into the mint without assay until, in 1808, the mint contractor reported that he found he was not getting as many rupees from the dollars as had previously been the case[337]:

We beg you will be pleased to report to the Honble the Governor General in Council that the mint contractor lately complained to us that he had just detected a deficiency in his accounts of not less than 1500 rupees, which on further enquiry he found to arise from the coining of rupees from new dollars.

The dollar is a coin so long established and its value has been so faithfully preserved that they pass here to any amount by number and without enquiry into their weight or standard. In like manner they have always been received by tale at the mint. That the dollars received of late dated 1800, 1, 2, 3, 4, 5, 6 are a fraudulent coinage it is impossible for us to doubt for we have made very particular enquiry into their real value, and find it somewhat less than it

---

[335] Bombay Public Consultations. IOR P/343/36, p. 4747. Resolution at a meeting held on 9th September 1806.

[336] Bombay Public Consultations. IOR P/343/55, p. 804. Letter from the mint master (Watkins) to government, dated 4th February 1808.

[337] Bombay Public Consultations. IOR P/343/56, p. 1445. Letter from the assay master (H Scott) and mint master (Watkins) to government, read at a meeting on 26th February 1808.

ought to be, both in respect to the proportion of silver and the weight of each dollar. The deviations from the true standard are but small but they are uniform and on that account bear more strongly the marks of design…

Another source of silver bullion was China. This also caused problems from time to time. In 1808 Dyal Boolakidass believed that he had been short-changed from some of the Chinese silver he had sent to the mint[338]:

…It is not entirely without reason that Dyal complains of this sycee silver for, until a year or two past, the Chinese always sent it pure or with but very little alloy. They now however adulterate it considerably as will appear by the mint assays of very large quantities. Such is the confidence acquired by time that I have no doubt but that Dyal could have sold in the bazar all this sycee silver as pure silver, but still the assays are true and I believe can never be controverted.

In November 1808 a dispute over the value of silver bullion arose with another merchant who had sent silver to the mint[339]:

I have the honor to acknowledge your letter under date the 18th instant accompanied with a recommendation by the sub-treasurer that a re-assay of the silver purchased from Ardaseer Dady should take place and to which you were pleased to assent.

On receiving from the treasury the pieces of silver reserved for this purpose I naturally expected that the same pieces which were originally cut by Mr Scott for assay would have been preserved but in this I was disappointed and found that most, if not all, of them had been coined.

I find by Mr Scott's memorandum that he had taken from each box containing 40 to 50 pieces, two pieces, one from the top and the other from the bottom of the package, and that the medium fineness of these two pieces was taken by him as that of the contents of the box. I find however that the same precaution has not been observed in regard to the pieces now presented for assay, but that four pieces have been taken from each box promiscuously, after they had been unpacked for the purpose of weighing.

I have thought it my duty previously to my executing the intended assay to state the above circumstances to your Honble Board for the follow reasons:

1st from a consideration that if they had been known, your Honble Board would have hesitated at granting a new assay, for such it really must be, and not a re-assay as requested by Ardaseer.

2nd from the few trials I have made, I have every reason to believe that a new assay will not in its result agree with that formerly made; nor yet were I to divide the new into two separate

---

[338] Bombay Public Consultations. IOR P/343/58, p. 2938. Letter from the assay master (H Scott) to government, dated 26th April 1808.

[339] Bombay Public Consultations. IOR P/344/4, p. 7994. Letter from the acting assay master (R Stewart) to government, dated 29th November 1808.

assays, would they agree with each other; and this is unavoidable from the difference in regard to fineness between the pieces contained in the same box, which I have observed to exist.

The regular manner in which every assay of this silver has been entered in Mr Scott's book in his own handwriting, and which I have carefully examined in case there might be an error in calculation, leaves me in no doubt with regard to their accuracy, but I can easily show that the quality of the silver in question is so irregular as to render a partial assay but at least doubtful and only an approximation of the truth.

Should your Honble Board still deem another assay desirable, I shall take the liberty of proposing that Ardaseer Dady in place of abiding by it shall abide by the result of it compared with that which has already been made, or the mean of the two.

The assay master did conduct a second assay and the silver was found to be purer than shown by the first assay[340]:

…The letter to which I have alluded conveys the acquiescence of your Honble Board in the application of Ardaseer Dady for a further assay of syce silver sold by him to the Honble Company on condition that the medium of the result of the second assay compared with that formerly made by Mr Scott should be accepted as the criterion for fixing the value of the silver in question.

In my communication on this subject under date the 29th November, I stated to your Honble Board my expectation that a second assay was not likely to agree with that made by Mr Scott owing to the same pieces which were assayed first not being procurable, as well as to the irregularity that had been observed in the silver, this expectation my late trials have [been] simply justified.

After a carefully repeated assay of 84 pieces, I find the medium alloy to be 1.25 per cent or 1¼ per cent.

The amount of alloy by Mr Scott's assay was according to his books	*3.04 per cent*
By second assay of new pieces	*1.25*
	4.29/2
Leaving a medium of	*2.145 per*
cent	

Or in round numbers 2⅛ per cent on the whole purchase…

Rupees from surrounding areas were sometimes re-coined into Surat rupees. For instance, in 1809, a batch of Broach rupees was examined and ordered to be re-coined[341]:

I have the honor to acknowledge [Secretary] Gordivin's letter under the date the 18th ultimo, transmitting enclosures from the collector of Surat respecting the accumulation of Broach

---

[340] Bombay Public Consultations. IOR P/344/7, p. 509. Letter from the assay master (R Stewart) to government, dated 14th July 1809.

[341] Bombay Public Consultations. IOR P/344/17, p. 6996. Letter from the assay master (Stewart) to government, dated 20th October 1809.

rupees in the treasury and from the deputy accountant general at the presidency containing the tender of a shroff for one lack of the above rupees at the rate of 94 Surat rupees for one hundred Broach, and desiring me to state what I conceive to be the best means of turning the rupees in question to the best account.

Having fully considered the statement of the mint master of Surat respecting the high price of silver bullion in the market, and the probability of its becoming still higher as well as the low rate of exchange between this place & Surat at present, I have no hesitation in recommending that the whole of the rupees of the Broach mint may be re-coined into Surat standard rupees as the most advantageous for the public, whether considered in a mercantile or political point of view…

As with the gold bullion, Messrs Forbes & Co often submitted silver bullion for coinage. An entry of 1809 shows that 42 chests of bullion were sent to Surat[342]:

I have the honor to report to your Honble Board that I have assayed the silver bullion contained in forty two chests purchased from Mesrs Forbes & Co and now under consignment to Surat and find it to contain one and one third per cent alloy or to be of 98⅔ touch.

In 1811 coins were sent to Bengal for assay[343]:

I have the honor to hand up specimens of the Bombay coinage taken out of the mint of this Presidency for transmission to the Supreme Government, amounting to rupees 225 as follows:
No 1 contains 10 gold mohurs each at 15 rupees
No 2 ditto 10 gold puncheas at 5 Rs each
No 3 ditto 10 gold rupees
No 4 ditto 10 silver half rupees
No 5 ditto 10 silver rupees…

The Bombay assay master wrote a letter to the Calcutta Government about the standard of some silver coins in 1823 and this revealed the differences between the Bombay and Calcutta standards, which could cause confusion[344]:

…The first letter of the Assay Master of the Bombay mint, dated the 28th April, related to the supposed difference in the assay reports of the Calcutta and Bombay mint, the silver called 15½ Br in the former appearing to be but 13½ Br in the latter.

It is unnecessary however to discuss the apparent difference as Mr Noton concludes his letter by accurately conjecturing the cause of the variation. We refer in the Calcutta mint to our own standard. At Bombay the English standard is referred to. The English standard is

---

[342] Bombay Public Consultations. IOR P/344/23, p. 1500. Letter from the assay master (R Stewart) to government, dated 19th March 1810.

[343] Bombay Public Consultations. IOR P/344/38, p. 1333. Letter from the mint master (GC Osborne) to government, dated 4th March 1811.

[344] Bombay Consultations. IOR P/411/41, 1823, p. 47. Letter from Calcutta government to Bombay government dated 30th July 1823. Also Letter from the acting mint master at Calcutta (H H Wilson) to the Calcutta mint committee, dated 15th July 1823

already 2 dwt better than the Calcutta standard. Consequently 13½ dwt better than English standard is 15½ better than Calcutta standard and the two denominations mean the same thing. The assays at Bombay therefore precisely correspond with those at Calcutta…

Counterfeit Silver Coins

In August 1801, the mint and assay masters discussed Mr Constable's report on the coinage[345]:

We have perused Mr Constable's report on the coinage. We approve much of the regulations that he proposes for protecting the coins against the risk of being counterfeited and we think that what he says in paragraph 23rd is the most deserving of attention. These, no doubt, will have their effect, but unless we can stamp our coins in a way that cannot be imitated in India, all the regulations that can be adopted against false coiners will be insufficient.

A false coinage made its appearance here some months ago. It probably came from a Maharatta mint where we had not the power of getting satisfaction. All that could be done was to stop it where it could be found in circulation. If our coins were impressed by Europe machinery this could not possibly have happened…

In 1811, counterfeit coins believed to have originated in Bhaunagar, were examined. Whilst they agreed with the regulations proposed against counterfeiting by the judge & magistrate of Surat, the Bombay assay master believed that forgery would never be stopped until European machinery was introduced[346]:

I have the honor to report on your letter of yesterday's date giving cover to one from the judge and magistrate of Surat with a rupee accompanying, said to be a counterfeit coin of the Bombay currency, for examination.

The coin in question was first submitted to the examination of the undertakers for the mint, who immediately declared that it was not struck at the Bombay mint, nor the stamps made use of, engraved at Bombay. On more minute inspection they made no further observation than that they believed it to be the manufacture of Bhownagar.

In point of weight, the coin was exactly of the Bombay standard of 179 grains, but on cutting it for assay it was immediately discovered to be a piece of copper with an extremely thin coating of silver, so thin as certainly as not to exceed one fiftieth part of its weight, which rendered any further examination unnecessary.

I have only further to observe that I agree entirely in the opinion of Mr [.....] that the manufacture of the counterfeit is so well executed as very likely to impose on and prove extremely injurious to the public, while at the same time it affords a convincing and also an alarming proof of the facility with which our coinage may be imitated whilst it continues on its present footing.

---

[345] Bombay Public Consultations. IOR P/342/49, p. 2751. Letter from the mint master (J.A. Grant) and the assay master (A. Scott) to government, dated 31st August 1801.

[346] Bombay Public Consultations. IOR P/344/36, p. 531. Letter from the assay master (R Stewart) to government, dated 29th January 1811.

The Bombay authorities determined on taking forceful action:

Ordered that copies of the correspondence on the subject of the preceding letter be referred to the Acting Resident at Baroda with instructions to inform the Thacoor of Bhownagar of the suspicions thus entertained of the fabrication of base coins in semblance of the Bombay rupee being carried on in his town; such as it is accordingly expected and required that he adopt immediate and effective measures to put a stop to and to detect the falsifiers, in default of which Government may, with whatever reluctance, be obliged to interfere in the research in a manner which it is expected the Thackoor will not by any supiness on the present occasion, afford any ground for.

A plated forgery has been discussed above (p. 115) when examining the XRF analysis of the coins and this seems to have been a common way of forging silver rupees.

Copper Pice – 1802 to 1829

Double pice, 1825

On 15th November 1802, the mint and assay masters addressed the Bombay Council about the copper coinage. They drew the Council's attention to the fact that the Soho-minted coins dated 1791 and 1794 (see chapter 11) had almost disappeared and a new copper coinage was needed. However, they pointed out that the current price of copper at Bombay would produce a loss if the pice were coined at the same weight as the then existing pice, and recommended that the weight be reduced to 164 grains. They also recommended that the 1½ pice value should no longer be coined, as it could easily be mistaken for the double and single pice and served no other useful function (e.g. for the accounts) [347].

The scarcity of copper money has become so great that it is now very difficult to pay the troops or marine, or for the people in the buzars to carry on their small transactions. The price of copper is usually from 14 Rs to 16 the Bombay maund in the buzar, but it now sells for 17.1 while the Company's price is 19.3.50.

If at the lowest of these rates (17.1 per maund) we were to coin copper money here of the same weight and fineness with the present coin, a considerable loss will arise to the Honble Company. A maund of 28 lb is coined into 980 pice which are worth 20 rupees. But a maund costs Rs 17.1. Charges and losses on coining Rs 6.2. Total Rs 23.3. This would therefore produce a loss to the Company of Rs 3 An 2 on each maund.

In order to obviate this loss & at the same time supply a copper coinage we would recommend a reduction of weight in the coin so that a maund may be coined into 1200 pice instead of 980. Twelve hundred pice are worth 24 rupees so that the Company will be very little more than indemnified for this coinage.

An Avoirdupois pound contains 7000 grains, which, multiplied by 28 gives 196,000 or the number of grains in a Bombay maund. If therefore, as we propose, this be coined into 1200 pice each pice will weigh 163.3333 etc grains or 164. At present a pice weighs 200 grains.

---

[347] Bombay Public Consultations. IOR P/342/57, p. 3778. Letter from the mint master (P. Le Mesurier) and assay master (H Scott) to Bombay government, dated 15th November 1802.

139

The present copper coinage consists of four values. 1ˢᵗ double pice worth 8 reas each. 2ⁿᵈ pices worth 6 reas each. 3ʳᵈ single pice or 4 reas each. 4ᵗʰ half pice or two reas each.

We would further recommend that the pieces of 6 reas be no longer coined for they are easily mistaken for the 8 or 4 reas pieces & they are quite unnecessary for accounts.

The discussion about the weight of the pice requires some explanation because the weight of the 1791/94 pice was 100 grains and the proposed weight of 164 grains would obviously not result in a reduction, rather the opposite. Pridmore explained this by saying that the mint and assay masters were using the term pice in its generic sense and were actually referring to the double pice of 200 grains being reduced to 164 grains. This seems to provide a sensible explanation since the rate of exchange of the single pice was changed from 100 to a rupee to 50 to a rupee[348].

The recommendations were approved and the mint and assay masters were instructed to take the necessary action. The design was copied from the earlier Soho pice, and the first pieces were dated 1802, implying that work must have started almost immediately.

From 1802 to 1804 the denominations consisted of a four, two, one, and half pice. The four pice coin was very heavy and clumsy and was discontinued after 1804. Later a quarter pice denomination was added to the series. The exact date of introduction of this last denomination is not known, but the earliest recorded specimen is 1816. However, the use of dies larger than the flans, means that dates on coins of lower denominations are often not visible so that, although the coins were issued in large numbers, they are often difficult to find with clear dates. Thus quarter pice could have been issued earlier than known dated specimens. Many forgeries occur, some apparently produced by local native rulers (see chapter 8, p. 242 ff.).

1803 Copper Coinage. Square Copper Coins

In 1803 the cost of producing the copper coins was discussed and a decision was taken to strike square coins[349]:

Charges on Japan copper

The warehousekeepers charge	*Rs 16.-.70*
Burnage	*-.3.87*
Minters charges for smiths charcoal etc	*5.1.50*
	22.2.07
The above will yield in pice	*Rs 24*

It is however to be observed that those pice will be square like the Mahratta pice and not round. I suppose this is very immaterial. If they are to be made round the 3ʳᵈ charge will be increased by Rs 1-1-50. This is owing to the necessity they are under for melting the Japan

---

[348] Proclamation of 9ᵗʰ March 1831 50 pice to a rupee. Taken from Pridmore.

[349] Bombay Public Consultations. IOR P/343/9, p. 4320. Letter from William Crawford (mint master) & H Scott (Bombay assay master) to Bombay Board, dated 12ᵗʰ November 1803.

copper before they make it into round pice which additional melting they avoid for square. From the above statement it appears that the Japan copper is more advantageous for the purpose of pice than the sheet copper.

This proposal from the mint master was accepted:

The mint master was on the 16th instant ordered on the ground of the preceding statements to coin to the value of a lack of rupees from Japan copper into square pice and annas or sixteenths of a rupee in the proportions of 2/3rds of the former and one third of the latter, which copper coins were to be paid into the treasury as speedily as possible.

That would amount to about 50,000 annas (4 pice) and 3.2 million pice but no obviously square copper coins are known.

Copper Coinage – 1810

Pice 1810

An entry of 1810 refers to the production of copper coins simply to keep the mint workers employed[350]:

I had indented on the Import Warehousekeeper for 600 maunds of copper but as he informs me Government have ordered the remains of that article in store to be conveyed to Bengal, I request you will be pleased to move the Governor in Council to direct the Import Warehousekeeper to deliver to my order 100 maunds of copper. My object in this application is to give employment to the mint workers until the gold and silver bullion from China is landed. If the mint had not employment, the mint contractor would discharge the workers immediately, the consequence of which would be the reduction of the mint from its present unprecedented effective condition to its former inefficiency.

The mint contractor would not willingly incur the smallest certain loss for any contingent profit.

The warehousekeeper was ordered to deliver the copper to the mint. Because the Bombay mint would use all of the copper in the warehouse, Bengal was informed

---

[350] Bombay Public Consultations. IOR P/344/24, p. 2373. Letter from the mint master (GC Osborne) to government, dated 1st May 1810.

that no copper could be sent there[351]:

…I have examined the copper fit for coinage in the Honble Company's warehouse and find that the quantity does not exceed 375 Surat maunds, which is not more than is required at the mint of this Presidency. It will therefore be impossible to supply the demand at the Presidency of Fort William until the arrival of the expected ships from England.

Copper Coins to be sent from England

In 1808, consideration had again been given, in London, to the possibility of producing coins in England for India, including the Bombay Presidency[352].

The principle of executing in England a copper coinage for Bengal and other parts of India having occupied our attention for some considerable time, and the price of copper in the London market having been lately much reduced, it appears that the present is a favourable opportunity for effecting a copper coinage on a larger scale.

We have accordingly bestowed much consideration on the subject and have forwarded our views thereon to the Governor General. We have determined that 64 copper pice weighing 7425 troy grains shall circulate in exchange for one sicca rupee and that there shall be also half pice coined at the rate of 128 to the rupee…

…We have also determined that the copper coin for Bengal shall have for an impression on one side the Company's arms & motto, with the date of year when struck (say 1809) and also the value of the coin (say 64…128) and on the reverse an inscription in Persian, Nagaree & Bengalee, indicating the value of the coin.

As we are of opinion a coin of the above weight will answer for the circulation of Bombay as well as for that of Bengal & that the arms etc are as applicable for the one as the other, it becomes necessary that we should be put in as early possession as practicable of your views on the fittest division of the coin and also as to the most proper inscription and characters for the reverse, together with the quantity you deem necessary to be sent in the first instance, & also the probable annual quantity which may be required afterwards.

It is our intention, if we receive your reply in time, to ship for your Presidency in the season 1809/1810 whatever quantity of copper coin you may indent for, executed on the principle we have before stated, and which we doubt not will be found very convenient for the circulation of Bombay and its subordinates.

Nothing ever seems to have come of this proposal but in 1813 the mint and assay masters discussed various other suggestions made from London[353]:

---

[351] Bombay Public Consultations. IOR P/344/25, p. 2258. Letter from the assay master (Stuart) to government, dated 4th May 1810.

[352] Dispatches to Bombay. IOR E/4/1023, pp. 258-259. 7th September 1808

[353] Bombay Public Consultations. IOR P/344/63, p. 3368. Letter from the Mr Coward (Acting mint master), Mr Kaye (accountant general), Mr Wedderburn (sub-treasurer), Mr Noton (assay master) to government, dated 8th June 1813.

We have now the honor to reply to Mr Secretary Newnham's of the 31ˢᵗ of May…desiring us to consider and report on the expediency or otherwise of conducting a coinage of copper at this Presidency, and on the propriety in the former case, of applying to Bengal for the requisite machinery or, in the latter, for a supply of copper pice.

With regard to the first of these points we are decidedly of opinion that it will be much better both for the sake of our own credit, as well as the profit derivable from the operation, to coin our own copper, and with respect to the second, that as we have now a fair prospect of being supplied with a complete coining apparatus from Madras, it will be unnecessary to seek for any aid from Bengal. In the meantime the present system may be allowed to continue, by which the mint is enabled to supply the treasury with copper pice sufficient for its ordinary wants, of rude manufacture it is true, but not more than our gold or silver coinage.

As the Honble Court's orders seem quite peremptory respecting the division of the rupee into 64 instead of 50 pice, we refrain from offering any objections to the change, but there is one circumstance that would appear to have been overlooked by them, which in our opinion is an insuperable bar to the immediate introduction here of the Bengal weight for the pice, namely that the half pice or 4 rea piece of the European coinages now in circulation is the same, or very nearly the same, weight as the Calcutta whole pice, or what would be here at the rate of 64 pice to the rupee, the 6¼ rea piece.

Provided, however, there be no more coined than is actually required for the circulation, we see no great objection to the immediate reduction to the weight of our copper coin by coining for instance, forty (40) pice to the seer when each 6¼ rea piece will weigh troy grains 122½ , nearly which at 64 per rupee will make 7840 troy grains of copper instead of 8175 as heretofore (a diminution of above 4 per cent) represent a rupee.

Thereafter when the new coinage shall have thoroughly displaced the old, we may, if it should be thought expedient, reduce the weight still further, though it would perhaps be politic to avoid attempting even the diminution above mentioned, or indeed any other change, until we have secured the aid of machinery, lest the profit, already 7 per cent to the Company, should only seem to encourage fraudulent imitations.

Copper Coinage – 1813

An indication of the amount of copper coin produced was given by the mint master in 1813[354]:

In acknowledgement of the receipt of your letter of the 28ᵗʰ ultimo, I have the honor to enclose for the information of the Right Honble the Governor in Council an account of copper received from the Warehouse Keeper with the balance required to complete the amount of copper coinage directed to be made by the orders of Government.

The quantity which remains to be received is 767 Cwt or Bombay maund 3070.

---

[354] Bombay Public Consultations. IOR P/344/62, p. 2857. Letter from the Mr Edward (Acting mint master) to government, dated 2ⁿᵈ July 1813.

	Rs worth of copper coined
January 2ⁿᵈ (1813)	12,217
January 20ᵗʰ	50,000
February 10ᵗʰ	50,000
	112,217

Copper Coinage – 1816

Pice 1816

In 1816 orders were given for a further coinage of copper coins[355]:

The balance of copper pice within the General Treasury being reduced very low, I beg to recommend a new coinage being ordered to the extent of twenty five thousand rupees.

Growing Demand for Copper Coins

In 1817 the Bombay mint committee discussed the possibility of introducing a new copper coinage into the Presidency, following a request for copper coins to be sent to the Kaira district[356]:

We have the honor to acknowledge the receipts of Mr secretary Newnhams letter dated the 31ˢᵗ December last…

…Copper coins in all countries bear a nominal value very different from their intrinsic, and it is already within the knowledge of Your Honble Board, from the report of the Treasury Committee of 13ᵗʰ March 1813, that at the Presidency, copper pice weighing only 166 grains troy, have equal currency with others weighing 200 grains, without any perceptible preference of one above the other.

Viewing therefore the present as the most favourable opportunity that has yet occurred for commencing the introduction of an uniform copper currency into the districts subordinate to this Presidency, as proposed some years ago by the Honble Court, we have held it to be our duty to consider the subject with more than usual care before we ventured to recommend any final measures to the adoption of Your Honble Board.

---

[355] Bombay Mint Procedings. IOR P/411/37 (1816), p. 17. Letter from the sub-treasurer to government, dated 8ᵗʰ March 1816.

[356] Bombay Mint Procedings. IOR P/411/37 (1817), p. 8. Letter from the mint committee to government, dated 15ᵗʰ February 1817.

They went on to discuss the number of pice that should pass for a rupee as well as the weight of the pice:

Under these impressions and with a view of giving our opinion in the most deliberate manner on the best weight, division and inscription for this new copper coinage, which is eventually to become the only copper currency under this Presidency, we have carefully reviewed and reconsidered all the documents on our records that seemed likely to throw any light on the subject. We have consulted also with the Mint Contractor, as well to ascertain the terms on which he might be willing to undertake the new coinage (which if the division is to exceed the present of 50 pice to the rupee, will be proportionately more expensive) as the ability of his native engravers to execute any new inscription.

The conclusion we have drawn from this view is that the division of 64 pices to a rupee , though not free from objections, is certainly upon the whole the best, but we still adhere to the opinion offered in the 4th paragraph of our letter of the 15th of July 1813 in regard to the weight, which we think should be fixed at 122½ grain troy each pice, 40 of the new pice will then weigh a Bombay seer, 1600 a Bombay maund or 28 lbs avoirdupois, exactly, and at 64 to a rupee 7840 troy grains of copper, instead of 8175 as heretofore, will represent a rupee.

Below this we do not think it would be safe under present circumstances, to reduce their weight and as the heavy pice of the European coinages of copper for the use of this Presidency, have now almost disappeared from circulation, and the contractor is willing to undertake the new coinage at the moderate advance of (Rupee ,,– 3 – 50) three quarters of a rupee and fifty reas per maund on his present charges (at which rates and the current prices of copper, the gain to the mint will still be 8 per cent) we accordingly take the liberty of recommending that the new copper coinage for Kaira, as well as for all future coinages of copper either for the Presidency or subordinates, should be executed on the principles laid down in the preceding paragraph.

Having discussed the weight and division of the coins, they went on to consider the design. They agreed with the Court of Directors that the inscription should be in English and Persian. This should accompany a simple design such as that on the then current coins:

With regard to the inscription which we have also attentively considered though we fully appreciate the value of the opinion given by the assistant in charge of the Kaira Collectorship, in the 8th paragraph of his letter that it should be in English and Guzeratee, yet, as the Honble Court have in the 11th paragraph of their orders of the 18th of December 1812, distinctly preferred on general grounds, the Persian to all other native languages, we do not feel at liberty to recommend any deviation in that particular, from their instructions.

The English and Persian should therefore be the only languages employed, but as there seems no prospect under existing circumstances, of the Courts object of rendering the pice coined here universally current at the same value throughout the whole of their possessions, being fully accomplished, and as the native engraver is not qualified to execute in any good style the inscription suggested by the Court, we are inclined to think the more simple mark,

145

as it is commonly called, of the Company on one side and the seals on the reverse as at present, with the addition of the date and denomination in English and Persian would be better adapted to our means and circumstances…

They considered the introduction of machinery into the mint to be a prerequisite to the successful introduction of a lower weight coin. They went on to examine the cost and it seems to have been the conclusions drawn from this discussion that led to the machinery built by Dr Stewart (see chapter 6):

..It is the machinery employed in the mint that enables the Government of Bengal to disregard the weight of their pice, secure in the superiority of their workmanship from all danger of counterfeits it is absolutely of no consequence what the intrinsic value of their pice may be. Copper coins in this respect resemble very much the notes or tokens of a bank, which have often little or no intrinsic value in themselves, and owe their currency entirely to their convertibility into whatever may be the legal currency of the realm…

…The first cost of erection [of machinery] *seems then to be the only obstacle to the accomplishment of so very desirable an object, and we cannot resist therefore the present opportunity of remarking that very nearly the whole expense might be defrayed by the mere introduction by its* [means] *of the Bengal weight of copper coin into the districts subordinate to this Presidency.*

Estimating the amount that would in the first instance be required at each of the four stations of the Presidency, Surat, Broach and Kaira (see map on next page), at the moderate allowance of half a Lack of rupees worth, the total amount of copper pice immediately necessary would be two Lacks of rupees worth. These the mint (the establishment of which would under the new system be a fixed monthly charge) might easily be employed, during intervals of leisure in coining, without adding at all to its expense and being issued at double their intrinsic value, which is about the proportion in the Bengal pice, would only cost one Lack, and thus a measure pointed out by the Honble Court as a most beneficial one, might be carried into effect, not only without any additional expense, but with a positive gain to the mint of at least a Lack of rupees…

…We may add that we are unwilling to be left behind our neighbours in the race of improvement. Bengal and Madras have long had machinery in their mints, but we have even had the opportunity lately of seeing coins struck in Persia by an apparatus erected there by Mr Armstrong, in a style of execution that would not disgrace any mint in Europe. This is a theme on which it would be very easy to enlarge but we believe and hope that we have said enough and, trusting that the importance of the subject on which we have been treating will plead our excuse for the length to which this report has extended.

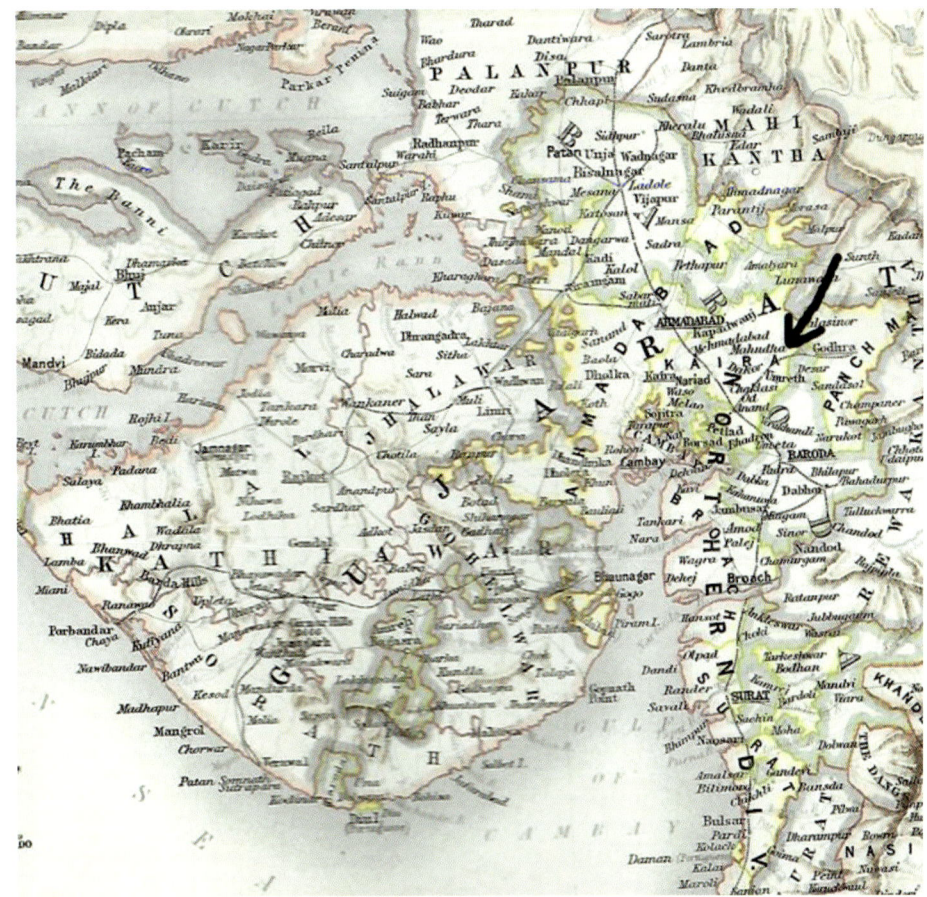

Location of Kaira

Request to Calcutta for Copper Coins – 1817

Bombay Government decided that since no machinery was available they should ask Calcutta to provide the copper coins:

The Honble the Court of Directors not having authorized the construction of a new mint at Bombay on the plan submitted to them in the 166 & 173 paragraphs of the letter from this Government dated the 14th October 1813, and the want of a machinery for conducting the coinage in an improved form precluding us from authorizing the coinage of the copper currency required for the district of Kaira and from adopting generally the suggestions of the Mint Committee, resolved that the expediency of copper pice to the extent of fifty thousand rupees being coined at Calcutta and consigned to Bombay by the first opportunity that may offer, be submitted to the consideration of the Supreme Government.

However, Bengal were unable to supply the copper coins[357]:

---

[357] Bombay Mint Procedings. IOR P/411/37 (1817), p. 33. Letter from Bengal (Governor General) to Bombay government, dated 25th April 1817.

…The Governor General in Council desires me at the same time to remark that independent of the above circumstances which thus renders it necessary to postpone a compliance with the wishes of the Bombay Government, some inconvenience would result from the proposed coinage being undertaken at the mint of this Presidency at the present moment when the officers of that establishment are engaged with a considerable coinage in silver…

The Governor General at Calcutta criticised the Governor of Bombay for not having installed machinery:

Honble the Governor General in Council cannot help regretting that the Right Honble the Governor in Council should have felt himself constrained to postpone for so long a period the adoption of a measure which appeared calculated to be of so much public benefit as the establishment of an efficient mint at Bombay and which instead of being a source of expense appears likely in every view to produce ultimately a considerable increase of revenue…

However, the Governor of Bombay pointed out that the Court of Directors had instructed him not to incur costs in building a new mint at Bombay because they would be able to provide a cheaper mint from England.

…In the 159th paragraph the Court state that "we approve of your determination in declining to incur any expense respecting mint apparatus or buildings till furnished with our deliberate opinion on the subject, as we are satisfied the necessary apparatus could be supplied in a cheaper and better manner in London than in India…"

So the problem remained unresolved and slowly got worse.

Copper Coins Sent to Malwan

Not only were copper coins required for the region of Kaira but the introduction of the Bombay copper coins into Malwan was recommended in 1817 meaning there was even greater pressure to make more in the Bombay mint[358]:

…Under these circumstances we have no hesitation in recommending the Bombay pice to be, as soon as possible, substituted for the country pice, as proposed by the Resident. Mr Hale, in requesting a supply, does not name any particular amount, but we do not think that ten thousand rupees worth can be too much for the whole district.

The Accountant General has therefore in consequence of the [Emaad] being under orders to sail so immediately, taken the liberty, in concert with the sub-treasurer, to substitute copper pice, of which there is an abundant supply in the General Treasury, for silver rupees to that extent in the consignment of thirty thousand rupees lately ordered for Malwan, and which was to go down in that vessel, which it is hoped will not meet with the approbation of the Right Honble the Governor in Council…

---

[358] Bombay Mint Procedings. IOR P/411/37 (1817), p. 119. Letter from the mint committee (Best, sub treasurer, Wedderburn, accountant general, Steurt, mint master, Noton, assay master) to government, dated 6th October 1817.

Location of Malwan

The shortage of copper coins got even worse with demand for more copper coins in 1818 and this prompted the Bombay authorities to consider introducing a new copper coinage (see also chapter 6)[359]:

I am directed by the Right Honble the Governor in Council to transmit to you copy of a letter from the Collector of the Eastern Zillah north of the Myhee, regarding the copper currency of that division and copies of a further letter from the Judge and Magistrate at Surat repeating the application for a supply of copper currency for that city.

The Ann having arrived from England since my letter to you of the 21st ultimo and not having brought out any instructions from the Honble Court regarding the mint, some measures must be immediately adopted for supplying the copper currency so much required in the various districts subordinate to this Government.

The great extent of the demand affords an eligible opportunity for introducing an improved coinage and the Governor in Council is disposed therefore immediately [to] adopt the division

---

[359] Bombay Consultations. IOR P/411/38, p. 141. Letter from Bombay government to the Bombay mint committee, dated 20th June 1818.

recommended in the 7th para of your letter of the 15th February 1817 on being informed of the present ability of the mint establishment to comply with the demand.

You are therefore requested to consider the subject and report what means can be adopted for providing an improved copper currency with the greatest promptness and whether the machinery alluded to in the 3rd para of your letter of the 3rd instant can be procured in Bombay.

More copper was received in 1819 and stored in the warehouse[360]:

The Commander of the Susan having reported that he has a quantity of copper on board consigned to this Presidency for the use of the mint, resolved that the Warehousekeeper be directed to land the same as soon as the Commander may report himself ready to discharge it, and to keep it in store until required by the Mint Master.

The Warehousekeeper is to report the quantity thus received.

However, not all the copper in the warehouse was used by the mint and some was sold for profit[361]:

…Ordered that Mr Goodwin be informed that as the whole of the copper received by the Susan cannot be wanted for the mint before a further supply arrives from Calcutta, any part required by the Public Departments should be issued to them accordingly, but it is not to be sold to individuals.

Ordered that the Mint Master be advised of the arrival of this supply of copper and of the disposal of a part.

and thick copper sheets were also needed for other purposes[362]:

I beg to report for the information of Government that I have not the means of complying with an indent which I have just received from the Commissary General for thick sheet copper for the use of the Marine Department. If Government should be pleased to sanction a transfer from the consignment on account of the mint, to the extent of the exigencies of the public service, It will, I hope, be in my power to replace it on the arrival of the [Ernaad]. I do not imagine a purchase could be now effected in the bazar unless on very unreasonable terms.

Ordered Mr Goodwin be referred to the reply returned to his letter of the 6th instant.

---

[360] Bombay Consultations. P/411/39, p. 76. Minutes, dated 7th July 1819.

[361] Bombay Consultations. P/411/39, p. 76. Letter from the Warehousekeeper to government, dated 6th July 1819.

[362] Bombay Consultations. P/411/39, p. 78. Letter from the Warehousekeeper (Mr Goodwin) to government, dated 8th July 1819.

Chapter 5 – Bombay Mint 1800 to c1830 – Mint Operations

Summary

This chapter deals with the people in the mint and the method of operating between 1800 and the introduction of machinery early in the 1830s. The mint buildings themselves are also discussed.

Mint Output – 1800 to mid-1820s

There does not seem to have been any very consistent way in which the mint output was reported. Various records have been discovered reporting the value of coins produced and these give some indication of the mint activities but no complete record for the entire period has been put together.

In June 1802, the mint master reported the mint output for the year as being 484,303 rupees and 2,354 mohurs[363]:

… I beg leave to submit to you for the notice of the Honble the Governor in Council an account of coinage in the mint at this Presidency during the last year…

From this statement it will appear that the coinage of silver during that period amounted to Rupees 484,303 . 2 . 25 and of gold to Mohurs 156,942 Rupees or 2,354 . 1 . 23 and that on the entire amount a duty of 3 per cent has been collected, out of which ½ per cent on silver and ¾ per cent on gold have been realized on account of the Honble Company, whilst the residuary 2/4 per cent on silver and 1/4 per cent on gold have been appropriated by the native overseer in payment of wages to himself and to those employed by him as authorized by the orders of Government of 2nd May 1801…

In 1805, in reply to various criticisms from a Mr Henshaw, the mint and assay masters discussed the output of the mint over the previous thirty or more years. They stated that the mint output from 1800 to 1804 had been over five million rupees worth, whilst the preceding twenty years had only produced about half that amount[364]:

…Considering therefore the first of these queries we beg leave to refer to a report, copy of which is annexed, which was furnished to Mr Henshaw under the 24th October last, and which shews that the total of gold coinage in the mint of Bombay amounted from the year of account 1770/1 to 30th September 1804 to Rupees 7,659,122, of which the coinage since November 1800 when the present mint regulations were introduced, or in four years is 5,017,382 and shewing the amount coined in the previous 20 years as rupees 2,641,740.

With the evidence of this statement it may be deemed unnecessary for us to follow Mr Henshaw thro' the causes he has assigned for the <u>deficiency of circulating medium</u> from which he apprehends such incalculably ill effects. It is perhaps enough for us to prove that the

---

[363] Bombay Public Consultations. IOR P/342/54, p. 1471. Letter from PA Grant, mint master at Bombay to Bombay Board dated 24th June 1802.

[364] Bombay Public Consultations. IOR P/343/22, p. 2186. Letter from William Crawford (mint master) and Helenus Scott (assay Master) to government, dated 19th April 1805.

position he has assumed is fundamentally erroneous, and we here shew that the mint regulations of 1800, instead of occasioning a decrease in circulating medium, has produced a very considerable addition.

In 1810, the mint master published a table showing the total output of the mint since 1800. This showed the value in rupees of both gold and silver coined[365]:

Statement exhibiting the annual operations of the mint for the last 30 years, Viz from 1780/1 to 1809/10 [only 180-1810 shown here]

Date	Rupees	Annas	Reas
1800/1	1,586,340	1	42
1801/2	1,255,586	2	50
1802/3	555,084	0	16
1803/4	736,527	0	66
1804/5	1,666,942	3	71
1805/6	632,549	0	67
1806/7	3,721,642	3	28
1807/8	874,870	3	49
1808/9	984.029	3	40
1809/10	795,206	3	10

In 1811 another table was issued by the new mint master, this time showing the breakdown into gold, silver and copper[366]:

From 1st Jan to 31st Dec each year	Gold Mohurs (in rupees)	Gold rupees	Silver (in rupees)	Copper (in rupees)
1801	2,170,458	121,265	100,217	
1802	91,048	121,599		
1803	472,953	252,588	4753	104,201
1804	2,083,385			
1805	265,509			
1806	717,065		665,141	
1807	798,439		265,373	
1808	132,844		515,332	
1809	220,452		36,401	6795
1810	1,554,891		67,709	61151

A report dated 15th September 1819[367] stated that during the years 1809-1819 the

---

[365] Bombay Public Consultations. IOR P/344/36, p. 430. Letter from the mint master (GC Osborne) to government, dated 31st December 1810.

[366] Bombay Public Consultations. IOR P/344/43, p. 4618. Letter from the acting mint master (J Wedderburn) to government, dated 27th July 1811.

[367] Report of 15th September 1819 giving number copper coins issued. Taken from Pridmore.

copper coinage by the mint contractor amounted to 277,357 rupees value, producing a total number of pieces in pice, halves and quarters of 17,179,650. The coins continued to be issued until 1829.

Other entries in the records show mintage figures for various years throughout this period and have been compiled into the following table:

Date	Gold (Rs value)		Silver (Rs value)		Copper (Rs value)
	For the EIC	For Individuals	For the EIC	For Individuals	
1814[368]	19,050	1,931,425	10,417	10,220	
1815[369]	280,121	669,774	165,455	10,035	9,486
1818[370]	734,684	72,897	188,847	156,278	
1819[371]	900,772	2119	693,651	1,692,805	57,603
1820[372]	1953	72,991	17,337	482,579	
1822[373]	365	0	7426	16905	

(All numbers rounded to nearest whole number)

Mint Master

In 1815, regulations for the operation of the mint were discussed. Up until that time the jobs of the mint and assay masters had not been clearly specified. The Bombay mint committee stated that they had considered the information received from the Madras and Calcutta mints about the regulations for operating the mints there, and had produced draft regulations for the conduct of the Bombay mint[374]. This draft was modified by the Bombay Government and issued a little later[375]. The role of the mint master was:

…The mint master shall have the general superintendence and control of every department of the mint,

The mint master shall establish such checks to prevent gold or silver bullion being coined

---

[368] Bombay Mint Proceedings. IOR P/411/37 (1816), p. 5. Letter from the mint master (R. Stewart) to government, dated 27th January 1816 (actually says 1815).

[369] Bombay Mint Proceedings. IOR P/411/37 (1816), p. 5. Letter from the mint master (R. Stewart) to government, dated 27th January 1816 (actually says 1815).

[370] Bombay Consultations. IOR P/411/39 7th, p. 38. Letter from the mint master (R. Stewart) dated 18th May 1819.

[371] Bombay Consultations. P/411/40 (1820), p. 4. Letter from the mint master (Henderson) to government, dated 19th January 1820.

[372] Bombay Consultations. P/411/40 (1820), p. 4. Letter from the mint master (Henderson) to government, dated sometime after 31st December 1820.

[373] Bombay Consultations. IOR P/411/41, 1823, p. 2. Letter from the Acting mint master (J Bourchier) to government dated 4th January 1823.

[374] Bombay Mint Procedings. IOR P/411/36, p. 113. Letter from the Bombay Mint Committee to government, dated 7th September 1815.

[375] Bombay Mint Procedings. IOR P/411/36, p. 128. Revised Regulations by Bombay Council.

in or out of the mint without his knowledge, or other frauds, as he may deem expedient.

The mint master is to keep a register specifying the quantity of bullion delivered into the mint for coinage, the date under which it was received and the name of the proprietors.

The gold mohur or silver rupee of the Surat or Mogul impression, now current, being of the following weights and standard shall continue to be the established coins and none others shall be coined without the special orders of Government, and the gold mohurs third, commonly called the panchia, and the single gold rupee, and the halves and quarters of the single rupee shall continue to be coined of the same standard and of proportionate weights.

Gold mohur or Silver rupee

Troy weight	179 grains
Pure gold or silver	164 grains 64 pennyweight
Alloy	14 grains 32 pennyweight

Touch or parts of pure gold or silver in 100	92
Alloy	8

If the gold coins shall turn out to vary no more in weight and touch taken together than ⅓ per cent, or the silver coins no more than ½ per cent (the remedy or allowance for error within the King's mint being above ⅔ per cent for the former and above ⅘ per cent for the latter) over or under the standard fixed, they shall be deemed good, but if they shall vary more in gold or silver than the limits above prescribed, the coins shall be re-melted and alligated to the proper standard at the sole charge and expense of the contractor.

The mint master shall keep regular accounts of all the bullion coined and take care that the proper return of standard coins is made to the bullion owner by the contractor after deducting the established duties.

A duty of 2½ per cent shall be levied on the gross out turn of all gold bullion and 3 per cent on the gross out turn of all silver bullion coined exclusive of any charges that may hereafter be established for refinage.

After deducting from the amount of the duties collected the allowances due to the contractor, agreeably to the terms of his contract, the balance shall be paid by the mint master into the general treasury.

Name	Start Date
Mr Grant	1802
Mr Le mesurier[376]:	1802
Mr Crawford	
Charles Watkins[377]	1805

Mint masters of the Bombay mint

---

[376] Bombay Public Consultations. IOR P/342/56, p. 2693. Letter from Mr Grant and Mr Le Messurier to Bombay Council, dated 9th September 1802.

[377] Bombay Public Consultations. IOR P/343/22, p. 2604. Letter from Charles Watkins (mint master) to government, dated 10th May 1805.

G C Osborne[378]	1809
J Wedderborn[379]	1811
H Munro[380]	1812
Mr Edward[381]	1813
Mr Coward[382]	1813
Dr Stewart[383]	1815/16 Date not certain
J Henderson[384]	1819

Mint masters of the Bombay mint

Assay Master and Mint Committee

The roles of the assay master and mint committee were also defined at the same time as that of the mint master[385]:

When the coins are stamped, the produce of the different meltings must be kept as much as possible apart from each other, under the custody of the mint master and notice be given to the assay master whose duty it will be to take promiscuously two or more pieces from every thousand to weigh and assay the specimens of each melting separately and to enter the result in a register.

If on examination the coins so weighed prove of the proper weight and standard or within the remedy allowed, the assay master shall give a pass note for the whole number stamped, but before they are issued the mint master shall give notice of the circumstance to the mint committee who shall attend at the mint and collect therefrom such number of coins as they think proper, or pix specimens, of which they are to forward a portion half yearly to Government for transmission to Bengal and England, the specimens to be deposited in the interim in the treasury under the keys of the committee.

If on the contrary the coins in question prove to be beyond the remedy or allowance for error prescribed in the 4th clause, the assay master shall report the same to the mint master in order that the whole of the coins from which the assay specimens were taken may be melted

---

[378] Bombay Public Consultations. IOR P/344/13, p. 3852. Letter from the mint master (GC Osborne) to government, dated 3rd July 1809.

[379] Bombay Public Consultations. IOR P/344/39, p. 2413. Letter from the acting mint master (J Wedderburn) to government, dated 16th April 1811.

[380] Bombay Public Consultations. IOR P/344/51, p. 2248. Letter from the mint master (H Munro) to government, dated 13th July 1812.

[381] Bombay Public Consultations. IOR P/344/62, p. 2519. Letter from the Mr Edward (Acting mint master) to government, dated 8th June 1813.

[382] Bombay Public Consultations. IOR P/344/63, p. 3368. Letter from the Mr Coward (Acting mint master), Mr Kaye (accountant general), Mr Wedderburn (sub-treasurer), Mr Noton (assay master) to government, dated 8th June 1813.

[383] Bombay Mint Proceedings. IOR P/411/37, (1816). p. 5. Letter from the mint master (R. Stewart) to government, dated 27th January 1816 (actually says 1815).

[384] Bombay Consultations. IOR P/411/39 7th, p. 38. Letter from the mint master (J Henderson) dated 22th May 1819.

[385] Bombay Mint Procedings. IOR P/411/36, p. 128. Revised Regulations by Bombay Council.

down and re-coined of the proper standard at the expense of the contractor as already provided for, and if he should see reason to suspect that unfair advantage was attempted to be taken of the remedy or allowance for errors, he is to apprize the mint master thereof in order that he may give a suitable caution to the contractor.

The assay master shall also from time to time, at his discretion, but four times a month at least when there is any coinage going on, take coins from the hands of the workmen and assay them and report the result to the mint master.

The assay master shall assay all bullion and coins belonging to the Honble Company that may be delivered over to the mint for coinage, and report the result to the mint master for the information of the contractor, who must receive the same by his report.

The assay master shall likewise assay the bullion or coins of individuals when called upon so to do, in consequence of any disagreement between them and the contractor respecting the standard, provided the party or parties consent to have the same melted into government ingots for that purpose.

The assay master shall assay and report to the mint master the standard of all bullion sent from the mint for refinage and repeat the process when it is returned to the mint in a refined state.

The mint committee shall proceed to the mint at least once in each month and oftener if an extensive coinage be going on, without giving any previous notice of their intention, & take indiscriminately from the hands of the workmen such number of coins as they think proper, and deliver them to the assay master who shall forthwith examine them and report the result to the committee.

Name	Start Date
Helenius Scott	Before 1800
Dr Stewart[386]	1809
Mr Noton[387]	1812

Assay masters at the Bombay mint

The assay masters often seem to have been concerned about their pay and their staff. For instance in 1810 Dr Stewart, when he was assay master, wrote to the Bombay council complaining[388]:

…That to the office of assay master, the Honble the Governor General in Council has never to my knowledge offered any establishment of servants, assistants or any allowance for necessary attendance on it and that, of consequence, I cannot afford any detailed account of expenses that have been entirely defrayed by myself without having kept any memoranda.

---

[386] Bombay Public Consultations. IOR P/344/11, p. 3128. Resolution dated 16th May 1809.

[387] Bombay Public Consultations. IOR P/344/55, p. 4061. Letter from the Mr Noton to government, dated 23rd October 1812.

[388] Bombay Public Consultations. IOR P/344/36, p. 97. Letter from the assay master (R Stewart) to government, dated 29th December 1810.

That I conceive no gentleman of education or principle would have applied for any such allowances under the liberal salary of Rupees 1000 per month, which the Honble the Governor in Council had awarded to that office under my immediate predecessor, a person whom no one can name without the feeling of respect, due to honor and integrity and which, after minute investigation, was sanctioned with the full approbation of the Honble Court of Directors in as much as that after the Honble Court has by their own authority reduced the salary of Rupees 1000 per month first granted by the Honble the Governor in Council, to Rupees 500, they, upon the representations of that gentleman, sanctioned by the approbation of the Honble the Governor in Council, not only restored the original salary, but also the difference between it and the reduced salary during the intermediate period.

That the salary of Rupees 1000 per month annexed to the office of the assay master was on 1st January 1809, while I had acted without pay for Mr Scott, from the month of May 1808 till March 1809 reduced to rupees 500 per month.

That I have from motives of necessity caused by a greatly impaired state of health and for the support of my family after a period of 22 years service, continued to hold a situation of great honor, of great importance and of great responsibility, and at the present time of great labour, without an adequate salary.

I have taken the opportunity which Mr Secretary Farish's letter seems to afford me, of stating these few facts for the information of the Honble the Governor in Council and also for that of the Honble the Court of Directors in preference to sending to the latter a formal memorial, trusting that this letter will be forwarded to them, as such, by the Honble the Governor in Council, on the Exeter, but if not that I may have due notice to enable me to comply with the orders of Government as advertised in the Bombay Courier of the 22nd instant.

…Resolved that the preceding address be sent home…

Whether or not Dr Stewart received any money as a result of this is not known but he was promoted to mint master later on (see next chapter). In 1812, Mr Noton, the next assay master, also wrote to the Bombay Government[389]:

Understanding that the allowances which are made to such of the Honble Company's civil servants as are out of employ are invariably paid to them at the exchange of 2/3 (two and three pence) per rupee, and that the adjustments of the commercial transactions of this Government and the Court of Directors, as well as of the short delivery accounts of the vessels employed in their service, are all regulated by the same exchange, I take the liberty of requesting you to submit to the Right Honble the Governor in Council my respectful application to be allowed to have my salary converted into Bombay currency at that rate…

This was granted.

---

[389] Bombay Public Consultations. IOR P/344/56, p. 4748. Letter from the Mr Noton to government, dated 18th December 1812.

In 1813, Mr Noton discovered that Mr Ryder, the assay master at Madras, received an allowance for rent and asked that he should be granted the same amount[390]:

Having lately received a letter from Mr Ryder, Assay Master at Madras, in which he informs me he receives (35) [five] and thirty pagodas a month for house rent and having received my appointment to this Presidency from the Honble Court of Directors under exactly the same circumstances as Mr Ryder did, I beg leave to enclose you his letter requesting you to submit that statement to the Right Honble the Governor in Council with my respectful application for a similar indulgence for house rent.

This time his request was denied:

Ordered that Mr Noton be informed that as the Honble the Court of Directors have already fixed his allowance as stated in his indentures, we cannot increase them, unless some further explanation of their intentions be communicated when the regular notification of his appointment shall reach this Presidency.

Special Apparatus Required for Assays

Not all apparatus was available locally, particularly that needed for the assay office[391]:

We beg that you will be pleased to order from England for the use of the mint, one set of assay scales & weights and one ditto for silver.

The mint contractor having made several applications to us to procure for him a quantity of crucibles for the melting of gold in consequence of the very great loss to be constantly felt from the badness of such as are to be procured here. We are induced to solicit that you will likewise be good enough to order a supply of 10,000 crucibles from England by the first ships, each crucible should be capable of melting 60 tolas of metal or 109,40 grains. For the expense of them he agrees to reimburse the Honble Company.

The apparatus requested from England arrived in January 1808[392]:

In consequence of the representation which I formerly made to Government, we received from England by the ships of this season a set of assay scales and weights and also a beam with scales and weights for weighing silver in large quantities.

All those articles are of an excellent kind and have already enabled me to adjust some doubtful and disputed points in the most satisfactory manner.

I have on former occasions represented that the people of this country have not the means of determining the weight of anything to a great degree of accuracy. The beams which the merchants use for gold and silver are still more inaccurate. Several kinds of tola differing from

---

[390] Bombay Public Consultations. IOR P/344/58, p. 385. Letter from the Mr Noton (assay master) to government, dated 23rd January 1813.

[391] Bombay Public Consultations. IOR P/343/1, p. 4223. Letter from Le Messurier & Scott to Bombay Board, dated 15th December 1802.

[392] Bombay Public Consultations. IOR P/343/54, p. 785. Letter from the assay master (H Scott) to government, dated 25th January 1808.

each other by some grains are in use in Bombay and the [waal] the weight next below it is altogether without precision…

In December 1811 more articles were requested from London but not before remarking on the inadequacy of the crucibles previously sent[393]:

…It may be precautionary and not irrelevant to the present subject to notice that several chests of crucibles sent out by the Honble Court about six or seven years ago, for the use of this mint, remain still on hand, having proved on trial of so very inferior a quality, as to be altogether unserviceable…

The articles requested were:

…2 sets of assay scales with [touch] weights for both gold and silver. Carat, grain and quarter weights for gold and assay pound, ounce, pennyweights and grains for silver. The unit or assay pound for gold to weigh 12 grains troy and that for silver eighteen grains ditto.

2 sets of small scales capable of weighing one pound troy with grain weights from five thousand (5000) grains downwards to tenths of a grain

2 sets of scales for gold capable of weighing from ten (10) to fifteen (15) pounds troy with proportionate weights.

2 ditto for silver capable of weighing a hundred (100) pounds troy with proportionate weights from 100 pounds downwards.

One thousand (1000) nests of black lead crucibles…

Even when the apparatus did arrive it was liable to get damaged in unusual ways. In 1813 the assay master reported that white ants had eaten part of the balance in his office and asked for it to be repaired[394]:

I request you will do me the favour to state to the Right Honble the Governor in Council that in consequence of the white ant having got into the assay balance in my office, it is requisite to be repaired, and to request an order may be forwarded to the Civil Engineer's Department for effecting the same…

People Employed in the Mint – 1805

In 1805, the mint master reported on the number and cost of people directly employed by the Company in the mint[395]:

Purvoes [i.e.writers] *2 Viz:*
1 Purshohim Mungajee   25-1-33
1 Dadajee Sumkerseljee   8

---

[393] Bombay Public Consultations. IOR P/344/46, p. 6224. Letter from the acting mint master (J Wedderburn) to government, dated 3rd December 1811.

[394] Bombay Public Consultations. IOR P/344/64, p. 3759. Letter from the Mr Noton (assay master) to government, dated 2nd September 1813.

[395] Bombay Public Consultations. IOR P/343/23, p. 2950. Letter from Charles Watkins (mint master) and H Scott to government, dated 30th May 1805.

Assayman:
1 Arzam Ragojee	4	
Sepoys 4 Viz:		
1 Dhurma Gunpatill	4	
2 Nanna Appajee	4	
3 Mados Shullia	4	
4 Shikh Ahmud	4	

53-1-33

Sometimes bureaucracy got in the way. In 1806 the mint seems to have been working later than usual and the sepoy guard would not allow bullion to enter the mint after a certain time[396]:

The officer on guard at the castle gate having evinced a disinclination lately to let the bullion pass thru' from the mint [past the ... hour], I am to request an order be issued that the bullion may be allowed [past] without impediment at any hour within [the] evening as the work people at the present [time of] unusual exertion will very often be kept [until a] late hour.

Mint Contractors – 1801

By April 1801 the mint contractor had been persuaded to accept changes to the terms of his contract[397]:

In pursuance of your Honble Boards commands of the 27th January last we have, after much hesitation and delay got the present mint contractor, Narondass Toolsidass to agree to carry on the business of the coinage and to pay all its expenses (except such servants as have been usually kept up by the company) and at the following rates:

For gold he is to receive for every 100 mohurs that he coins, one and one quarter, but out of this he is to furnish the silver alloy.

For silver he is to receive for every 100 rupees that he coins two and one half rupees

For the due performance of his duties he agrees to enter into a penalty bond with proper securities for a lac of rupees. This bond should specify that he is responsible for issuing no base coin; for keeping it as near as possible to its standard; and for returning to the mint master the whole of the gold or silver that he receives from him.

This is the best agreement we can at present make with Toolsidass; nor do we think considering the importance of his situation that his profits can be much too great...

In December the mint and assay masters reported on the contract with Narondass Tulsidass[398]:

---

[396] Bombay Public Consultations. IOR P/343/31, p. 1682. Letter from Charles Watkins (mint master) to government, dated 18th April 1806.

[397] Bombay Public Consultations. IOR P/342/47, p. 1009. Letter from the mint and assay masters, April 1801.

[398] Bombay Public Consultations. IOR P/342/50, p. 3699. Letter from the mint master (J.A. Grant) and the assay master (A. Scott) to government, dated 16th December 1801.

In our letter of the 28ᵗʰ April last, we had the honor to report to you that Narondass Tulsidass, the principal native overseer in the mint, was ready to enter into a penalty bond, with proper securities to the amount of a lac of rupees, for the due performance of his duties, but having afterwards found it impracticable from the largeness of the sum to fulfil that engagement the deed still remains to be executed. It has, however, been lately intimated to us that Mr Henry Fawcett is willing to become surety for Narondass Tulsidass in the sum of rupees fifty thousand, an offer which we beg leave to recommend the acceptance, being satisfied that the amount is sufficiently considerable to answer every necessary purpose.

The bond should specify that the native overseer is responsible for issuing no base coin; for keeping it as nearly as possible to its standard; re-coining of a proper standard at his own expense all that shall be discovered to be exceptional; & for returning to the mint master the whole of the gold and silver that may be delivered to him

Mint Contractor – 1807

In 1807, the mint contractor died and his grandson asked to take over the contract[399]:

I am concerned to announce to you that Tappidass Nunsidass, the person who used to conduct the business of the mint, died yesterday evening after a short illness. Nurbaram Bhowanydass, the grandson of Narrondass Tulsidass, and the representative of that house which has heretofore managed the coinage, is here present. I am to request to be honored with your decisions in consequence of the death of Tappidass.

This was passed to the mint master who discussed the suitability of the late contractor's grandson. This extract reveals the complicated manner in which the mint contract seems to have been drawn up in the name of a particular individual even though the contractor actually seems to have been another family member[400]:

…in reply beg leave to acquaint you that Nurbaram Bhowanydass, the grandson and representative of Narrondass Tulsidass acquaints me that his age is about 32 years, his place of residence within the fort in the principle street of the bazar, opposite the shop of Gopalldass Manordass. Permit me also to inform you that the existing contract entered into with Government, Nurbaram Bhowanydass and not the late Tappidass Nunsidass, signed, in the name of Narrondass Tulsidass, which has been made use of in every engagement of the kind since the first contract in 1793 (which the late Tappidass Nunsidass signed in like manner). The securities are the house of Messrs Bruce, Fawcett & Co.. The contract paper I am to observe, is not in my office.

---

[399] Bombay Public Consultations. IOR P/343/46, p. 3861. Letter from the mint master to government, dated 30ᵗʰ May 1807.

[400] Bombay Public Consultations. IOR P/343/46, p. 4094. Letter from the mint master (Watkins) to government, dated 8ᵗʰ June 1807.

In 1807 the mint contractor was obliged to find some other security to replace Messrs Bruce, Fawcett & Co[401]:

In compliance with the instructions conveyed to me in Mr Secretary Warden's letter of the 22nd instant I intimated to the mint contractor, Nurbaram, the necessity of his providing other security in lieu of the firm of Bruce, Fawcett & Co.

I have the honor to report in consequence that Nurbaram is prepared as security to deposit in the treasury, Government obligations to the amount of fifty thousand rupees, which he trusts will be approved by the Honble Board.

At the same time there were discussions about the amount of security provided by the mint contractor[402]:

Agreeably to the directions conveyed in Mr Secretary Warden's letter of the 29th ultimo, I called upon the mint contractor to provide security to the amount of one lac of rupees.

The house of Ransondass Tulsidass are ready to deposit fifty thousand rupees as a security, which is the amount heretofore required but they assure me that it is not in their power without materially [affecting] their [...] to appropriate a larger sum.

They may get some of the wealthy natives to be security for them to the amount required by Government but I think it my duty to call the notice of the Honble the Governor in Council to the ill effects that were formerly found to arise from permitting a security of this kind to be established. It appears to be a custom among the natives to consider the person standing for them as security, as a kind of partner, entitled to a certain share of the profits on that account. On settling the security some years ago, for the mint, all security by natives were rejected, for at the time it was discovered that several of the monied men who had engaged in this way for the mint contractor had forced him to give them a part of what he gained, a practice which led, and which evidently has a tendency to lead, to improper gain and fraud. From the above considerations, I respectfully submit to Government whether it may not be better to relinquish the additional security required, provided the mint contractor finds it impossible to get one of the European houses to assist him. This he will attempt to accomplish if indulged with a little longer time.

Mint Contractor – 1810

In 1810 the mint contractor was found to be too lazy to get the work done at a reasonable pace[403]:

I have the honor to hand up an indent from Messrs Forbes & Co for the coinage of a quantity of bullion equal to four lacs of rupees.

---

[401] Bombay Public Consultations. IOR P/343/49, p. 7748. Letter from the mint master (Charles Watkins) to government, dated 26th September 1807.

[402] Bombay Public Consultations. IOR P/343/50, p. 7956. Letter from the mint master (Charles Watkins) to government, dated 8th October 1807.

[403] Bombay Public Consultations. IOR P/344/22, p. 566. Letter from the mint master (GC Osborne) to government, dated 29th January 1810.

I can advance from the treasury without inconvenience, one lac of rupees on account of this bullion which will satisfy the above firm until the mint is placed in such a state of efficiency as to coin at the rate of 20,000 rupees a day.

The Honble the President is aware that I have been using every exertion to attain this desirable end, which is however, no easy matter owing to the inactivity of the present mint contractor who is decidedly adverse to any alteration in his dilatory habits. I have hitherto trusted by perseverance to overcome his obstinacy and to induce him to carry on his work with more energy but, having completely failed, I see no other recourse than to retain a new contractor who should be a man of enterprize, intelligence and personal activity, qualities in which the present contractor is notoriously deficient…

The threat of replacement goaded the mint contractor into action[404]:

…I request you will state to the Honble the Governor in Council that I have at last induced such improvement in the conduct of the present contractor as to render any change unnecessary for the present.

In respectfully submitting this opinion to the notice of the Honble the Governor in Council I beg leave to state that the mint now coins at the rate of 17,000 silver rupees and 10,000 pice per diem which is double the produce that it has yielded in past years, when the mint coined at the rate of 8,000 and very seldom of 10,000 rupees per diem.

The actual amelioration has been introduced gradually and not without continual battling with the contractor. My utmost vigilance shall be exerted to keep the mint in its present state of efficiency. It yielded last month a clear surplus revenue of Rs 4000 after defraying all expenses (including the salaries of the mint and assay masters) and, if the coinage had been gold instead of silver, the net revenue for last month would have been 8,000 rupees…

Mint Contractor – 1811

In January 1811, the mint master agreed to present a shawl to the mint contractor in recognition of the work he had done. He also suggested that the manager of the mint should receive the same recognition[405]:

I shall present to the mint contractor in the name of Government the shawl which the Honble the Governor General in Council has been so gracious as to authorize me to give him in testimony of the Honble Board's satisfaction at the activity displayed in the late operations of the mint.

I beg leave on this occasion to state that the manager of the mint, named Cooshall, is entitled to great credit in removing all difficulties which a person less zealously disposed to meet the wishes of Government might have reasonably raised to the recent rapid coinage.

---

[404] Bombay Public Consultations. IOR P/344/23, p. 1287. Letter from the mint master (GC Osborne) to government, dated 5th March 1810.

[405] Bombay Public Consultations. IOR P/344/36, p. 134. Letter from the mint master (GC Osborne) to government, dated 9th January 1811.

I respectfully request therefore that I may be allowed to present Cooshall with a similar mark of the Honble Board's high approbation.

Anticipating the liberal compliance of the Honble the Governor in Council, in this humble request, I hand up the enclosed bill.

This was agreed.

Mint Contractor – 1813

In 1813, two members of the staff of the assay office asked to join a fund named the Purvoes fund, presumably some sort of pension scheme[406]:

I have the honor to inform you that two of the Purvoes of the mint office named [Purshotun Mungajee] and Dadajee Sunkersett have requested me to make application for them to be admitted as subscribers to the Purvoes fund. They have stated to me that they did not perfectly understand the principles on which the fund was established at the time it was instituted and the beneficial effects to be derived to them and their families by becoming subscribers, but being now better acquainted with the advantages of this institution they request to be admitted as members of the fund and they agree to pay whatever subscription may be required of them.

Mint Contractor – 1814

In 1814 a new mint contractor was appointed[407]:

…[we] have now the honor to submit the draft of an agreement to be entered into with Pestonjee Bhicajee on his undertaking the management of the mint, framed in conformity to the orders issued to Mr Stephenson under date the 14th September last, and providing as far as is practicable both against embezzlement and fraud…

Mint Contractor – 1815

In 1815, at the same time as the roles of the mint master, assay master and mint committee were defined, so was that of the mint contractor[408]:

The contractor to deposit a lack of rupees in Government securities in the Honble Company's treasury accompanied with a bond, as a security for making the coins of proper standard, and for the due performance of the contract.

To receive all gold and silver bullion, and all foreign coins that may be tendered for coinage by their weight and touch, and to give in an attested daily account of the same to the mint master.

To make such gold and silver coins and of such standard as the Right Honble the Governor in Council shall direct.

To coin copper pice for the Honble Company exclusively.

---

[406] Bombay Public Consultations. IOR P/344/65, p. 4047. Letter from the Mr Edward (Acting mint master) to government, dated 10th June 1813.

[407] Bombay Mint Procedings. IOR P/411/36, p. 1. Letter from the Bombay Mint Committee to government, dated 20th December 1814.

[408] Bombay Mint Procedings. IOR P/411/36, p. 128. Revised Regulations by Bombay Council.

To give the bullion owners their just return of specie.

To observe the following rules in calculating the quantity of standard metal in bullion Viz

If 92 tolas of pure metal are equal to 100 tolas of standard (of 92 touch), then 100 tolas of fine metal must be equal to 108 tolas 965 penyweight of standard.

To keep the coins as near as possible to the standard and melt down and re-coin at his own expense and charge all coins that the assay master on examination find to deviate too much from the proper standard.

To conduct every part of the coinage in the mint buildings provided by the Honble Company for that purpose.

Not to receive either directly or indirectly any other gain as emolument for coinage over and above the regular percentage specified in his contract.

The alloy for gold to consist of pure silver and for silver of pure copper.

To forfeit the contract and become liable to the penalties therein prescribed on the infringement of any of the above conditions.

It shall be the duty of the mint master to see that the contractor be not in making his deliveries in any instance influenced by favor or affection towards anyone, but that he makes his deliveries to the bullion owners on principles of fairness to all parties, and the mint master shall also be held responsible that the mint shall be in such a state of efficiency as to be capable if required of returning in specie to the extent of rupees […] within […] when employed on a gold coinage and of returning within a like period rupees […] when employed on a silver coinage, being on the former case at the rate of rupees […] and in the latter at the rate of rupees […] per diem, commencing in both instances from the commencement of the process of coinage.

This draft was sent to the Bombay mint committee, who informed Government in October 1815 that it was the responsibility of the mint contractor to determine how many people were employed in the mint[409]:

…In reply we request you will have the goodness respectfully to bring to the notice of the Right Honble the Governor in Council that as it rests with the contractor to entertain workmen in such numbers and at such times as suits his convenience, it is wholly out of the power of the mint master to keep the mint in any certain state of efficiency.

Had the contractor been bound by the terms of his contract to maintain a permanent establishment, the only mode by which certain returns could have been ensured, he could not, it is obvious, have undertaken the coinage at the same low rates as at present, when he is allowed the privilege of hiring and discharging his workmen according to the state of the business in the mint…

The proposed changes were made to the regulations, which were then issued.

---

[409] Bombay Mint Procedings. IOR P/411/36, p. 145. Letter from the Bombay mint committee to government, dated 21st October 1815.

Yet another mint contractor was appointed in 1815[410]:

In acknowledging your letter of the 9th instant authorising the coinage of one lac of rupees in panchias and gold rupees I have to request the further instructions of the Right Honble the Governor in Council relative to the present mint contractor in view to his contract expiring at the end of the present month, in order to avoid any confusion or dispute that may arise before the present coinage can be carried into effect.

The mint contractor informs me that a month and a half will be required to finish the coinage in question and to enable him to clear his accounts and to dispose of his stock of materials, which will extend the period of his contract beyond the middle of February.

The contractor is willing to execute the proposed coinage at the rates specified in his last tender, Viz one and a half per cent on Panchias and one and three quarters on gold rupees, which is on each one eighth per cent higher than the tender of Pestonjee Bhickajee.

Under these circumstances it appears necessary that either the present contract should be extended to the 1st of March next or that the proposed coinage should not be begun until the execution of that of Pestonjee Bhiccajee, as the urgency of the case may appear to the Honble the Governor in Council to require.

The new gold coins were urgently required so the then current mint contractor was ordered to finish work on those and the new contractor was to undertake the copper coinage that was also required[411]:

Mint Contractor – 1818

A new mint contract was put out to tender in 1818 and it is interesting to note that it was not just the cost that was taken into consideration on this occasion[412]:

…Resolved under the circumstances stated by the Committee that the proposal of Narondass Tulsidass for conducting the coinage of the mint (although on a less advantageous terms in a pecuniary point of view to Narsidass Purshotunass) be accepted for a period of three years on the terms of his former contract, determinable on six months previous notice at any time within that period at the option of either party.

Mint Contractor – 1824

In 1824 the mint contractor died and Sambal Hurrybaye petitioned to take over the work[413]:

---

[410] Bombay Mint Procedings. IOR P/411/36, p. 6. Letter from the Bombay mint master (R Stewart) to government, dated 11th January 1815.

[411] Bombay Mint Procedings. IOR P/411/36, p. 8. Letter from the sub-Treasurer to government, dated 16th January 1815.

[412] Bombay Consultations. IOR P/411/38, p. 226. Letter from Bombay mint committee to Bombay government, dated 9th September 1818.

[413] Bombay Consultations. IOR P/411/42, 1824, p. 33. Letter from the Acting mint master to government, dated 2nd April 1824.

It is with great regret that I have to announce for the information of Government the death of Nurberam Bhowanidass, the mint contractor, who had served the Honble Company in that capacity for a number of years with the greatest integrity and in times of emergency as shown in the mint records, so much to the satisfaction of the mint officers as to obtain from Government very gratifying testimonies of its appreciation.

The petitioner having, as stated in his petition, been the active manager at the mint for some years past, must be competent to continue the same upon his own responsibility. I have no hesitation therefore in recommending him to the Honble the Governor in Council as a proper person to be entrusted with the mint contract until such time as Government shall have erected the new mint, and be prepared to take the coinage into their own hands, when it may be found very convenient to engage his further service as a native assistant in the melting department.

Mint Buildings – 1800-c1835

Throughout the early part of the nineteenth century, the mint buildings continued to be in a state of disrepair and work was constantly needed to maintain them. In April 1800 payments were made for the repair of the mint buildings[414]:

…The following allowances are also authorized, Viz

To the Mint Master the sum of 280 rupees per annum for keeping the building under him in repair…

In 1802 the mint master reported that the roof of the mint had collapsed and a wall appeared to be falling down. He requested permission to get it repaired. This was granted[415]. The superintending engineer reported on the damage and gave an estimate of the cost of repairs and it was agreed that the work should be put out to tender[416]. A number of proposals were received and that of Ragoonath Wittorjee was accepted[417]. A contract to repair various parts of the mint building was duly drawn up[418].

There is a coloured plan of Bombay Castle which shows, *inter alia*, the position of the mint in 1803 (see p. vii). The plan was produced following a major fire[419]. Following this, the mint buildings required further repair[420]:

The time draws near when the public buildings of the Honble Company should be put into sufficient state of repair at least to withstand the inclemency of the approaching monsoon.

---

[414] Bombay Public Consultations. IOR P/342/42, p. 935. Resolution 18th April 1800.

[415] Bombay Public Consultations. IOR P/342/54, p. 1618. Letter from PA Grant, mint master at Bombay to Bombay Board dated 16th July 1802.

[416] Bombay Public Consultations. IOR P/342/54, p. 1671. Letter from the Superintending Engineer to Bombay Board dated 24th July 1802.

[417] Bombay Public Consultations. IOR P/342/55, p. 2012. Proposals reviewed at meeting of 11th August 1802.

[418] Bombay Public Consultations. IOR P/342/56, p. 2520. Contract between Ragoonth Wittojee and the EIC, 31st August 1802.

[419] Bombay Public Consultations. IOR P/343/4, p. 1079. Site of the Bombay mint, 1803

[420] Bombay Public Consultations. IOR P/343/5, p. 1686. Letter from Le Messurier to Bombay Board, dated 29th April 1803.

Permit me therefore to respectfully represent the present decayed state of the roof of the mint house, which absolutely requires being put into some immediate kind of repair so as to render it tolerably habitable for the several workmen during the rains. The damage which it has sustained in consequence of the late disastrous conflafration tho' not very considerable, yet it is the chief cause of my soliciting your sanction of expending the sum of rupees 300 on the Honble Company's account in addition to my annual allowance of rupees 280, which I trust will not be considered extravagant. You may rely that the greatest attention will be [paid] to the strictest economy on my part.

The charges were sanctioned by Council.

Payment of Carpenter

In 1805 a carpenter petitioned for payment for work he said he had done on the mint buildings[421]:

In reply to your letter of the 23rd instant forwarding for my report copy of a petition from Waman Ballajee carpenter, I request you will be pleased to acquaint the Honble the Governor in Council that this practitioner has been in the practice of making the annual repairs to the mint buildings, that instead of applying for the superintending engineer's certificate, which is a necessary voucher to pass his bill, he entirely neglected this form (with the necessity of which he was well acquainted) in the last year until the monsoon was entirely over and when it was consequently out of the power of the engineer to say whether the work for which he required to be paid had been really executed.

It remains for the Honble the Governor General in Council to decide on the sum which he will be allowed to receive. The amount of his claim is Rs 280 but as far as I am capable of judging, I do not think that the petitioner expended one half of this sum in the last year.

The whole of the mint buildings are now in such a general state of decay as to require a thorough repair to prevent them falling in during the next monsoon and as these repairs are under the late orders of Government to be made by Captain Brookes, it will be necessary that he should examine their present condition, when he will be able to form a more correct judgement than I possibly can of the sum which is justly due to the petitioner.

The engineer could not find what work the carpenter was referring to, but reported that the mint buildings were in a poor state. In fact one, at least, appeared to be falling down[422]:

In reply to your letter of the 28th ultimo, enclosing a copy of a letter by the mint master, I beg that you will inform the Honble the Governor General in Council that I have looked at the mint and that I find that some repairs have been made to a back veranda. It is however, now impossible for me to say what the contractor alluded to, ought to have [been done].

---

[421] Bombay Public Consultations. IOR P/343/21, p. 1724. Letter from William Crawford (mint master) to government, dated 27th March 1805.

[422] Bombay Public Consultations. IOR P/343/21, p. 1815. Letter from William Brookes (Captain of Engineers) to government, dated 1st April 1805.

The old building is in a most dangerous state for the walls are pressed outwards and the rafters in one place have drawn from the wall plate. This part must therefore be taken down or it will certainly fall…

Proposed Enlargement of the mint, 1806

In 1806 a slight extension of the mint buildings was proposed but was rejected because of plans to move the mint to another site[423]:

In reply to your secretary's letter of yesterday's date, just received, informing me that the appropriation of the ravelin occupied with military stores, for the mint, is to be postponed, I beg leave respectfully to intimate that, should you think proper to sanction the measure, an apartment adjoining the refining room (the walls of which are standing) might be roofed in at a very trifling expense, which would obviate the necessity of having recourse to any other buildings as a temporary [suceedarevum?]. The room alluded to with the other plans in the mint already prepared for the work-people would afford space for the whole number we are likely to collect.

I beg leave to add that no danger could reasonably be apprehended from fire in bringing this portion of the old building into use again.

Ruinous State of the Mint and Proposed Relocation, 1807

By May 1807 the mint was in a 'ruinous' state and could not operate very effectively[424]:

In answer to the second question of the Honble the Governor in Council, we can say that the mint in its present state is very unequal to the supply of a considerable quantity of silver coinage. We can hardly coin 8000 rupees a day, or 240,000 a month. This is owing in great measure to the ruinous state of the mint, which some time ago fell down suddenly, leaving no more than one small room for all the purposes of the coinage. We are at all times however, confined in our operations from the want of machinery, everything here being done by the hands of men, and it frequently happens that a sufficient number of such artists cannot be procured.

The town committee was asked to propose a site for the mint outside of the fort:

It was, on the 6th instant, observed that by order of the 13th May 1806 one of the ravelins was offered to be assigned to the mint master in aid of the insufficiency of space at the mint office, and to call upon Mr Watkins to report why that had not proved available.

The town committee were at the same time to give their opinions as to the most eligible spot to erect a mint on, without the fortifications and to present a plan thereof with an estimate of the expense and the time in which, in their opinion, it might be got ready for the purposes of the coinage.

---

[423] Bombay Public Consultations. IOR P/343/31, p. 1835. Letter from Charles Watkins (mint master) to government, dated 25th April 1806.

[424] Bombay Public Consultations. IOR P/343/45, p. 3112. Letter from Charles Watkins (mint master) and H Scott to government, dated 1st May 1807.

Lack of Space in the Mint, 1807

In September 1807, the mint and assay masters reported on the inability of the mint to produce more coins. This was mainly caused by the lack of space in the mint buildings[425]:

…That our coinage can be carried on but to a very limited extent is too true, and this arises chiefly from the want of machinery for coinage here. The coins are made entirely by the hand so that the amount of the coinage must be exactly in proportion to the number of smiths that we can hire in Bombay. We have at present at work sixty smiths and forty more might be procured in Bombay. This is the greatest extent of our coinage and is impossible to extend it. Smiths might be found from Surat but the employment for them in the mint is very uncertain as the silver coinage depends on the cheapness of silver bullion in the market, which for some years past has continued but for a short time. If we could assure the mint contractor that he could find a regular employment for a considerable space of time he would agree to bring down a number of smiths from Surat, but this we cannot do.

If the mint were not in a ruinous state we could easily accommodate all the smiths to be found in Bombay and a much greater number. We can, as we have said, get forty more smiths only, and when the rains are over we can employ them all as they can then work in the open air…

…The ravelin* of which we were put in possession last year was found not to answer the purpose and it was relinquished at the entreaty of the contractor. It held twenty five men. By his business being divided between the mint and the ravelin, he was not able to protect himself from theft & to our certain knowledge he suffered very serious losses from that cause…

Mint Moved but Still Delapidated, 1810 & 1811

In 1810 the south west ravelin was assigned to the mint but needed repairs[426]:

The south west ravelin having been assigned pro tempore for the Honble Company's mint, I request you will repair the buildings situated in that work, with the least possible delay.

In 1811 the mint was again found to be in a ruinous state[427]:

The dilapidated state of the mint has so often been brought under the notice of your Honble Board that it may be superfluous to do more on the present occasion than simply to advert to its ruinous condition as being a circumstance perfectly established and notorious.

Your Honble Board was pleased on the arrival of the bullion from Madras on His Majesty's ship Caroline to authorize me to hire additional premises for carrying on the coinage.

---

*   A ravelin is a triangular fortification or detached outwork, located in front of the innerworks of a fortress. Definition taken from Wikipedia.

[425] Bombay Public Consultations. IOR P/343/49, p. 7552. Letter from the mint master (Charles Watkins) and the assay master (H. Scott) to government, dated 23rd September 1807.

[426] Bombay Public Consultations. IOR P/344/21, p. 114. Letter from the mint master (GC Osborne) to Major Brookes, no date (about Jan 1810).

[427] Bombay Public Consultations. IOR P/344/37, p. 896. Letter from the mint master (GC Osborne) to government, dated 14th February 1811.

Anxious however, to avoid any additional expense that might not be indispensibly necessary, I did not avail myself of this permission of your Honble Board, but I now find it my duty to recommend that some spacious warehouses may be immediately hired for the purpose of carrying on the silver coinage.

There can be no doubt that the mint will have to work throughout the monsoon, and I am of opinion that the present state of the mint building precludes all hope that it will be available to any adequate extent during the rainy season.

Even during the fair season, it does not afford sufficient accommodation for carrying on an extensive silver coinage, no more than 20,000 per diem can be coined in it, which is by no means equal to the demand for its labours…

…The arrangements I find it my duty to recommend are necessarily attended with some expense, but by no means approximating in proportion to the increased revenue the Honble Company will derive from the mint department in consequence of its increased activity and efficiency…

Estimate of the probable expense that will attend the present proposed arrangement.

1ˢᵗ	*Rent of buildings for the mintage*	*500*
2ⁿᵈ	*Temporary extra establishment of two purvoes and 6 peons*	*186*
		686

However, the amount of bullion to be coined was much smaller than expected so a new building was not required[428]:

The quantity of silver bullion imported from China is so much smaller than was expected that it is not probable the mint master will derive much employment from the merchants and other inhabitants…

In 1811 a request was made to build a shed over the area where the stamping part of the process took place[429]:

I request you will have the goodness to procure an order from the Honble the Governor in Council to the Superintending Engineer for the erection of a shed over the platform used at the mint for the operation of stamping.

As the shed in question will not be at all exposed to the action of fire and does not therefore require to be composed of very solid materials, expense can be but trifling compared with the very desirable object of giving every possible degree of efficiency to the mint in the extensive coinage in which it is engaged.

Further work was requested a little later when the mint master asked that the platform for stamping should be extended as well as the shed built over it. The engineer was asked to inspect it and the work was approved[430].

---

[428] Bombay Public Consultations. IOR P/344/38, p. 1792. Letter from the mint master (GC Osborne) to government, dated 17ᵗʰ March 1811.

[429] Bombay Public Consultations. IOR P/344/41, p. 3306. Letter from the acting mint master (J Wedderburn) to government, dated 6ᵗʰ June 1811.

[430] Bombay Public Consultations. IOR P/344/41, p. 3693. Letter from the acting mint master (J Wedderburn) to government, dated 21st June 1811.

A little later in 1811 the mint master discussed the possibility of a completely new mint building but considered that this should not be built until it had been established whether or not a new mint was to be sent from England[431].

In 1812 Mr Noton was appointed to the post of assay master and one of the first things he did was to request that a new assay office should be built[432].

Thus, the ruinous state of the mint buildings and the lack of machinery was a constant problem for the officers of the mint. Repairs to the existing buildings continued to be necessary, but the idea of a new building was overtaken by the plans for a new mint to be brought from England and was not put into effect until 1830 (see chapter 7).

---

[431] Bombay Public Consultations. IOR P/344/43, p. 4618. Letter from the acting mint master (J Wedderburn) to government, dated 27th July 1811.

[432] Bombay Public Consultations. IOR P/344/55, p. 4162. Letter from the Mr Noton to government, undated but about 4th November 1812.

Chapter 6 – Bombay Mint, Dr Stewart's Machinery

Summary

The EIC mints at Calcutta and Madras had both been mechanised in the early 1790s or early 1800s respectively. However, Bombay continued with the old hammered method of coin production for many more years. In 1817 or 1818 the Bombay mint master, Dr. Stewart, had begun to investigate the possibility of building machines that could be used to strike the coinage for that presidency. However, probably due to illness, Stewart had to leave India and the project passed to the new mint master, Henderson, who spent several more years trying to perfect the machinery. Because the directors of the EIC decided to ship a new mint from Europe, the local production of machinery was limited to a few machines for striking copper coins and was eventually halted altogether and it never went into full production. A number of pattern coins for a proposed new copper coinage were produced and are discussed in this chapter.

Introduction

In 1997 a group of copper pattern coins was offered for sale by Bonhams[433]. These coins were machine struck for the Bombay Presidency, with denominations of one anna, half anna, quarter anna and one pie (twelfth anna) and dated 1820 or 1821. This group greatly extended the known denominations and dates that had been recorded previously by Major Pridmore[434].

The Coins and their Context

Following the final war with the Marathas in 1817, the British added large tracts of territory to their Bombay Presidency. This expansion required a larger number of coins in circulation to meet the demands of the increased population, and the authorities were obliged to keep working those mints that they had acquired with the territory. These mints have been called 'transitional' mints and have been discussed in some detail elsewhere[435] (see chapter 9).

In addition to keeping these transitional mints working, the Bombay Council, at a meeting on 23rd September 1818, ordered that the Bombay mint committee be asked whether or not they could build machinery capable of meeting the new demands. They also believed that they could make sufficient profit on a copper coinage to cover the cost of building a new, machine-driven, mint[436]:

The direct ships of the season having arrived without bringing us any instructions from the Honble Court regarding the mint, it becomes [imperitively] necessary that we should without

---

[433] Bonhams (1997), 26th March, sale 27299, lots 413-421.

[434] Pridmore F, The Coins of the British Commonwealth of Nations. Part 4, India, Vol. 1 East India Company Presidency Series c1642-1835. Spink & Son Ltd, 1975.

[435] Stevens PJE, JONS 179, 181 & 182.

[436] Bombay Consultations. IOR P/411/38 p. 237. Resolution of Council, 23rd September 1818.

further delay adopt some measures for remedying the great inconveniences under which we at present labour from the want of an efficient mint.

The quantity of <u>copper coin alone</u> required for circulation in the new extended districts of this government cannot be estimated at less then five lacs of rupees, and if this were coined by means of machinery, there would as shewn by the mint committee in their letter of 30ᵗʰ April last be "a gain of nearly two lacs and a half of Rs on the first issue of the pice which will be much more than sufficient [to cover?] the expense of any mint that it can be deemed advisable to erect".

This fact, which cannot be disputed, is sufficient to authorize Government to proceed in the erection of a mint without further waiting for the Court's orders, independent of the great gain to be derived from an improved silver coinage. The circumstances of this Government are so much changed, that the reasons which may at one time have operated to delay the erection of a mint can now have no influence.

Ordered therefore that the mint committee be called upon to report on the reference made to it on the 20ᵗʰ June in regard to the means now available for preparing an improved copper currency. The Committee are at the same time to state whether complete machinery for all purposes of a mint can now be prepared at Bombay, or whether an application for such should be made to Bengal.

The mint committee are at the same time to report the difference which would have accrued to the Honble Company, supposing the extensive recoinage which has for sometime past and is now carrying on, including the expected consignment of 15 lacs of dollars, had been conducted by machinery, under the improvements contemplated, instead of the rude manner in which the coinage is now formed.

To enable us likewise to judge of the evils of our present currency which can now so easily be counterfeited by any common mechanic, the mint committee should lay before us a return of the quantity of uncurrent and debased coins of the Bombay and Surat mints found in the several consignments of treasure from the Coast since we have been furnished with funds from that quarter.

Ordered also that the Court of Petty Sessions report the number of cases brought before it, since its institution, of persons charged with counterfeiting or debasing the public currency of this Presidency.

A similar return to be prepared by the Register of the Sudder Adaulut of convictions in the subordinate courts.

The other Presidency mints at Calcutta and Madras had already constructed machinery to produce their coinages some years earlier (Calcutta in the early 1790s and Madras in 1807) and had been successfully producing milled coins for some time.

The mint master at Bombay, Dr Stewart, reported that *'for some time past'* he had been considering building such machinery but in order to continue the work he would need help from the gun carriage manufactory[437]:

I request that you will have the goodness to inform the Right Honble the Governor in Council that I have for some time past turned my attention to the practicability of improving the coinage of this Presidency by means of machinery prepared at this place without having recourse to the other Presidencies, and that from what I have seen I am of the opinion that the attempt may be attended with success.

In order, however, for me to determine this point with precision, I request that the Right Honble the Governor in Council may be pleased to direct that I may be supplied with such assistance as may be procurable from the Department of the Gun Carriage Manufactory as may be necessary, consisting chiefly of the occasional use of the foundry and the labour of two European artificers belonging to that department.

By these means I trust the mint committee will be enabled to answer your letter of the 20th June in the course of a few weeks, and to accompany it with a specimen of the coins proposed.

In response the Bombay Council resolved:

That the military Board be ordered to instruct the gun carriage department to afford such aid to the Mint Master as he may require in the trial now in progress connected with the manufacture of mint machinery.

Stewart received the help of matross[438] Mulholland and sub-conductor[439] Hughes as well as access to the foundry in the gun carriage manufactory. In fact, Stewart appears to have been working on the machinery for more than a year (i.e. since at least 1817), and Hughes and Mulholland had been helping on a casual basis. This distraction seems to have annoyed the officer in charge of the gun carriage manufactory, Captain Mackintosh, who had ordered Hughes and Mulholland to stop helping Stewart. In November 1818, Stewart wrote[440]:

I have the honour to acknowledge receipt of your letter dated the 25th instant with its accompaniments from the secretary to the Military Board, and the Agent for Gun Carriages, calling on me to state for what period I require the services of Matross Mulholland and sub-conductor Hughes, in the preparation of machinery for the use of the mint, and whether workmen equally qualified for the same duty cannot be obtained elsewhere.

In reply I beg leave to state for the information of the Right Honble the Governor in Council, that the period for which the services of Matross Mulholland may be required will greatly depend upon the success or otherwise of the experiment on which he is now engaged, and which, in reference to my letter to you of the 2nd instant, I expected would be concluded

---

[437] Bombay Consultations. IOR p/411/38, p. 303. Letter from the mint master (R. Stewart) to government dated 2nd November 1818.

[438] Matross = low ranking artillery soldier

[439] Sub-conductor = private in the logistics corp

[440] Bombay Consultations. IOR p/411/38, p. 323. Letter from the mint master to government dated 30th November 1818.

in a few weeks. This man was sent to me on 24th instant and I think that I can now state confidently that the point in question will be finally determined by the first or second week of January next, provided that no interruption takes place. With regard to sub-conductor Hughes, there is so little required in his department, that I am [of] opinion that a day or two in each week or a week in each month, as may be best suited to the conveniency of the Gun Carriage Department, is the utmost extent of his services that can be required even on the supposition that a complete set of mint machinery should ultimately be determined on by Government. It will hence, I trust, appear that so far as this man's services are concerned it can scarcely be termed an interference with the Gun Carriage Department.

In reply to the concluding part of your letter, I have only to state that I know of no person capable of performing the services I require of Matross Mulholland otherwise I should have carefully avoided any requisition of them while I am at the same time fully satisfied that others may be found capable of performing all that is required of him in the construction of gun carriages, of which the work is of the plainest kind, and I may add coarse in comparison to that which is required in the construction of coining machinery, on the accurate workmanship of which its success exclusively depends.

Stewart went on to discuss Captain Mackintosh's interference in the matter of the two workment helping at the mint:

It remains for me to make a few observations on the nature of the objection stated by Captain Mackintosh, in his letter to the Military Board, and also in one to myself dated the 26th instant (copies of which I now enclose) in answer to an application which I made to him on that day, for the labour of sub-conductor Hughes for three days, and that Government may fully understand the circumstances which have led to the present discussion. I shall premise that it is now upwards of a year since I first directed my attention to the machinery in question, the progress of which has been delayed from time to time by various causes, but chiefly from the want of workmen to execute anything to my satisfaction. During this period however, until lately, I had the occasional assistance of both the mechanics in question, on Sundays and sometimes on Hindoo holidays when the Gun Carriage Manufactory was necessarily shut up by the non-attendance of the native workmen. I had also the assistance of Matross Mulholland by Captain Mackintosh's permission for a few days in the latter end of September, or beginning of October last, when the Gun Carriage Manufactory was removed to Colaba, and consequently the labour of this man suspended for a time. On the latter occasion I was so satisfied that the services of Matross Mulholland were so indispensably necessary to the completion of my plan, that I ventured to speak to Major General Bailie, and also Captain Mackintosh, of obtaining his discharge from the military, with the view of employing him under Government both for making and keeping in repair the machinery with which I was engaged. So far however was this application from forwarding my purpose, that, from that time, the men in question were strictly prohibited, by an order of Captain Mackintosh, from working anywhere but in the department. Thus deprived of the casual assistance I formerly had from these men, the alternative remained to me of relinquishing altogether the plan [on] which I had already made considerable progress, or by an application to Government, to obtain such assistance as I thought absolutely necessary towards its completion and from the department where alone it was to be found.

I am ignorant of the nature of Captain Mackintosh's objections to permitting these men to work anywhere but at the manufactory, but I can with great truth assert that during my intercourse with them I observed nothing but the most orderly conduct, united to a laudable desire of improving by their labour, the humble condition in which they are placed, and I shall only add that if Captain Mackintosh's statement proves anything they appear also to prove too much, as, on general principles, it seems difficult to conceive the state of a department of such importance and extent as the Gun Carriage Manufactory, the efficiency of which should in any considerable degree depend on the exertions of any individual whatever, but more especially on the fortuitous circumstance of a private of the battalion of artillery, having been bred a turner in metals, and who, I believe, has not now completed one year of service in that department.

It is unnecessary for me to occupy the time of Government on the necessity which has long existed, for some reform in the state of the coinage of this Presidency. Their records during the last three years bear ample testimony both of that and the desire they have evinced of carrying it into effect. It therefore remains for them to decide whether it shall now be relinquished or carried into exertion, even at the risk of occasioning a small degree of inconvenience to another department, which, in the nature of things, cannot be of long duration.

Dr Stewart now got the help that he needed and was able to report that the investigatory work would be complete by January 1819. Unfortunately, Mulholland, who appears to have been the person with the necessary skills to build the machinery, fell ill and the whole project was delayed as revealed in a letter dated January 1819[441]:

I have the honor to report for the information of the Right Honble the Governor in Council that Matross Mulholland, whom Government had directed to be employed under me for the purpose of preparing machinery for the mint, has been unfit for any kind of duty ever since 28th November last in consequence of a severe attack of Dysentery from which he is only now recovering.

Government will hence perceive that so far as this man's services are concerned, little progress can have been made in my present undertaking. In other respects the work has been going forward as I could wish.

Captain Mackintosh continued to complain that he could not find workmen of the standard of Mulholland. In February 1819 he wrote[442]:

---

[441] Bombay Consultations. P/411/39. 20th January 1819, p. 4. Letter from the mint master (Stewart) to government, dated 10th January 1819.

[442] Bombay Consultations. IOR P/411/39, 25th January 1819, pp. 13/14. Letter from R. Mackintosh (Gun Carriage Dept.) to Captain Bellasis (Secretary to the Military Board), dated 11th February 1819.

I have the honor to acknowledge receipt of your letter of the 27th ultimo and in reply request that you will have the goodness to report to the Military Board that I have within the last fifteen days obtained from the artillery two men as metal turners, but they are of such inferior capacity that their work is not only badly executed, but both are not capable of performing in two days what Matross Mulholland would complete in one. I am however at the present under the necessity of employing these, and a double expense is thus incurred, until Matross Mulholland be directed to return to his duty in the department

but the Bombay Government continued to believe that Mulholland was better employed in the mint than in the gun carriage department[443]:

Ordered the Military Board be informed that as no person equally capable with Matross Mulholland to prepare the superior description of machinery required for the mint can be procured, there is no alternative than to allow that person to remain in the mint so long as his services may be required.

In May 1819, Stewart set sail for England (probably due to ill-health) and a Mr Henderson was appointed mint master on 20th May[444]:

Doctor Stewart having signified his intention of returning to England in the course of a few days, it was my intention to have proposed to the Board [that?] under the orders of the Honble Court the office of Mint Master is to be filled by a Civil servant, that Mr Newnham should succeed to that situation, but understanding on a private communication I have had with him that he would wish to decline the acceptance of that employment, I propose that it may be conferred on Mr Henderson.

The members below the chair concurring in the President's nomination of Mr Henderson as successor to Doctor Stewart in the office of Mint Master, resolved that he be appointed accordingly and directed to receive immediate charge of the department from Doctor Stewart who is on the point of embarking for England on the Blenden Hale.

Stewart's departure seems to have been very rushed, leaving Henderson little time to pick up knowledge of what had been happening in the mint[445]:

I have the honor to acknowledge the receipt of your letter of the 27th instant, referring for my examination and report, an account of Mr Stewart's expenditure for certain mint machinery, which he was authorised to construct experimentally without my previous estimate of the expense.

In reply I request you have the goodness to state to the Right Honble the Governor in Council, that the document transmitted appears to be an abstract of bills incurred by the late Mint Master, amounting, in aggregate, to Rupees eleven thousand four hundred and twenty

---

[443] *Ibid.* Minutes 19th February 1819.
[444] Bombay Consultations. IOR P/411/39 7th April 1819. Minute by the President dated 20th May.
[445] Bombay Consultations. IOR P/411/39, p. 44. Letter from the Accountant General and Civil Auditor to government, dated 31st May 1819.

eight, three quarters, and 74 reas, unaccompanied indeed by any vouchers, but being correct in additions, and solemnly attested on honor, it may, I think, on an undertaking of such a nature, be deemed unobjectionable, and is accordingly retained in this department, to await the orders of Government.

and the Bombay Government agreed to accept the expenses as described by Henderson[446]:

Resolved under the explanations afforded by Mr Wedderburn, that the account of Mr Stewart's expenditure for mint machinery amounting to rupees 11428..3..74 be passed and discharged by the proper officer.

One of Henderson's first actions was to take an inventory of the machinery that had been constructed[447]:

I have the honor to transmit to you for the purpose of being laid before the Right Honble the Governor in Council, the accompanying inventory of mint machinery etc to which Mr Stewart's letter of the 22nd ultimo refers.

I have the honor also to report that agreeably to the direction conveyed in your letter of the 27th ultimo, the establishment for constructing the mint machinery has been reduced to the numbers of workmen specified by Mr Stewart. The Europeans discharged are Privates Edward Jones and William Parker, who have been sent to the depot of the Honble Company's European regiment.

There then follows a detailed list of all the equipment built by Dr. Stewart. In summary:

Cutting Presses
Milling Presses
Stamping presses to be contained in wooden frames, length 5 feet, breadth 7 feet, height 6 feet 6 inches

> *4 Fixing beds & 14 screws complete*
> *3 ditto without screws*
> *4 slides and brass boxes with bolts*
> *8 iron screws & 4 brass boxes incomplete*
> *1 ditto extra*
> *1 pr dies complete*
> *1 ditto in hand*
> *2 ditto ready to be sunk*
> *4 ditto ready to be turned*

Laminating mills each to work 2 rollers

---

[446] Bombay Consultations. IOR P/411/39, p. 44. Minute 5th June.

[447] Bombay Consultations. IOR P/411/39 p. 46. Letter from the mint master (Henderson) to government, dated 1st June 1819.

Various pieces of metal of different types (iron, steel, brass, lead, zinc)

…

From this it can be seen that one pair of dies had already been completed by then (June 1819).

Henderson was asked to report what further work was necessary and what assistance he would need[448]:

Ordered Mr Henderson be called upon to report whether the present establishment of his department is capable with further assistance of completing the machinery still required, as specified in the inventory. If so, Mr Henderson will state what further aid will be necessary, and likewise the probable expense of rendering the machine complete.

He considered that the required machinery would be 8 cutting presses, 8 stamping presses, 4 milling presses and 4 laminating mills at an estimated cost of Rs 8000-9000, and that these would be ready by the end of the year (1819)[449]:

I have the honor to acknowledge the receipt of Mr Acting Secretary Simson's letter, dated 5th instant, calling on me to report whether the establishment of workmen allowed for constructing the mint machinery be capable of completing it, with further assistance; and if so to state what additional aid will be necessary and the probable expense of rendering the machinery complete.

I would beg leave in the first instance to refer to Mr Stewart's letter of the 22nd ultimo, by which it appears that the establishment reduced to its present scale will in his opinion be sufficient for the purpose, although the time is not mentioned by which it may be expected to be finished. Mr Stewart also estimates the further expense likely to be incurred on account of the machinery at 7 or 8000 rupees.

From the inventory which I did myself the honor of submitting on the 1st instant, the Right Honorable the Governor in Council will have perceived that the machinery was intended by Mr Stewart to consist of:

8 Cutting Presses

8 Stamping Presses

4 Milling Presses

4 Laminating Mills

From the inventory it will also be seen that although many of the different parts of the machinery were in progress, Mr Stewart was unable to finish more than 4 cutting presses and 1 milling press previously to his departure. I believe that Mr Stewart at one time entertained an expectation that the cutting presses could be made to answer also the purpose of stamping presses, but it was found more powerful machinery would be required.

---

[448] *Ibid.* Minute 5th June.

[449] Bombay Consultations. IOR P/411/39, p. 79. Letter from the mint master (Henderson) to government, dated 12th June 1819.

Since Mr Stewart's departure one stamping press has been nearly completed, of a more solid structure then the cutting presses, and also one laminating mill. But as the stamping press is contained in a wooden frame whereas, according to the description of a gentleman well acquainted with the Tower mint, with whom I have lately had an opportunity of conversing, they are now made generally, if not always, of cast iron, and as the laminating mill is on a new or at least on an unusual principle, it may probably be expedient before any more of either be constructed on the same plan to await the result of a trial of the two nearly finished, and which will be ready in the course of a very short time.

Should the machinery on the principles followed by Mr Stewart be found to answer and no alteration be required, it would no doubt be in the power of the present establishment to complete it by the end of the present year at furthest. Such is the expectation of the principal workman who seems to be capable of finishing it, with the assistance of the other people employed. But it will be perceived that it would not be possible for me to offer an opinion whether any further assistance or expense, than what has been stated by Mr Stewart, may be necessary, until the result of a trial of one set of the machinery, when perfectly complete, can be ascertained.

In a minute of 24th July 1819 the Bombay Council stated[450]:

For the reasons given in the concluding part of the 5th Paragraph of the preceding letter, it would appear unadvisable to complete the second stamping press only before it can be satisfactorily ascertained how far the presses as now constructed will answer all the purposes.

and on 27th July they added a further minute about the site of a building for the machinery to operate in[451]:

The President remarks that as the machinery will be ready in the course of the present year, it will be necessary to take measures for the preparation of a mint. The Bomb Room suggested by Doctor Stewart on the examination of a common observer, will not, he conceives, answer the purpose, having personally inspected it with the chief engineer, and some other place must be found.

The President also states that he can see no objection, in a military point of view, to one of the Ravelins being appropriated to this purpose since one of them has already been assigned to the forging the machinery, and there is, in the Governors opinion, recollecting what the mint is in the Tower, sufficient room for every necessary building.

However, in August 1819, a letter was received from Captain Hawkins, who had been sent to England to investigate the new steam driven machinery produced by Boulton at his Soho mint and then used in the Royal Mint. Hawkins appeared to be making good progress in persuading the Court of Directors at '*India House*' to have a

---

[450] *Ibid.*
[451] *Ibid.*

new mint built in Bombay[452]:

I have made some progress at the India House in furthering the design which you patronised of building the Town Hall Mint and Main Guard in one line on Bombay Green. You will, long ere this arrives, have heard of the Court's grant of ground for the Hall and perhaps know more about it than I do myself as the India House is not the readiest place of obtaining correct information. But as to the mint from Mr Tompson having taken up my plans very warmly, I believe I can speak very fully. The idea of the Court of Directors seems to be to make the coin of the same stamp and value all over India beginning with Bombay as being the most in want of [a] mint. The art of coining has been brought to wonderful perfection in the Royal Mint, particularly in laminating or fine rolling the metal, which is done by the power of a steam [engine] applied to improved rollers, which so compress the metal as to render its specific gravity uniform throughout. The cutting out stamp has also been carried to great perfection so that from the improvements on fine rolling and cutting out the coin, any subsequent adjustment is almost entirely superseded. This improvement has caused a wonderful saving in labour, time and metal and the quantity of coin turned out of the Royal Mint in one day, over and above the former plan, is quite incredible. The thing we have most to combat introducing the improved plan into India is the expense of machinery which from the plan already submitted to the Court will cost about thirty thousand pounds, but I have hopes of bringing it down fully one third, which sum the Court appears inclined to grant. If this can be done our mint at Bombay will, I have no doubt, be the first in the world.

This letter made the Bombay Government review the idea of building machinery locally for all the gold, silver and copper coins and, in a minute of 2nd August, they ordered the mint master to concentrate on producing machinery for the manufacture of copper coins alone[453]:

Resolved the Mint Master be informed that by the receipt of this intelligence, it becomes necessary that no expense should be incurred in providing machinery in this country. In regulating therefore his proceedings under this intimation, Mr Henderson is to be called upon to state the probable expense at which the machinery begun by Doctor Stewart, could be so far completed as to be rendered available for the manufacture of a copper currency, leaving the improvement in the silver and gold until the arrival of the more perfect machinery expected from England.

In July, a Mr Atkinson had written to the Bombay Government offering his services[454]:

Having been given to understand that it is in agitation to establish a mint at this Presidency, upon a new principle, and being at the same time led to believe that the machinery has been

---

[452] Bombay Consultations. IOR P/411/39 p. 86. Extract of a private letter from Captain Hawkins, dated the 19th March 1819.

[453] Bombay Consultations. IOR P/411/39 p. 86. Minute 2nd August.

[454] Bombay Consultations. IOR P/411/39, p. 84. Letter from James Atkinson to government, dated 22nd July 1819 and Minute 27th July.

left in an imperfect state by Dr Stewart on his departure for Europe, I am induced to offer my services, either to assist in the completion of the undertaking which has commenced, or to make improvements upon it, after the principle of the mint in London.

I beg leave, Right Honble Sir, to state that my pretensions to perform this piece of service rest upon having been regularly apprenticed under my father, who has the immediate superintendence of the coining department in His Majesty's mint in London, and I consequently have had an opportunity of witnessing, and assisting, in all the operations necessary in conducting that establishment.

Bombay Council wanted to know the terms on which Mr. Atkinson could be employed:

Ordered that Mr Atkinson be called upon to state the terms in which he would undertake to complete and make improvement in the mint machinery in the event of the government accepting his offer.

But, in the end, they decided that they would not need his services because of the imminent arrival of the new mint from England as discussed in the letter from Captain Hawkins quoted above[455]:

Under the above information which, though not official, may in some degree be relied on as correct, it is thought proper that Mr Atkinson should be informed that letters received from England by the Bombay Merchant rendering probable that machinery for the mint will shortly be sent out to this country, the Governor in Council will no longer have occasion to avail himself of his services in that department.

Henderson, the mint master, now felt that he needed 2 rolling mills, 4 cutting presses and 6 stamping presses at a cost of about Rs 1000. This machinery would be capable of the following output:

- 10 pieces could be struck per minute
- 6 hours per day = 3600 per machine
- 6 machines = 21600 per day
- 300 working days = 6,480,000 per year

He estimated that this should be sufficient to meet demand based on the fact that the output of pice, half pice and quarter pice over the previous ten years had been 17,179,650 pieces[456]:

…The quantity of machinery which it appears to me would be wanted to execute a copper coinage within any reasonable time, will be as follows:

2 Rolling Mills

4 Cutting Presses

6 Stamping Presses

---

[455] Bombay Consultations. IOR P/411/39 p. 86. Minute 2nd August.

[456] Bombay Consultations. IOR P/411/39 p. 134. Letter from the mint master (Henderson) to government, dated 31st August 1819.

From an estimate of the wood and iron which will be required and which might be supplied from the warehouse and Marine Store Departments, on the usual terms, it may be reckoned that the expense of completing the above machinery, will not exceed 1000 rupees, in addition to the expense of the establishment employed, and after the sale of some of the articles now under my charge, which are not required, I think the Honble Board may rely on that sum being sufficient.

The following are the grounds on which I think this extent of machinery will be necessary:

From the manner in which the stamping press has been constructed, I find that about 10 pieces only can be struck by it in minute. Supposing therefore that 6 stamping presses were completed for the copper coinage and were constantly at work for 6 hours out of 12, allowing the rest of the day for all delays, the result would be each day 21,600 pieces, or for 300 working days in the year 6,480,000.

In the course of the last 10 years a copper currency has been executed by the mint contractor to the extent of Rs 277,357. The total number of pieces struck in pice, half pice and quarter pice being 17,179,650, so that it will be perceived that probably a third only of that sum could be coined in the course of one year, taking the above calculation of the powers of the 6 presses, and supposing the same divisions of the pice were to be continued.

2 Rolling mills and 4 cutting presses would appear to be sufficient to keep the stamping presses fully employed

However, Henderson stated in the same letter that he was having difficulty in rolling copper to the correct thickness:

…I expected to have been able to report sometime ago the completion of one set of the machinery and the result of a trial of its efficiency; but from the delay arising from the alterations which have been found necessary, I have been prevented hitherto from submitting any report on the subject. The trial has also, in consequence of Mr Simson's letter now acknowledged, been chiefly confined to its power of coining a copper currency. The Honble Board may probably be aware that the whole of the machinery, with the exception of the milling press, will be required to execute a copper coinage, and in fact as much strength in the parts and as much nicety and perfection in the workmanship will be necessary for coining the former as the latter. In the three processes also of rolling cutting and stamping, the two first must be executed with much precision to obviate the necessity of a subsequent adjustment, the expense of which a copper coinage could not well bear.

The copper plates which are now coining in the mint, are of a considerable size and thickness, and even if cut into small bars, I am doubtful whether all the parts of the mill as it has been constructed, could for any length of time perform what is called the breaking-down rolling, without sustaining injury. Indeed I understand Mr Stewart never contemplated a coinage from copper plates unless a supply of large rollers were sent out from Europe, that the coinage would be made of sheet copper. An experiment however of two or three bars of silver, rather smaller than the size of the Tower mint Moulds, had certainly no visible effect on the mill, after the final alterations were made, but unless one on a much larger scale and for a continuance of time were undertaken, it would be difficult to determine the point.

He went on to say that if copper could be obtained in the form of sheets this problem might be overcome:

If however a sufficient quantity of sheet copper were always procurable, this objection would be obviated, since by far the greater part of the breaking-down rolling would be superseded, and I have little doubt that the mill would easily answer the purpose of rolling down sheet copper.

Supposing a sufficient quantity of sheet copper to be procurable, the question for consideration would then be, whether the mill as now completed, could bring it to a size of that exactness, that none of the blanks when cut out should deviate in weight beyond a very few grains on either side of the proper standard; and I have little hesitation offering an opinion from our experiment which has been made on a small quantity of sheet copper, that with a proper pair of finely turned adjusting rollers, with due attention of the part of the workmen employed, and to the state of the cutters in the cutting presses, that deviation would not be more than between 5 & 6 grains in any of the pieces at the utmost, taking the standard at 100 grains.

Indeed the result of the experiment made with the machinery as it stands, although on a small scale, did not give a greater difference, and I should think it possible that after the workmen shall have had a little experience it may not exceed 4 grains. It would however be probably the province of the mint committee to offer an opinion whether such a deviation or a smaller remedy only ought to be allowed in the coinage.

With respect to the cutting press, it appears to answer the purpose fully. The stamping press has also to all appearance been now constructed of a sufficient strength, nor does it appear in any degree injured from the frequent trials which have been made of its powers…

In a minute of 10th September 1819, the Bombay Council authorised Henderson to complete the machinery:

Ordered that Mr Henderson be authorized to complete the machinery to the extent stated in the 11th paragraph of the preceding letter, a requisite for conducting a copper coinage, at the further estimated expense of Rupees one thousand.

Mr Henderson is to be called upon to state the period in which the machinery may be expected to be completed, and what arrangements appear to him necessary before it can be set to work in the preparation of a copper currency

In the same letter (August 1819), Henderson stated that he had actually produced coins from the new machinery:

The Honble Board will be able to judge from the specimens which I have the honor to hand up, what description of coinage can be executed by the machinery. These have not been particularly selected but have been struck one after the other in the press.

The dies have been cut by a private in His Majesty's 65th regiment and should they be considered sufficiently well executed, his services might be permanently engaged by allowing him to exchange with a private of the Honble Company's European regiment.

Pridmore speculated that the private who cut the dies may have been Robert Gordon[457].

In a minute of 10th September, the Bombay Council resolved:

…that the mint committee be directed to offer their opinion on the specimens of copper coins…

No coins dated 1819 are known so perhaps these still await discovery.

Henderson at first reported that the machinery would be ready for the production of the new copper coinage at the beginning of 1820[458]:

I have the honor to acknowledge the receipt of your letter dated the 10th instant authorizing the completion of the machinery considered to be required for conducting a copper coinage at the estimated expense of Rupees 1000, and calling on me to state the period by which it may be expected to be finished, and what arrangements appear to be necessary before it can be set to work in the preparation of the coinage.

I request you will be pleased to acquaint the Right Honble the Governor in Council that I have reason to expect the greater part, if not the whole of the machinery, will be in a state of readiness about the commencement of the ensuing year; and as it appears to be perfectly impracticable to carry on a copper coinage with machinery in the present mint, it would be necessary that some building would be rented and prepared for the purpose if there be no suitable public building unoccupied. There will not indeed be more than sufficient space for the coinage of gold and silver in the mint, the workmen being much crowded at present, and the contractor having complained of the inconvenience which he suffers from the limited extent of the buildings.

It would perhaps in the first place be advisable to ascertain whether if the ravelin until lately appropriated for the foundry, or that which was occupied by the Assay Master for refining gold and silver, be not otherwise required for the public service, the temporary buildings contained in either might not be so far added to and altered as to admit of their receiving the machinery, which may prove to be the least expensive plan upon the whole.

and the Bombay Council agreed with this suggestion[459]:

Ordered Mr Henderson be informed that we are not aware of any objection to either of the ravelins which have buildings on them suited for conducting a copper currency being appropriated to the services of the mint. Mr Henderson is therefore in communication with the superintending engineer to examine them and send in an estimate of the expense that

---

[457] Pridmore p. 134.

[458] Bombay Consultations. IOR P/411/39 p. 150. Letter from the mint master (Henderson) to government, dated 26th September.

[459] Bombay Consultations. IOR P/411/39 p. 150. minute 1st October 1819

would be incurred in rendering either of them available for the purposes required by Mr Henderson.

By November Henderson had to move the date that he could start the new copper coinage, back to February or March 1820. This was due to the fact that the private soldier who had prepared the dies had been sent back to England with his regiment. In addition, Henderson had realised that once the machinery was completed some time would be required to train the workmen[460]:

I have the honor to acknowledge the receipt of your letter of the 28th ultimo, calling on me to report when the machinery now constructing may be likely to be ready to begin a copper coinage if a place be appropriated for the purpose.

In my letter of the 26th ultimo, I offered an opinion that the machinery would be in readiness about the commencement of the ensuing year, but under the 4th paragraph of your letter to the mint committee of the 10th ultimo, it is probable, as improvements may be introduced, that its final completion will be delayed beyond that period.

The private of H.M. 65th regiment employed as a die sinker having been obliged to embark with the corps, this part of the work will be suspended until another can be procured. On the completion of the machinery it may likewise be sometime before the workmen to be employed can be sufficiently instructed in its operations.

I therefore request you will be pleased to acquaint the Honorable the Governor in Council that, under all these circumstances, the commencement of a copper coinage, if undertaken with the machinery authorised to be completed for the purpose, would in all probability be delayed until the month of February or March next.

A second problem facing Henderson was the fact that there was not enough room in the mint for the new machinery to operate. Various existing buildings, including the ravelins mentioned above, had been considered but rejected by the superintendent of engineers[461]:

In reply to your letter directing me to examine in communication with the Mint Master, the building in the ravelin lately appropriated to the foundry and in that which was occupied by the Assay Master, and to report if either be suited to the purposes required by Mr Henderson etc etc, I have the honor to state to you that I have examined with Mr Henderson both ravelins and the machinery for which accommodation is required, and am of the opinion that the buildings are not adapted to the purposes of Mr Henderson.

Mr Henderson is of opinion that by building in the ravelin for the accommodation of the machines for rolling copper, some of the old sheds now standing may be converted to minor uses, the magazine has been given up for furnaces etc, and should it be thought proper to

---

[460] Bombay Consultations. IOR P/411/39 p. 158. Letter from the mint master (Henderson) to government, dated 2nd November 1819.

[461] Bombay Consultations. IOR P/411/39 p. 196. Letter from R. Bentley (Superintendent of Engineers) to Lieutenant Co. Brookes (Chief Engineer), dated 23rd November 1819.

appropriate one of the ravelins of the place permanently in this way, the machinery I have seen may be accommodated.

I beg leave to submit that it may be within your recollection, the Cumberland ravelin has been contemplated as an airing ground for the convalescents of the garrison/hospital, which has never been adopted to ground immediately opposite to it, and is now upon reference to the Honble the Court of Directors for approval. This work has been also temporarily given by Government to me as a depot for my stores and a working place for my artificers.

and the mint master was asked whether he could find somewhere else (minute dated 4th December):

Ordered that the Mint Master be called upon to report whether there be no other place suitable for conducting a copper coinage as one of the outworks in the fort cannot be appropriated for the purposes of a mint.

By May 1820 no suitable building had been found and the machinery itself was still not ready[462]:

With reference to your letter under date 4th December last, I request you will acquaint the Honble the Governor General in Council that I do not know of any public or private building unoccupied within the fort, which would answer for the reception of the mint machinery. Among those occupied however one will probably be found of the required description, and (if private property) which the owners would agree to rent to the Government. The house formerly the property of General Jones appeared to me on inspection to be likely to answer with some alterations but it is appropriated by Messrs Remington & Co, to whom it now belongs, to particular purposes.

The Honble the Governor in Council will perhaps not feel disposed to sanction the erection of any buildings for this machinery under the expectation of machines being sent from Europe, which may entirely supersede the use of that now preparing, and would require a large building of peculiar construction. But if it should be considered inexpedient to rent a private house at probably a high rate, or appropriate for the purpose any of the public buildings now occupied, which I conclude cannot be done, I am not aware of any other plan that can be adopted. If the expense of erecting substantial buildings cannot be incurred, some of a slighter structure might be added to those in which the coinage is at present conducted, and which are of the same description. But it would be requisite that very particular precautions should be taken for the safety of the machinery etc.

In the event of this being resolved upon in preference to renting a building, it will no doubt be advisable to ascertain in the first instance, that there is no apparent possibility of the machinery failing in its operations, which cannot be known until its final completion and repeated and more extensive trials be made of its powers.

---

[462] Bombay Consultations. IOR P/411/40 p. 59. Letter from the mint master (Henderson) to government, dated 19th May 1820.

Not only was Henderson having difficulty finding a building to house his equipment, but the gun carriage department still wanted their men and equipment returned and he was asked when this might happen[463]:

Ordered that the Mint Master be called upon to report how long he will require the use of the foundry and artificers of the Gun Carriage Department under the permission granted to his predecessor under the date 10th November 1818

and in July 1820 he replied[464]:

I have the honor to acknowledge the receipt of your letter dated the 8th instant calling on me to report how long the use of the foundry and the artificers of the Gun Carriage Department will be required by this department, it having been represented that if their use be continued, it will be necessary for the Agent to have recourse to the Coppersmith in the bazaar.

In respect to the use of the foundry, I have not been called upon to state the extent of the assistance latterly afforded by it to the mint. It will be necessary only to report that the models of the articles required to complete the machinery have been since the 8th March at the Foundry, and that I am not aware that it will occupy more than two days at most of the founder's time to cast the whole. It is possible however, if any further alterations in the machinery should prove necessary, as well as any repairs after it may come into use, that the occasional altho' very limited assistance of the foundry may be hereafter required.

In regard to the artificers of the gun carriage department, unless the founder be meant, this probably alludes to the chief workman employed on the machinery who was formerly in that department, but who cannot I conclude, have been on its list of establishment since he began to receive his salary from this department. I beg leave further to observe in respect to this person, whom I found employed on the machinery when I received charge of it, that the Government will have chiefly to depend on his practical mechanical skill for its completion, and for keeping it in repair after the coinage may commence.

By July 1820 the machinery appeared to be sufficiently advanced that the mint committee felt that they should reply to the letter received from Government the previous September asking their opinion of the pattern coins submitted the previous August (i.e. 1819). They were very positive in their recommendation[465]:

As the mint machinery may probably be soon completed, we have now the honor to reply to the letter from Mr Acting Chief Secretary Newnham of the 10th September last.

In the second paragraph we are called upon to report whether the specimens of coins which accompanied the Mint Master's letter to the Government of the 31st August, are sufficiently

---

[463] Bombay Consultations. IOR P/411/40 p. 67. Minute dated 8th July 1820.

[464] Bombay Consultations. IOR P/411/40 p. 71. Letter from the mint master (Henderson) to government, dated 15th July 1820.

[465] Bombay Consultations. IOR P/411/40 p. 71. Letter from the mint committee (consisting of: J Best, Sub-treasurer; J Wedderburn, Accountant General; J Henderson, mint master; B Noton, assay master) to government, dated 20th July 1820.

well executed to allow of their being sent in circulation.

However little these coins will admit of a comparison with the copper coins executed in England, some of which are still to be seen in circulation, there can be no difference of opinion as to their superiority over those executed in this country of which nearly the whole currency is composed. We should therefore have no difficulty in recommending their issue as the Government coin, if reliance can be placed (as we think it can) on the whole being executed as well as the specimens which have been submitted.

Much further improvement cannot, we apprehend, be expected with the means now at command, except possibly in the strength of the impression.

They further recommended that the new copper coinage should consist of a pice (pie) of 33⅓ grains, a pice of 100 grains (i.e. 3 pies) to be called a quarter anna to avoid confusion with the smaller '*pice of account*', a half anna and a one anna coin.

In the 3ʳᵈ paragraph we are desired to report whether the specimens correspond in weight and divisions with the principles laid down in the 7ᵗʰ paragraph of the Committee's report of the 15ᵗʰ February 1817, and whether the gain contemplated in that report will be realized from the issue of such a currency.

The seventh paragraph of the report recommended the division of 64 pice to the rupee as the best upon the whole, and the weight of 122½ grains troy each, as the lowest to which it would be then prudent to reduce them.

The reasons for considering the division of 64 to the rupee as the best will still operate, but it will be seen that the committee contemplate a considerably greater reduction in the weight, if machinery were to be employed in executing the coinage, and that they might be issued at double their intrinsic value. It was in reference to this opinion that the specimens were prepared, and the weight was meant to be brought as nearly as possible to 100 grains each pice. The principle that copper may be considered a subsidiary currency throughout our territory, being laid down, and inconvenience having occurred in Bengal, as far as our information goes, from the issue of a currency at a similarly reduced rate, this question seems to call for no further observation. If therefore the weight of what would thus be the pice were fixed at 100 grains, it would only remain to fix the weights of its subdivisions.

But as it appears to be a desirable object to introduce at this Presidency the denominations of the subordinate monies of account, prevalent in Bengal and Madras, we should propose in view to a correspondence with this new money of account, the following denominations and divisions to be adopted in the new copper coinage. The money of account would stand as follows

12 pice 1 anna

16 annas 1 rupee

which will therefore contain 192 pice, and this we should recommend as the lowest denomination of our currency, each pice to contain 33⅓ grains. Then 3 pice – 1 qr anna; a name which we should propose to be assigned to what would be the 100 grain pice above noticed, which would otherwise create a confusion with the pice of account; and then 2 qrs annas – 1 half anna; and 2 half annas – 1 anna; a change from which we do not think any public inconvenience can arise, since in fact at the present moment the copper payments in the market are always made as payment in annas.

Prospectively when a new silver coinage may be introduced, we should contemplate the following gradations in the silver coins Viz:

⅛ *of a Rupee – 2 annas*
¼ *of a Rupee – 4 annas*
½ *of a rupee – 8 annas*
1 rupee – 16 annas

but on this point it is unnecessary to dwell at present.

This is the first mention of the name 'quarter anna' for the 100 grain coin. Up until then, coins of this size had been referred to as 'pice'. The mint committee then went on to discuss the profit that might be made from a copper coinage:

On the question of the profit which may be realised from the coinage, the committee were of opinion that if a regular mint were established, in which the whole currency might be coined with machinery, the profits on a copper coinage would be very considerable, supposing that the establishment, which would be a fixed monthly charge, did not require to be increased, but continued the same, whether copper were coined in the mint or not; the profit on an issue of two lacks of rupees would be one lack.

It will be seen however that this calculation of the profit does not apply to the present state of things. The whole cost of the machinery and the whole expense of a separate establishment will have, perhaps, to be charged against the coinage. It would be extremely difficult if not altogether impracticable to frame an estimate of the possible profits, on which much reliance could be placed – a good deal will depend upon the expertise of the workmen in leaving the least possible quantity of sizel, and on the number of perfect blanks which may be turned out from the cutting and stamping presses. Much will also depend on the quickness of the process, on the number of the workmen to be employed, the price of the copper and sizel in the market and the article required in the operations of cleaning. But we may calculate on a greater profit than has been of late realised from the copper coinage at the Presidency, which is only 1.2.78 per cent.

Next, what improvements could be made to the machinery?

The 4th paragraph instructs us to avail ourselves of the opinions of any persons who may be able to suggest improvements in the machinery.

The Honble Board are aware that the late Dr Stewart was compelled to proceed to Europe from indisposition before he was able to complete even the outline of the machinery. Some instructions were left however with the head workman, and chiefly from these, from his own ingenuity and from the suggestions that have been offered from one or two persons whom we have been able to consult, the machinery stated in the Mint Master's letter of 31st August to be necessary for a copper coinage has been at length nearly completed.

In consequence of the little assistance which has latterly been afforded from the foundry, one rolling mill is unfinished, but this and the dies are all that remain incomplete.

The chief difficulties which appear to us to remain, are the execution of the dies, the apparent want of power in the stamping presses to make a sufficiently strong impression and the adjusting rolling.

The die sinker mentioned in the above letter was able only to afford his services occasionally, as it was found impracticable to transfer him from His Majesty's 65th regiment to the Honble Company's European regiment, and we have lately been deprived of them altogether. We have now however another on employment who will answer the purpose sufficiently. There has been considerable difficulty in getting any of the dies properly tempered, in consequence of which most of those yet tried have become useless after striking a few impressions. This has however now been surmounted in a considerable degree.

The mint committee went on to discuss the lack of depth of design that was achieved on the coins produced by the machines, as well as the design itself:

…It is rather difficult to say whether the present faintness in the impression arises from the mode in which the presses have been constructed or from a fault in the dies, but we are induced to think the former, because every alteration yet tried in the dies (which will if practicable be sunk with punches) has proved but little effect. It is possible enough that it may arise from the screws of the presses being only two threaded, and a model of a four threaded screw has therefore been prepared by the head workman, which when cast in the foundry, will be tried. If it arises from any general defect in the mode of constructing the press, we fear the hoped of remedy are but little. The only further observation which it seems necessary to offer in respect to the impression is that it should be rendered as difficult of imitation as possible, and we think that it will not be easy for any native artist to imitate successfully that struck on the coinage of 1804, sent out from Europe, which might therefore be adopted and which will no doubt sufficiently meet the wishes of the Honble Court on this point.

When the weight of the pice is to be so much reduced, coining would become so profitable an occupation that it might be imprudent to adopt any more simple impression.

and they went on to discuss the fact that the weight of each coin might vary by up to four grains (i.e. 4%):

In respect to the adjusting rollers, to which point our attention is drawn in the 5th paragraph, the last experiment which has been made, clearly shows that a less variation then 4 grains on each side of the standard weight, cannot be confidently expected with the means at our command. The rollers of the mill and the smaller ones intended to be used for the adjusting, have been turned with as much exactness as seems to be in the power of the head workman, whose skill must be considered to rank high.

Of about 190 blanks, cut out of seven or eight copper slips, passed through the rollers, a considerable number vary as much as 4 grains, and a trial of this extent may be held to have decided the question. A good deal of skill and attention, it is true, are required in the process, but we do not think much dependence is to be placed on a decrease of the variation, from longer practice on the part of the workmen, considering the inherent defects of machinery of this kind. We are therefore of opinion that a remedy to this extent must be allowed in the coinage.

The mint committee then went on to discuss how much copper might be required for the coinage:

In the concluding paragraph we are called upon to state what quantity of sheet copper should be provided, if we might be of opinion on completion of the machinery that the coinage ought to be undertaken. It appears that a considerable quantity of sheet copper had been ordered round from Calcutta for the use of the mint, and the Mint Master has been directed to receive charge of the whole, the cost of which is Rupee 258,385. The Mint Master has stated that until the extent of the coinage and the weights and divisions of the coins to be struck be decided upon, he could not form an estimate of the quantity which would be required. He was also unable to say with any degree of precision, when the coinage could be commenced in consequence of the improvements and alterations which might be made in the machinery, and he had before shown that the process of coining would be extremely slow.

We have submitted in paragraph 5 our opinion with respect to the weights and divisions of the copper coinage. In respect to its extent, the committee in their report of the 30th April 1818, entertained an expectation that 5 lacks of rupees may perhaps be eventually required, and the subsequent increase which our territory has received will of course add considerably to that sum. It would be a matter of much difficulty to obtain any correct notion of the extent of the copper currency at present in circulation throughout our limits, and it may be here observed that on whatever part of it may come into the Company's treasuries, sooner or later after the issue of the new currency, the loss will be the difference between its value as a coin, and its value when melted down and sold as copper, and must be deducted from the profits of the new coinage. After making an allowance for what may have disappeared from the wear and tear of the coins, and ascertaining the quantities issued from the mint, it would be necessary in calculating the quantity in circulation to ascertain what may have disappeared, by having been exported or melted down, and what may have been brought into circulation by private coiners, all of which may have depended on the price of copper in the market. On these points it is impracticable to obtain any accurate information.

They then discussed the changes to the machinery that might be necessary:

It will be seen that the machinery may be still susceptible of improvement before the coinage commences. We think it probable that the frame containing the four cutting presses will have to be altered, so as to have each cutter separate, for as it now stands, as soon as they come to be a little ground down which must occur frequently from the sharp edge breaking, the lever of one will impede that of the next. But this would not be a long operation.

From the improvements which have been introduced since the Mint Master's letter of the 31st August, the process of coining will we expect go on faster than was contemplated at that time.

Finally the mint committee stated that if a new mint was really to be delivered from

England then they did not think that Dr. Stewart's machinery should be used for a coinage:

Having thus afforded the information required by the Government as far as we have the means of doing, accompanied by such further observations as the subject seemed to call for, and shown the progress which has been made in the machinery, we are yet compelled to hesitate before we can recommend that the coinage should commence at the present moment, even if it was complete and its power of executing a proper coinage were placed (as we anticipate) beyond a doubt.

It will be seen from what has already been said, that no reliance can be placed on the coinage realizing any considerable profit to the Company if executed with this machinery under so many disadvantages, and as we are given to understand that there is a probability of the erection of a mint being sanctioned by the Honble Court, and that European machinery will be sent out to this Presidency, it would in our opinion be advisable to ascertain these points to a certainty in the first instance. For it may appear that a much greater profit would be realized from the coinage being executed by the European machinery, by the rapidity of the process and the saving of labour, and the supersession of the necessity of employing a separate establishment. On the other hand it may appear that the new machinery may be less calculated to execute a copper than a gold & silver coinage, and that its wear and tear might be greatly increased by employing it in the execution of an extensive copper currency, in which case the machinery completed here might come into use under fewer disadvantages then at present.

If however it be found that the expectation of our receiving European machinery is likely to be disappointed, we can have no hesitation in recommending that the coinage should be commenced upon with the other as soon as circumstances might permit.

In the meantime, and indeed at all events, we think it would be advisable that the mint should be relieved of at least two thirds of the Bengal copper, which not only exceeds in price what can be procured here, but is besides in quantity much beyond what will be required in the first instance, with reference to the period which the coinage will occupy. Should the Honble Board concur in this opinion, the warehousekeeper may be directed to receive charge and dispose of it accordingly.

The coins examined by the mint committee may have included the known patterns for a quarter anna and twelfth anna dated 1820 (and AH 1235), which came to light in the Bonhams' listing. It is conceivable that these coins were produced in 1819 and dated 1820 because the machinery had been promised for the end of 1819 and production was planned to begin in 1820. However, it is more likely that the 1820 dated coins were produced as trials whilst the machinery was under construction in 1820 and that these were the coins examined by the mint committee in 1820. They are certainly very weakly struck and this would fit with their comments. If this latter assumption is true, then the 1819 coins still await discovery as aleady mentioned.

On 28th July 1820 a resolution to suspend the copper coinage was passed[466]:

---

[466] Bombay Consultations. IOR P/411/40 p. 71. Minute, 28th July 1820.

Resolved that the copper coinage be suspended until we shall learn finally whether machinery for conducting the coinage is likely to be sent from Europe.

Ordered that the warehouskeeper be directed to receive back two thirds of the copper received from Bengal for the use of the mint, to be disposed of to the best advantage.

Quarter Anna 1820 (Bonhams lot 415, 420 & 421)

Pie 1820 (Bonhams lot 416)

This resolution was to continue in force until the decision about sending machinery from England was finally made, one way or another, and this seemed like the end of the trial to build machinery locally for the Bombay mint. But the story does not end there.

By November 1821 the mint committee was in a position to submit to Government its report on the reform of the coinage of Bombay[467]:

…Of course little can be done towards carrying these views, even if approved, into execution, until the actual arrival of the machinery from England, since it would be unsafe to commence building for its reception without more accurate knowledge than we possess of its dimensions, but it has occurred to us that we might, without interfering with, or impeding, the erection of the more perfect European machinery, which we would recommend to be reserved for the coinage of gold and silver exclusively, contrive to set in motion the machinery projected and begun by the late Dr Stewart, and which for some time past has been constructed [?] in this country for the coinage of copper.

As a proof of its powers, we beg leave to hand up for the inspection of your honble Board a few specimens of copper coins (Viz 6 annas, 6 half ditto, 6 quarter ditto, 6 pice), recently

---

[467] Bombay Consultations. IOR P/411/40, 1821, p. 95. Letter from the mint committee to government, dated 20th November 1821.

struck by it, which appear to us of highly respectable execution, and should any question arise as to the expediency of having two sets of machinery, we beg leave to observe that we consider it of the utmost importance that we should, both with a view to expedition, and of saving as much as possible the European machinery, which, in the event of accident, we should find it so difficult to repair.

What we would propose therefore is that, as Dr Stewart's machinery may now be said to be completed, since dies only are wanting, which can easily be supplied long before they will be required, a vacant space of considerable extent – say three hundred feet in length and fifty in breadth – be immediately enclosed simply by a wall, and that along the inside of the back wall of the quadrangle, a line of rough but substantial sheds be built, capable of containing the machinery in question, with one or two strong casements, for the safe custody of the copper in course of coinage.

This enclosure, we entertain no doubts from the general knowledge we possess of the dimensions of the European machinery, will afford ample space for both, and will even admit of the copper coinage proceeding whilst the buildings for the other machinery are erecting, which, if practicable, will obviously be a very desirable arrangement.

The site we would recommend for the enclosure, is that on which the new mint was formerly proposed to be built, namely the space to the eastward of the mint tank, between the rear of the town barracks and the north east angle of the castle, and we have only further to add that, as it has become indispensably necessary to provide some building for the reception of the machinery here at all events, the plan we have suggested can hardly prove a very expensive experiment, even should our expectations of receiving machinery from England be disappointed.

The Bombay Government initially agreed with the proposal to construct the buildings described by the mint committee[468]:

I am directed by the Honble the Governor General in Council to acknowledge the receipt of your letter dated the 20th of last month, on the subject of a general reform of the currency under this Presidency…

…The enclosing a space of ground is sanctioned as you have suggested and corresponding instructions have been issued to the commandant of the garrison and the chief engineer has been directed in consultation with you to build sheds for the reception of the machinery for copper coinage constructed by the late Dr Stewart, which you are authorised to be complete.

As can be seen from the above two extracts, although the Committee knew that machinery would be arriving from England, they recommended that Dr Stewart's machinery should be used to produce the copper coins, thereby saving the new European machinery for the gold and silver coinages. This would also have the advantage that the new copper coinage could begin as soon as an appropriate

---

[468] Bombay Consultations. IOR P/411/40, 1821, p. 95. To the mint committee from government, dated 4th December 1821.

building was found.

Despite agreement to rehouse Dr. Stewart's machinery, by December 1821, the machinery was still stored in the house originally occupied by Dr Stewart and was looked after by a Parsee specially employed for the job[469]:

[In?] the mint machinery constructed in this country still remains in the premises of the house formerly belonging to the late Dr Stewart, under the care of a respected Parsee, who has long been employed on that duty, and whose wages, sixteen rupees a month, have hitherto been defrayed out of a small balance remaining in the hands of the Mint Master, on account of petty supplies, but which is now exhausted, we beg to recommend that the Parsee in question may be placed on the strength of the mint establishment from the 1st instant, either until proper buildings can be erected for the reception of the machinery, or until further orders.

It was agreed that the man responsible for looking after the machinery should be put on the mint establishment from the 1st December 1821[470]:

Resolved on the grounds of the Committee's recommendation, that the Parsee employed in taking care of the machinery constructed by the late Dr Stewart, be placed on the mint establishment from the 1st of this month until proper buildings can be erected for the reception of the machinery or until further orders.

Thus, the mint machinery remained in Dr Stewart's house throughout 1821 and the pattern coins dated 1821 must have been produced there. These coins have an AH date of 1231 on the reverse. This equates with an AD date of 1815/16. Quite why the coins bear this anomalous Hijri date is not known. Pridmore has speculated that the final Persian numeral 1 may have been intended as a Persian 7. It is also possible that the only dies available were those from Dr Stewart's earliest experiments, which he appears to have started in 1817 (see above for list of equipment available in 1819 including dies). However, the quarter anna of this series is named as such and therefore probably the dies were produced after July 1820 when the Bombay Council agreed to this epithet for the coin. Neither of these explanations seems very good. Perhaps it was just ignorance on the part of the die engraver?

There seem to be two series of these 1821 coins. One with the denominations expressed as e.g. ONE HALF ANNA and the other with the denominations expressed simply as e.g. HALF ANNA. Some denominations are missing from these sets but this may be because they have not yet been discovered. Whether all of these coins were submitted to the Bombay Council at the same time, or not, is not clear. It may be that different sets were prepared as trials and only one chosen for submission to the Council.

---

[469] Bombay Consultations. IOR P/411/40 p. 117. Letter from the mint committee (including J Bouchier as Acting mint master) to government, dated 4th December 1821.
[470] Bombay Consultations. IOR P/411/40 p. 117. Minute, 12th December 1821.

Quarter Anna 1821 (Pridmore 335)

Half Anna 1821 (Pridmore sale, lot 560)

Anna 1821 (Bonhams lot 413 & 419)

Half Anna 1821 (Bonhams lot 414 & 419)

Pie (Twelfth Anna), 1821 (Bonhams lot 417, 418 & 419)

In February 1822, the chief engineer submitted a plan for the new building and this was estimated to cost between Rs 36,000 and Rs 42,000[471], which was considered rather high and was never proceeded with:

With reference to Mr Deputy Secretary Simson's letter of the 4th December, I now forward a plan and two estimates for enclosing a space for the new mint, with substantial sheds for the copper coinage. The instructions contained in the letter alluded to, direct rough but substantial sheds and, agreeably to that idea, the design and estimate marked No 1 has been prepared, the amount being rupees 36,402-2-49. The surrounding wall is proposed to be 12 feet high, which may perhaps be proper to secure the premises.

I enclose a copy of the Civil Engineer's report forwarded with his estimate, in which he suggests a different design marked No 2 at an expense of 42,286-3-07, framed agreeably to the opinion of the mint committee, and certainly if the machinery to be used is connected with the buildings, it may when in action have a tendency to shake and displace the tiles. In this view the terrace roof would be preferable.

On the estimates I have no remarks to offer.

This was passed to the mint committee:

---

[471] Bombay Consultations. IOR P/411/41, 1822, p. 25. Letter from the chief engineer (W. Brooks) to government, dated 26th February 1822.

Bombay Consultations. IOR P/411/41, 1822, p. 31. Letter from government to the mint committee, dated 12th March 1822.

In reference to your letter dated 20th November last, I am directed to inform you that the Civil Engineer has laid before the Honorable the Governor in Council an estimate of the expense that will be incurred in enclosing a new mint with substantial sheds of terraced roof for the accommodation of the machinery constructed under the superintendence of the late Dr Stewart for coining copper, amounting to Rupees 42,286..3..07.

The Honble the Governor in Council desires your opinion as to the necessity for incurring so heavy an expense under the prospects entertained of receiving complete mint machinery from England.

The plan and estimate transmitted for your inspection you will be pleased to return.

In July 1822, there was a suggestion that Dr Stewart's machinery should be moved temporarily to the mint[472]:

It will be in the recollection of the Honble Board that when the late Dr Stewart made over to the charge of Government some mint machinery which he had undertaken, it was permitted to remain on the premises where it then was to be completed and has remained there free of expense of rent to Government ever since.

Circumstances however requiring that everything belonging to the mint should now be taken away from thence as early as may be convenient, and Government having deferred erecting it for coinage for the present, I beg to suggest that I may be authorised to bring it to the mint in the first instance, to be stowed there until we commence coining again, and require the room, when some other place for its reception must be obtained.

and this was agreed:

I am directed by the Honble the Governor in Council, to acknowledge the receipt of your letter dated the 30th ultimo, and to authorise you to remove to the mint premises the machinery undertaken by the late Doctor Stewart as you suggest.

However, in the same letter the Governor was informed that a warehouse had been rented for the machinery at a cost of fifty rupees per month and Government was asked to sanction this expenditure:

I have the honor to acquaint you for the information of the Honorable the Governor in Council, that I have engaged a warehouse in town at the rate of fifty rupees per month, for the purpose of keeping therein the mint machinery, iron, steel etc, belonging to the Honorable Company, which were formerly in the house of late Doctor Stewart.

I request the Honorable the Governor in Council will have the goodness to direct the Civil Paymaster to discharge the bill for the rent of the said warehouse monthly, and instruct the Town Major to allow a Centry (sic) for watching it.

---

[472] Bombay Consultations. IOR P/411/41, 1822, p. 50. Letter from the acting mint master (J Bourchier) to government, dated 30th July 1822.

Bombay Consultations. IOR P/411/41, 1823, p. 20. Letter from the acting mint master (J Bourchier) to government dated 4th April 1823.

and this action was also approved:

I am directed to acknowledge the receipt of your letter dated the 4 instant and to inform you that the Honorable the Governor in Council approves of your having engaged a warehouse within the Fort for the mint machinery, iron, steel etc formerly kept in the house of the late Doctor Stewart.

The Civil paymaster has been instructed to discharge the rent amounting to rupees 50 per month from the date of the warehouse having been engaged.

As it is presumed the machinery is not to be in use while in warehouse it does not seem necessary to appoint a military Centry (sic) over it but you will adopt the same means as are found sufficient in other departments for the security of goods in warehouse.

In 1824 the machinery was moved into the mint[473]:

I have the honor to report for the information of the Honble the Governor in Council, that the buildings in the mint having been available for the reception of the machinery, Iron, steel, etc lodged in the warehouse, which I am authorized to engage under date the 8th of April last, I have given up the warehouse from the 29th of last month.

In 1825 it was suggested that the machinery should be broken up and disposed of to various departments, including, ironically, the gun carriage manufactory[474]:

We request you will have the goodness to submit to the Honble the Governor in Council that the article contained in the enclosed list belonging to the mint machinery constructed by the late Dr Stewart and which Captain Hawkins has examined and stated will be of no use in the new mint, be distributed to the several departments therein suggested, and that Mr B Mulholland, the European artificer now in charge of them, and who is a most able workman, be retained for the service of the new mint and placed at the disposal of Captain Hawkins

Articles to be transferred for the use of the Stamp Office, Gun Carriage Department and Civil Engineers Department

6 Stamp presses with 7 spare screws and their brass boxes complete	*For treasure and Stamp Office*
12 cast steel dies ready forged which may be made for treasury dies	
5 cutting presses with 6 spare male and female cutters of sizes	*For Gun Carriage Department*
2 rolling mills with 4 spare cog wheels	
1 slitting machine for slitting copper	

Continued on next page

---

[473] Bombay Consultations. IOR P/411/42, 1824, p. 33. Letter from the acting mint master to government, dated 30th March 1824.

[474] Bombay Consultations. IOR P/411/44, 16th February, No. 3, 4, 5. Letter from the mint committee to government, dated 5th February 1825.

1 large turning lathe with 1 large flywheel	
1 spare spindle and brass lock	
6 iron rests	
15 iron turning tools	
4 iron callipers	
1 brass ditto	
5 iron catches	*For Civil*
1 small turning lathe with 2 brass chocks	*Engineer*
10 tools for turning wood	*Department*
3 iron rests and fly wheel	
1 foot lathe with 5 caste iron chocks	
12 tools for turning brass	
2 iron rests	
1 screw cutting lathe with 1 additional regulating screw & brass box *Two popet* [a type of valve?]	

A quantity of unserviceable articles such as carpenter's and smith's tools stated in the inventory may be sold by public auction

87 dies ready sunk may be defaced

134 steel types can be defaced and sold for the worth of the steel

This proposal was accepted[475]:

I am directed to acknowledge receipt of your letter dated the 5th instant recommending that the articles belonging to the machinery constructed by the late Dr Stewart may be made over to certain departments and that the European artificer in charge of them should be retained for the service of the mint and placed at the disposal of Captain Hawkins.

The Honble the Governor in Council acquiescing in your recommendations authorizes you to give them effect.

Eighty-seven dies that had already been sunk were ordered to be defaced, so there were a lot of dies available, any of which could have been used to produce the coins described herein. In the same letter it was reported that Mr B Mulholland, the person who had built most of the machinery, would continue to be employed on the mint establishment and would help Captain Hawkins with the erection of a new mint due to arrive from England (see chapter 7).

---

[475] Bombay Consultations. IOR P/411/44, 16th February, No. 3, 4, 5. Letter from government to the mint committee, dated 5th February 1825.

Chapter 7 – Bombay Mint – Introduction of Steam

Summary

The Bombay mint was unable to supply the volume of coinage needed to meet the expansion of the Presidency following the third Maratha war. Both the machinery and mint buildings had been in a state of decay for years and a decision was finally made to send a major Hawkins to England to investigate the purchase of machinery from there. Eventually it was agreed that the steam driven machinery of the Soho mint in Birmingham would be purched from Boulton and Watt and this machinery was disassembled, packed-up and sent to Bombay together with a team of engineers capable of rebuilding it.

The reconstruction did not prove easy and it was not until 1832 that the first coins were produced.

Discussions about Replacing the Bombay Mint

The possibility of introducing machinery from England into the Bombay mint had been discussed for many years before any action was actually taken. As early as August 1801, the mint and assay master had discussed a report on the coinage produced by a Mr Constable and they had proposed the introduction of machinery[476]:

…We have, Honble Sir, recommended before now, in the strongest manner, the adoption of Europe stamps such as the machinery of Bolton and Watts for our coinage. If this recommendation should be adopted, we beg leave to remind you of W. Goodhew who is not only extremely well qualified to execute such a scheme (and he has offered to do it without additional expense to the Honble Company but who has some claim to your favour from the attention he has paid to the subject). Nobody knows our wants better than he does, nor is any person better qualified to satisfy them.

Again, in 1811, the Bombay mint master had considered the possibility of obtaining a steam-driven mint but nothing further was done at the time (see chapter 5, p. 172).

In 1817 the Bengal Council considered the state of the Bombay mint but stated that any decision to change the mint there would have to be taken by the authorities in Bombay itself[477]:

…The sentiments entertained by this Government [i.e. Bengal] of placing the mint of Bombay on a proper footing entirely correspond with those conveyed in the dispatch from this department under date the 20th April last, but under the present circumstances of this Government, the Right Honble the Governor in Council will recognise the force of the considerations under which the Honble the Vice President in Council feels himself constrained

---

[476] Bombay Public Consultations. IOR P/342/49 p. 2751. Letter from the mint master (J.A. Grant) and the assay master (A. Scott) to government, dated 31st August 1801.

[477] Bombay mint Proceedings. IOR P/411/37 (1817). p. 81 Letter from Bengal (Governor General) to Bombay government, dated 18th July 1817.

to leave the practical question, which forms the subject of your dispatch, to the decision of the Government of Bombay.

The Bombay Council inserted a minute in the records ordering that the subject of placing the Bombay mint on a proper footing should be brought to the notice of the Court of Directors in London and this must have had some effect because the Bombay Council next learnt of the intention of the Board in London to buy a new mint in 1819 (see chapter 6, p. 181). In 1821 the Bombay mint committee sent a letter to the Bombay Council discussing the plans that needed to be made if and when this came about[478]:

Information on which, though unofficial, we conceive reliance may be placed, having lately reached us through several private channels that the Honble the Court of Directors have actually ordered a set of the most improved modern machinery for the services of the mint at this Presidency, we are induced again to revive the subject, and represent the expediency of undertaking a general reform of our currency, which we have never indeed entirely lost sight of, but which the little prospect there seemed to be of our ever possessing the means of accomplishing has, for some time past, discouraged us from bringing under discussion.

In their letter the mint committee stated that it was obvious that a new uniform system of coinage was needed but that they had been unable to take the necessary steps to rectify the problem because of the cost. However, since the Board had now decided to buy a new mint, the cost was not now an impediment:

That a different currency prevails in almost every different district subordinate to this Presidency, and the inconveniences both public and private that must attend such a state of things, are already fully known to your Honble Board. It is not therefore our intention to repeat here, nor to endeavour to strengthen the arguments so often urged by us in former reports, in favour of an uniformity of system. The advantages of such a system, both to the financial arrangements of Government, and the interests of commerce, hardly at any time need illustration. The real question was whether these advantages were likely to compensate the immediate expense involving the erection of a new mint, and the cost of machinery necessary to carry the measure into effect.

But as even this point may now, from the step taken by the Honble Court, be considered as decided in the affirmative, all that apparently remains to be discussed is the standard that should be adopted for the new currency, together with the best means of introducing it into circulation.

The letter went on to discuss the idea that Bombay should adopt the same currency standards as Bengal and Madras both for circulating coin and for their money of account:

---

[478] Bombay Consultations. IOR P/411/40, 1821, p. 95. Letter from the mint committee to government, dated 20th November 1821.

So many inconveniences attend all alterations in the standard of the current coin that had we only the circumstances of this Presidency to consult we should be much disposed to recommend that none should be made, but it would be taking a very narrow view of the subject, on an occasion of such general concern, not to have reference to what has been done at Bengal and Madras.

We have accordingly reperused with attention, the several documents quoted in the margin and, finding that the standard proposed by the Honble Court in their orders of 25th April 1806, for the whole of British India (which differs indeed very little from the present Bombay standard) has, after the most mature deliberation, been adopted at both these Presidencies, and as the alteration will not materially affect either existing contracts, or the expenses of the Government, we are of opinion in the event of the reform we contemplate in our currency taking place, that it would afford a most favourable opportunity, and one that ought not to be neglected, of introducing the same standard here.

With the view of assimilating still more the monetary system of the three Presidencies, we would propose to adopt at the same time, the same divisions as now obtain on the other side of India, for our money of account, namely rupees, annas and pice, instead of Rupees, Quarters and Reas, but in all other respects to consult as much as possible, local convenience, as for instance in the sub divisions and denominations of the coins with which, as given in the 6th paragraph of our letter of the 20th July 1820, our native subjects are already in practice sufficiently familiar.

They produced a table (not shown here) showing the proposed new system and, in particular, proposed that the gold rupee should be dropped:

The accompanying tables of the weight and assay of the coins, of the exchangeable value and of the money of account, will exhibit at one view, the whole of the proposed new monetary system which, whether regard be had to the smallness and regularity of the subdivisions, or the adaptation of the money of circulation to the money of account, appears to us better suited to the wants and conveniences of the lower, and therefore most numerous, orders of the community, than any other with which we are acquainted. The only coin in the whole that seems likely to objection, and that chiefly on account of its small size, which renders it inconvenient, is the gold rupee, and we would therefore recommend its issue to be restricted to cases of urgent necessity.

The letter went on to discuss in principle how they might get the new coins into circulation and that coins produced by other polities in the area would have to be stopped. As will be seen, both these matters came to cause much concern when the new coinage was actually produced:

With regards to the best means of introducing the new system into general operation, much previous enquiry and correspondence with the local authorities will be necessary before the course of proceeding can be exactly defined, for which however there will be ample time and opportunity before the mint can be completed, and other necessary preparations be made. All that we can pretend to offer at present are a few general remarks on the principles that should be observed on the occasion.

We assume as a matter of course that your Honble Board would not wish to make any alteration in the metal (silver) that is actually the principle circulation medium, nor that the circulation of the gold coins should be extended beyond the Presidency and its immediate neighbourhood, to which they are at present confined for, although the gold coin has long been considered, and has lately been declared by [some] to be the standard currency at home, it seems quite clear that the general wealth of our native subjects is not such as to require so valuable a material for the purpose. The new copper coin as a subsidiary currency, we conclude, would be introduced universally.

The stoppages of all other coinages and the abolition of all other currencies, are obviously necessary conditions to the successful introduction of the new system, though it will depend on the result of the enquiries referred to in a preceding paragraph, whether we shall be able to introduce it into all our districts simultaneously, or whether we must be contented to do it gradually, district by district. We must also trust to the same enquiries to guide us with regard to the amount of gold, silver or copper coin, as the case may be, that will be required for each district and the time that should be allowed for withdrawing the old currencies from circulation.

The subject of the exchange rate was then discussed. For the coins struck in silver and gold, the exchange of old coins for new would be straight forward, but the new copper coinage was to be, in effect, a token coinage and the mint committee, rightly as it turned out, considered that this might cause a problem. They proposed that all copper coins, whether produced before the arrival of the EIC or during their time in power, as well as those produced unofficially, should be exchanged for their nominal values:

…Even here however, as far as regards the gold and silver currencies, the value of which in circulation must always depend ultimately on their intrinsic value, we hold the rule that Government should bear the expense of the re-coinage, and the old currencies should be held exchangeable for the new, according to their respective intrinsic values, to be both clearly equitable, and that usually followed in well ordered states. But as it is to be otherwise with the new copper currency, which is to circulate at a nominal value considerably above its intrinsic value, it will be necessary to lay down other rules for its exchange with the old currency.

The experiment of issuing a copper currency on these principles having completely succeeded in Bengal, doubtless from the superiority of the execution, and the impossibility of the natives of the country imitating coins struck by machinery, and from their issue being limited to the real wants of the community, it must be unnecessary for us to enter into any arguments to prove the practicability of the measure, and we shall confine our enquiries therefore to an examination to the best means of effecting the change, that is to say with the least expense to Government and the smallest loss or inconvenience to the subject.

The local copper currencies will generally, we believe, be found to consist of several different descriptions, namely of such as have remained from former times or such as have been coined under the immediate sanction of Government since the district came into our possession, and of others of private manufacture which the wants or convenience of the community have admitted into circulation.

With regard to the two former descriptions, it seems but common justice that the holders should not be subjected to loss by the introduction of the new system, and as the last could hardly maintain their ground, unsanctioned by authority without an high intrinsic value, it cannot be foregoing any great advantage, whilst it would be an act of liberal consideration on the part of Government, to admit the holders to an equality with the others.

We would accordingly propose that all three descriptions of the old copper currencies shall be held exchangeable for the new, at their respective nominal values, that is to say that the number to be held equivalent to a rupee in the new currency, shall be given for the number usually passing current for a rupee in the old, without regard to their weight.

As can be seen, they proposed that all copper coins, whether official or otherwise should be exchanged at their nominal values. The exchange of the copper coins on this basis could be liable to fraud and caution would be necessary in this regard:

Even in effecting this exchange, however, it will be necessary for the local authorities to use great caution to prevent frauds, in regard to the number of old copper coins usually exchanged for a rupee, as well as in regard to the metal of which they are composed, which, though professedly copper, is, in fact, occasionally lead and of little or no value. These last should, of course be rejected though they are more likely to prove counterfeits than coins acknowledgedly current.

The mint committee recognised that whilst gold and silver coins could be re-coined, the cost of doing this with the copper coins would be too great and these would have to be sold for their metal content:

The old local gold and silver coins, which the introduction of the new system will cause to accumulate in the different public treasuries will, of course, be sent to the mint for re-coinage, whilst the old copper coins must, we apprehend, be disposed of for what they will fetch as old copper merely, since any attempt to recoin them would be attended with an expense wholly disproportionate to the object.

Because the old copper coins were heavier and contained more copper than the new, the mint committee believed that they would be exported or used for other purposes:

We entertain confident expectations however, that the circumstances of the superior intrinsic value of the old copper coins will occasion them to be exported, or converted to other uses, rather than exchanged for the new currency. Of the probability of this the local authorities will perhaps be the best judges, but at all events the effect cannot, after operations are commenced, remain uncertain, and our subsequent proceedings cannot be regulated accordingly.

Following this, in December 1821, the mint committee was asked to obtain the views of the several Collectors throughout the Presidency[479]:

I am directed by the Honble the Governor General in Council to acknowledge the receipt of your letter dated the 20th of last month, on the subject of a general reform of the currency under this Presidency.

The Governor in Council requests you will be pleased to draft and submit a series of distinct queries as the most effectual mode of obtaining from the Commissioner in the Deckan and the several Collectors such information as they can collect on the subject to which it refers, as well as their opinion generally on the question…

Building the New Mint

Doty has given a detailed description of the introduction of machinery into the Bombay mint[480]. On 21st June 1821, Captain JohnJohn Hawkins wrote to Thomas Reid, Chairman of the Court of Directors, concerning the state of the mint at Bombay and declaring that the need for improvement was even greater than that at Calcutta, given that the only tools then in use for minting coins at Bombay were '*Hammer, Chisell and Punch*'.

Negotiations with Boulton, Watt and Co. for a new mint for Bombay (as well as Calcutta) had begun in 1820 and, as early as this, one of the options considered was for the EIC to purchase the working mint at Soho, disassemble it, ship it to Bombay and re-build it there.

Hawkins was the representative of the Bombay authorities in this matter and had arrived in England either late in 1820 or early in 1821. He visited Soho in May 1821 and saw the mint striking the St. Helena coinage and was completely enamoured of the apparatus and totally convinced that this was what was needed for the Bombay mint.

On 25th June 1822, the EIC asked Boulton, Watt & Co. for an estimate of the cost of shipping the Soho mint to Bombay and also asked them to act as the primary contractor. The total cost came to £37,824 which was agreed, although work did not start until February 1823 by when the price had increased to £40,016.

In a letter dated June 1823, the Court of Directors confirmed to Bombay that new coining machinery had been purchased and would be delivered to London on 24th April of the following year. The mint committee was informed of this in December 1823[481]:

---

[479] Bombay Consultations. IOR P/411/40, 1821, p. 95. To the mint committee from government, dated 4th December 1821.

[480] Doty R., (1998), The Soho mint & the Industrialization of money, Smithsonian Institution with Spink & the British Numismatic Society

[481] Bombay Consultations. IOR P/411/41, 1823, p. 83. Letter from Bombay assay master (Noton) to Bombay government dated 26th December 1823.

In reference to your letter of the 20th September last, to the Mint committee transmitting the copy of a letter from the Honble the Court of Directors dated the 4th June last stating that they had purchased for this Presidency a complete set of coining machinery which would be delivered to them in London in the month of April 1824…

Hawkins sailed for India on 18th April 1824. On 13th September 1824 the Bombay authorities were informed that the machinery for the mint had been loaded on two ships with a number of mechanics who would build and operate it[482].

The whole of the machinery intended for the mint at Bombay being entirely completed, it is now loading on the ships Florentia and England which we have taken up for that service.

The particulars of the several parts of the machinery with the numbers, weights and marks of the package are inserted in the invoices of those ships, to which we refer you for full information.

We have engaged the several mechanics selected by Messrs Boulton Watt & Co named in the margin to aid in setting up the machinery and to assist in its operations afterwards at the salaries therein mention.

[in the margin}:

Per Florentia
George Caddenhead, Foreman mechanist £400 pa
James Howard £250
JohnJohn Clough £250
Henry Bellamy £250
Henry Ingles £250
Henry Enderwick £250

Per England
JohnJohn Scott, Foreman millwright £300
Joshua Humphreys £250
George Bilton £250

…It is our desire that the machinery now advised as loading for your mint, be landed immediately on its arrival and that it be stored in places as free from damp and as much secured from the sun as possible, that it may be preserved from rust and every other damage 'till the buildings of the intended new mint are ready to receive that same.

We have ordered of Messrs Boulton Watt & Co several articles which have been deemed necessary for the immediate use of the mint. Should the whole of these be got ready in time they will be shipt on the Florentia and England, but if all should not be completed early enough for that purpose, those which are not shipt on either of the vessels above mentioned, will be forwarded by the earlieat opportunity. The invoices will contain the particulars of the articles shipt on the Florentia and England.

---

[482] Dispatches to Bombay. E/4/1045. pp. 51-56. 13th September 1824.

We have ordered several articles for your assay department referred to in your Financial Letter of 24th March last…

The Florentia sailed on 14th September 1824 and the England on 1st October.

When Hawkins arrived in Bombay he found that nothing had been done to prepare for the arrival of the new mint. Not even the site had been selected. He immediately began work on securing what he needed and the foundation stone of the new mint was laid on 1st February 1825. The Florentia arrived on 12th February 1825 and the England by the end of March.

As well as supplying the machinery Boulton & Watt were responsible with their sub-contractors, for supplying the men necessary to get the mint working in India. Their fates are shown in the following table:

Name	Fate
George Cadenhead	Died in Bombay in 1827
James Howard	?
JohnJohn Clough	?
Henry Bellamy	Dismissed 1826
Henry Ingle	Sent home due to illness 1829
Henry Enderwick	Became head engineer in the new Bombay Mint
JohnJohn Scott	Dismissed 1826. Died in Bombay in 1827
Joshua Humphreys	Returned to England 1829
George Bilton	Took to drink 1827

Hawkins soon ran into trouble with the people who had come out to help him. Cadenhead had taken to drink, whilst the refusal of the Bombay authorities to provide adequate accommodation caused a great deal of unnecessary ill feeling amongst the entire group. He worked hard to drive the project forwards to the extent that he made himself ill and even collapsed once during 1825. By the end of that year most of the buildings were complete and the heavy machinery was in place. However, that was not the end of his staff problems. In 1826 he had to dismiss JohnJohn Scott and Henry Bellamy and chose to appoint and train men from local regiments to replace them, rather than calling for replacements from England.

Not only did Hawkins have problems with his own staff, but the Bombay mint committee seemed dead set on making things as difficult as possible for him by imposing all kinds of bureaucratic hurdles for him to jump as well as failing to deliver materials when he needed them.

Trials of parts of the equipment began early in 1827 but Hawkins suffered another serious illness in November of that year. Nevertheless, by 6th January 1828 he was able to report that the machinery was ready but he was still waiting for metal pipes from England to channel water into the mint. This may have been the time when the copper pattern or trial coins were struck.

Copper pattern prepared in 1828. These three designs were used in various obverse and reverse combinations.

Most of 1828 and 1829 was spent recruiting and training staff and awaiting the necessary material from England. Henry Ingle, who had come out from England with the original team, was made foreman of the coining operation and Enderwick, another member of the original team, was made head engineer. However, Hawkins was constantly losing staff due to illness. Four of the soldiers that he had trained died and he was obliged to recruit and train yet more. In July of 1829 Hawkins was promoted to the rank of major.

At the end of 1830 striking of copper coins finally started although, by then, Hawkins was very ill. He was sent to the Cape to recuperate but died at sea on 19th February 1831.

Closure of the Old Mint

On 28th April 1831, the mint master (J. Farish) informed the Bombay Government that the silver coinage in the old mint had been stopped and all the people who worked there had moved to the new mint[483]:

I request you will have the goodness to inform the Right Honble the Governor in Council that the silver coinage in the old mint is now brought to a close, that the old buildings will be made over to the engineer officer, and the establishment removed altogether to the new mint from the 1st May, in which alone the coinage will hereafter have to be carried on.

This transfer involves a change from conducting the coinage by contract, to taking under the direct management of the officers of Government.

In my letter of the 21st September last, I had the honor of submitting a statement of establishment which I considered to be necessary under this change of circumstances for conducting the duties of the Mint Master's office, the Assay Master, the Refining Mint Master's Assayer and Melter's Department. I have the honor to transmit an extract from the statement in question embracing this part of the establishment, amounting to rupees 1199, exclusive of occasional extra hands, which must however be considered liable to extension or modification as experience may show this to be necessary. A part of this which has been

---

[483] Bombay Consultations. P/411/50. No. 169 (4th May 1831) Letter from the mint master (J Farish) to government, dated 28th April 1831.

sanctioned by your letter of the 22nd November 1830, amounting together with the present Establishment of the Mint Master and Assay Master (as shown in the comparative statement accompanying my letter of 21st September) to Rupees 613, is included in the statement enclosed. It was stated in your letter that the subject was under reference to the Supreme Government, but it is obvious that circumstances will not admit of further delay and I have therefore most respectfully to request that the establishment as at first proposed may now be authorized.

The new establishment was authorised.

The New Mint. Operation and Output

A letter from the mint master to Government dated 31st December 1831, enclosed the output of the Bombay mint for 1831. The total copper coined into quarter annas was 197,450 rupees worth. This letter also showed the annual salaries of the principle people at the mint[484]:

	Rupees (rounded)
Mint Master	20,000
Deputy Mint Master	6000
Assay Master	15000
Mint Engineer	11455
Assistant Mint Engineer	4170
Mint Master's Establishment	7592
Assay Master's ditto	958
Mint Engineer's ditto	42584

On 3rd April 1832 the mint engineer (McGillivrey) sent a long letter to the mint master discussing the operation of the mint and the people required to run it[485]:

The Bombay mint having now been at work for more than a year, and having during the latter months of that period been brought to perform more than the quantity of labour which the contract of its makers (Messrs Boulton, Watt & Co) engaged that it should execute, the experience thus acquired enables me to determine with tolerable precision the number of people required in each department in order to make the establishment (what at present it is not) fully efficient for the discharge of all its duties.

---

[484] Bombay Consultations. P/411/51. No. 4 (25th January 1832). Letter from the mint master to government, dated 31st December 1831.

[485] Bombay Consultations. P/411/51. No. 104 (9th May 1832). Letter from the mint engineer (McGillivray) to the mint master, dated 3rd April 1832.

Quarter Anna, 1833

He showed that the mint output exceeded that which had been promised by Boulton and Watt:

The contract of Messrs Boulton and Watt specified that the performance of the Bombay mint should be equal to the production of 100,000 pieces of money in a days work of 8 hours. During the month of February last and several preceding months more than 96,000 pieces of good money were daily struck, while copper enough for more than 100,000 pieces was daily operated on. This performance is considerably above the contract as it is the produce of a days work which, tho' consisting nominally of 6 hours is, when stoppages are considered really only 5½ which time, at the contract rate of 12,500 pieces per hour is only engaged to produce about 70,000 pieces, so that the mint has really done more work daily by 26,000 pieces than the contractor engaged it should perform.

but, to achieve this, he had been obliged to employ people from the bazaar, something that he considered unsatisfactory:

To enable it however to perform this work, I have been obliged as a temporary expedient to have recourse to two measures, both of which I consider very objectionable in such an establishment. The first is that we have hired men from the bazar as their services were required, and made a charge for their wages in the contingent bill, but this plan is objectionable as it is the means of introducing strange labourers into the mint, whose honesty cannot be so much depended on as that of men regularly employed.

In addition he had had to distribute the apprentices throughout the different departments where they had to stay, rather than having the opportunity to move around and learn all the different aspects of the running of the new mint. He was not happy about this:

The other measure to which I allude is that the want of hands has compelled me to distribute all the apprentices through the different departments for the performance of duties from which they can learn little or nothing that can conduce to their eventual usefulness and which duties could be performed equally well after a little practice by labourers of an inferior class.

The consequence of this necessity is that the beneficial instruction of these apprentices in such knowledge as they must become possessed of before they can be considered fit to hold a situation of any trust, has for some time been suspended, nor can it be resumed until the establishment is rendered independent of any aid from their labour and fully efficient in itself to the discharge of all its duties.

To remedy these issues he firstly proposed a new mint establishment:

It is for these reasons and with an earnest wish for the correction of such evils that I have now the honor to submit for your approval and, I hope, the sanction, of Government, the draft of a revised establishment upon a scale which will make it fully competent in itself to carry on the work of any copper coinage.

It is framed upon the principle of being perfectly independent of the labour of apprentices who, until their time of service is elapsed should in my opinion be considered as merely under instruction. After having made a few remarks in explanation of the proposed establishment, I shall then detail the plan which I would propose to be adopted for educating these apprentices.

1. General Department

		Cost		
		Rupees	Quarters	Reas
1	Foreman	427	3	30
1	Millwright	340	3	47
1	Storekeeper	150		
1	Accountant	60		
1	Clerk of the Tally	30		
1	Under ditto	20		
1	Muster Clerk & Writer	30		
2	Carpenters	33		
2	Bricklayers	26		
1	Belt maker	15		
2	Storemen	15		
4	Peons	24		
4	Summerhead Boys	20		
1	Overseer	8		
5	Labourers	27	2	
3	Boys	12	2	
1	Water Brahmin	5	2	
1	Sweeper	6		
		1251		77

In the General department marked 1 in the draft, little or no alteration is proposed with the exception of transferring the millwright from the rolling department to it, to which his services more properly belong, and adding a sweeper and additional labourer whose pay is now always charged in the contingent bill.

2. General Workshop

		Cost		
		Rupees	Quarters	Reas
1	Superintendent & Die Multiplier	340	3	47
1	Die Sinker	100		
1	Assistant	38		
1	General Turner	38		
1	Die turner	38		
2	Under Die Turners	50		
1	Die Polisher, European	38		
1	Ditto, native	6		
1	Annealer	25		
6	Vicemen	90		
2	Boys	9		
		772	3	47

All apprentices to be attached to this department and any received must be supernumerary to the establishment

In the General Workshop, to which it is proposed all apprentices should in the first place be attached, a reduction is proposed equal to 29 rupees. This arises from the omission of one turner, the number specified in the list being considered sufficient.

3. Smith's Shop

		Cost		
		Rupees	Quarters	Reas
1	European Smith	50		
1	Native Smith	25		
4	Hammermen	30		
4	Bellows Boys	18		
		123		

In the Smith's shop an increase has been made of 11 Rs 2 Qr. This consists of an increase of pay proposed to be given to the Head Smith, who has been a long time in the mint and is a good workman and a steady man. I here take the opportunity of stating that I have assumed 50 rupees per month as the ultimate rate of pay to which soldier artificers or apprentices can look forward until placed in charge of a department. At present the former class is placed upon a salary of 38 rupees per mensum when they first join, and they cannot look forward to any increase of pay with length of service. This renders them in many cases discontented. I therefore propose that when soldier artificers first enter, their pay should be somewhat less than 38 rupees so that upon their becoming useful and qualified workmen it should be increased to 38 rupees and that a few situations should be paid at the rate of 50 rupees per *month, to which they might look forward on promotion in consequence of long service, superior usefulness or good conduct.*

4. Engine Department

		Cost		
		Rupees	*Quarters*	*Reas*
1	Engineer	340	3	47
1	Second Engineer	50		
1	Third Engineer	30		
4	Lascars	44		
5	Stokers	40		
		504	3	47

In the Engine department there is an increase of 11 rupees which is caused by increasing the pay of the second engineer to 50 rupees on the principle above stated.

5. Rolling Department

		Cost		
		Rupees	*Quarters*	*Reas*
1	Superintendent and in charge of copper hold	110		
1	Assistant and Adjuster	50		
7	Lascars to breakdown	90		
8	Bigaries ditto in breaking down and in annealing and cross cutting	52		
2	Stokers	14		
1	Furnace Boy	5		
8	Boys for second rolling and adjusting	48		
4	Gaging Boys	36		
4	Boys for trial presses	18		
1	Shroff	10		
8	Scrubbers	44		
1	Boy to boil cocum	4	2	
Roller Lathe and Lap and Stone				
1	Turner	20		
1	Lapper	15		
1	Lascar	8		
		524	2	

It is in the Rolling department, No 5, where the heaviest work and that of most importance to the mint, is carried on, that I recommend the principle alteration and increase be made.

As the establishment is constituted under the present sanction, the sum allotted to this department after the Millwright is thrown into the General one (to which his services strictly belong) only amount to 255 Rs 2 Qr. This sum, even exclusive of any allowance for superintendence is inadequate to the payment of the mere labourers required in this department, and I have in consequence been under the necessity of sometimes employing as many as 15 or 20 extra hands from the bazar.

As I consider it an objectionable measure to admit any strange workmen into an establishment like the mint, I propose that the number of workmen in this department shall be so increased as to render it fully efficient, and the number of working people stated in the accompanying draft, I have found from experience to be as few as are able to carry on the work properly. I also propose that Robert Bishop, who has had acting charge of this department since January 1830, and who has since that time given great satisfaction in every respect, should be confirmed in its charge on a consolidated salary of 110 rupees per month. He now receives of pay, 105 rupees per mensum, Viz 15 rupees for having charge of the copper hold, and an acting salary of 90 rupees, which has been drawn from the pay of the Millwright, whose allowance since the departure of the late Millwright (Mr Humphreys) for England, has not been drawn. As the successor to Mr Humphreys is daily expected, Bishop must lose this pay and would then (unless Government sanction a salary for having charge of the rolling mill) merely draw his allowance as a soldier artificer, and this although I consider Bishop's experience qualifies him for this charge far better than any Millwright could be expected to be until after many months practice. I have no hesitation in stating that this charge involves the most responsible duty and hardest work in the mint. I likewise propose that the assistant in the Rolling mill should receive 50 rupees per month, to equalise his situation with that of smith and second engineer and that he should have immediate charge of second rolling and adjusting, which is an employment requiring great attention. This situation could be looked forward to by a serving soldier artificer or clever apprentice after time of servitude had elapsed.

The proposed arrangement will render the rolling mill very efficient.

6. Cutting Out and Milling

		Cost		
		Rupees	Quarters	Reas
1	Superintendent	340	3	47
1	Assistant Superintendent	50		
1	Viceman	15		
2	Lascars	20		
9	Cutting out press boys	72		
1	Shroff	10		
4	Pickers	20		
1	Miller	12		
1	Assistant ditto	8		
3	Boys	18		
		565	3	47

In the Cutting out, the increase of 36 rupees is caused by an increase of 12 rupees to the Assistant's pay to equalise it on the principle stated para sixth, with those of second engineer, smith and Assistant Roller. A Viceman has likewise been allowed to assist in roughing down in the General workshop of this department.

7. Shaking, Annealing and Pickling Department

		Cost		
		Rupees	Quarters	Reas
1	Overseer	50		
1	Rough Shaker	8		
1	Under ditto	5	2	
1	Furnace Lascar	11		
1	Pickler	6		
1	Smooth Shaker	8		
2	Second Smooth Shakers	11		
		99	2	

8. Picking Department

		Cost		
		Rupees	Quarters	Reas
1	Shroff	15		
2	Pickers	11		
		26		

9. Coining

		Cost		
		Rupees	Quarters	Reas
1	Head Pressman	340	3	47
1	Assistant Pressman	250		
1	Under ditto	30		
1	Lascar	10		
1	Viceman	15		
8	Press Boys	64		
1	Pump Lascar	10		
2	Ditto boys	9		
		728	3	47

10. Packing

		Cost		
		Rupees	Quarters	Reas
1	Weigher and Packer	25		
2	Shroffs	20		
2	Assistants	11		
1	Gate Porter	10		
		66		
	Total	4662	2	65

The other 4 departments remain much as they did, both as to amount and division of labour.

With the establishment sanctioned as now proposed, I have no doubt the mint will be very efficient in all its departments, and able to carry on the current work of any coinage. In operating on the precious metals, the only difference would be that after having been cut out the blanks must be individually weighed and adjusted to standard, before passing through any of the other processes. These operations will require a set of weighers and filers, but it is the only addition that need be anticipated in the working departments.

Recruitment and Training of Apprentices

The mint engineer went on to discuss the recruitment and training of apprentices:

I have already given it as my opinion that all apprentices should be attached in the first instance to the general workshop, and that until the expiration of their apprenticeship, they ought to be considered as merely under instruction and supernumerary to the establishment. The necessity of this arrangement arises from the circumstance that if they are in the regular performance of any duty in a working department, they cannot be spared from it for the purpose of acquiring other useful and necessary information.

It has also been already mentioned that since the mint has commenced regular work, the apprentices have been all attached as workmen to the different departments, since which period they have been acquiring dexterity at only one description of manual employment. Before that time the only instruction which, as far as I can learn, had been communicated to them was merely to practice them in the manual operations of forging, turning or fitting, as each individual should [have] a disposition to take readily to any or all of these employments, but no attempt had been made to teach them any principles and (with a very few exceptions) these boys are quite illiterate and utterly ignorant of the causes which regulate the action or adjustment of any part of the machinery, which they see daily in operation.

He presumed that the intention behind employing apprentices was to replace the skilled and expensive employees obtained from England:

It is presumed that when Government ordered a system of instruction or apprenticeship to be organized, they were desirous that boys should be taught enough to enable them eventually (with a few exceptions) to perform duties now necessarily executed by a class of qualified machinists, obtained at very great expense from Europe, for had such not been the intention and were vacancies as they occurred to be always filled up by procuring qualified individuals from Europe, there would be little necessity for retaining any apprentices, because supernumerary machinists must then be obtained to fill vacancies from unforeseen casualties, and merely manual dexterity in turning, filing etc where qualified workmen are already retained on an establishment, can very soon be acquired by native or PortuguesePortuguese boys for whose remuneration, even as qualified workmen in these branches, 25 rupees per month would be always sufficient.

If it was indeed true that the apprentices should be trained to a level where they could replace the skilled workmen from Europe, then the training necessary would be far more extensive than that then currently undertaken because the apprentices were entirely uneducated:

Assuming then that it is the intention of Government that apprentices instructed at the mint should eventually become qualified to fill the situations held by machinists, or as engineers to steam vessels, I have no hesitation in stating that it seems to me very improbable the great majority of the class of apprentices hitherto received, can under any system of instruction ever be expected to become qualified for these situations, because from their entire want of anything approaching to education, it is quite impossible to communicate to them any definite idea of many things in themselves partly of an abstract nature, but which it is necessary they should understand in order to enable them to comprehend the mode of action and due regulation of machinery, and without a knowledge of which, it would be idle to assert that they could ever be fit to perform the work now done by our regular machinists, or a steam vessel engineer.

The information to which I allude is of the following nature. In instructing boys for instance in the management of a steam engine, it is necessary that they should understand something of the nature of the agent whose power they are directing. They must know how steam is generated, and understand the principle of the contrivances by which its strength is measured. They must know the manner in which it performs its work in the cylinder and how it is got rid of after its work is done. They must understand the mode of action of the pump which draws off the air and condensed vapour, as well as the operation of the common pump which draws water for condensing steam and of the force pump which feeds the boiler, but all these points, simple as they may appear, are not to be comprehended without an elementary knowledge of at least three branches of natural philosophy.

The knowledge necessary to the comprehension of this species of information must be possessed by every person who wishes to benefit by instruction in the practical management of machinery, and tho' in consequence of the diffusion of knowledge and superior intellectual abilities among the labouring classes in manufacturing towns in England, it being by them acquired almost unconsciously and without much effort, yet in this country from the want of these advantages, it cannot be learnt unless it be communicated by regular instruction.

Selection and Training of Apprentices

The mint engineer then went on to discuss in detail such things as the age at which they should be recruited, the level of education they should have attained before recruitment, the further education they should receive, and the hours they should devote to work and study:

Having I hope shown from the reasons above stated that the present system of instruction is not likely to produce useful workmen, I shall now proceed to describe the system of education which in lieu of it I would propose to be adopted for the instruction of apprentices.

I propose that the number of boys received in the mint as apprentices or pupils, inclusive of those received for the steam vessels, should not exceed twelve.

That the age of these boys should not be more than 16 nor less than 14 years.

That previous to being received as apprentices they must be able to read English fluently, write a fair hand and understand arithmetic as far as vulgar and decimal fractions, to ascertain which point they ought to undergo an examination.

That during their apprenticeship in the mint, they should go through a course of instruction of the following nature: to be made perfect in arithmetic and to receive instruction in logarithms, practical geometry and mensuration of planes and solids including artificers work.

That they should be taught the elements of plane trigonometry and mechanics including hydrostatics and pneumatics.

This course ought to be combined with practical instruction as workmen in forging, turning, fitting and acquiring a practical knowledge of the machinery, to effect which the first hours of the day, viz from 9 to 12 might be devoted to study and the latter hours from 1 till 4 O'clock, to work.

Length of Training

In the opinion of the mint engineer, the apprenticeship should last for five years, with the first year being probationary:

As it is not probable that every boy received will turn out a subject likely to be eventually useful, it would be desirable that the first year of their apprenticeship should be probationary and that at any time during that period, a boy might be discharged, who might not turn out to be useful.

I would propose five years as the term of their apprenticeship, for I do not think that less time would be sufficient to enable them to become competent workmen. They ought to be engaged under regular indentures like apprentices at home, and a certain penalty ought to be attached to their leaving their employment without permission, or breaking their indentures.

Finally, he considered that the apprentices should be bound to work in the mint for a number of years, although it should be made clear to them that the apprenticeship would not certainly lead on to a permanent job in the mint:

As the instruction they would receive during their apprenticeship would be a very great benefit to them, they ought to be bound down to give their services to Government at reasonably fixed rates for some years after its expiration, but if their number should be greater than Government has occasion for, they should be led to understand that their apprenticeship in the mint gives them no claim to constant employment afterwards.

With a system of education of this description, combining what is necessary of theory with practical instruction steadily persevered in for some years, I doubt not that several boys might be instructed who, after they had acquired some practice and experience would become very competent machinists or steam vessel engineers, but without teaching a man enough theory to enable him to attach a definite idea or meaning to the names of the different forces which he will hear described as producing motion in a machine, I conceive it will be impossible to make him fitted for these duties, although he may be a good manual workman and know individually every bolt and nut in an engine.

Provided Government approve this or some similar arrangement for the education of apprentices, the details of the plan can be settled at a future date.

The increase in the establishment was sanctioned and the proposal for the apprentices was approved of and an even more detailed plan was asked for.

Silver and Gold

In May 1831 the mint master, J. Farrish, announced that the new mint was ready to begin producing silver coins[486]

In regard to the point noticed at the close of your letter, as to whether the new mint is ready to commence a silver coinage directly, I request you will inform the Right Honble the Governor in Council that there is in the Treasury reserved for coinage in the new mint, bullion to the value of about rupees 218,22?, which was brought for coinage to the old mint too late to be undertaken. I have requested the Acting Mint Engineer to make arrangements to be prepared for the coinage of silver and I am not aware of anything to prevent our proceeding as soon as working dies can be provided from the matrices which we have, and beds, punches and collars turned. When these arrangements are made, I hope we shall not be delayed in consequence of insecurity of the premises. At present, until the buildings required to complete the inner enclosure are finished, it would not be safe for the mint engineer to proceed with the precious metals.

While these preparations are making, the Establishment have to learn the use of the apparatus with which they must work and to acquire a knowledge of the method of refining and melting according to the mode to be hereafter followed. I consider it to be necessary that the mint should without delay be placed in a state of efficiency to coin whatever bullion may be sent to it by individuals or Government, and it is a favourable circumstance that the

---

[486] Bombay Consultations. P/411/50. No. 178 (18th May 1831). Letter from the mint master (J Farish) to government, dated 5th May 1831.

removal of silver from the old to the new mint occurs at a period of the year when there will necessarily for a short time be comparatively little coinage to conduct.

The mint master suggested that now that the old mint was closed and the people transferred to the new mint, they should be directly employed by Government instead of by the mint contractor:

In the new establishment it is necessary that many of the experienced persons employed by the contractor should be employed by the Government. It was worth his while to keep them in regular pay that he might be secure of their services and he was remunerated by the commission he received. The commission or seignorage will now go to Government and, on the same grounds, it must be for the public interests to receive the parties into the public service from the 1ˢᵗ of this month when their claim on him cease.

In my last letter I requested that the establishment might be sanctioned as proposed on a former date and I have then explained that the persons to be newly engaged would be taken into employ only as found to be required. Under these explanations I trust the Right Honble the Governor in Council will be pleased to sanction my suggestions of the 28ᵗʰ ultimo

By the 15ᵗʰ July 1832 the mint committee were able to send a rupee that had been struck at the new mint to the Governor and suggest that a number of foreign coins could now be melted and re-coined in the new mint[487]:

We have the honor to acknowledge the receipt of your letter of the 24ᵗʰ instant with enclosure respecting the disposal of about 18 lacs of foreign coins which have accumulated in the Treasury.

We request you will be pleased to inform the Right Honble the Governor in Council that the dies having been prepared in the new mint bearing the inscription of the rupee now in use, in conformity with the directions given in para 4ᵗʰ of the Honorable Court's letter of the 17ᵗʰ March 1829, we have the honor to submit a specimen of the rupee struck therewith, and we are not aware of any objection to the uncurrent coins in the Treasury being re-coined in the new mint accordingly.

---

[487] Bombay Consultations. P/411/51. No. 209 (15ᵗʰ August 1832). Letter from mint committee to government, dated 25ᵗʰ July 1832.

Silver rupee issued from the new mint
Obverse: sikka mubārak bādshāh ghazi shāh alām 1215 (= The auspicious coin of the
victorious Emperor Shah Alām, AH 1215).
Reverse: ẓarb surat sanah 46 julūs maimanat mānūs (= Struck at Surat in the 46th year of
tranquil prosperity).

This letter includes a memorandum by the secretary recording the fact that the silver coins would be the same design as those struck at Calcutta for Bombay in 1823 but they would have a plain edge:

…In answer the Secretary with the Governor General in his letter of the 10th February 1831, states the following as the construction which the Governor General places on the orders of the Court of 27th March 1829 and the course to be pursued under them…

…"In the present state of the question therefore, the Governor General thinks it will be best that the Mint master at Bombay should be directed to coin from the old impressions and issue no new coin of any kind"

The only difference (independent of the execution) between the specimen coins now submitted by the committee, and the Surat rupees struck in Calcutta and sent round for circulation in 1823 to the amount of 30 lacs of rupees, is that the former have a plain milled edge, while the latter are serrated or corded. Both coins have the complete impression of the die contained on the face of the piece.

There seems no reason therefore to consider the specimens now submitted to Government as <u>new coins</u> under the meaning of the letter from Bengal and an order for the re-coinage in this form of the uncurrent money now in the Treasury may perhaps be issued.

The rupee design was approved and by October 1832 the minting of silver coins was in full swing:

Resolved, the silver coinage in the new mint being in progress, and a quantity of rupees having been delivered into the treasury for circulation…

and a proclamation was issued[488]:

---

[488] Bombay Consultations. P/411/51. No. 296 (17th October 1832). Minute of the Governor, dated 17th October 1832.

PROCLAMATION

Whereas the Right Honorable the Governor in Council has been pleased to direct the coinage at the Bombay Mint, of Gold and Silver Coins, of improved form and impression, but of the same weight and standard as the present current money of Bombay, it is hereby notified that such coin of the denomination hereinafter mentioned shall be current and received as legal tender in the Town and Island of Bombay, and throughout the provinces subject to the Presidency.

GOLD COIN

The Bombay Gold Mohur of fifteen Rupees

The Bombay Ten rupee piece

The Bombay Panchia or five rupee piece

SILVER COIN

The Bombay Rupee

Ditto Half Rupee

Ditto Quarter Rupee

Ditto Eighth of Rupee or two anna piece

No eighth rupee/two anna pieces were struck.

Up until that time, Bombay had received blank dies from Soho and engraved them at Bombay. For instance, in July 1825 they received 750 rupee-sized dies from Soho but in 1831 it was decided that in future all (matrix) dies would be engraved in Calcutta and then sent to Bombay. This did not actually happen until at least the end of 1836 and Bombay continued to receive blank dies from Soho and engrave them locally.

From 1832 until 1835, Bombay issued machine-struck coins in the Moghul-style bearing the mint name of Surat.

Pattern/Trial Mohur/Rupee 1828 (see p. 211 for photos)

On 15th April 1827 Robert Gordon was transferred to the mint from 2nd Battalion, Bombay Artillery[489]. He was employed as a diesinker and may have been responsible for production of the copper Lion and Palm patterns produced at about this time. Pridmore speculated these may have been patterns for the gold or silver coinage but no direct reference to this has been found in the records. Pridmore also speculated that Gordon was responsible for the dies of the pattern coins produced during the 1817-1821 period (see chapter 6).

Doty provides an interesting extract from the Boulton papers. In February 1829 Hawkins wrote to Boulton[490]:

---

[489] Pridmore stated that on 15th April 1827 Robert Gordon transferred to the mint. His source for this information has not been found.

[490] Doty R. (1998), The Soho mint & the Industrialization of money, Smithsonian Institution with Spink & the British Numismatic Society, p. 222. He refers to the Boulton papers No. MBP404.

I have sent you a few pice coined a few weeks since in the old mint, & some pieces of copper struck from blank dies in our presses last month. I had hoped to have sent you others, with the Lion and palm on one side & star and inscription on the other, of the same size, done by a lad of my instruction here, but they are not ready – You must not expect them to be perfect, it is only a first attempt –

Pattern Mohur – Shah Alam – 46 San. Issued 1833

Silver pattern for the gold coinage

In October 1833, the mint master suggested to the mint committee that in addition to the colour of the metal, gold and silver coins should have some feature that would distinguish one from another. He suggested adding a milled edge to the gold coins[491]:

…I had at one time an idea of striking gold mohurs with the same dies as half rupees, but this would be objectionable in as much as by gilding a half rupee it might be passed off as a gold Mohur. It will therefore be necessary to have new dies engraved for this coinage, one pair for each description of money.

I beg to suggest that I conceive it would be desirable, in order to make a still greater difference between the gold and silver coin, both having the same device, that the edges should be corded like an English Sovereign. This will constitute such a marked difference between the gold and silver money as to make it very unlikely that it will not be remarked by every person.

A pattern mohur struck in silver, with the obverse struck from the pattern rupee die of 1831, but with a milled edge, exists, and may have been shown to the mint committee at this time.

On 29th November 1833[492] the mint master was instructed to add a milled edge to any gold coins produced. However, no gold currency coins appear to have been struck, and only the silver pattern of the gold mohur is known. However, gold coins

---

[491].Bombay Consultations. IOR P/411/52. No. 412 Letter from F. McGillivray (mint engineer) to the mint master (James Farish), dated 30th October 1833

[492] Bombay Consultations. IOR P/411/52. Nos. 454 &455. Letter from the mint committee to government dated 19th November 1833 and letter from government to mint master dated 29th November 1833.

may exist because Atkins[493] lists three denominations in gold of this new design as mohur, half mohur and quarter mohur under his numbers 5, 6 and 7 with upright milled edges and 8, 9 and 10 with plain edges. Johnston[494] also lists the mohur with straight milling (No 165) and plain edge (No 167). The whereabouts of these coins is not known.

The coinage continued until the end of 1835 and the coins were finally demonetised from 1st June 1878[495]:

In exercise of the power conferred by section 28 of "the Indian Coinage Act, 1870", the Governor General in Council is pleased to call in, with effect on and from the 1st day of June 1878, all silver coins coined and issued by the authority of the Government of India before the 1st day of September 1835.

Until the said 1st day of June 1878, such of the coins called in by this notification as are now legal tender will continue to be legal tender in payment or on account, under the conditions which now apply to them, and on demand, current coins of recent date will be given in exchange for the same at any Government treasury, or at the Presidency banks and their branches.

On and from the said 1st day of June 1878, all silver coins so called in will cease to be legal tender; and, if tendered to any officer authorized to act under section 16 of the Indian Coinage Act, 1870, will be dealt with in accordance with the provisions of that section.

Copper Annas – 1830 to 1833. Proposals of 1824

A proposal for a new copper coinage had been discussed as early as 1824 but had not been put into practice[496]:

…The only alteration from the system of currency therein recommended, which subsequent reflection and experience have induced us to think, would be an improvement of the division of the anna into sixteen instead of twelve pice, but as this would require a corresponding alteration in the money of account, which is intended or proposed to be the same at all the three Presidencies, the change would require the express sanction of the Supreme Government.

There can be no manner of doubt that a decimal division throughout would better suit our arithmetic, but on the other hand the division by sixteenths is practically more simple and complete, as well as much more congenial to the habits and usages of the people of this country. For the rest there is high authority for the opinion that the minute subdivisions of the lower coins has a tendency to cheapen commodities to the poorer class.

---

[493] Atkins (1889), The Coins and Tokens of the Possessions and Colonies of the British Empire, p. 136, nos. 5,6,7,8,9,10.Published by Bernard Quaritch, London.

[494] Johnston No 165, 167. Cited by Pridmore on p.138 but I don't know to whom he refers.

[495] Bombay Consultations. IOR P/967. Notification by government of India. December 1877 p. 78.

[496] Bombay Consultations. IOR P/411/42, 1824, p. 80. Letter from the mint committee to government, dated 27th September 1824.

The following would under such an arrangement be the system of our copper currency instead of that given in the tables accompanying our report above quoted.

Anna Troy weight	*400 grains*
Half anna	*200*
Quarter anna	*100*
Double pice	*50*
Single pice	*25*

4 pice = one quarter anna
8 pice = one half anna
16 pice = one anna

Money of account
16 pice = one anna
16 annas = one rupee

Copper Coins – 1829

The weight of the new copper coins had been fixed by the Court of Directors in 1829[497]:

We have determined that the copper money to be coined in your mint do consist of three denominations, namely half anna, quarter anna and one pice (or twelfth anna) pieces, the first (or half anna) to weigh 200 troy grains, the second to weigh 100 troy grains and the third to weigh 33⅓ troy grains, that is 6400 troy grains copper (or 64 quarter anna pieces) are therefore to be equivalent for one rupee of silver, according to the proportion established by the Bengal Government and to which we desire you to conform.

The Bombay mint committee consultations, 21st October 1829 record[498]:

There appears to be no material objection to the old impression for our copper coinage (we mean of those formerly coined at the Soho mint) being continued.

The new mint started operations on 22nd November 1830, with the first coins being the quarter annas followed by twelfth annas in 1831. The coins were announced by proclamation in November 1830[499]:

PROCLAMATION
Whereas it has been deemed advisable to fix an uniformity of division, and to prescribe a

---

[497] Bombay Consultations. P/411/50. No. 401 (15th November 1831). Extract from a letter from the Honble Court, dated 27th March 1829.

[498] 29th November 1830 proclamation declaring copper coins current.

[498] Pridmore. I have been unable to find his source for this extract but it can probably be found in IOR P/411/49

[499] See Bombay Consultations. P/411/50. No. 407 (15th November 1831). Letter from the mint committee to government, dated 11th October 1831. This contains a copy of the proclamation. Also IOR, P/411/49, 1st December 1830, No. 4.

specified weight for a new copper coinage intended to be introduced into the Town and Island of Bombay and throughout the territories of this Presidency; The Honorable the Governor in Council is pleased to announce the following resolutions, which have been passed for the purpose, under the orders of the Honble the Court of Directors.

The following copper coins shall be struck at the Mint of Bombay namely –

The Pie – weighing (33⅓) grains thirty three grains and one third, twelve of which pie shall pass current for one anna.

The Quarter Anna piece – weighing (100) one hundred grains

The Half Anna piece – weighing (200) two hundred grains

Such copper coins shall be issued from the Public Treasury at the rate of thirty-two half anna pieces, or sixty four quarter anna pieces for one rupee, & twelve Pies for one anna; at which rates they are to be received as legal tender to the amount of a rupee, and its fractional parts, in all public and private transactions throughout the provinces subject to this Presidency.

Copper Coins – 1831

In October 1831 the mint master reported the number of quarter annas that had been produced[500]:

I have the honor to acknowledge the receipt of your letter of yesterday's date and to transmit for the purpose of being laid before the Right Honble the Governor in Council, a statement of the quantity of new quarter annas which have been struck and paid into the treasury.

I beg respectfully to refer to the sub-treasurer to whose department the duty belongs, for information regarding the disposal of the new copper coin and what Collectors have been supplied, and as your call is urgent I have transmitted to that officer an extract of your letter that he may report thereon at once to Government.

From my letter of the 22nd March last, His Lordship in Council will be aware that though the aggregate of the Collectors estimates was upwards of Rupees twenty five lacs, my opinion that half that quantity was probably nearer what would be required. The new mint is now coining at the rate of twenty five thousand per month and at that rate therefore, if nothing occur to prevent it, it would require between three and four years to complete the small quantity.

It is evident therefore that one cause which has prevented the whole quantity being coined is that there has not been sufficient time for the purpose. At the commencement of operations, coining did not proceed so rapidly as it is now doing, which will appear from the statement. With regards to the future, the causes which may retard the copper coinage are, the mint being required to coin silver and the want of those working stores which can only be obtained from England. Indents have been duly sent home but I have received no intimation that any are to be supplied in the present season and, if not, great inconvenience and delay must arise. Indeed

---

[500] Bombay Consultations. P/411/50. No. 404 (15th November 1831). Letter from the mint master (J Farish), dated 7th October 1831.

it is to be feared that from want of some essential stores, the mint may be unable to continue working unless the supply indented for should arrive.

No. Quarter Annas Produced. 1831

	Value (Rs)
January	17850
February	3050
March	3550
April	21150
May	8400
June	5150
July	15300
August	34650
September	32000

Half Annas – 1833 to 1844

Half annas were not struck until 1832, and then only proof specimens, which were shown to the mint committee on 23rd July 1833[501]:

I have the honor to enclose for the purpose of being laid before the Right Honorable the Governor in Council specimens of the half Anna ordered to be executed which I trust will meet with the approbation of Government

The design was approved, and twelve specimens were sent to London to be shown to the Court of Directors. The coins were not struck for currency until 1834 (see next page).

Following the approval of the design for the half anna by the mint committee on the 23rd July 1833, the mint master requested, on 29th July[502], that a matrix die be obtained from Calcutta. This had come about because the die sinker, Mr Clarke, had effectively resigned in a fit of pique. The mint engineer wrote to the mint master[503]:

Mr Clarke, the die sinker in the mint, having thought fit to request his discharge from employment (I presume from thinking that his services were indispensable) because I found fault with him for his extreme irregularity in attendance, it becomes necessary to adopt other measures for having our matrix dies for copper money renewed against the time our stock wears out.

It is not unlikely that Mr Clarke, as soon as he fairly feels the consequences of his having relinquished employment, may solicit to be again retained, in which case it might be desirable

---

[501] Bombay Consultations. IOR P/411/52. No. 293. Letter from the mint master to Bombay government, dated 23rd July 1833.

[502] Bombay Consultations. IOR P/411/52. No.298. Letter from the mint master to the mint committee, dated 29th July 1833.

[503] Bombay Mint Proceedings. P/411/52. No. 299. Letter from the mint engineer to the mint master, dated 29th July 1833.

to re-engage him but upon such terms as would subject him to a severe forfeiture in addition to loss of employment in the event of his again misbehaving.

In the meantime, and to prevent the possibility of the occurrence of any delay in work from this cause, I beg to suggest that in conformity with the orders of the Honorable the Court of Directors, a complete set of matric dies for copper money be indented for without delay from Calcutta…

The request for matrix dies was sent to Calcutta together with specimens of the Bombay copper coins and orders were issued to the Calcutta mint in August, to prepare matrix dies for Bombay[504]

On 7th February 1834, the Calcutta mint master reported that the matrix dies for the Bombay copper coins were ready and named the people who had undertaken the work[505]:

…Mr Delacombe was occupied for a month in engraving the arms on a matrix and the scales for the reverse and in re-touching the punches taken from his original (arms) matrix of the half anna piece and I propose that sicca rupees 200 should be paid him for the work done.

Cossinath engraved the matrix of the arms & of the scales on the reverse of the Pyce piece, and was occupied about the same length of time. His work is decidedly superior to that of either of the other engravers, and he expects to be paid at the same rate as Mr Delacombe, which I think is but reasonable.

Hurree engraved two matrices of the arms and two of the scales of the pie piece, the engraving of the first being found on trial of the pieces to be too deep, and has from the 29th of August up to the 3rd instant been engaged in the mint in engraving two matrices for the scales of the Pyce piece and one for the Half Anna, the originals executed by Cossinath and Mr Delacombe having given way in multiplying, and also in retouching other punches and matrices. I would recommend that he be paid for that period at the rate of 50 rupees per month.

Half anna 1834

---

[504] Bombay Consultations. IOR P/162/49. Letter from the Calcutta mint master to Calcutta council dated 7th February 1834. Meeting of 24th February 1834, No. 1.

[505] Bombay Consultations. IOR P/162/49. Letter from the Calcutta mint master to Calcutta council dated 7th February 1834. Meeting of 24th February 1834, No. 2.

The matrices, punches and dies was shipped to Bombay in February 1834[506]

I have the honor to report for the information of the Committee and of Government that I have delivered to Captain McDougall, commander of the ship Edmonstone, one box containing 40 dies for half anna pieces, 29 Dies for Pice pieces and 31 dies for pie pieces of the Bombay Currency for consignment to Bombay

Copper coins of this design continued to be issued from the Bombay mint until 1844, well after the introduction of the Uniform Coinage for the whole of British India in 1835.

---

[506] Bombay Consultations. IOR P/162/49. Letter from the Calcutta mint master to the Calcutta mint committee, dated 21st February 1834. Meeting of 10th March 1834, No. 2.

Chapter 8 – Getting the Copper Coins into Circulation

Summary

Having the ability to manufacture the coins with machinery turned out to be only the first step in the new coinage. Getting the new copper coins into circulation proved to be very difficult for a number of reasons. Firstly, they were a token coinage and did not contain their intrinsic value of copper. Secondly, there were a number of copper coins produced by local polities in the surrounding area, and they did contain their intrinsic value of copper (or, at least, were heavier than the new coins) and it was feared that these would compete with the new coins and prevent their circulating. Thirdly, there were a large number of copper coins already in circulation and these had to be exchanged for the new coins. All these issues had to be addressed.

Silver and gold coins, being the same intrinsic value as the old ones, did not face the same challenges.

Local Native Mints in the Deccan

As the Bombay Council had discussed as early as 1821, the fact that copper coins were produced by several other polities in the area was likely to cause problems with getting the new copper coins into circulation. In 1831 the Junior Principal Collector of Poona reported his worries about local mints striking copper coins [507]:

In reference to your circular of the 27th ultimo on the subject of introducing the new currency into this Presidency, I have the honor to bring to the notice of the Right Honble the Governor that some measures probably should be adopted to prevent the Punt Suchen at Bhore and His Highness the Rajah of Sattarah and other places coining pice which we shall be unable to prevent coming into our districts as the stamp on each is the same as that used in the Poona mint and consequently our district treasuries will continue receiving the coins as that of our own manufacture. It appears that so long as the Poona mint continued to coin copper, none was coined either at Bhore or Sattara. I understand that they are just about to commence at both places and a consignment of copper has actually left Poonah for that purpose. For two years and upwards they have not coined at Bhore, the capital of the Punt Suchen Territories, and I do not think it would be very severe to prevent him doing so now. At any rate, if the power cannot with justice be withheld, the coin and stamp should be altered to enable us to recognise it from the Company's old currency, and the alteration should be made in the Rajah's states. I beg to suggest however that a letter be sent to the Resident immediately to prevail upon the Rajah either to stop coining altogether in his states, or to limit the same to his own immediate states and mint, if absolutely necessary, which however was put a stop to by the Paishwa, [and] as paramount lord to prevent the Punt Suchen coining at all. He can have no right to do so of himself, nor do I think the Rajah of Sattara has any right as it was stopped by the Paishwa.

---

[507] Bombay Consultations. P/411/50. No. 281 (27th July 1831). Letter from the Junior Principal Collector, Poona, to government, dated 11th July 1831.

The mint at Phultun should also be stopped and that at Wattar also. These belong to the Nimbalkur. The Rajah I believe has attached these towns and territories at present.

One interesting comment in the above letter is the observation that pice struck at Poona and Satara were indistinguishable from one another.

Poona/Satara pice

Another interesting observation from the extract is the number of different mints in operation in the area.

The mint committee supported the proposals of the Collector of Poona in a letter to the Bombay Council dated July 1831[508]:

We have the honor to acknowledge the receipt of your letter dated 21ˢᵗ instant with one from the Junior Principal Collector of Poona proposing certain measures for preventing the native chieftains in the Deccan from coining copper pice, and in reply to state for the information of the Right Honble the Governor in Council, that we entirely concur in the Collector's suggestions and accordingly beg to recommend their adoption.

However the Governor was worried about interfering in the affairs of Satara and wanted to hear the views of the Resident there:

Before we adopt the opinion of the Committee, I should wish to refer the question as stated by the Junior Principal Collector of Poona to the Resident for his opinion. I confess it is to me very doubtful whether we ought to interfere in the internal management of the Rajah of Sattara's administration so far as to prevent his coinage.

The resident at Satara was asked for his opinion[509]:

I am directed by the Right Honble the Governor in Council to transmit for your opinion the accompanying copy of a letter from the Junior Principal Collector of Poona dated the 11ᵗʰ ultimo, proposing that certain native chieftains in the Deccan be prevented from coining and

---

[508] Bombay Consultations. P/411/50. No. 302 (17ᵗʰ August 1831). Letter from Bombay mint committee to government, dated 25ᵗʰ July 1831.

[509] Bombay Consultations. P/411/50. No. 304 (17ᵗʰ August 1831). Letter from Bombay government to the Resident at Sattarah, dated 11ᵗʰ August 1831.

to call your attention to the suggestion offered by Mr Giberne at the conclusion of the 1ˢᵗ paragraph.

and he replied in September 1831. He believed that the mint controlled by the Raja could be stopped without too much difficulty[510]:

I have the honor to acknowledge receipt of your letter dated the 11ᵗʰ instant and to report for the information of the Right Honble the Governor in Council that there does not seem any objection to order the pice coinage at Bhore, Watar and Fultun immediately to cease and I shall therefore request His Highness to give orders to this effect.

On enquiry I have learnt that the mint at this place has recently been set a going on a contract with a coiner for several years but His Highness does not seem to attach much importance to its continuation though he does not like, without cause, to abrogate the engagement he has come under. He however states there is little doubt a good plea in breach of contract on the part of the contractor will occur in the course of the next three or four months or even before, in attempting to issue pice of an inferior weight or debased metal, and that he will embrace such an opportunity as his agreement authorizes, to suspend further operations.

As this mode of meeting the wishes of the Right Honble the Governor in Council holds out a near prospect of getting rid of the mint altogether, it may not be necessary to require any change in the die in use here for so short a time, especially as the coinage is after all, very limited.

This was forwarded to the Junior Principal Collector at Poona.

Meanwhile the junior principal collector at Poona had noticed the arrival of a large quantity of copper coins from the very areas he was most concerned about[511]:

I have the honor in reference to my letter of the 11ᵗʰ ultimo to state for the information of the Right Honble the Governor in Council that I have received information that a large consignment of copper pice have been received by the merchants in camp at Poona from the Sattara and Punt Suchen's territory. I should wish to be informed whether immediate steps should not be taken to prevent the supply of copper pice which the foreign mints have and will continue to afford. The pice will find its way into our territory, there can be little doubt, and the only mode I conceive as likely to remedy the evil, is to stop the mint in those territories or to require another stamp to the coin, which I suggested in my letter alluded to above.

I would further request to be instructed whether I am authorized to issue instructions to all the Nakadars to prevent the import of pice into our territories.

---

[510] Bombay Consultations. P/411/50. No. 333 (21ˢᵗ September 1831). Letter from the Resident at Satara to government, dated 26ᵗʰ August 1831.

[511] Bombay Consultations. P/411/50. No. 350 (12ᵗʰ October 1831). Letter from the junior principal collector of Poona to government , dated 19ᵗʰ August 1831.

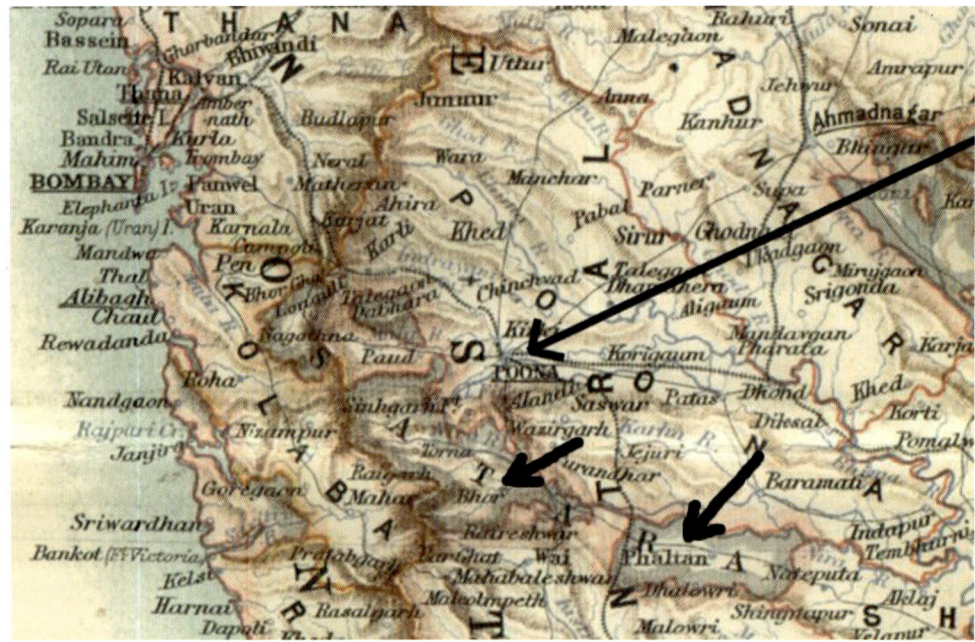

Map of Poona and surrounding areas

By October 1831, the resident at Satara was able to report that all the mints in the area had been closed[512]:

I have the honor to reply to your letter dated the 26ᵗʰ of last month concerning the pice mints in the territories of His Highness the Raja and his Jagherdars, to report for the information of the Right Honble the Governor that His Highness by a memorandum No 76 dated 13ᵗʰ instant, has advised me that he has put a stop to the manufacture of pice at this place and has ordered that all the other mints in his territory be closed.

Should the Collector of Poona ascertain therefore that any of them is still clandestinely carried on, I shall on his appraising me of the same, take measures against the offending parties.

Local Native Mints – Bhaunagar

To the north of Bombay there was a mint at Bhaunagar and it was thought that this might cause problems. In 1831 the principal collector at Ahmadabad wrote[513]:

I have the honor to bring to the notice of the Right Honble the Governor in Council that the Rajah of Bhownugher has a mint in the town of Bhownugher for coining copper pice and which are sold by him and pass current through the Western Districts.

---

[512] Bombay Consultations. P/411/50. No. 391 (9ᵗʰ November 1831). Letter from the resident at Satara to government, dated 16ᵗʰ October 1831.

[513] Bombay Consultations. P/411/50. No. 314 (24ᵗʰ August 1831). Letter from the principal collector of Ahmadabad (J Vibart) to government, dated 26ᵗʰ July 1831.

I called upon the Rajah sometime since on the subject, requesting him to state on what grounds he rested his right to issue coin and beg submit his answers on the point.

I shall feel obliged to your furnishing me with the instruction of the Right Honble the Governor in Council as to what steps should be taken with regard to this mint on the introduction of the new copper coin into those districts, whether the mint should be stopped or merely the coin declared not current in this Zillah

Map of the Gulf of Cambay showing Bhaunagar and the surrounding area

Vibart, the magistrate at Ahmadabad, had obviously written to Bhaunagar about their mint because in August 1831 he received the following letter from there[514]:

---

[514] Bombay Consultations. P/411/50. No. 315 (24th August 1831). Translation of a letter from Rawul Nujjasungjee and son Koonvursee Bhowsee to John Vibart esquire, magistrate of the Zillah of Ahmadabad.

Your letter dated the 14th of [Jestvud] has been duly received and I have understood its contents. You have written that it has been reported to the Sircar that I had established a mint in the town of Bhownugur for coining copper pice and calling upon me to state by whose authority I had done so, from what year and on what right. I beg to state that this mint has not been recently established by me but has been [Coeval] with the town that the coining of copper pice has been carried on previous to the time of the late Wuckhutsingjee and that according to which, it still continues. The mint has not been established on any new grounds, as the management of the Mehaul of the Bunder has been under my ancestors, so has also that of the mint.

I rely on your protection and goodness

These two letters were sent to the Mint committee who forwarded them on to the Bombay Government with a covering letter. They were unsure of the politics involved in stopping the mint at Bhaunagar. Firstly[515]:

We have the honor to acknowledge the receipt of your letter of the 19th instant with copy of one from the Principal Collector of Ahmadabad and its enclosures respecting the mint in the town of Bhownuggur, the coins issued from which are current in the Western Districts of the Zillah.

Secondly:

We have the honor to acknowledge the receipt of your letter of the 19th instant with copy of one from the Principal Collector of Ahmadabad and its enclosures respecting the mint in the town of Bhownuggur, the coins issued from which are current in the Western Districts of the Zillah.

We request that you will bring to the notice of the Right Honble the Governor in Council that it appears to us to be a question depending upon the nature of our political relations with the Rajah of Bhownuggur whether he should be allowed to coin copper or not and if not, whether any compensation should be given him for relinquishing his privilege. It would certainly be desirable to prevent him coining pice if it can be done without injustice.

Should this however be impracticable or the objections and difficulties be greater than the advantages to be secured, we request you will submit our opinion to His Lordship in Council that the course suggested in para 3 of the extract accompanying the Government Circular of the 27th June last in regard to the coinage of foreign states should be followed.

The revenue commissioner's view was solicited[516]:

In transmitting to you the enclosed copy of a letter from the Mint committee dated the 24th of last month and of the one from the Principal Collector of Ahmadabad therein referred to, I am desired by the Right Honble the Governor to request your opinion on the question therein submitted, regarding the copper coin issuing from the mint at Bhownuggur.

---

[515] Bombay Consultations. P/411/50. No. 372 (19th October 1831). Letter from the Bombay mint committee to government, dated 24th August 1831.

[516] Bombay Consultations. P/411/50. No. 373 (19th October 1831). Letter from the Bombay government, to the revenue commissioner, dated 5th September 1831.

and the revenue commissioner replied in October 1831 stating that he felt sure that the mint could be closed[517]:

I have the honor to acknowledge the receipt of your letter of the 5th ultimo with enclosure and calling on me for my opinion regarding the copper coin issuing from the mint at Bhownuggur. The Circular of Government of the 27th June last with accompanying extract has not been sent to me, so that I do not know to what measure the Mint committee allude in the 3rd paragraph of their letter, neither has the Bhownughur Thacore's answer to Mr Vibart been sent, but Bhownughur has long been known as a place where false and debased coins of different descriptions were fabricated*. It is however situated within our limits and is subject to our authority so that there cannot, I presume, be any doubt of our right to prevent coining of any kind there, if Government should so determine, but I am not sufficiently acquainted with Katteewar rights to be able to say whether the Thacore might not be entitled to coin at Leehor if he chose to transfer his mint to that place…

However the Bombay Government was unsure of the closeness of relationship with the Thacoor of Bhaungar and asked the collector at Ahmadabad for his opinion[518]:

I am directed by the Right Honble the Governor in Council to acknowledge receipt of your letter dated 26th July last to the address of Mr Chief Secretary Norris soliciting instructions respecting the copper coinage struck in the mint at Bhownuggur and to convey the request of the Right Honble the Governor in Council that you will report the exact relations subsisting between this Government and the Thacore of Bhownuggur and whether they are such as to admit of steps being taken for stopping the mint at that place

The collector of Ahmadabad replied in October 1831 that he believed that the Bombay Government had the right to close the mint at Bhaunagar[519]:

I have the honor to acknowledge the receipt of your letter of the 18th instant, calling upon me to state precisely the relations on which the Government stand with regard to the Rajah of Bhownuggur, and beg to inform you that the Rajah is precisely on the same footing with regard to his possession etc in the Goga Purganna as any other Gamettee. I do not find from any of the records that the Rajah ever claimed any sovereign rights in the Goga Purganna previous to its cession by the Paishwa to the Honorouble Company by the treaty of Bassein, and it fully appears by a letter from Mr Chief Secretary Warden dated 23rd April 1811, that the Government did not recognise any further rights than those enjoyed by other Gamettees on our taking possession of the Purganna.

---

[517] Bombay Consultations. P/411/50. No. 374 (19th October 1831). Letter from the revenue commissioner to government, dated 7th October 1831.

* My underlining

[518] Bombay Consultations. P/411/50. No. 375 (19th October 1831). Letter to the principal collector of Ahmadabad from government, dated 18th October 1831.

[519] Bombay Consultations. P/411/50. No. 448 (31st December 1831). Letter from the principal collector of Ahmadabad to government, dated 29th October 1831.

The town of Bhownuggur is subject in every way to the operation of the regulations and I conceive Government would be fully authorized in suppressing or, what would be equivalent to the same, declining to admit the coin as current in our district.

The Rajah in his letter which I did myself the honor to lay before Government, rests his rights on the length of time that the mint has been in operation, upwards of 50 years.

but the Governor also wanted information from other sources and wrote to the political agent in Kathiawar[520]:

I am desired by the Right Honble the Governor in Council to request you will reply to my letter dated 18th October last calling upon you to report the exact relations subsisting between this Government and the Thacore of Bhownuggur, and whether they are such as to admit of steps being taken to prevent that chief from maintaining a mint.

The Bhaunaggar question was raised again in April 1832 when the Political Agent in Kathiawar finally got around to replying. His opinion was somewhat at odds with that of the Collector of Ahmadabad, believing that the mint at Bhaunagar had been in existence for many years and could not therefore be closed at the demand of Bombay[521]:

In acknowledging the receipt of your letter of the 18th October last and the 22nd ultimo, I have the honor to inform you that as far as the tributary relations subsisting between the Thakore of Bhownuggur and the British Government are concerned, I should conceive that they would not admit of taking any steps beyond those of persuasion to prevent that Chief maintaining a mint as it appears to have existed many years before the permanent settlement was made by the late Colonel Walker and the agreements then entered into only require the tributaries to conform to existing usages.

A great many of the Thakore's villages and the capital Bhownuggur itself are however under the jurisdiction of the Honorable Company, both revenue and judicial, and as such subject to the Collector of Ahmadabad. This may confer on the British Government the power of putting down the mint at Bhownuggur, but the Thakore would no doubt in that case petition for permission to establish it in one of his independent villages and, should we prevent his doing so, he would have great reason to complain of this measure being enforced against him alone. Some of the Chiefs of less consequence still being allowed to keep up their mint.

He went on to discuss the fact that the copper coins of Bhaunagar had been banned from use in the Company's territories when an EIC mint had been established at Dholera in 1811/12 (see chapter 9). This had apparently worked effectively and he suggested that the same might be done again:

---

[520] Bombay Consultations. P/411/50. No. 449 (31st December 1831). Letter to the political agent in Kathiawar from government, dated 22nd December 1831.

[521] Bombay Consultations. P/411/51. No. 62 (17th April 1832). Letter from the acting political Agent for Kathiawar to government, dated 3rd January 1832.

The Thakore's Wakeel states that some correspondence took place between Mr Rowles and the Thakore on this subject about the year of Samvut 1867/68 (ad 1810/11) when the mint was established at Dholera. I have desired their Wukeel to produce any letters which may have passed but he has not yet done so, and I therefore beg to suggest that I may be favoured with copies of Mr Rowles' letters to Government on this subject, which will enable me to form a more correct opinion. It must, I think, admit of a question whether our jurisdiction over Bhownuggur as one of the Goga Barra Villages, extends to the power of putting down the mint as it was established so long before that jurisdiction seems to have been exercised either by the Mogul, Peishwa or Gaicawar authorities to the extent it now is. The Thakore complains much of our extension of it but in this point I beg to refer you to Mr Blane's letter to the chief Secretary of the 16th May 1829 handing up a petition on the subject.

When the mint for coining pice was established at Dhollera the currency of the Bhownuggur coin was prohibited in all our districts of Goga, Raunpor and Dhunduka. This I am informed lasted about five years after which coining at Dhollera was discontinued and the Bhownuggur coin became again more or less current in all the above places. A strict prohibition of this would render the Thakore's mint less valuable to him and he would thereby be more easily persuaded to discontinue it.

All of the local chiefs who had mints in the area placed great value on the privilege of coining their own money but the Political Agent thought that it might be possible to buy them off:

The Chiefs who have mints in this province value the privilege very highly, but should it be an object of Government to introduce the Bombay coins they might perhaps be induced to accede to our wishes by offering them a reduction in their tribute equal to the amount they may be considered to realise from their mints. On this subject, however, I speak with the greatest diffidence, not having made any enquiries from the chiefs concerned on the subject, and being quite ignorant whether putting down the mints in Kathywar would be of sufficient importance to induce the British Government to make the pecuniary sacrifices which such a move would no doubt render necessary.

There then follows several minutes on the subject from different people but concludes with a minute from the Governor[522]:

A full consideration of the question leads me to think that the Bhownuggur mint should be suppressed, of the propriety of which measure Mr Sutherland, I observe, entertains no doubt. The right of coinage belongs to us as sovereigns, but as the measure will be disagreeable to the Thakore, I would not recommend it, had I not strong reasons for doing so. In bringing our new coinage into circulation Government has met, is meeting and will probably continue to meet with many obstacles and those obstacles I feel assured for what I have observed at Poona

---

[522] Bombay Consultations. P/411/51. No. 69 (17th April 1832). Minute of the governor (Clare) dated 17th April 1832.

and elsewhere will increase to a very embarrassing extent unless we overcome them by a consistent course of decided measures steadily pursued and firmly enforced.

This appears to have put an end to the matter since no more entries have been found in the records concerning this. Presumably the Bhaunagar mint in question was closed.

Local Native mints in the Concan

In May 1832 the Collector in the Concan reported to Government that there were several mints operating under Angria's control[523]:

I have the honor to acknowledge receipt of your letter dated the 1st instant with copy of one from the Collector in Candeish reporting that a coinage of copper pice (Dubhoo) is in progress at some mints near Panwell.

There are five mints for coining copper coins in Angriah's country and established and farmed by him. They are as follows:

Cusba Apta		2 mints established in July and September 1831
Mouza Kopur	Turuf Ourwuleet	1 mint established in August 1830
Mouza Dar pulee	Turuf Ourwuleet	1 mint established in December 1831
Mouza Gowan	Turuf Ourwuleet	1 mint established in August 1831

The following statement will show the number of coins struck off, and the distance of these places from Panwell

Places	Distance from Panwell	Amount Coined (Rs)
Cusba Apta	5 Coss	13,000
Mouza Kopur	1 Coss	30,000
Ditto Dar pulee	1 ½ Coss	2,000
Ditto Gowan	4 Coss	10,000
Amounting in all to fifty five thousand Rupees, 55,000		

The copper coins are represented as being of an inferior description.

Angria has I presume the full power of establishing mints in his territory, but it will be obvious to Government that if his copper coins are circulated in the Provinces belonging to the British Government that they must materially interfere with the new Government currency as remarked by Mr Boyd's [letter]. Measures should therefore be taken to suppress the mints and all others which may exist in Angria's territory, either by directing Angria to discontinue the coinage or by prohibiting by proclamation the receipt of the copper coins into the Company's territories in payment of revenue.

The Bombay Government resolved that a letter be sent to Angria asking him to shut the mints:

---

[523] Bombay Consultations. P/411/51. No. 141 (6th June 1832). Letter from the acting principal collector in the Concan to government, dated 18th May 1832.

The Acting Persian Secretary is requested to write to Angria informing him that Government has been apprized of the number of mints which have been lately established by him in the Concan, pointing out the inconvenience which arises from the excessive issue of copper pice from them and its importation into the Honble Company's territory, especially at a time when it is the intention of Government to introduce a copper currency of a different description, and requesting that the mints may all be stopped with the exception of such as may be necessary to supply the circulation within his own districts.

An interesting letter from the Collector in the Concan states that the copper coins issued from Angria's mints were identical to those issued by the EIC and so issuing a proclamation banning Angria's coins would be impossible to enforce[524]:

With reference to your letter of the 1st instant in reply to Mr Mills' letter of the 18th ultimo, and directing me to issue a proclamation prohibiting the receipt in payment of revenue of the copper pice issued from the mints established in Angria's territory, I have the honor to state for the information of the Right Honble the Governor in Council that there is no difference between the Honourable Company's pice current, and Angria's, excepting that the latter are newly coined, the die being the same, so that it is impossible to check the receipt in payment of revenue. If Angria cannot be prevented coining, which however I should think we have every right to do, it would, I respectfully beg to observe, be advisable to require him to use another die.

Exactly which of the Company's copper coins is meant by the above statement is not clear but, assuming it refers to the balemark coinage of 1802-31, it might help explain the existence of coins with unreadable crude dates (see chapter 4).

Double pice with strange date (1816 inverted?) and inverted letters in balemark

Despite the Collector's reservations, he was ordered to issue the proclamation:

I am directed to acknowledge the receipt of your letter dated the 29th ultimo, reporting that owing to there being no difference between the Honourable Company's current pice and that coined by Angria, it will be extremely difficult to check the receipt of the latter in payment of the revenue, and to convey to you the instructions of the Right Honble the Governor in

---

[524] Bombay Consultations. P/411/51. No. 171 (11th July 1832). Letter from the principal collector in the Concan to government, dated 29th June 1832.

Council, nevertheless, to issue a proclamation as directed in my letter of the 1st of last month, as it may have the effect of discouraging the import into our districts of the pice coined in Angria's territories.

As the new copper currency is shortly to be introduced, His Lordship in Council deems it unnecessary at the present time either to put a stop to Angria's mints or to request him to adopt a different stamp.

The Collector in the Concan had written to Angria asking that either the copper mints should be closed or the circulation of the pice issued therefrom should be confined to his own territories. In June 1832 Angria replied that he had issued orders to stop the circulation of his coins in British territories. In the letter he gives an interesting insight into how the mints were moved around[525]:

I have received your letter dated 1st June and (after recapitulating substance) have to state in reply that there have been mints for the issue of copper pice established, not recently, but of old in my state which are moved from one village to another according to the convenience of the merchants. There has always been a constant traffic of pice between the merchants of the British territories and those of Colaba. I have issued orders to prevent the circulation of Colaba pice in the British Territories and request that the Bombay Government would issue similar orders.

but in July of 1832 several mints continued to operate[526]:

…In reply I beg to state for the information of the Right Honble the Governor in Council that it has not ceased. One manufactury of pice is at work in Coper, 2 in Aptah, 1 in Dapewlee and one in Gonhan…

However, by August Angria had agreed to shut all but one mint[527]:

I have had the pleasure of receiving your Lordship's letter dated 4th August, requesting that I should take measures to stop all mints but one in my territories.

In reply I beg to state that I have issued injunctions to the managers of mints according to the answer which I sent to your Lordships former letter.

With respect to the present letter, though I shall suffer loss by the reduction of the number of mints, yet as I am unwilling to do anything which might inconvenience the British Government, I have complied with your Lordship's request. But I request that such an arrangement may be made that the mint which I have retained may not meet with obstruction for the future from any public officer.

---

[525] Bombay Consultations. P/411/51. No. 175 (18th July 1832). Translation of a letter from Raghojee Angria, chieftain of Colaba to government, dated 23rd June 1832.

[526] Bombay Consultations. P/411/51. No. 203 (8th August 1832). Letter from the principal collector in the Concan to government, dated 26th July 1832.

[527] Bombay Consultations. P/411/51. No. 254 (19th September 1832). Substance of a letter from Angria, Chieftain of Colaba, dated 30th August 1832.

This seems to have resolved the problems of the local mints issuing copper coins that were interfering with the distribution of the new copper coinage. However, this had only solved one of the problems faced by the Bombay authorities.

Getting the New Pice into Circulation

Having overcome the challenges of installing the new machinery, learning how to operate it, producing the new copper coins and attempting to control the mints owned by other local chieftains, there was still the problem of how to get the new copper coins accepted by the local populace. This problem was largely caused by the fact that the old circulating pice varied in value according to their weight and availability and this issue had been foreseen by the mint committee in 1821 but nothing appears to have been done about it. This difficulty is illustrated by the junior principal collector at Poona who pointed out challenges that he faced in the Deccan[528]:

...I also beg to bring to the notice of Government that the intrinsic value of the old pice and new pice is almost as one half more in favour of the former which weighs 9¾ massee. The new pice weighs 6¼ ditto, so that about 90 new pice would be required for 60 old. On issuing the proclamation directed in the 7th paragraph of the enclosure to your Circular of the 27th June, it is necessary to fix the rate at which the old pice is to be received in lieu of the new. The nominal number of old pice to the ankosee rupee here is 64 but this varies considerably according to the supply of pice in the market.

The number of new pice (quarter annas) fixed as an exchange to the ankoosee rupee in the Government Circular dated the 3rd June last is 62. I beg to know therefore whether the old pice are to be received as old 64 for 62 new, or whether the exchange is to be fixed more in reference to their respective intrinsic value. I fear there will be some difficulty in the exchange as long as the old and new pice, being of such very different value are in currency together, and I should wish to be instructed what authority is to be exercised in compelling persons to receive the currency now introduced as a legal tender, for I foresee much opposition on the part of many in this city. For instance, if a shopkeeper or merchant declines receiving 62 pice of the new currency for an ankoosee rupee and chooses to demand a number equal in value to the number of the old pice I should beg to be acquainted with the authority I am to exercise, as the regulation allude only on this subject to the unlawful coining and issue of the same, vide sections of Regulation XIV AD1827...

...My opinion is that the old should be exchanged for the new at the rate now fixed without regard to the intrinsic value of the copper, but some punishment will be necessary to those who refuse to receive the legal tender. It is probable that if this is the case, the greater part of the old currency will find its way gradually out of the Company's territory. Were we to pay the full value of the copper with the new currency, the loss to Government would be great as it is impossible to distinguish the copper coined in the Sattarah states from that coined in ours.

---

[528] Bombay Consultations. P/411/50. No. 350 (12th October 1831). Letter from the junior principal collector of Poona to government, dated 19th August 1831.

In the same entry in the records there then follows a long discussion about the points raised including the comments of the Governor (Clare) as follows:

This should be referred in the first place to the Mint Committee and they should report whether there is a sufficient quantity of the new pice coined ready to be issued to meet the demands in the several districts. If there is, the Collectors should be supplied with the quantity required by them and they should call in the old pice and exchange them for the new pice and after a certain day the old pice should not be received, but I apprehend a Regulation will be necessary as there is, I apprehend, no obligation of anyone at present to receive the coin issued by Government. This I have already suggested in a former minute.

I do not see how the present difficulty can be met at Poona except by adopting the suggestion of the Junior Principal Collector, but to enable him to carry his plan into effect, he should have a large supply of the new coin.

The Governor wanted to know how many new pice had been issued and whether this was sufficient to meet requirements. If not, how long would it take to do so. In addition be believed that the customs officers on the frontiers should be instructed to prevent importation of foreign copper coins into the territory of the EIC:

I wish the Mint master to be called on to state what quantity of the new pice he has issued, whether he has supplied the Collectors with the quantity they stated they would require and which was, I believe, communicated to him, and if not, when he will be prepared to do so and what causes have hitherto prevented him from issuing the quantity required.

I think Nakadars and the officers stationed on the frontier should be instructed not to allow the importation into our territory of pice coined at Satara or at any other foreign mint, tho' this question has been referred to the Revenue Commissioner for his opinion. I think prompt measures are necessary to check the evil complained of. Having given my sentiments on this subject, it is of so much importance to issue the necessary orders, I beg they may be issued from the Presidency. If, in the details of the question, any better arrangement shall be approved of by my colleagues, I shall be satisfied to abide by their decision.

The revenue commissioner believed that a notice should be issued as well as local mints being stopped in addition to stopping the importation of pice[529]:

…The preventive measures on which my opinion is required are, the stoppage of foreign mints and preventing the import of pice into our territories.

The former of these will no doubt tend to reduce the quantities of pice in circulation and may be accomplished with states entirely dependent on us, but wherever our neighbours are of sufficient rank or power to have mints of their own, as the Guikwar in Guzerat, the Nizam in the Dekhan, the PortuguesePortuguese settlements etc, such a measure could not be resorted to, and these exceptions are sufficient to derange plans for introducing a new coinage by stopping other mints.

---

[529] Bombay Consultations. P/411/50. No. 364 (12th October 1831). Letter from the revenue commissioner to government, dated 1st October 1831.

The second measure proposed for preventing the importation of pice would also have some effect, but it would be extremely difficult to enforce the prohibition if the people continued desirous of obtaining foreign pice, which will no doubt be the case until the Banyans and dealers can be prevailed on to receive the new coinage, without which it can be of no use to the people. I would therefore suggest that some measure should be adopted to declare the new pice a standard currency and to oblige all persons to receive them, under such penalties as Government may be pleased to appoint.

He suggested that the following proclamation be issued:

Be it known to all persons that the Honble Company's Government having observed that the poor have hitherto been subjected to great loss by variations in the numbers of pice current for each rupee, and being desirous to prevent this for the future, determined to coin a copper currency in numbers and denominations corresponding with the divisions of rupees established in the country, of a description which could not be imitated and containing a smaller quantity of metal than could be procured for their nominal value, in order that while false pice could not be coined, there might be no temptation at any time to melt or otherwise dispose of them, and thus occasion similar mischiefs of differences in pice. And whereas it has already been made known by former public notifications that these pice have been coined, this advertisement is now issued to make known the objects of Government in adopting this measure, to remove all doubts respecting it. The pice are merely a token or representation of the value stamped on them and will always be received in the public treasuries at the same rates as they are issued in payment of revenue or any other transactions with Government.

The Governor agreed that the notice should be issued:

…The proclamation may, I think, be issued immediately being translated and lithographed, 500 copies at least should be distributed, of which 100 may be sent to Poona. This proclamation cannot interfere with any ulterior measures to be hereafter decided on.

The mint committee agreed that a new proclamation might help get the new pice into circulation at Poona[530]:

We have the honor to acknowledge the receipt of your letter of the 6th instant with enclosures from the Junior Principal Collector of Poona, reporting the opposition offered by the inhabitants of Poona to the introduction of the new copper coinage.

A reference to Steels's summary of Hindu law and customs (Page 327, near the foot) will at once explain the origin and motive of the opposition of the Poona Shroffs to the introduction of the new quarter annas, which they artfully endeavour to impute to the Ryots. We have very little faith in the efficacy of prohibitions and penalties in such cases, and think that the only means of any avail will be to supply the Collector with a sufficiency of the new quarter annas, to exchange for the old, and then to fix a date beyond which the latter should not be current.

---

[530] Bombay Consultations. P/411/50. No. 407 (15th November 1831). Letter from the mint committee to government, dated 11th October 1831.

In the meantime Mr Giberne might be instructed not to press the issue of, but to comply with all demands for, the new quarter annas…

…We beg to submit to the consideration of His Lordship in Council, whether it would not be expedient to pass a regulation to the effect of the proclamation of the 29th November 1830.

There then follow two proclamations, one of 29th November 1830 stating that the new copper coins were to be struck and the second of the 3rd March 1831 stating that the old pice would continue to pass current

In October 1831 the registrar of the courts provided the opinion of the judges on the legality of issuing the new pice in the way that was planned[531]:

I am directed by the judges of the Sudur Dewanee and Sudur Fuojdaree Adalut to acknowledge receipt of your letter of the 22nd instant and enclosures, calling upon the judges for their opinion whether it is necessary a Regulation should be enacted declaring the new copper pice the standard coin of this Presidency and receivable at the value at which it is issued.

In reply the judges ask me to state that they have no doubt of the new pice being legal tender without any specific law in the strict sense of the expression, as a civil court would certainly hold a dependent exonerated on offering payment in a coin issued formally and at a determinate value by the Government, always excepting any circumstances from which obvious and reasonable objection may arise, for instance offering payment of a lack of rupees in copper coin when other was easily to be had.

The present question however is of a different nature. The Collector appears to contemplate obliging individuals to hold dealings in an article which they do not wish to deal in, to take the new pice not in payment of debts but as a capital to carry on business with, and such an object is not likely to be well or safely obtained by a simple act of authority.

The information furnished by the Collector shows so great a deficiency in the intrinsic value of the new pice that the Honble Board of Council will probably consider the matter as requiring other consideration than belongs in the judicial department.

Also the opinion of the acting advocate general was given in November 1831. He had some doubts about some aspects of the process particularly the fact that the new copper coins contained so much less copper than the old coins[532]:

I have the honor in reply to your letter of 22nd instant to state that I am inclined to doubt the legality of the late issues of copper pice at Poona on the point of intrinsic value and the small proportion it seems to bear to the nominal imposed on the coin by Government but on that ground alone.

---

[531] Bombay Consultations. P/411/50. No. 399 (15th November 1831). Letter from the acting register of the court of sudder adawlat to government, dated 26th October 1831.

[532] Bombay Consultations. P/411/50. No. 400 (15th November 1831). Letter from the acting advocate general to government, dated 31st October 1831.

The prerogative of coining new money or adopting what comes from foreign countries and fixing the value, belongs to the Executive Government here exercizing the sovereignty with which the law has invested the East India Company and this prerogative is as well derived from Royal Grant as from the powers incidental to all sovereigns, of protecting and regulating trade and commerce in their dominions, towards which object a properly established currency is so great an auxiliary.

The Government here therefore ought to possess that power to the same extent as the executive at home exercise it, and it should also be linked by the same constitutional bounds. Now one of these is always to observe a certain proportion between the intrinsic value of the coin and that which is represented by it under the authority of the proclamation. The Government should not admit of a greater departure from the identity of these two valuations than a small seignorage, sufficient to protect the coin from being made an object of trade and speculation and bought up or otherwise [removed] from circulation.

How far the very great difference of intrinsic value or perhaps I should say weight in the new coin and the old has been judged necessary, I cannot pretend to say, or whether it has any reference whatever to that subject, but in case it should not, I should feel great reluctance in recommending to Government the adoption of any compulsory measures to procure a circulation of what seems to me to be a depreciated currency, for such it must be called if the ankosee rupee when in juxtaposition with the new and the old coin is intrinsically worth 90 of the former but 60 of the latter, a fact which ought to have prepared the Collector fully for all and even greater difficulties than he has encountered in pressing the new coin into circulation.

In addition he drew attention to the fact that in England there was a restriction on the amount of copper coin that could be passed in any single transaction:

I shall mention another restriction which has been frequently adopted at home in the issue of a copper coinage Viz: that it shall not be tendered with legal effect, in a greater quantity than makes up the value of the lowest piece of silver money in circulation. In one payment thus no more than 12 half pence or 24 farthings making up six pence shall be offered in one payment, nor of penny or two penny pieces than 12 and 6, being equivalent to one shilling. A similar limit has been put to payments in silver money which cannot however hold an analogy here as our gold has disappeared and the rupee has no superior in our circulation.

However, he believed that Government did have the right to impose the new coinage if they chose to do so. In his opinion, they might have difficulty in enforcing any criminal charges against people doing things wrong because of the token nature of the coinage:

I have little hesitation in declaring that issues by Government of all coins are sufficiently legalized by proclamation and that a regulation is not required. His Majesty exercises his Royal prerogative by proclamation in the case of a new coinage, such as was the late one of sovereigns etc, but for the issue of an accustomed coin such as half crowns, shillings and six pences, a proclamation even has been judged unnecessary.

As to the power which the King is said by some (and among them is found the respectable name of Mathew Hale) to have, of giving a currency at an arbitrary value to a debased circulation, Lord Coke and Sir William Blackstone, denying such to [appear] in the Royal Office of our constitution, the reason seems plain enough Viz: that a power which is given for the benefit of the subject should never be exercised to their loss and detriment.

But however legally the Government may issue coin by the force of their proclamation, I must be permitted to doubt that they can lawfully render penal any offences or malpractices in respect of the present issue on account of the inherent defect of intrinsic value. At the same time I must remind you that as all my objections to the legality of this issue are founded on an hypothesis that may be in reality false, they must be received subject to this qualification.

A circular was then sent to all Collectors asking them to compare the intrinsic values of the new copper coins to the old.

Having collected all these views, the Bombay Government sent their ideas to Poona. The Collector was authorised to establish shops at which the new coins would be received and to take steps to prevent the importation of foreign copper coins. In addition, once he had been provided with sufficient new coins he was to declare the old pice uncurrent[533]:

I am directed to acknowledge the receipt of your letter of 19th August and 13th September last to the address of Mr Secretary Bax on the subject of the new copper currency and to acquaint you that the right Honble the Governor in Council is pleased to authorize your establishing shops at which the new coin will be received, if the shopkeepers still refuse to receive it, and you are satisfied that the measure will have the desired effect, notwithstanding the opposition which you apprehend will be offered to it by the shroffs.

His Lordship in Council desires me at the same time to request you will instruct the Nakadars and officers stationed on the frontier, not to allow the importation of copper money coined in foreign mints.

In order to facilitate bringing the new copper coin into circulation the Right Honble the Governor in Council deems it desirable that the old pice should be declared not current, but not until you are provided with a sufficient quantity of the new to exchange for it. You will therefore be pleased to ascertain in communication with the sub Treasurer, the probable period when a sufficient supply can be obtained for that purpose, and report the date beyond which you would recommend the old copper money should not be current.

It was not just Poona where there were difficulties with the new copper coins. Problems were also encountered at Ahmadnagar. The Collector there suggested that an experiment be tried of choosing just one district and sending all available new pice to that district, and then declaring the old pice uncurrent. He wanted to try it in

---

[533] Bombay Consultations. P/411/50. No. 410 (15th November 1831). Letter to the junior principal collector of Poona from government, dated 12th November 1831.

just one district so that he could effectively flood the market with new coins and if it didn't work it would only affect that one area. In November 1831 he wrote[534]:

I have the honor to inform you that having received a supply of 15,000 Rupees worth of copper quarter anna pieces, my attention has been directed to the circulation of them and that I feel assured from the enquiries I have made that the intention of Government will be effectively opposed by the shroffs and the people until the Collectorate is filled with a supply of the new currency equal in number to the old. My opinion is that an experiment should be tried, in any one district, of sending it all the coins that fall from the mint and none to other places, until that district is completely supplied. That the Collector should send supplies to his Shekdaurs and to Cusba towns equal to the demand for their ranges and when everything is thus ready he should issue a proclamation declaring the circulation of old pice illegal, and at an end. That the old pice would be exchanged for their corresponding weight in new pice (provided they were of the standard and bona fide of the old constituted currency). That the rupee of the district would be exchanged at so many new pice for a rupee and that it was optional [for] withholders to melt down the old pice into utensils etc.

It is not necessary to enter into a history of the reasoning by which I have arrived at these conclusions or a dissertation on so intricate a question. I may content myself by stating that I feel assured a successful opposition will be made to every arrangement for insinuating the new currency by degree, and that Government will at some time have to enter the field with a veto of the kind I have suggested, and the provision of a perfect facility [for] obtaining the new coin. A more suitable scale for exchanging the old copper coins may occur to you, but the main features of the plan will perhaps be best found in those I have recommended. I should advise the measure also in one district only at first, in case it should prove abortive or be met by too much popular discontent.

He also recommended choosing a district some distance away from Bombay:

I should also advise the selection of a district where there are the fewest great shroffs or influential bankers and perhaps the further from Bombay the better, Candeish for instance.

Jageerdaurs and Enamdaurs within the Collectorate should be furnished with the new currency and it should be made obligatory on them to support the measure to the fullest extent.

This was passed to the mint committee who thought that it was a good idea in principle with some exceptions and the Collector of Ahmadnagar was asked how much copper coin he would need to conduct the experiment in his Collectorate.

The Bombay Consultation of 25th January 1832 contains letters from the collectors of Candeish (No 20), Poona (No. 21), Concan (No. 22), Surat (No. 23), Ahmadabad (No. 43) and Dharwar (No. 24) discussing the new copper coins[535].

---

[534] Bombay Consultations. P/411/50. No. 426 (23rd November 1831). Letter from the principal collector of Ahmednuggur to government, dated 10th November 1831.

[535] Bombay Consultations. P/411/51. No. 4 (25th January 1832). Letter from the mint master to government, dated 31st December 1831.

In addition to the problems of the new pice, some districts had other problems with copper coins. For instance, in March 1832 the sub-collector of Dharwar wrote[536]:

I have the honor to acknowledge your letter of the 13th instant transmitting a communication from the Budamee Mamlutdar for my report.

The Mamlutdar accounts for the large proportion of copper in his remittance to Dharwar by the fact that the rate of pice in the bazar has fallen below the Government rate enabling the Ryot to purchase 48 pice for one rupee, while the Government rate is fixed at 46.

By this variation between the bazar price and the rate at which copper is payable into the public treasury the Government apparently loses two pice per rupee and whether the gain is the Ryot's or the Sowkar's from whom he buys the money wherewith to pay his rent, there seems no remedy so long as the present rate remains fixed at 46 pice per Surat rupee.

But there is another and a direct loss to Government in the expense of transporting copper over silver money. One bullock carries usually 5000 rupees in silver and only 150 Rs worth of pice, showing a difference of more than thirty to one in favour of silver in transport.

The districts of Indee, Moodebehall, Hoongoond, and Budamee lie contiguous to the Nizam's provinces and a considerable traffic goes on between the subjects of the two states, the pice current on both sides [of] the frontier being the "Shahee Pice", the Government rate of which was altered in 1829 from 48 to 46 per Surat rupee throughout the Dharwar territories. But the silver money from the Nizam's side, owing to its inferior quality, is not payable at our treasuries as the copper is; so that sellers from our districts prefer payment in copper, and hence one cause of the plenty that has reduced the value of pice as compared with silver, in this part of the country…

The army was also having difficulty with the new pice. In April 1832 the army paymaster wrote to Bombay[537]:

I respectfully beg to bring to the notice of the Right Honble the Governor in Council that the new copper quarter anna pice has been issued in large quantities from this office during the last 3 months at the rate of 64 the rupee in conformity with the Government Proclamation 13th October 1831. The shroffs, merchants and retail dealers in the regimental bazars, and in the towns of Belgaum and Shapoor have gradually increased the number which they demand for a rupee from those with whom they deal and have this day raised it to seventy three.

All these problems caused the mint committee to recommend, at a meeting held in May 1832, that the pice should first be introduced into Bombay using the method first suggested by the Collector of Ahmadnagar[538]:

---

[536] Bombay Consultations. P/411/51. No. 49 (28th March 1832). Letter from the sub-collector of Dharwar to the acting principal collector, dated 8th February 1832.

[537] Bombay Consultations. P/411/51. No. 75 (17th April 1832). Letter from the army paymaster to government, dated 27th March 1832.

[538] Bombay Consultations. P/411/51. No. 81 (2nd May 1832). Letter from the mint committee to government, dated 30th March 1832.

Having called upon the Acting Collector of Ahmednuggur to report what measures had been taken in that Collectorate for the introduction of the new copper coinage under the orders of 15th December last, we request you will be pleased to lay before the Right Honble the Governor in Council the accompanying excerpt of his reply dated 22nd instant from which it appears that no further measures have as yet been adopted and we therefore beg to submit for the consideration of His Lordship in Council that the course which has been authorized for that district should in the first instance be adopted in Bombay…

This was agreed and the acting collector of revenue at Bombay suggested that the new copper coins could be distributed from the General Treasury rather than from several shops set up around the island[539].

By May 1832 the acting advocate general seems to have reconsidered his legal position with regard to the coins and stated that it would be legal for Government to declare the old copper coins not legal tender from a particular date. He was asked for more information about this. His ideas were sent to the mint committee[540].

In July 1832 the mint committee gave their opinion[541]:

We have the honor to acknowledge the receipt of your letter of the 20th instant, with copy of one from the Acting Advocate General, and calling on our opinion on the suggestions of that officer with regard to the measures most desirable to be adopted for bringing the new copper currency into circulation at the Presidency.

We request you will inform the Right Honble the Governor in Council that we cannot concur in the Advocate General's opinion that exchanging the old for the new coins for weight, "does not infer any loss for Government in the transaction", since the cost of preparing a superior coin is at least equal to the difference of intrinsic value, not to mention that Government would thereby depreciate their own coin. Eighty one of the quarter annas are about equal in weight to fifty of the old pice, which are equivalent to one rupee and, if issued at this low valuation, the object of Government would not be attained, for the new coin could hardly ever be expected to acquire the nominal value of 64 to the rupee, which they are intended to bear. The new quarter anna, it should be remembered is a token [only] but from the weights given in the margin it will be seen that the new copper coin for this Presidency is nearly of the same weight as the corresponding value in English copper money.

They suggested that Government should buy-up the old pice and then issue the new pice with the help of shroffs. By recruiting the very people most opposed to the new coins presumably they hoped to overcome some of the opposition:

---

[539] Bombay Consultations. P/411/51. No. 116 (16th May 1832). Letter from the acting collector of revenue at Bombay to government, dated 1st May 1832.

[540] Bombay Consultations. P/411/51. No. 135 (30th May 1832). Letter from the acting advocate general to government, dated 15th May 1832.

[541] Bombay Consultations. P/411/51. No. 227 (29th August 1832). Letter from mint committee to government, dated 27th July 1832.

Every legal difficulty as to an equitable exchange rate would however be overcome by Government offering to buy up the old pice for silver and the proclamation suggested in our letter of the 30th March should be altered in this respect.

It would be desirable to render it the interest of the shroffs who may be employed as suggested in Paragraph 8 of that letter, to aid the views of Government by the mode of remunerating them, and secure as far as possible the aid of persons already pursuing the trade of shroffs. Such persons should be employed and remunerated by a small monthly payment not exceeding perhaps 5 rupees and a per cent on the amount of old pice which they may pay into the Treasury. When employed in this duty by Government, they should engage to give the full exchange in conformity with the proclamation.

Should any shroffs offer to establish shops in the neighbourhood of those employed by Government, it might be desirable for the Government shroffs to be withdrawn.

They suggested offering a five percent premium for old pice with a value of one hundred rupees or more:

We would further recommend that a premium of 5 per cent should be offered in the public proclamation for any sum not less than rupees one hundred in pice which may be brought to the Treasury before the expiration of two months, unless previously ordered otherwise.

It appears to us immaterial whether the old pice be bought up with silver or with the new copper coin, provided only that they be bought up. For in whatever way they are withdrawn from circulation, other copper coin, viz the new quarter annas, must take their place and the silver will return to the Treasury. It will not however be consistent with the arrangement in the preceding paragraph to give the offer of exchanging the new coin for silver as was proposed in the proclamation, and it should be altered in this respect.

From the forgoing observations, His Lordship in Council will perceive that we do not consider it desirable to purchase the old coin at the market price of sheet copper, and it would not be the interest of the public to accept any such offer. It may be for consideration at a future time, whether it would be expedient to announce that after a certain date the old coin will no longer be exchangeable at the Treasury at a higher rate than the value of the copper.

The difficulties, if any should be experienced, will, we are led to believe, be rather occasioned by the change from 50 to 64 pieces per rupee in the division of the copper money, than in the reduction of weight, but as dealers will be without remedy if they refuse to receive payment for their goods from parties tendering it within the limited amount in the new coin, when it shall have been duly constituted a legal tender, we trust the inconvenience arising from this and from the non receipt of the old coin by the departments of Government, in conjunction with the arrangements providing facilities for equitably exchanging the old coin as submitted in our report of the 30th March last and in this letter will, if steadily persevered in, be found effectual.

To achieve this they proposed issuing a proclamation stating that from a certain date the new copper coinage would be the legal copper money of Bombay. They further proposed that shroffs would be employed to undertake the distribution of the new coins and the collection of the old and that this would take place at various places throughout the Island at rates that were already established (e.g. 50 old pice for one rupee).

The Governor asked the mint committee to provide more information. He immediately agreed with some of their ideas but he wanted to know if there were enough new pice available and if the five per cent premium could be offered on smaller sums of old rupees. He also wanted to know when the old pice would become uncurrent[542]:

The Mint committee should state whether there is a sufficient quantity of new pice for circulation in the island of Bombay and if there is, when the arrangements recommended by them in their letter of 27th July can be completed and what period they would propose to fix after when the old pice will not be received by the public officers of Government.

They may be asked whether there would be any objection to giving a premium of 5 per cent for a less sum than rupees 100 worth of old pice. If the same premium was offered even for so low a sum as rupees 10 worth of old pice it would, I should think, facilitate the withdrawal of them from the market.

The Mint committee may also state why they would confine the offer of a premium of 5 per cent to those only who bring their old pice to the General treasury and whether they consider that it would be objectionable to authorize the Government shroffs at the different stations in the island to give the same premium.

The suggestion of the Mint committee in paras 4 & 5 may be approved and they should state what percentage they will recommend to be given to the Govt shroffs on the amounts of old pice brought by them into the treasury.

The mint committee replied to the Governor's requests and stated that there was plenty of copper coin available to replace the old coin in Bombay and that the date would be fixed when the blank space at the beginning of the proclamation was filled in and the old coin should be returned within two months. This could be extended if necessary.

There was no objection to giving the 5 per cent premium to sums as low as 50 rupees worth of old pice[543].

On 24th October 1832 a proclamation was issued declaring the new copper coins to be the legal money of Bombay town and Island[544]:

The Right Honble the Governor in Council is pleased to declare that from the 24th instant the new copper coinage, as announced in the proclamation dated 29th of November 1830 is the legal copper money of the town and Island of Bombay and no other will be received by the public officers of Government.

A premium of 5 per cent will be given for any sum not less than rupees 50 in good pice of the

---

[542] Bombay Consultations. P/411/51. No. 228 (29th August 1832). Minute of the governor, dated 29th August 1832.

[543] Bombay Consultations. P/411/51. No. 259 (26th September 1832). Letter from the mint committee to government, dated 28th August 1832.

[544] Bombay Consultations. P/411/51. No. 315 (24th October 1832). Proclamation, dated 24th October 1832.

old currency which may be brought by individuals or the shroffs employed by Government to the treasury before the expiration of two months from this date, unless previously ordered otherwise.

For the convenience of the public, the Governor in Council has been pleased to cause shroffs to be employed for two months or until further orders at the under mentioned places, for the purpose of exchanging the new quarter annas and pies for good pice of the old currency, who will give in exchange without any deduction for exchanging

1 rupee (silver) for 50 pice

64 quarter annas for 50 pice

64 quarter annas for 1 rupee

3 new pies for 1 quarter anna

Places at which money will be exchanged by Government shroffs

The General Treasury

The Civil and Marine Pay Offices

The military Pay Office

Collector's Office

Custom House in the Fort

Custom House – Musjeed Bunder

Custom House – Mahim

The Principle Bazar in the Fort

The green market without the fort

Near Mumbadave

The Bazar near Jamsetjee Jeejeebhoy's House

Pydownee without the fort

Bhendy Bazar (near the Durga)

The bazar in the neighbourhood of the jail

Near Musjeed Budar gate

The Bazar near the washerman Tank

Chinch Bunder

The Bazar near the slaughterhouse

Kamatty Poord

Duncan Road in the Bazar

The bazar near Mr G Higg's stable in [Girojoun..]

The Bazar in Mazagon

The bazar in Mahim

The bazar in Colaba

Summary of Activities Undertaken to get the Copper Coins into Circulation

None of this went down very well with the authorities in London. In 1837 they summarised all this activity to get the new coinage into circulation and were very critical of the approach adopted by the Bombay authorities[545]:

---

[545] Dispatches to Bombay. E/4/1061. 187-197. 10th May 1837.

In our dispatch 1 this department, dated the 27ᵗʰ March 1829, we directed that a copper coinage should be struck similar to that prescribed for Bengal, both in weight and denomination but it appears that the first issue of such a coinage did not take place till the early part of the year 1831.

The first mistake made had been to assume that it would be possible to allow the old and the new copper coins to circulate concurrently when it should have been obvious that the difference in intrinsic value between the coins was so great that this could never work. This had meant that the early attempt to get the coins circulating in Bombay had failed:

It was your intention that for a time the new and the old currency should circulate concurrently, but the difference between the nominal and actual value in the new coins was much greater than the corresponding difference in the old, and there was naturally an indisposition to receive the former, so that the quantity issued at the Presidency during a period of several months was inconsiderable.

The same problems were encountered when efforts were made to introduce the coins into the various collectorates. Furthermore, having decided upon a particular course of action in Ahmadnagar, the action was not undertaken because of the absence of a particular member of staff, whose job should have been filled by someone else during his absence. Eventually this course of action was tried successfully in Bombay itself and then rolled out to various collectorates:

In the various collectorates and especially that of Poona, a similar feeling seems to have prevailed, and the reception of the new coinage into circulation was thereby seriously retarded. After various expedients had been tried and had failed, you determined to provide each district in succession with the full amount of new coinage required to meet the wants of the inhabitants and to fix an early period for putting an end to the circulation of the old.

Even this measure was delayed by your failing to carry it into effect in the district of Ahmednuggur (where you intended first to introduce it and had made arrangements accordingly), in consequence, as you state, of the absence at the Neilgherries of Major Robertson, the Collector. This is a most unsatisfactory reason. The public service ought not to have been obstructed by the omission to appoint in Major Robertson's place an officer capable of executing, during his accidental absence, all the duties of his station. At length the plan was tried at the Presidency in October 1832. To facilitate the desired operation a premium was offered for the old currency, if brought to the mint in sums of a certain amount before the expiration of two months, after which the old coin was to be received only at its metallic value. By this course the circulation of the new coinage was established at the Presidency, and it was extended by similar means to the islands of Salsette and Caranja without much difficulty. In the remaining districts of the Tanna Collectorate some obstructions occurred but we learn from your latest communication on the subject that the new coinage had been brought into circulation throughout that Collectorate and also in those of Rutnagurree, Poona and Ahmednuggur, that it was then in course of introduction into the Southern Maratha Country and that you anticipated in the districts remaining to be supplied, the same success which had attended your endeavours in those just named.

Although this proved satisfactory, the Board was not happy about the efforts to suppress the various local mints run by native rulers:

These results and expectations are satisfactory but we feel it necessary to advert briefly to some of the measures which you adopted with the view of facilitating the establishment of the new coinage. We observe that one of those measures was the suppression of certain mints belonging to native chieftains, the operations of which were adding to the difficulties with which you had to contend. That it was desirable to get rid of these establishments we do not question, but we deem it necessary to express our anxious hope that in effecting this object, the engagements and relations subsisting between the Company and the chiefs to whom those mints belong, were duly respected, and we desire that such information may be furnished as will remove all doubt upon this point.

They then went back to criticising the Bombay Government for believing the old and new coins could circulate together:

We are suprized that it should ever have been thought possible that the two currencies could circulate together and that the inevitable inconvenience and distress consequent upon an attempt to establish such joint circulation could have been overlooked. A large portion of the opposition manifested to the new coin might possibly proceed, as you believed, from Shroffs and interested persons, but the effects extended to the community generally and more especially pressed upon that part of it least able to bear them. The poor would naturally be dissatisfied with a currency with which they were unable to procure the necessities of life, and they ought to have been spared the suffering thus occasioned.

They thought the plan to open shops in Poona was *futile*:

The plan of opening shops as at Poona, for the receipt of the new copper money was futile in the extreme as the money was not thereby kept in circulation. The shops afforded to those who held it the means of returning it upon the hands of Government, and the system thus established consequently ended where it began.

They disapproved of the fact that there had been several attempts to force the new coins onto the poorer classes of people:

While noticing some of the errors which you were led to commit, we cannot refrain from expressing our disapprobation of the several instances in which the new currency was forced upon the humbler dependents of Government in discharge of a portion of their pay and allowances. Such attempts should not under any circumstances have been made and their obvious inexpediency is aggravated by the certainty that they must always prove abortive.

The Bombay authorities should not have wasted so much time on the various projects that they tried but should just have got on with the job. Because of the time wasted, the Board noted that even by 1836 the new copper coins had only been introduced into half the areas under the control of the Bombay Presidency:

You were in error also in wasting so much time and labor on projects for overcoming the difficulties with which you had to contend, difficulties of your own creating and which would not have occurred had you resolved on making arrangements at once for exchanging the new copper coin for the old. Had you acted promptly and vigourously there is no reason to doubt that the desired object would have been attained at a much earlier period, but owing to the delays which have been suffered to occur in carrying this important measure into effect, nearly seven years had elapsed from the date of our orders when your letter of 29th of February 1836 was written informing us that at that time the new copper currency had scarcely been fully introduced into half the territories under your Government. Such promptitude was the more imperiously pressed upon you by the superabundance of copper in circulation. To add to the amount and to delay so long the withdrawing of the old currency was needlessly to augment your difficulties.

Finally they considered that care should be taken in allowing too many copper coins into circulation and that these should only be accepted for values up to half a rupee:

The point last mentioned leads us to a subject which we feel incumbent upon us to press most earnestly upon your attention. The importance of guarding against any excess of the issue of copper coin from the Public Treasury. The difference between the nominal and actual value of the copper coinage will be productive of our public convenience, so long as that coinage is restricted to the place which it ought to occupy in the currency, that of representing small fractions of silver coin; but if unduly forced into circulation to an extent beyond the necessities of the community, depreciation will ensue, accompanied by its unavoidable consequences of distress among the people, especially the poorer classes and embarrassment to the Government.

For the purpose of averting such evil it is highly desirable that copper money should at the earliest possible period, cease to be a legal tender for sums exceeding half a rupee. We have fixed this amount for the territories under the Presidency of Bengal and it will be obviously beneficial to extend the same rule to those subject to your Presidency. One effect of the change will be an increased demand for silver coins of small value and it will be necessary to provide for this by the preparation and distribution of an adequate supply of half and quarter rupees. We also direct that a smaller silver coin than you have yet issued be fabricated and put into circulation as soon as practicable. Its weight should be 22½ grains troy and its value will be one-eighth of a "Company's Rupee"…

By 1836 the uniform currency for all of British India had been introduced, so it is interesting to note that London instructed Bombay, rather than Calcutta, to issue a coin denominated one eighth rupee. In fact, eighth rupees were not issued until 1841.

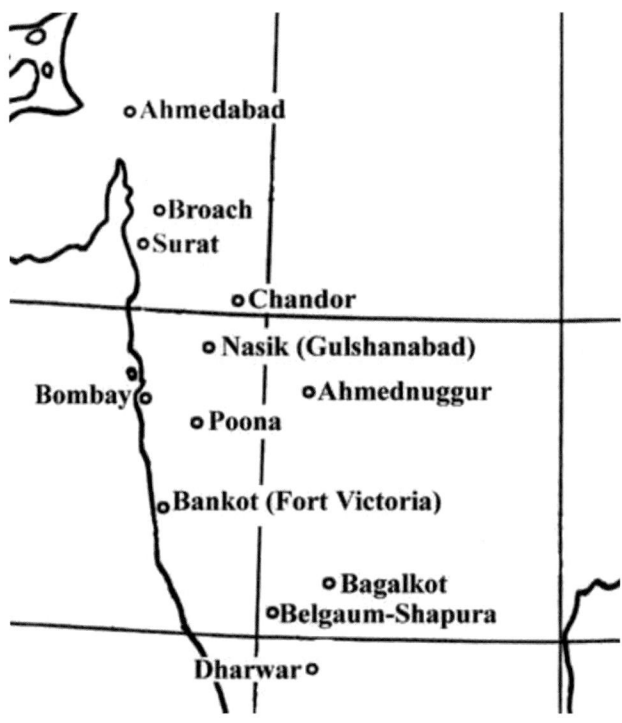

Mints of the Bombay Presidency

Chapter 9 – The Local and Transitional Mints of the Deccan and other places

Summary

As the British extended their control of India during the late eighteenth and early nineteenth centuries, a number of areas that had active mints fell under their management. Some of these mints were kept in operation for a number of years after they were taken over by the British. Bhandare has used the term 'transitional' to describe mints of this type[546], and that convention has been used here, although the term 'provincial' is sometimes used in the records. There are a number of examples of this happening on the western side of India, where various territories came under the control of the Bombay Presidency in the first half of the nineteenth century. Pridmore has recorded the coins of some of these mints (e.g. those of Surat), but, for some reason, he chose to ignore others, even quite major mints such as Poona and Ahmedabad. Some publications[547] give listings of coins from these mints with headings such as 'EIC', but provide no supporting documentary evidence for the attributions and these are sometimes incorrect. A study of the records stored in the India Office Library has therefore been undertaken to fill some of this gap.

Inland from Bombay was the area known as the Deccan, with the mints of Poona, Nasik/Chandore and Ahmadnagar, which were all acquired in 1817/1818. To the north lay the mints of Surat, Ahmadabad and Broach and to the south were the mints of the "Southern Maratha Country", Bagalkot and Belgaum-Shahpur. Bankot, though not strictly a 'transitional' mint, is included here because it behaved as a local mint. Bhakkar, in Sind, is also covered in this chapter. The records are not completely clear about the operations of these mints, but what archival evidence does exist can be combined with knowledge of the coins themselves to produce a much clearer picture.

Circulatory context

One important consideration in a discussion of the transitional and local mints is the fact that the coins issued from the mints that came under British control, together with those that remained under the control of native rulers, circulated together with many older types of coin in any one area. Local money-changers or shroffs found a niche for themselves in exchanging one type of coin for another at a rate that allowed them a profit. This rate of exchange is referred to in the records as the "bazar" rate. Once the British had gained control of the different regions, they instructed their local officials to collect examples of all the coins circulating in these regions and send them to Bombay for assay. The assay master at Bombay published two tables, one in 1817[548] (covering the Northern districts) and another in 1821[549] (covering the whole Presidency),

---

[546] Bhandare S. Talk presented to the Royal Numismatic Society 2001
[547] Bruce C.R., Deyell J.S., Rhodes N., Spengler W.F. The Standard Guide to South Asian Coins and Paper Money since 1556 AD. Krause publications, Iola, Wisonsin (1981).
[548] Bombay Consultations, IOR P/408/31, p. 211, 5th March 1817.
[549] Bombay Consultations, IOR P/411/40 p. 32, 13th August 1821.

establishing an official exchange rate between all of the different coins in circulation, allowing the local officials to accept the coins in payment of taxes. As the grip of the British tightened on the territories in their possession, the number of different coins that were acceptable in payment of taxes was gradually reduced and hence the coinage gradually became more standard. However, standardisation throughout the Bombay Presidency could not be achieved until the mint at Bombay had acquired the capability of meeting the demand of the entire Presidency and it could not do this until a new steam-driven mint was introduced at the beginning of the 1830s. Even then, the coins of the neighbouring states crossed into British controlled areas and continued to be used by the local population. The old (pre-steam) mint at Bombay could not meet the demand for the whole Presidency and this provides the explanation for the existence of the transitional mints. They were essential in providing sufficient currency until about 1834/35, because the Bombay mint could not satisfy the demand, although many of the transitional mints were closed before then.

Coins in circulation in the Bombay Presidency in 1820 are shown in the appendix at the end of this chapter[550].

Ahmadabad Mint

Ahmad Shah I, sovereign of the independent state of Gujarat, founded the city of Ahmadabad in AD 1411 and it became the capital. Akbar annexed Gujarat in 1572/3 and from then on Ahmadabad was an important mint town of the Moghuls, the majority of the emperors having coins struck there.

Moghul rule continued until the end of the reign of Ahmad Shah Bahadur. The city was then taken by the Marathas who, in 1755, were ejected by a Moghul army under Momin Khan, who restored the rule of the emperor, at least nominally. In 1757 Momin Khan surrendered Ahmadabad to the Marathas, an event that ended all Moghul connection with the place. Between 1757 and 1817 the city was either in the hands of the Marathas or held on lease by the Gaikwars of Baroda. In 1817 an agreement was struck between the Gaikwar and the British to hand over Ahmadabad to the latter. This was duly implemented and the British took over the city including the mint[551].

However, the British had been established in the city for many years before 1817. A Company of 32 Englishmen, led by Mr Aldworth had arrived at Ahmadabad in 1613 and a house had been bought and a factory established in 1614[552], but they had not obtained any right to coin money. They were obliged, therefore, to have their bullion coined at the local mint and several references exist in the records concerning the problems that this caused (e.g. the cost)[553].

After the British took control of the city in 1817, the Collector, Mr. Dunlop, found the mint

---

The table was published by Stevens in ONS Newsletter No. 180, p. 27.

[550] Bombay Consultations, IOR P/411/40 p. 32. Letter from the assay master to Government, dated 13th August 1821.

[551] Wiggins K.W. Acquisition of Indian Mints by E.I.CO. Numismatic Panorama, New Delhi, 1996.

[552] Bombay Gazetteer (1879), Vol. IV, Ahmadabad, p. 253. Government Press Bombay.

[553] Foster W., The English Factories in India 1618-1621. Clarendon Press, Oxford, 1906.

Foster W., The English Factories in India 1624-1629. Clarendon Press, Oxford, 1909, p. 325.

closed and the supply of circulating medium so low as seriously to impede trade[554]. This is confirmed in a letter from Dunlop to Government in which he proposed to abolish a nominal currency called *"Aunt"* (sometimes spelt *Ant*) and in which he explained the background to the problem. He stated that in 1780/81 the mint had been closed and sicca rupees had become scarce, so the merchants resorted to transfers in each other's books as a method of mutual payment. This was referred to as *"dealing in aunt"*. In 1805/06 this had been prohibited and this prohibition had continued all the time that sicca rupees were available. However, the mint had been closed again (no date given) and dealing in *"aunt"* had restarted and still continued in 1818 when Dunlop wrote the letter[555].

Dunlop appears to have re-opened the mint in December 1817[556]:

In reference to your letter of 20th February approving of my proceedings with respect to the Sicca mint at this place, I have the honor to transmit for information of Government an abstract statement of the sums coined, and showing also the amount of profit, which has been brought to the credit of Government.

The system reported in my letter of 28th December was continued until the end of February, when the receipt of your letter above referred to, directing me not to seek a higher rate of profit than might be sufficient to cover all expenses, determined me to fix the same rate of mint charges as that taken at the mint in Bombay, namely three per cent, which is considerably cheaper than the natives have been accustomed to get their bullion coined, so that the small advantage which accrues to Government on this rate, did not appear more than sufficient to cover incidental expenses, or more than should reasonably be paid for coin to secure it from being melted up for common purposes.

The amounts allowed both for wastage or melting and forming the coins were found by experience to be too large and have been accordingly reduced, but the contractors for smelting, I have reason to believe, have gone rather too far, and that some small increase to the present allowance will be requisite, the bullion now melted at 3 rupees per thousand less than the rate formerly reported to Government.

Every savings of this description is immediately carried to the credit of Government, and the whole profit is up to the end of June amounting to Rupees 31421.1.82, and the mint continues to be supplied with bullion, so that there does not appear any prospect of the working being stopped.

It seems only requisite for me to notice the large amount of profit which appears during the first months, the Mint had not been worked before for a considerable time, siccas had consequently obtained an artificial value, from their scarcity, and bullion sold from this cause at a very low price, as compared with sicca rupees.

Several other causes concurred to produce the same effect. Dollars have been imported freely for inland speculations, which were all abruptly stopped by the war, so that there was a great competition at that time to have them coined, as the only means of saving the interest, or disposing of their commodity.

---

[554] Bombay Gazetteer, Vol. IV, Ahmadabad, p. 72. Government Central Press, Bombay, 1879.

[555] Bombay Consultations, IOR P/411/38 p. 119, 13th May 1818.

[556] Bombay Consultations, IOR P/411/38, p. 216, 9th September 1818. Letter from the Collector at Ahmadabad to Government, dated 8th August.

Under the circumstances of trouble and responsibility to which the coinage of upwards of twelve lacs and a half of rupees, has subjected me, and the large profit which has resulted from my superintendence, I have the honor to request you will submit my claim to Government for remuneration.

The duties of Mint Master were long performed by the Collector at Surat, for which, I am informed, he received a monthly salary, and I request that Government may be pleased to grant me an allowance, either on this principle or such other as may appear most advisable to the Right Honorable the Governor in Council.

Details of the amount of coin produced at the mint are also shown in this extract and have been summarised in the following table:

Month	Value (Rs.Qtrs.Raes)
Dec 1817	95067.02.00
Jan 1818	211556.03.30
Feb 1818	218083.02.98
Mar 1818	206785.00.00
Apr 1818	205668.02.00
May 1818	177324.00.00
Jun 1818	150124.02.00

Amount of Silver Coin Produced at Ahmadabad

In February 1818, the mint committee in Bombay, whilst agreeing with Dunlop's actions in restarting the mint, suggested that the Judge and Magistrate (one person) at Ahmadabad should visit the mint two or three times a month and indiscriminately take a few coins and send them for assay at Bombay. Thenceforth this provided the means of controlling the quality of the coins issued from the mint[557]:

…As a means of placing the mint however, as far as possible under the control of the mint officers at the Presidency, in the same manner as the Surat mint formerly was, the Judge and Magistrate should be instructed to proceed without any previous notice two or three times in the month, at the least, to the mint and oftener when much business is going on, and to take a few pieces indiscriminately from the hands of the workmen – say not fewer then ten – and dispatch them under his seal at the end of the month, to the Mint Master at the Presidency for examination.

---

[557] Bombay Consultations, IOR P/408/36, p. 314, 25th February 1818.

Silver rupee of Ahmadabad. Date to right and above top line on obverse

Silver rupee of Ahmadabad. Date to left and below top line on obverse

Obverse: sikka mubārak bādshāh ghazi muḥammad akbar shāh (AH) (= the auspicious coin of the victorious Emperor Muhammad Akbar Shah [AH]).
Reverse: ẓarb ahmādābād sanah (RY) julūs maimanat mānūs (= Struck at Ahmadabad in his [RY] year of tranquil prosperity.

In October 1818, the mint committee recommended that the coinage should continue but the Financial Committee resolved that the Ahmadabad authorities should be asked for their opinion on the necessity for this, given that a new uniform coinage (for the Bombay Presidency) would soon be issued following the installation of a new mint at Bombay[558]. Of course, the new Bombay mint did not actually become operational until the 1830s, when a steam driven mint started operations, but, in 1818, consideration was being given to the possibility of building a local machine-driven mint (see chapter 6.).

As far as the copper coinage was concerned, Dunlop found that there was a shortage in 1818, but that this was caused by the shroffs deliberately taking the coins out of circulation. He therefore immediately began striking copper pice at the mint, with the effect that the hoarded copper was released into the market and minting was stopped[559]:

In reference to my letter of 6th May, I request you will have the goodness to acquaint the Right Honorable the Governor in Council that the shroffs of this place had so completely engrossed all the former pice

---

[558] Proceedings of the Bombay Financial Committee, IOR P/408/39, p. 1409, 21st October 1818.

[559] Proceedings of the Bombay mint committee, IOR P/411/38 p. 167, 8th July 1818. Letter from the Collector at Ahmadabad to Mr Secretary Newnham dated 22nd June.

coinage, with the view of [forcing] the people to accept of a much smaller number than had been fixed for the rupee, that no change was to be obtained in the city.

Finding it impossible to ascertain the persons by whom this monopoly was made, it became necessary for me immediately to coin other pice, for which purpose I purchased one hundred maund of copper, on the best terms procurable (an account of which shall be afterwards forwarded) and yesterday began making pice of the same weight as those now current here, and I am happy to say with the very best effect, as pice are today in sufficient numbers at every shop for the established rate of 64 per rupee.

The object I had in view being thus answered I shall not carry the experiment any further at present, than the quantity of copper already purchased (with the approbation of Government) than may from time to time be necessary to defeat similar interested combinations of shroffs.

Copper pice of the Ahmadabad mint.
Obverse: falūs akbar shāh [AH].
Reverse: ahmādābād [RY] julūs

The copper coinage of Ahmadabad was discussed by Wiggins in 1981[560]. He believed that copper pice were only struck dated 1234 and 1236 and that those given the date 1233 (1817/18), by Masters[561], were the result of an incorrect reading because this date was too early for the EIC. However the letter from Dunlop (above) would seem to refute this and coins dated 1233 are included in the Stevens catalogue[562] (indeed Wiggins had one of these in his collection, so his view may have changed after writing his paper). Pice dated 1232 and sold in the Noble sale (Noble (1995), sale 48, lot 2170) must be pre-EIC or may be a mis-reading. Unfortunately, there were no photos of these coins in the sale catalogue. Coins dated 1235 have been reported by Masters and in the Noble sale so this date is included in the catalogue[563].

In 1819 the standard for the Ahmadabad rupee was established by the assay master at Bombay[564]:

I am not aware that the professed standard weight in troy grains or quantity of pure silver in the Ahmadabad sicca rupees has hitherto been declared,…; perhaps the best standard would be weight 181 troy

---

[560] Wiggins (1981) ONS Newsletter 73.

[561] Masters (1914), Numismatic Supplement No. XXII, pp. 153-173.

[562] Stevens P, The Coins of the East India Company. Presidency Series. (2017), pp. 280-283.

[563] 563 Stevens P, The Coins of the East India Company. Presidency Series. (2017), pp. 280-283.

[564] Bombay Consultations, IOR P/411/39, p. 20, 3rd March 1819.

grains and purity or touch 85⅛ per cent. Each coin would thus contain 154 grains and a small fraction of no importance, of pure silver. I suggest this standard because it is very nearly the actual average of the coins of last year.

There are further references to the results of assays of the coins from the Ahmadabad mint in 1821[565], and in 1828 the Collector was able to report[566]:

…there is no other coin current in this collectorate except the Ahmadabad sicca rupees which are always received in revenue payments and struck by the Government at this place.

No record of the date of final closure of the Ahmadabad mint has been traced. By 1832 the mint had stopped producing copper coins because a proclamation was issued in that year concerning the rate of exchange of the new Bombay quarter annas for the old Ahmadabad pice[567]:

The Right Honorable the Governor in Council is pleased to give notice that the old pice called Ahmadabad, being genuine coin and not counterfeits, shall continue until further orders to be current throughout the several Purgannahs comprizing the Ahmadabad collectorate and will at all times be exchangeable for the new copper currency to the extent of the supply in the revenue treasuries of the district and Sudder station at the rate noticed below.

Sixty new quarter anna pice for 68 Ahmadabad pice.

Rupees and half rupees exist dated 1249 (1833/34) so the mint cannot have been closed before then, and Masters[568] lists coins dated 1250 and 1251 so the mint may have continued in operation until 1835, although no coins of these dates have been seen by the current author.

Gold third? mohur of the Ahmadabad mint

The coins themselves consist of silver rupees and copper pice dated from AH 1233 to AH 1249 (1817 to 1834). The silver coins come in two varieties, one with the date to the right and above the top line on the obverse, the other with the date to the left and below the top line on the obverse. There is also a small gold coin that appears to emanate from this mint. The weight of the three known examples (3.07g, 3.0g and 3.10g) is less than would be expected if the coin was denominated as one-third of a mohur (3.6-3.9g) and more than that of a quarter mohur (2.7-2.9g).

---

565 Bombay Consultations, IOR F/411/38, p. 119, 13th May 1818. Letter from the assay master to Government.

566 Bombay Consultations, IOR P/409/6, 9th April 1828. Letter from the Collector of Ahmadabad to Government, dated 27th March 1828.

567 Bombay Consultations, IOR P/411/51, 24th October 1832. Letter from the Principal Collector at Ahmadabad to Government, dated 3rd February 1832.

568 Masters (1914), Numismatic Supplement No. XXII, pp. 153-173.

A possible explanation is that these three coins are third-mohurs and that the low weight can be accounted for by some event in their lives such as mounting into jewellery and subsequent removal causing loss of metal.

Ahmadnagar Mint

There is no clear reference to the site of a mint operating under British jurisdiction in Ahmadnagar. There was a Maratha mint at Wabgaon (Vaphgaon), which is close to Ahmadnagar[569], so perhaps this mint was operational during the 1820s. In any case, an entry in the records does suggest that a mint was operational [570].

Mint	Number	Comments
Candeish	*80,000*	
Ahmednuggur & Nassick	*205,000*	*Chandore rupee*

Average annual coinage for 10 years prior to 1833/34 at the Presidency and subordinates.

Alternatively, the table might simply refer to coins supplied to the Nasik and Ahmadnagar collectorates from the Chandore mint. The design of the coins is not known.

Pattern Coins for Ahmadnagar

In 1820, consideration was given to a request to establish a mint at Ahmadnagar by Captain Gibbon[571]. The mint was to produce coins for the whole Deccan with Captain Gibbon himself acting as mint master. The coins were to consist of silver rupees (double, single, half, quarter and eighth) and copper pice (double, single and half) and specimens of the rupee and pice were sent to Bombay. In the event, the proposal was rejected on the grounds that a serving officer could not undertake such work and there were no plans to establish a mint master for the Deccan. However, a specimen of a copper pattern rupee for the Deccan dated 1820 exists in the Prince of Wales Museum in Bombay and was published by P.L. Gupta[572]. There is a high likelihood that this is an example of the pattern rupee submitted to Government by Gibbon.

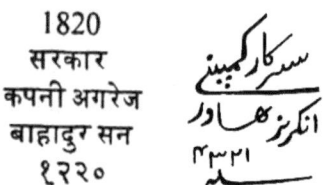

1820
सरकार
कपनी अगरेज
बाहादुर सन
१२२०

No photo of the rupee is available but the inscription on the coin is shown above.

---

[569] Bhandare S. Personal communication. See also Maheshwari & Wiggins.

[570] Bombay Consultations, IOR P/411/54, No. 5 & 6, 1835. 21st January 1835.

[571] Bombay Consultations, IOR P/408/45, p323, 26th April 1820.

[572] Gupta P.L. An Unknown Rupee Pattern of East India Company. Numismatic Digest Vol.1, part II, 1977.

Obverse: The date, 1820, above a Nagari inscription surrounded by the legend THE HONBLE EAST INDIA COMPANY. *Sarkar/Kampany Angrez/Bahadur San/1220 (or, more probably, 1221)* = (Money of the Honourable English Company).

Reverse: A Persian inscription surrounded by the legend BRITISH INDIA DECCAN ONE RUPEE. *Sarkar Kampany/Angrez Bahadur/4321 Sanah* (= Money of the Honourable English Company).

Bagalkot, Belgaum, Shahpur and Dharwar Mints

The British knew the area in the south of the Bombay Presidency as the "Southern Mahratta Country", which contained mints such as Shahpur, Belgaum, Bagalkot and Dharwar that were acquired in 1817/18.

Bagalkot rupee
Obverse: *sikka mubārak taban mihr-o-mah azizuddin shāh alām ghazi bādshāh* (= Struck the auspicious coin shining like sun and moon. Aziz-ud-din Shāh Alām, the Warrior and Emperor).
Reverse: żarb dar-al-khilafat shāhjahānābād bagadkut sanah julūs maimanat mānūs. (= Struck at the seat of the Caliphate Shahjahanabad Bagalkot in the RY reign of tranquil prosperity).

There are fewer references to these mints in the records, particularly later in the 1820s, than there are for some of the other mints and the analysis of those coins that were produced, where and when, is therefore rather scant.

The first reference to the mints in what the records refer to as the "Southern Mahratta Country" occurs in 1820 when the commissioner for the Deccan referred to a problem encountered in paying the troops with so many different types of coin in circulation. He recommended that a new mint should be established to replace those at Shahpur and Bagalkot[573]:

I have the honor to submit together with its enclosures, the copy of a correspondence with the Acting Principal Collector and Political Agent in the Southern Mahratta Country which has taken place in consequence of the complaints that have been preferred by the troops of the losses sustained by them in the depreciation of the currency in which they are paid.

---

[573] Bombay Consultations, IOR P/408/46,. 8th November 1820. Letter from the Commissioner in the Deccan to Government dated 18th October 1820.

I have instructed Mr Thackeray to make such immediate alteration to the rates at which coins are paid into his treasury as may be most likely to check the fluctuation which is experienced in the values of the currency, and I beg leave to submit to the consideration of the Honorable the Govr in Council the arguments by that Gentleman in favour of establishing a new mint, that may supersede the coinage of the old ones at Buggrekotta and Sharpore.

By 1821 some action had been taken on this proposal and a new mint had been established at Belgaum[574]:

I have the honor to enclose for your inspection one of the first coins struck at the mint which was lately transferred from Sholapoor [I presume that this is Shahpoor] to Belgam. The impression of the new coin differs from that of the old only in bearing the date of the present currency, and the same weight and proportion of alloy are still observed…

The Commissioner was able to report to the Bombay Government in May of 1821[575]:

I have the honor to forward for the information of the Honble the Governor in Council, copy of correspondence with Mr. Thackeray in regard to the mints and coins in the Southern Maratha Country.

In concluding our final settlement with Chintamun Row, in which the relinquishment of his mint at Shahpoor was an express condition, it became necessary to consider the best means of supplying its place, particularly as the Shahpoor rupee is also coined by the chief of Kittoor. I, in consequence, suggested to Mr Thackeray to stop the mint at Kittoor as well as Shahpoor, and instead of supplying their place by a new mint of the same coinage at Belgaum, to abandon our own mint at Bagrekotta [= Bagalkot], and establish one new mint for the whole at Dharwar.

The rupees of Bagalkot and Shahpur were well respected in the area:

As the Shapoor rupee is at present to be coined at Belgaum, I trust that no great inconvenience will be felt by the merchants who used to carry their bullion to Shapoor and Kittoor. The management of the late Shapoor mint are far more respectable than those of any other mint in the Dooab. They merely coin the silver that is brought to the mint, without having any other concern in it, so that the satisfaction that they give to the owners of the silver is the best test of the integrity of the coin. This security and the rules which have been laid down, will I hope, under a [regular] superintendence, prevent any abuse in the new mint at Belgaum.

In my letter of the 7th October last, I endeavoured to point out the evils to be apprehended from any sudden innovation with respect to the mint. Further experience has convinced me that it would be inexpedient to stop the coinage of either the Bagulkota or Shapoor rupee, until a superior currency is ready to supply their places in the markets of the Dooab. Much pains have been taken to prevent the depreciation of these coins, and the very favourable rates at which they exchange in remote and foreign bazars is the best proof of their intrinsic value – in the bazar of Sholapur the local currency is far less acceptable than

---

[574] Choksey R.D., (Ed.), (1945), Selections from the Deccan Commissioner's files. Period of Transition (1818-1826). My thanks to Shailendra Bhandare for drawing my attention to this publication.

[575] Bombay Mint Proceedings IOR P/411/40 p. 12, 28th May 1821. Letter from the Commissioner in the Deccan to Bombay Government.

the rupees of Shahpoor and Bagulkottah. If therefore we abolish these coins, before they are superseded by the natural operation of a superior currency we shall only make a blank in the circulation, which will be filled up by an inferior substitute.

I would therefore submit the expedient of continuing the coinage of the Shahpoor and Sicca rupees at Belgaum and Bagulkotah.

The idea of establishing a mint at Darwar, proposed above, was discussed further in the same letter:

With respect to the expediency of re-establishing a mint at Dharwar, although Darwar itself is not a place of much trade, its situation is central, it is near the large trading town of new [Hoobly?], and it is the seat of an ancient mint. The coin originally struck here was the Darwar Pagoda and as the revenue of the adjacent Talooka were formerly collected exclusively in this coin, its value was perhaps overrated. In Tipu's time the Bahaduree Pagoda was struck at Dharwar and the general currency of this coin both here and in Mysore would make it far preferable to the Darwar Pagoda, if it were thought advisable to re-establish a gold coinage.

There are indeed several considerations which would make it desirable to coin the Bahaduree Pagodas at Darwar – it is money of account in many parts of the district, it is more acceptable than any other coin in some of [the] countries that trade with the Dooab and its parent mint in Mysore is said [to] be losing its character for integrity. Much of the gold that supplies the mint of Mysore is carried from Goa through the Dooab, and if there were a mint to keep it here, a new channel of commerce would be opened between the district and the coast. The situation of Darwar would also be more favourable for a gold than a silver currency as the former is much more portable.

For these and other reasons, I think a mint for Bahaduree pagodas might be set up at Darwar, and tried for one year. It could at any time be stopped, it would be attended with little expense, and no inconvenience that I am aware of, and until the experiment be tried, it is difficult to judge whether it would be better to adopt the old gold coin of the place or a new silver one.

The integrity of the coin will be best supported by the kind of security noticed in the 2nd paragraph of this letter and if the coiners are prevented from working on their own account it will be easy to check abuses in the mint…

…To check this evil I would propose that a proclamation should be immediately published, excluding all coins from the revenues of the ensuing Fasli, except the Madras pagodas and rupees; the Bahaduree or Ikeree and Darwar pagodas, the Soortee or Bombay rupees, the Sicca or Bagulkotah, and Belgaum (cidevant Shapoor) rupees. Objections may I know be made to this measure but all that have struck me are counterbalanced by its advantages.

The proposal to reduce the number of coins accepted into the treasury was adopted almost immediately [576] and by 1823 the desired effect had been achieved[577]:

---

[576] Bombay Mint Proceedings IOR P/411/40 p. 30, 21st June 1821. Letter from the mint committee to Mr Secretary Farish dated 14th June 1821.

[577] Bombay Mint Proceedings IOR P/411/41 p. 13, 19th March 1823. Extract of a report from the Commissioner in the Deccan 25th August 1823? Transferred from the Revenue Department.

Adverting to the state of the currency, I beg leave to solicit the attention of the Honble the Governor in Council to Mr Thackeray's observations on the subject of mints and to his former correspondence on this head, which has been already laid before Government.

It appears that a great improvement has been brought about by the abolition of the Kittoor and Moodhal mints and the transfer of that of Shapoor belonging to Chintamun Row, to Belgam. The exclusion also of the inferior coins from the collections, a measure which Mr Thackeray had judiciously adopted, has had the good effect of silencing also the mints of Kolapore and of the Jageers, and Mr Thackeray is of opinion that what is now chiefly wanted, is the substitution of one uniform coinage for the currency of the Belgaum and Baggrecotta [Bagalkot] mints.

Belgaum/Shahpur rupee

Obverse: sikka zad dar jahan balutf-i-ilah bādshāh zaman muḥammad shāh (= Struck coin in the world by favour of God, Muhammad Shah, Emperor of the Age).

Reverse: ẓarb azamnagar sanah [RY] julūs maimanat mānūs. (= Struck at Azamnagar in the [RY] reign of tranquil prosperity).

The Bagalkot mint is believed to have closed about 1833[578].

The earlier proposal to establish a mint at Dharwar in the Doab appears to have been accepted[579]:

With regard to the proposal of establishing one regular mint at Darwar for the whole of our possessions in the Southern Maratha Country, we see no material objection to the measure, providing the several cautions adverted to in the 3rd and 6th paras. of this report be kept in mind and that the receipts are likely to cover the charges.

and there is an entry referring to the number of coins produced at Dharwar from 1823.

Mint	Number
Dharwar, including the Rajah of Colapoor	266,000

Average annual coinage for 10 years prior to 1833/34 at the Presidency and subordinate[580].

---

[578] Maheshwari & Wiggins, Maratha Mints and Coinage, Indian Institute of Research in Numismatic Studies, monograph 2, 1989, p. 45.

[579] Bombay Financial Proceedings, IOR P/408/54 p. 366, 7th May 1823. Letter from mint committee dated 26th April.

[580] Bombay Consultations, IOR P/411/54, No. 5 & 6, 1835. 21st January 1835.

This seems to imply that coins were produced at Dharwar throughout the 1820s, at least from 1823, until at least 1833/34 though exactly what coins were produced there is not known. Presumably, They were gold pagodas of some sort, as proposed by the commissioner in his letter above

Bandar Dholarah Mint (see p. 237 for map)

Introduction

Dholarah or Dholera is an old port city, located in Dhandhuka Taluka of Ahmadabad district in the modern state of Gujarat. Dholera's commercial importance dates back to the 18th-19th centuries. The creek on which it stands was then open to shipping, so it was quite an important, though small, port on the Gulf of Khambhat (Cambay). This part of the Kathiawar peninsula first came into the possession of the EIC in 1802 as a result of treaties signed with the leading political powers in the region, namely the Gaikwads of Baroda and the head of the Maratha Confederacy, the Peshwa. During the American civil war (1862-65), Dholera emerged as the chief port for cotton export in Gujarat, supplying cotton from upcountry cotton-growing regions to Bombay. However, by the end of the nineteenth century the port had silted up and was no longer used. Attempts to revive it are under way.

Archival References:

In 1816 the Collector of Kaira (Mr Rowles), the district under which Dholera was jurisdictionally located, wrote to the Governor in Council at Bombay informing him that there was a shortage of copper coins in the area and asking to be allowed to re-establish a 'pice manufactory'[581]:

I request you to represent to the Right Honble the Governor in Council that the copper currency within the Kaira Collectorship is extremely bad and that the lower orders of society, whose labor is compensated by a daily payment in pice, are considerable sufferers from this circumstance.

In addition to the badness of the pice, a further inconvenience is experienced arising from the different degrees of value set upon them, and not only in different towns and villages are pice of different weights and value in circulation, but even in the same place.

The class of society that benefits from this want of uniformity in the copper circulation are the many changers who speculate with the commodity, as a merchant with any article of traffic, and thus obtain an advantage in addition to what they are justly paid on exchanging copper for silver or vice versa.

The copper currency in the districts subordinate to the Guicowar, the Peshwa, the Nawab of Cambay and in fact throughout the province generally, with the exception of this jurisdiction, is brought under control, either by the establishment of manufactures or by sanctioning such pice only to pass in circulation as are of a certain weight, which is ascertained at an office fixed for that purpose and the approval is notified by a stamp [the countermarked coins of the area].

---

[581] Bombay Mint Procedings. IOR P/411/37 (1816) p. 31 from the collector at Kaira (Mr Rowles) to government, dated 9th July 1816

273

The pice in circulation in this jurisdiction are chiefly manufactured at Bhownugur by a class of people called Purjea Soonees, and are of a very inferior description with regard to the metal they are composed of, as well as their weight. Consequently they are much cheaper than any other pice, and the poor person who may receive payment by a given number of pice, instead of a certain proportion of a rupee is a material sufferer from the depreciation.

The reason why no measure has hitherto been adopted to remedy this evil within the Kaira jurisdiction, originates in a measure proposed by the Honble the Court of Directors, communicated in their letter of the 7th September 1808, and replied to by my predecessor on the 13th April 1809, when it was suggested that 50,000 rupees worth of pice of British manufacture should be forwarded for the use of these districts, but the suggestion has not since been adopted.

Under date the 25th August 1810, I had the honor to submit a petition relative to the establishment of a pice manufactory at Dollerah, to which the sanction of Government was communicated on the 10th of the following month permitting me to make an experiment of the plan proposed.

The manufactury was accordingly established and about four hundred and nineteen maunds of copper were worked into pice and circulated at the proposed rate of 64 for a rupee.

As the experiment was only extended to Dollarah and its vicinity, this quantity of pice proved sufficient for the circulation and I stopped the manufactory, fearful that a more extensive issue might tend to detract from the value of the pice and thereby not only be productive of a loss but also baffle that part of the object which was to keep the exchange at a given number of pice for a rupee of a given value.

The pice above stated to have been manufactured for Dollerah are now become inadequate to the demand and it would be expedient to set the manufactory again on foot, provided the objective is not extended and rendered applicable to the whole of the jurisdiction.

A sense of the benefit that will accrue, both to Government and to the Public, from the establishment of a regular pice manufactory, makes me solicitous to submit the subject for the consideration of the Right Honble the Governor in Council, and to request his sanction to the introduction of a manufactory at this place for the use of the jurisdiction generally.

The Governor passed the request to the Bombay mint committee who replied that they were not in favour of copper coins being produced anywhere in the Presidency except in the Bombay mint but that they would like to have specimens of all the copper coins in the district sent to them[582]:

We have the honor to acknowledge the receipt of your letter dated the 1st instant giving cover to the copy of one from the collector of Kaira and desiring us to suggest the most advisable means to be adopted for supplying the collectorship of Kaira with copper pice.

In reply we request you will have the goodness to state to the Right Honble the Governor in Council that in our opinion it is not desirable to sanction private coinages of any description and that as all our other mints are now abolished, not only the Kaira Collectorship, but all the districts subordinate to this Presidency should in future be supplied with copper pice from the Bombay mint.

To ascertain how this might be effected in the best manner, it was necessary that we should inform

---

[582] Bombay Mint Procedings. IOR P/411/37 (1816) p. 44. Letter from the mint committee to government, dated 24th August 1816

ourselves of the actual value of what Mr Rowles appeared to consider the best description of Pice in circulation in the Kaira district and we have accordingly been endeavouring, but in vain, to trace any account on our records of the expense or outturn of the four hundred and nineteen (419) maunds of copper stated, in the eighth paragraph of that gentleman's letter, to have been coined into pice at the pice manufactury at Dollera in 1810.

Under these circumstances we beg to recommend that the collector be directed to send down by an early opportunity specimens to the number of sixty four (64) of each sorts of the different kinds actually current within his district for examination, and in the meantime, judging from the description Mr Rowles has given of them, we may state that we have little doubt that a superior coinage may be introduced of a weight sufficient to secure a regular supply from this mint without incurring loss even in the event of the price of copper becoming much higher than it is at present.

A copy of this was passed to the Collector at Kaira with instructions to send examples of the copper coins in circulation there, to Bombay.

In December of 1816, the assistant collector of Kaira replied to the mint committee's request and sent the copper coins as ordered[583]:

I have the honor in reply to your letter dated 30th August last, with copy of a letter to your address under date the 24th of that month from the mint committee, on the subject of a coinage of pice for this jurisdiction, to transmit specimens to the number of sixty four of each sort of the different kinds of pice now current within this collectorship.

I beg leave to refer the Right Honble the Governor in Council for every information which seems requisite in regard to these specimens (ten in number) to the annexed memorandum.

In reference to the 3rd paragraph of the Committee's letter to your address, I have the honor to submit a statement exhibiting the result of the manufacture of pice which Mr Rowles, in the 8th para of his letter of the 9th July last, reported to have been carried out at Dhollera, under the authority of Government dated 25th August 1810. The quantity of copper coined did not exceed 330 maunds, 1 quarter, 1 pennyweight...

In the same letter he provided a list of the different types of pice sent to Bombay:

Bhaunagar, old
Bhaunagar, new
Goga*
Dhundroka*
Dollerah*
Dholka
Kaira
Mondeh
Nerriad
Naupar

---

[583] Bombay Mint Procedings. IOR P/411/37 p. 52. Letter from the assistant collector at Kaira to government, dated 14th December 1816

He stated that those marked with a * were of the Dolerah coinage of 1811 & 1812. They are place names, marked on the map as Dhandhuka and Gogo (as well as Dholera). Exactly what this means is not entirely clear, but it will be discussed further below. He also added a statement of the number of pice produced:

330 maunds 11¼ [gr] copper coined into pice at 64 per rupee, yielding 725,990. Value rupees 11,343 . 2 . 37

This whole event provoked considerable discussion within the Bombay mint committee about the necessity to improve the coinage of Bombay but as far as the Kaira copper coinage was concerned, it was eventually decided that 50,000 rupees worth of pice should be sent to Kaira from Bombay[584] and no further pice coinage took place at Dholera.

The Coinage:

Pice of the Bandar Dholara mint 1225 at top and 1226 below

Recently, copper coins with mint-name 'Bandar Dholarah' were identified by Dr. S. Bhandare. The coins are rather crudely struck specimens on which, as is usual, only part of the legend can be seen. The date is rarely visible, but specimens have been found with clear dates AH1225 and 1226, both of which match exactly with the duration of the functioning of the 'manufactory' as indicated in the archival reference reproduced above. The coins weigh about 8-9g and have a diameter of about 19.5-21.5mm. A full-die impression, showing complete obverse and reverse dies, can be created:

---

[584] Bombay Mint Procedings. IOR P/411/37 (1817) p. 8. Letter from the mint committee to government, dated 15th February 1817.

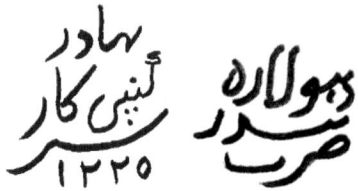

The obverse carries a Farsi/Hindustani inscription *Sarkar Kampani Bahadur* followed by the date, and the reverse carries a legend *Bandar Dholarah*. Both inscriptions are enclosed within circular borders – on some coins it is composed of a saw-toothed inward edge. On one coin, the saw-teeth are replaced with semicircles. There appears to be a difference in placement of legends – on coins dated AH1225, the word 'Bahadur' appears at the top, 'Kampani' and '..kar' in the word 'Sarkar' appear below it and the date is placed right at the bottom of the design, beneath a divider formed by 'Sar…' 'Sarkar'. On coins dated AH1226, the word 'Bahadur' appears after the word 'Sarkar' and it seems the word 'Kampani' forms the last horizontal divider at the bottom. Contrary to the issues of the previous year, the date 1226 appears right at the top. Depending on this variation, the coins may be classified as 'Type 1' and 'Type 2'.

There is also a noteworthy degradation noticed in surviving specimens of both types. On some coins, the legends are executed in retrograde, on others the words 'Sarkar', 'Kampani' etc. are ill-executed, the 'Ka' looking more like the Indian numeral '4'. This observation seems not in congruence with the fact that the 'manufactory' was run for a relatively short time only as an 'experiment', and one would presume the issue was not long enough lived to induce so many die-variations and executional changes in the design.

Another significant aspect to be noted is that at least two of the known coins are overstrikes. The under-type in one instance is a copper falūs, struck in the name of Muhammad Akbar II, issued by the Maratha government mint at Ahmedabad. It is listed as T6 for the Ahmedabad mint by Maheshwari & Wiggins[585]. It is plausible that the second piece also has the same under-type, although it is not as clear as it is in the first instance. This is interesting inasmuch as both coins have the 'Dholarah' overtype of reasonably crude calligraphy. The under-type is listed by Maheshwari & Wiggins as bearing RY9 and AH1232/RY10. It appears to have been struck during a period of a temporary re-occupation of the city by the Peshwas after almost ten years of control by the Gaikwads of Baroda (for further discussion on Ahmedbad coins, see Shailendra Bhandare - 'Maratha Issues of Ahmedabad', ONSNL 184, 2005 and Alfred Master – 'The post-Mughal coins of Ahmedabad, or a Study in mint-marks', JASB-NS, vol. XXII, 1913). The fact that the under-type is dated to AH1232 clearly indicates that the issue of 'Dholarah' coins, albeit of a cruder execution, went on for at least seven years after the Company's 'manufactory' situated there struck coins in AH1225 and 1226. These later coins would fall into the category of 'Katchha' pice, as identified by Barry Tabor[586], and have been discussed in more detail by Bhandare & Stevens[587]. It is possible that these coins were struck at one of the other mints mentioned in the list above.

[585] Maheshwari & Wiggins, Maratha Mints and Coinage, Nasik, 1989, p. 41.
[586] Tabor B, JONS 205, pp. 33-35.
[587] Bhandare & Stevens (2012) JONS 213 pp. 17-22.

Bankot (Fort Victoria) Mint

Around Bombay itself, and down the coast, was the area known as the Concan which had a Northern and Southern district, some of which came under British control as early as the mid-eighteenth century, but mostly fell under their control after about 1817.

The British are not known to have produced any coins in the Northern Concan and this area will not be discussed further. However, this is not true of the area known to the British, in the early nineteenth century, as the Southern Concan. This district lay on the west coast of India to the south of Bombay (Mumbai). Bankot, with its fort and nine surrounding villages, had been ceded to the British by the Peshwa in 1755 and 1756 but it was not until 1819, following the final Mahratta war and the acquisition of further territory, that the area was formed into the separate collectorate of the Southern Concan. Initially Bankot, which was also known as Fort Victoria, was the headquarters of the collectorate but in 1820 this was transferred further south to Ratnagiri, and in 1830 the three subdivisions to the north of Bankot Creek were transferred to the Northern Concan collectorate and the Southern Concan was reduced to the rank of sub-collectorate. This situation only lasted for two years and in 1832 the Southern Concan was again raised to the status of collectorate[588]. The Southern Concan was also known as Ratnagiri after the place of its headquarters.

The currency of the Concan was mixed, the brisk sea trade bringing into the district every sort of Indian coin. Up until 1835, the main coin was the Chinchoree rupee (struck at Poona), and later the Surat rupee (struck at Surat and Bombay), supplemented by various older rupees known as Chanvad, Doulatabad, Hukeri, Chikodi and the Emperor Akbar's Chavkoni, or square rupee. After 1835, the Company's rupee gradually superseded this heterogeneous currency until, by 1880, the Imperial currency was the sole circulating monetary medium[589].

Following the creation of the collectorate in 1819, a copper coinage was issued to meet the needs of local tradespeople and Pridmore catalogued the coins[590]. They are crudely struck, consisting of three denominations: double pice, pice and half pice, and variously dated 1820 and 1821. Similar coins dated 1828 and 1829 will be dealt with in the section on the Rahimatpur mint.

The Coins and their Use

On the 30th June 1820, Mr. Pelly, the collector responsible for the Southern Concan, wrote to the Governor and Council of the Bombay Presidency stating that the people of the area were suffering considerable inconvenience because of the lack of copper coins available for everyday commerce. He believed that this was caused because the copper coins were exported more profitably for their metal content rather than being exchanged for rupees. He had tried to intervene by sending pice from areas where there were fewer difficulties, to those where the problem was most acute, but this had not succeeded. He therefore proposed that a copper coinage should be undertaken, either locally or in Bombay, consisting of pice and half pice

---

[588] Bombay Gazetteer (1880). Volume X, Ratnagiri & Savantvadi, p. 200. Government Central Press Bombay.

[589] Bombay Gazetteer (1880). Volume X, Ratnagiri & Savantvadi, p. 154. Government Central Press Bombay.

[590] Pridmore

exchangeable at the rate of 64 and 128 to the rupee respectively. Pelly's proposal was referred to the mint committee who agreed that it seemed sensible, given the circumstances, and recommended that the contract for striking the coins should be open to competition and that, before authorising the coinage, the collector should send specimens to Bombay for examination [591]:

I beg leave to represent for the information of the Honble the Governor in Council that for some months past considerable inconvenience has been experienced in this Zillah owing to a scarcity of copper coin, which has been withdrawn from circulation principally owing to the course of exchanges having rendered its exportation the most profitable remittance that could be made, to other quarters – at Malwar when the fixed quantity of copper exchangeable for a rupee was largest, the inconvenience has naturally been most severely felt. I have endeavoured to lessen it, by sending thither supplies of pice from other Tallookas – but this expedient if long pursued would obviously be merely shifting, not removing the evil. What appears to be required [is] the issue of a sufficient supply (perhaps half a lack) of this circulating medium, at such a rate as may stop its exportation. And I would respectfully suggest that a coinage of copper pice of 64, and half pice of 128, to the rupee, be undertaken for this Zillah, either here or at Bombay – I venture to recommend the half pice, because the inferior classes of inhabitants who are the greatest consumers of trifling retail articles, are always sure to suffer by the lowest denomination of coin in a Country, being of comparatively high value, since scarcely anything they buy is charged lower than the smallest current coin – and probably would not be charged much higher, even if its intrinsic value were far less. The numbers have been selected from the convenience they afford of each of them dividing by the annas in a rupee, without a remainder – they possess moreover this further advantage, that as the pice now commonly current are not generally widely different from this same standard value, inconvenience from the introduction of the proposed new pice is not, I think, to be apprehended.

Ordered that a copy of the preceding letter be transmitted to the Mint Committee with directions to offer their opinion on the suggestions offered by Mr. Pelly for relieving the scarcity of copper coin in the Southern Concan.

The mint committee responded [592]:

We have the honor to acknowledge the receipt of your letter of the 11th instant, referring to us one from the Collector in the Southern Concan dated the 30th ultimo and desiring our opinion on the suggestion offered by Mr Pelly for relieving the scarcity of copper coin in that district.

In reply we request you will do us the favour to state to the Honble the Governor in Council that under the circumstances stated by the Collector, we are not aware of any better mode of supplying the deficiency than by adopting Mr Pelly's suggestion of undertaking, or rather authorizing, a coinage of copper, to a certain extent, on the spot.

---

591 Bombay Consultations, IOR P/411/40, p. 67, 12th July 1820. Letter from the Collector in the Southern Concan (Mr Pelly) to Bombay, dated 30th June 1820.

592 Bombay Consultations, IOR P/411/40, p. 74, 26th July 1820. Letter from the mint committee to Mr Secretary Farish dated 15th July 1820.

The rules we would recommend would be the same as for the Broach copper coinage, namely that the division should, as Mr Pelly proposes be 64 whole, or 128 half, pice per rupee, and the privilege of coining should be assigned to a sort of competition to the person who may be willing to coin the heaviest pice to be exchanged at that rate, but without requiring any share in the profits. Before, however, finally authorizing the coinage, it might be advisable that a few specimens of the proposed coin should be forwarded to the Presidency for examination.

Ordered that instruction be issued to the Collector in the Southern Concan to invite proposals for coining copper pice comformably to the Mint Committee's suggestions.

Bankot pice

Accordingly, in September 1820, Pelly advised the Bombay Government that he had issued an advertisement inviting tenders for making the new copper coins but that he had received only one reply, from Sootoophoo Din Purkar, who had recommended that 25,000 rupees-worth of each of three denominations should be struck[593]:

Pursuant to the instructions conveyed in Mr Farish's letter dated the 21ˢᵗ July last, advertisement (as per accompanying translation) were issued, inviting tenders for coining copper pice to the extent of seventy five thousand rupees which will probably be required, the population of this zillah amounting to nearly six and half lacks of person; and the export of copper pice being a common mode of remittance by sea during the fair season.

Of the only tender which has been received in consequence of the above notification, I enclose a copy on its merits. With reference to the Bombay currency, I am not able to offer any decisive opinion, because I do not know the standard weight of copper, which there ought to be in each Bombay Rupees worth of Bombay pice. Those pice are not current here but having collected 50, and weighed them, I found they fluctuated from about 41 to 42½ tolas of copper for a Bombay rupee – the present tender offers a weight of 41 tolas of pure copper per Chinchoree rupee, a coin rupees 3..2..52 percent inferior to the Bombay rupee.

I enclose, as desired, specimens of the proposed coin. They seem, I think, better executed than the Bombay coin. Besides the pice and half pice, I would recommend to be coined about twenty five thousand rupees worth of the double pice, or half anna, as per specimen no. 3, which will be a great convenience and

---

[593] Bombay Consultations, IOR P/411/40 p. 115, 15ᵗʰ September 1820. Letter from the Collector in the Southern Concan to Mr Chief Secretary Warden, dated 4ᵗʰ September 1820.

in no way objectionable that I can perceive, since, like the pice and half pice, a rupee worth of them may be divided by the annas in a rupee, without a remainder.

The contractor, it will be observed, expects that the copper (which is a British staple), should be allowed to be imported into this zillah free of customs. The Honble the Governor in Council can best determine whether this can be complied with; any abuse of the privilege (if conceded) might easily be guarded against by giving the contractor dustucks for the exact weight of copper necessary for the fulfilment of the contract and no more.

The security offered is wholly unexceptionable. The contractor will probably solicit an advance of 20 or 25,000 rupees.

PS Specimens of three kinds of coin are enclosed as follows:

No. 1 double pice or half anna, 32 to the Chinchour rupee.

No. 2 whole pice, 64 to the Chinchoree rupee

No. 3 half pice, 128 to the Chinchoree rupee

Sootoophoo Din Purkar's offer was as follows[594]:

Your Honor having made notification that sealed tenders will be received in Southern Konkan Collector's Sudder Kutcherry for the coinage of copper pice on the 26th day of August 1820 to the amount of seventy five thousand rupees in the proportions of one third whole, one third half and the remaining third double pice, the whole pice to contain sixty four and the half pice one hundred and twenty eight and the double pice thirty two for each Ankosee Chinchoree rupee.

I wishing to have undertake the coinage of the seventy five thousand rupees in copper pice and tender to your honor the weight of copper for each rupee as follows Viz: for every Ankosee Chinchoree rupee received I engage to deliver forty one tola of copper in pice, or in English weight, seventeen ounces one quarter Avoirdupois, the half and double pice to weigh the same for each rupee.

I have accompanying this tender sent muster of the different sizes of the coin in whole, half and double pice as I perceived was ordered in your Honor's notice.

I mention my friends Abdull Guffoor and Dayen Khaun, they having agreed to become security for my due performance according to agreement.

I also wish to make remark your Honor, this pice exceeds the Bombay average and I hope equally so in other respects as to execution etc.

I beg to mention to your Honor that I make so much weight in my tender because I hope and conclude your Honor not expect customs for the copper employed in this business, upon importation here.

Ordered that copies of the preceding papers together with the specimens of the copper coin accompanying them be referred to the Mint Committee.

The three proposed denominations were double pice, single pice and half pice, specimens of which were sent to Bombay, via Pelly, as had been requested by the mint committee. The original advertisement called for denominations of pice and half pice, and it is clear that the addition of the double pice denomination originated with Sootoophoo Din Purkar, although Pelly

---

[594] Bombay Consultations, 15th September 1820. Letter from the Collector in the Southern Concan to Mr Chief Secretary Warden dated 4th September 1820. IOR, P/411/40 p115.

subsequently supported it.

A translation of the actual advertisement appears in the records as follows[595]:

Notice is hereby given

That at noon on the twenty sixth day of August, corresponding with Suravan sood 3rd Shalewan 1742 and 16th Zilkand 1235 Hejree, sealed tenders will be received at the Southern Konkan Collector's Sudder Cutcherree, for the coining of copper pice.

The coins must be rendered in whole or half pice, the former consisting of sixty four (64) the latter one hundred and twenty eight pice (128), to the rupee.

A specimen of each kind of coin must accompany the tender, and the contractor must give in the names of two sufficient sureties for the due performance of this engagement.

The tender must contain in words, written at length, the weight of copper in Bombay seers, which the proposer will undertake to deliver for each Ankoosee Chinchoree rupee, at sixty four whole, and one hundred and twenty eight half pice to the rupee.

The tender offering the greatest weight (if in other respects approved of) will be accepted; and the whole profit of the transaction will be the contractors.

The contractor will be required to deliver at least one thousand rupees worth of copper pice per week in the proportion of half in whole, and half in half pice; to undertake to coin in the whole to the value of seventy five thousand rupees, 37,500 in half and the same quantity in whole pice, and he must desist from coining when that quantity shall have been completed.

The pice must be made of pure copper, and not mixed with any other material; each pice, and half pice cast, must be of uniform weights, should there be found any differences in weight, the contractor will be punished.

The mint committee was very complimentary about the process that Pelly had used to get the proposal from Sootoophoo Din Purkar and they considered the terms *as advantageous to the community as could be wished or expected*. The quality of the copper and the workmanship in the specimens submitted to the committee *will do great credit to the individual undertaking the coinage, if the whole shall be completed in the same style*. To ensure that future coins were of the same standard, Pelly was asked to send specimens, regularly, to Bombay for assay[596].

Sootoophoo Din Purkar had signed the contract by November 1820, and Pelly requested permission to advance him 25,000 rupees so that he could begin work on the first batch of coins[597].

Adverting to the 5th paragraph of my letter dated the 4th September last, and yours of the 2nd ultimo, I beg to report that the contractor for the coinage of copper pice for the use of this zillah, having executed his deed of agreement under proper security, I request authority to advance him the sum of twenty five thousand rupees, as mentioned at the conclusion of the paragraph above referred to.

---

[595] Bombay Consultations, 15th September 1820. Letter from the Collector in the Southern Concan to Mr Chief Secretary Warden dated 4th September 1820. IOR, P/411/40 p115.

[596] Bombay Consultations, IOR P/411/40 p. 126, 4th October 1820. Letter from the mint committee to Mr Secretary Farish, dated 23rd September 1820.

[597] Bombay Consultations, IOR P/411/40 p. 137, 28th November 1820. Letter from the Collector in the Southern Concan to Mr Secretary Farish, dated 18th November 1820.

Ordered that Mr Pelly be authorized to issue to the contractor for the coinage of copper pice for the use of his zillah an advance of rupees 25,000.

By early May of 1821 he had produced about 20,000 rupees worth of the pice and permission to start issuing the coins was sought and received[598].

With reference to your letter of 20th July and 2nd October last relative to the new copper coinage in this zillah, I have now the honor to report that the contractor has delivered upwards of twenty thousand rupees worth of pice into the treasury at this station, and as great inconvenience has for a considerable time past been felt throughout the different districts in the Southern Concan, from the scarcity of copper coin, I beg to solicit the permission of the Honble the Governor in Council to issue the quantity already received at the rate of sixty four pice, or one hundred and twenty eight half pice, per rupee.

Ordered that Mr Burnett be authorized to issue the copper pice received from the contractor at the rate of sixty four pice or one hundred and twenty eight half pice [per] rupee, of which the Mint Committee is to be informed.

In that month he was advanced another 25,000 rupees for the next batch of pice and the final 25,000 rupees in early November 1821[599].

I have the honor to report for the information of Government that the contractor for the coining of pice in this zillah has delivered copper coin to the amount of the sum advanced to him agreeably to the orders conveyed in your letter of the 28th November last and now beg to request the permission of the Honble the Governor in Council to make a further advance of twenty five thousand rupees on account of this contract.

Ordered that Mr Burnett be authorized to advance the sum of twenty five thousand rupees to the contractor for the coinage of pice on account of this contract.

In November 1821, Sootoophoo Din Purkar asked for another contract for a further 50,000 rupees-worth of pice on the grounds that he had all the people and tools necessary to undertake the coinage, which meant that it would be cheaper to strike another batch immediately, rather than have to start again[600].

Petition of Sootfooteen Purkar to J.J. Sparrow, dated 10th November 1821.

Represents that my present contract for coining copper pices nearly completed and I hope to your satisfaction, I therefore offer, if you are desirous of coining more copper pice to undertake the same on the terms of my present contract, because I have at present workpeople and mint implements, and if the former are once dispersed they cannot without great trouble be collected together, in which case I should not be

---

[598] Bombay Consultations, IOR P/411/40 p. 11, 18th May 1821. Letter from the Acting Collector (A. Burnett) in the Southern Concan to Mr Secretary Farish, dated 5th May 1821.

[599] Bombay Consultations IOR P/411/40 p. 23, 31st May 1821. Letter from the Acting Collector in the Southern Concan to Mr Secretary Farish, dated 18th May 1821.
Bombay Consultations, IOR P/411/40 p. 91, 17th November 1821. Letter from the Accountant General to Mr Secretary Farish.

[600] Bombay Consultations, IOR P/411/40 p. 88, 10th November 1821. Letter from the Collector in the Southern Concan to Mr Chief Secretary Warden.
Petition of Sootfooteen Purkar to J.J. Sparrow, dated 10th November 1821.

able to undertake the contract at the present low rates. I therefore pray that you will take this petition into your serious consideration and issue such orders as you may deem proper.

However, the Accountant General had noticed the final advance of 25,000 rupees and drew the attention of the Bombay Government to the fact that no specimens of the new coinage had been received at Bombay for examination since the original specimens sent before the contract had been agreed[601].

With reference to your letter of the 6th instant, apprizing me of a further advance having been authorised to be made to the contractor for coining pice in the Southern Concan, to the extent of twenty five thousand (25,000) rupees, and having ascertained from the Assay Master that no further specimens of the pice have been transmitted to the mint officer at the Presidency for examination since those received with your letter of the 15th of September 1820, to the address of the Mint Committee, I beg recommend that the attention of the Collector be called to this very important point in the orders conveyed to him on the 2nd of the following month.

Resolved that the corresponding orders be issued to the Collector in the Southern Concan.

Following this, the mint committee examined specimens in January 1822 and they reported that the quality of the coins was not equal to that of the specimens sent in September 1820, although they had to admit that the assay master was away, and that this was merely their opinion. However, they felt strongly enough to recommend that the coinage should be stopped and no further pice should be issued. The Bombay Government instructed the Collector to stop issuing the coins, but not to stop making more[602].

In May 1822 a further ten specimens were sent to Bombay and were again found to be of lower quality than the first samples and to be of slightly lower weight. This time the collector was instructed to stop the production of the coins and to report how many had already been struck[603].

I am directed by the Honorable the Governor in Council to acknowledge the receipt of your letter dated the 19th ultimo and to inform you that the ten specimens of the half pice of the new copper coinage accompanying it are found on examination not to be so well executed [as] former samples transmitted to Government nor to be of the full weight. They are a grain lighter than those received in February last.

The Honorable the Governor in Council thinks it expedient to direct you to suspend the further coinage of copper coins contracted for by Sootoophoodeen Purkar and to report the value of those already struck by the contractor.

---

[601] Bombay Consultations IOR P/411/40 p. 91, 17th November 1821. Letter from the Accountant General to Mr Secretary Farish. IOR,

[602] Bombay Consultations, IOR P/408/51 p. 64, 30th January 1822. Letter from mint committee, dated 14th January 1822.

[603] Bombay Consultations, IOR P/408/52, p425, 12th June 1822. Letter from the Collector in the Southern Concan (Mr Sparrow), dated 29th May 1822.
Letter to the mint committee from the Finance Committee, 6th June 1822.
From the mint committee to the Finance Committee, 13th June 1822.
From the Finance Committee to the Collector of the Southern Concan, 21st June 1822.
From the Finance Committee to the mint committee, 21st June 1822.

You will also be pleased to send up a number taken promiscuously of the different coins made under the contract for further examination by the Assay Master. The Mint Committee have been directed to suggest the number they may consider sufficient for this purpose.

He replied that of the original planned 75,000 rupees-worth, 70,897 rupees, 2 quarters and 44 reas worth had then been received into the treasury and that the greater proportion of the outstanding amount had already been struck and was awaiting delivery. Sootoophoo Din Purkar sent a petition to the collector for transmission to Bombay, in which he tried to explain why the coins were of lower quality than the original specimens and requesting that he should be allowed to complete the contract, which he was allowed to do[604].

However, getting the coins into circulation was not proving easy. In December 1821, the commander in chief of the Bombay Presidency raised the matter of the troops in the Southern Concan losing as much as a quarter of their pay because they were being forced to receive part of it in *the Bankote pice*. The exchange rate of 128 new pice per rupee (this must refer to the half pice denomination) compared unfavourably to the old exchange rate of 160 old pice per rupee, and the use of the new pice to pay the troops was stopped. This incident does reveal the fact that the new copper pice were struck in a mint established at Bankot. This is evident not only from the above quote but also a reference to *the new copper currency issued from Bancote* in the same series of correspondence[605].

By 1823 it had become obvious that it would be impossible to get more then a small part of the 75,000 rupees-worth of pice into circulation in the collectorate within a reasonable timeframe. The new collector in the Southern Concan, Mr Dunlop, gave serious consideration to various possible options. Firstly, he thought about reducing the value of the pice so that the number per rupee was increased from 64. This was rejected on the grounds that, once started, the value would continue to decrease until it reached the value of the intrinsic copper content, at which point the pice would be sold for scrap metal and the whole *raison d'être* for issuing them would be lost. In addition the reduction in value would cause a considerable financial loss to Government. The second option was to keep the pice in the treasury for a number of years and release them slowly, at the authorised Government rate of 64 per rupee, as the community

---

[604] Bombay Consultations, IOR P/411/41, 7th August 1822. Letter from the Assistant to the Collector in Charge of the Southern Concan (L.R. Read) to Government, dated 27th July 1822.

Petition from Sootfoodeen Purkar to the Collector in the Southern Concan, dated 11th July 1822. Ibid.

Letter from Government to the Assistant in charge of the Southern Concan, dated 6th August 1822. Ibid.

[605] Bombay Consultations, IOR P/411/41, 13th December 1821. Letter from Commander in Chief to Bombay Government, dated 13th December 1821.

Letter to Major Jackson from Lt Col Kennedy, 7th December 1821.

Letter from Sparrow (the Collector) to Kennedy (Officer commanding), 1st November 1821.

Letter from Kennedy to Sparrow, 7th November 1821.

Letter from Major D Campbell (Major in charge of the 2nd battalion 9th regiment) to Kennedy, 11th November 1821.

Proceedings of a Committee assembled by Captain Tweedy of 1st Battalion 4th regiment, held 16th November 1821.

Letter from Mr Gibbon, dated 12th November 1821.

Letter from Sparrow, 21st November.

needed them. This would also confer a financial loss on the Government[606]. However, this second option seems to have been adopted almost by default, and there was a very slow release of the coins into circulation over the next few years.

Fortunately, in 1824, the Judge at Surat had another idea. For some time there had been a shortage of copper coins in Surat and the Judge suggested that some of the surplus coins in Bankot, in fact 10,000 rupees-worth, could be used to fill the gap[607]. As soon as the Surat shroffs heard about this proposal they issued a petition stating that they had plenty of copper pice and could meet the requirements themselves if only the Government would allow them to over-stamp the coins with the Company's mark[608]. The British authorities did not trust the local shroffs and this petition was rejected[609]:

…that after a deliberate review of all the circumstances of the case, we are of the opinion that the native community of Surat cannot be in such great want of an addition to their copper currency as the money changers would wish us to believe and that it seems pretty plain that the object of the latter, in wishing to obtain the Government stamp on the pice in their possession, is to force a spurious coinage on the public at a rate above its marketable value.

That the copper circulation of Surat stands in need of a reform in common with that of every subordinate district, we do not in the least doubt, but conceive it would be idle, with the prospect of our efficient mint before us [this is a reference to the new steam-driven mint to be built at Bombay], to make the attempt with our present means, nor do we think it would tend to any good end, to allow of any further coinages of copper being undertaken, under the sanction of Government, as a private speculation.

We incline therefore to recommend, that the copper currency of Surat be left for the present as it is, that is, the old pice passing as heretofore, at their marketable value, and the circulation of the new (Concan) pice being under the proclamation which we presume has been issued, entirely optional, which will afford at least some sort of security to the lower classes against a worse currency being imposed on them, until we shall be able to supply them with an entire new coinage which cannot be imitated without machinery.

Ten thousand rupees-worth of Concan pice were shipped to Surat via Bombay, and a further 5,000 to Broach, which was also very short of copper coin. In fact the collector at Broach had already agreed a contract with local moneyers to strike 7,000 rupees-worth of pice, but was

---

[606] Bombay Consultations IOR P/411/41 p. 53, 11th September 1823. Extract of a letter from the Collector in the Southern Concan, dated 16th August, Paras 11 & 15 with enclosure transferred from the Revenue Department.
   Extract of a report from Mr Blane to Mr Dunlop, dated the 3rd July 1823.

[607] Bombay Consultations, IOR P/411/42, 28th January 1824. p. 7. Letter from J Farish (Secretary to Government) to the Accountant General, dated 2nd January 1824.
   Bombay Consultations, 18th February 1824.
   Letter from the Accountant General to Government, dated 5th February 1824. IOR, P/411/42 p. 8.

[608] Bombay Consultations IOR P/411/42 p. 37, 7th April 1824.Substance of a petition from Muncharam Nahana Lall on behalf of the moneychangers of Surat to the Honourable Mountstuart Elphinstone, Governor in Council, dated 5th March 1824.

[609] Bombay Consultations IOR P/411/42 p. 56, 12th May 1824. Letter from the mint committee to Government dated, 18th April 1824.

instructed to stop this, if possible, and wait for the Concan pice to arrive[610]. The pice were to be exchanged at 64 to the rupee, but the Surat shroffs refused to trade in the coins at that rate, and the experiment was not successful there[611]. However, in Broach there was no such resistance and the coins quickly gained acceptance[612].

In 1826, the shortage of copper coins in Surat was felt even more acutely, and the judge asked that the collector be given permission to strike copper coins locally[613]. However, the Bombay Government would not accept the proposition that the Bankot pice could not be used, basing their conclusion on the fact that they had been successfully adopted in Broach in 1824[614]. They, therefore, sent a further 10,000 rupees-worth of the Bankot pice together with a proclamation declaring that they would be issued at 64 to the rupee and would be accepted back at the treasury at 64 to the rupee. A further 5,000 rupees-worth was also sent to Broach[615].

This time the pice were accepted and the following year, 1827, a further 20,000 rupees-worth were requested although the records are not clear about whether or not they were actually sent[616]. A petition from the Surat shopkeepers of 1828 implies that they were not[617]. What is certain is that 5,000 rupees more were sent to Broach in 1827[618], making a total of at least 35,000 rupees-worth that were sent to Surat and Broach (and possibly 55,000), of the original 75,000 that were produced.

This exhausted the stocks of the pice in the treasury of the Southern Concan, and when further demands were made in 1828, the collectors at both Broach and Surat were instructed to strike pice locally, though exactly what type these would have been is not known[619].

---

[610] Bombay Consultations IOR P/411/42 p. 8, 18th February1824. Letter from the Acting Collector of Broach to Government. Letter to the Acting Collector of Broach from Government, dated 18th February 1824.
  Bombay Consultations IOR P/411/42 p. 24, 10th March 1824. Letter from the Acting Collector at Broach (Robert Boyd) to Government dated 28th February 1824.
  Letter from Government to the Acting Collector at Broach, dated 10th March 1824.
[611] Bombay Consultations IOR P/411/42 p. 43, 11th April. Letter from the Collector of Surat to Government dated 29th March 1824.
[612] Bombay Consultations, IOR P/408/65, 12th April 1826. Letter from the mint committee to Government dated 27th March 1826.
[613] Bombay Consultations, IOR P/408/64, 15th March 1826. Letter from the Judge at Surat to Government, dated 7th March 1826.
[614] Bombay Consultations 12th April 1826. IOR P/408/65. Letter from the mint committee to Government dated 27th March 1826.
[615] Bombay Consultations, IOR P/408/65, 3rd May 1826. Letter from the Collector in the Southern Concan to Government, dated 2nd May 1826.
  Letter to the Acting Sub-Treasurer from Government, dated 2nd May 1826.
  Letter to the Superintendent of Marine from Government, dated 2nd May 1826.
[616] Bombay Consultations, IOR P/409/1, 18th April 1827. Letter from the Judge at Surat to Government, dated 29th March 1827.
[617] Bombay Consultations, IOR P/409/5, 30th January 1828. Letter to the Judge at Surat from Doolubh Narun and other inhabitants of Surat dated 9th January 1929.
[618] Bombay Consultations, IOR P/408/68, 28th February 1827.
  Bombay Consultations, IOR P/408/68, 21st March 1827.
[619] Bombay Consultations, IOR P/409/6, 16th April 1828. Letter from the First Assistant in Charge of Broach to Government, dated 26th March 1828.

In 1831, a certain Nathooset bin Abaset sent a petition to Bombay asking for permission to open a copper mint at Penn in the Southern Concan. This petition was passed to the collector in the Southern Concan and he was asked for his opinion. He confirmed that all of the 1820/21 pice were now in circulation and that there was a need for more copper coins. Having spoken to Nathooset bin Abaset, he was able to confirm that the petitioner wanted to produce 50,000 rupees-worth of pice[620]:

…half to be of the description coined at Bankote by Mr George Pelly in 1820/21 at the rate of (64) sixty four per rupee, and half, Doodandees, or old Poona pice, at the rate of (60) sixty per rupee, weighing 57 [per] Chinchoree rupee.

Following this petition and its rejection, the whole focus of the mint committee fell on the new copper quarter annas (pice) produced in the new steam-driven mint supplied to Bombay by Boulton & Watt of Soho, Birmingham, England. Because of the great shortage of copper coins throughout the Presidency, the new mint concentrated first on meeting this need as opposed to the silver coinage. Once the mint was up and running so that the coins could be produced in sufficient numbers, a difficult enough process in itself (see chapter 5 and also[621]), it soon became clear that getting the coins into circulation was going to be yet another challenge. At first the coins were simply sent to the different collectorates throughout the Presidency in the expectation that they could be exchanged for the old pice when these came into the treasury. However, the rate of exchange of 64 quarter-annas for one rupee, inhibited this to such an extent that, for instance, in Bombay itself there was little or no demand for the new coins, with less than 50 rupees-worth having been issued by November 1831[622].

A new approach was taken in 1833[623], the intention being to target the collectorates one by one and offer favourable terms of exchange for a short period to get the new coins accepted. The Northern Concan was chosen as the first place for this new approach, which proved to be successful, and, in 1834, the second collectorate to receive the new coins was the Southern Concan, by then referred to as Ratnagiri[624]. This approach again proved successful. Henceforth, the copper coinage for the Southern Concan would be the uniform coinage of the Bombay Presidency eventually replaced in 1844 by the uniform copper coinage for all of British India.

Letter from Government to the first Assistant in Charge of Broach, dated 11th April 1828.

Bombay Consultations, IOR P/409/5, 20th February 1828. Letter to the Judge at Surat from Government, dated 14th February 1828.

Letter to the Collector of Surat from Government, dated 24th February 1828.

[620] Bombay Consultations, IOR P/411/49, 1st September 1830. Petition from Nathooset bin Abaset to Bombay Government.

[621] Doty R., The Soho Mint and the Industrialization of Money, Spink & BNS, London. 1998.

[622] Bombay Consultations, IOR P/411/51, 29th February 1832.

[623] Bombay Consultations, IOR P/411/52, 1833.

[624] Bombay Consultations, IOR P/411/53, 1834.

Bhakkar Mint

The province of Sind was conquered and annexed to British India in 1843 by Major-General Sir Charles Napier, whose reputed telegram *'Peccavi'* (Latin for 'I have sinned' i.e. Sind) was in fact a caption given to his picture by Punch magazine.

No entries in the records, referring to the Bhakkar mint, have been found, so the evidence at present relies mainly on the coins. The mint at Bhakkar, which had been a Moghul mint, then Durrani and then local mirs for many years, continued to issue coins and therefore falls into the category of a transitional mint from 1843 onwards. One type shows a lion, which is believed to represent the fact that the British had taken control, but the longest-lived type has a selection of floral ornaments amongst the Persian inscription.

Bhakkar rupee, lion and hare type

Bhakar Rupee, floral type
Obverse on both types: maḥmūd shāh (Durrani) surrounded by an unread Persian inscription.
Reverse on both types: ẓarb bhakkar sanah [RY] julūs maimanat mānūs (= struck at Bhakkar in the [RY] year of tranquil prosperity). Various floral designs in the legend.

Broach & Jambusar Mints

The port of Broach (Bharuch) on the river Narmada is a town of great antiquity and was an important centre of trade and commerce for a considerable time until superseded in importance by Surat. Broach was never a mint of the Moghul emperors. In the eighteenth century it was part of the private estate of the Governor of Gujarat.

A mint was established at Broach during the time of the second Nawab, Nek Alam Khan II, by permission of the emperor, Ahmad Shah Bahadur (1748-1754). In 1772 the Nawab of Broach was deposed by the East India Company, whose army took the city, the belief being that the Nawab was in alliance with the Gaikwars, who had designs on the Company's territory.

In 1782, by virtue of the treaty of Salbye, the Company made over the port of Broach to Sindhia of Gwalior.

Jambusar, a few miles to the north of Broach, was occupied by the British from 1775 to 1783 and contained a mint that issued coins during this time[625].

Coins struck at Broach between 1772 (AH 1186) and 1782 (1197) fall into the British series but later coins, up until 1803, belong to the Marathas[626]. Coins may have been issued from the mint at Jambusar during the time it was occupied by the British but whether or not they were also issued from a mint in Broach, itself, is not clear.

In 1803, after the treaty of Bassein, Broach once again became a possession of the EIC, who did strike coins there at this time.

Silver Coins

A rupee dated AH 1173 issued in the name of Alamgir II, regnal year 6, is known. However, no direct reference to mints operating in Broach under the British, during the period 1772-1782, has been found in the EIC records and no coins are known. However, there is a tangential reference in a record dated 1781[627]:

The President acquainted the Board that there is a quantity of private silver on the island [Bombay] brought by the freight ships from the Gulf of Mocha and that it would be of the highest benefit to the place if such an advantage could be held out to the proprietors as would induce them to continue their bullion upon the island & convert it into Bombay currency, otherwise that they will as usual export it to Surat and Broach where it will yield a larger return from the mints.

Although Jambusar features quite often in the EIC records, there is no mention of a mint operating. However, rupees have been reported with this mint name and dated RY 22 (1780/81)[628]. Kulkarni pointed out that this date could be fictitious and that the coin might be a Mahratta coin of a different time. The coins have a distinctive symbol in the *seen* of *julūs* on the

---

625 Bombay Consultations, IOR P/341/48, p. 532, 3rd October 1781.
626 Wiggins K.W. Acquisition of Indian Mints by E.I.CO. Numismatic Panorama, New Delhi, 1996.
627 Bombay Consultations, 3rd October 1781.
628 ONS Newsletter 132 (1992). Also list received from Stephen Album.

reverse[629].

Jambusar rupee
Obverse: shāh alām bādshāh ghazi sicca mubārak (= The auspicious coin of the victorious emperor, Shāh
Alām [AH]).
Reverse: ẓarb Jambusir sanah [RY] julūs maimanat mānūs (= Struck at Jambusir in the [RY] year of his
reign of tranquil prosperity). NB ornament in seen of julūs.

In 1803, the Company took over the mint at Broach and continued striking rupees and fractions (halves and possibly quarters) and copper coins. The coins formerly struck by the Nawabs had a flower as the predominant mark but the Company changed this to the cross of St. Thomas. Although the mark is often present on the coins, very few will be found with clear regnal years as they are almost always off the flan.

In a letter to the Bombay Government dated 31st October 1814, the Collector reported the value of rupees produced at Broach for each year from 1787 to 1803 under the control of Sindhia and then the value of those produced each year under British control[630]. This seems to clearly establish the years in which silver coins were produced at the Broach mint under EIC control with the silver mint being closed in 1814. A petition from local people to issue more silver rupees in 1820 was rejected by Government[631].

Date	Value of Rupees(Rupee. Quarters)
1803	959,686
1804	1,469,700
1805	1,837,597
1806	355,686
1807	662,228.2
1808	-
1809	24,283

Mintage of silver coins at the Broach mint, 1803-1809

[629] Kulkarni P. Indian Coin Society Newsletter, No. 10, September 1991.
Bhandare S. Personal communication.
[630] Board's Collections, IOR F/4/1016, 19th December 1806.
Bombay Consultations, IOR P/411/35, p. 103 onwards. Letter from the Collector at Broach to Government, dated 31st October 1814.
[631] Bombay Consultations, IOR P/411/40, p. 132, 25th October 1820.

Broach rupee
Obverse: sikka mubārak bādshāh ghazi shāh alām [AH] (= The auspicious coin of the victorious emperor, Shāh Alām [AH]).
Reverse: ẓarb Broach sanah (RY) julūs maimanat mānūs (= Struck at Broach in his [RY] year of tranquil prosperity).

Copper Coins

In 1820 a decision was taken to produce copper coins at Broach and to fix the exchange rate of pice at 64 to the rupee[632]. By April of 1820 the Collector at Broach was able to report that he had received a response to his advertisement for a contract for a copper coinage and he sent examples of the pice to Bombay for examination by the Bombay Government[633]. The assay master at Bombay reported that the coins weighed 139 grains 15 dwt each and their manufacture was *'wretched in the extreme'*[634]. The Collector at Broach was ordered to stop their production immediately. However, in 1821 the Broach authorities were informed that they could restart the coinage of copper provided that the quality of coins was improved[635].

In 1824 a contract for the production of 7,000 rupees worth of pice was granted to *'Chocksee Pranwallub Gokooldas, Ruseeckbhaee Bhugwandass, Khooshall Purmanund and Jugdees Mungul Pahruck on similar terms to those of 1821'*[636]. However, too many pice had been produced in the Southern Concan[637], and a decision was made to ship these *'Bankote'* pice to Broach to meet the need for copper coin, and the Collector was asked to withdraw from the contract that he had made. This he succeeded in doing, and the need for copper coin at Broach was met by the Bankot pice for the next few years.

By 1827, there were no further pice left in the treasury of the Southern Concan and the Collector at Broach was instructed to issue a contract for the production of pice locally, again,

---

[632] Bombay Consultations, IOR P/411/40 p. 13, 22nd March 1820. Letter from the mint committee to Chief Secretary Warden, dated 8th March 1820.

[633] Bombay Consultations, IOR P/411/40 p. 46, 26th April 1820. Letter from the Collector of Broach to Mr Secretary Farish, dated 19th April 1820.

[634] Bombay Consultations, IOR P/411/40 p. 52, 17th May 1820.

[635] Bombay Consultations, IOR P/411/40 p. 28, 13th June 1821. Letter from the mint committee to Farish, dated 12th June 1821.

[636] Bombay Consultations, IOR P/411/42 p8, 18th February1824.

[637] See section on Bankot mint. Also Stevens PJE, ONS Newsletter 179.

under the same terms as those used in 1821[638]. In 1828 the production of a further 10,000 rupees worth of pice was sanctioned[639].

In 1830 the Collector reported on the number of pice struck in the preceding three years[640]:

1827	May 31st sanctioned 15,000 rupees-worth
1828	April 14th sanctioned 10,000 rupees-worth
1829	April 11th sanctioned 10,000 rupees-worth

Value of copper pice produced at Broach

A further 25,000 rupees-worth were authorised for production in 1830[641], but with the opening of the new Bombay mint, the activities of the Broach mint were ordered to be stopped on 14th February 1831[642].

Copper pice with crudely engraved balemark on both sides, attributed to Broach

An interesting reference to the copper coins of Broach is found in a petition from the shroffs of Surat to the Bombay Government dated 1824[643]:

When a dispute arose sometime back, at Broach, concerning the pice of that place, Mr Prendergast ordered the pice of Broach to be stamped with the mark of the Sirkar, and from that time all disturbances concerning them ceased, and they were received as current.

This implies that at least prior to 1824 some of the coins of Broach bore the *'mark of the Sirkar'*, probably the balemark of the Company.

Jan Lingen has reported the existence of copper coins of Baroda (not far from Broach) over-stamped on coins with the Company's balemark on both obv. and rev. One of these coins is dated 1244 (1828/29), a date that fits very well with the production of coins at Broach earlier in the century.

---

[638] Bombay Consultations, IOR P/409/1, 6th June 1827.
[639] Bombay Consultations, IOR P/409/6, 16th April 1828.
[640] Bombay Consultations, IOR P/411/49, 17th March 1830.
[641] Bombay Consultations, IOR P/411/49, 23rd June 1830.
[642] Bombay Consultations, IOR P/411/50, No. 66, 16th February 1831.
[643] Bombay Consultations, IOR P/411/42 p. 37, 7th April 1824.

Baroda pice overstruck on Broach pice.

Pridmore reported a copper coin bearing the Company's balemark on both obverse and reverse (Pr. 300) and he assigned it to the Malabar Coast. Given the quote above, the fact that the copper coins of the Concan (bearing the Company's balemark) were so readily accepted at Broach, and the existence of Baroda coins over-stamped with the balemark of the Company, it seems reasonable to reassign this coin to Broach, with a probable date of issue sometime during the first quarter of the nineteenth century.

Nasik & Chandor Mints

Nasik became a stronghold of the Marathas in the mid-eighteenth century. Their first rupees were struck in the name of Alamgir II, and these were followed by coins with the name of Shah Alam II.

The old Moghul name of Gulshanabad was retained on the coins, although the name Nasik seems to have been used in all other matters once the Marathas had charge of the district. Coins were struck with the Shah Alam legend until 1818 (AH 1233) when the city fell into the hands of the British at the conclusion of the third Maratha war. Wiggins stated that the mint continued production of the same type of rupee and its fractions until AH 1249 (AD1833), when it was closed down[644].

---

[644] Wiggins K.W., (1996). Acquisition of Indian Mints by E.I.CO. Numismatic Panorama, New Delhi.

Rupee AH1206. Struck under authority of the Maratha Peshwa

In contradiction to this last statement, in 1823, the Commissioner for the Deccan stated that *'The only other mint in this part of the Deccan [apart from Poona] is that of Chandoor'*[645], implying that, by 1823, only the mints at Poona and Chandore were operating in the Deccan.

So, what about Chandore? The Bombay Gazetteer of 1880[646] states that:

the Chandore rupee coined at the Chandore mint in Nasik (this mint started about 175 years ago was closed soon after the British conquest) was current at the beginning of British rule, but it has now disappeared.

Although this was written fifty or sixty years after the event, it does imply that the mint in Nasik (presumably in the Collectorate of Nasik) might have been located at Chandor, not in the town of Nasik itself. This, together with the previous quote about the Chandor mint, suggests that there was a mint at Chandor and this was the only mint in the Deccan other than Poona.

There are therefore two possibilities. Firstly there may have been two mints operating, one at Nasik and one at Chandor, or secondly, there may have been only one mint, at Chandor, producing the coins identified as 'Nasik' type (Jaripataka) rupees. The first possibility seems to be the more likely for several reasons. Firstly, if the mint was in Nasik when the British took control, it seems unlikely that it would have been moved from that place. If it had been moved to Chandor, then the type of rupee produced would most probably have been the Chandori type rather than the Jaripataka type, which was strongly associated with Nasik. The Jaripatakas are known to exist with dates down to AH 1249 (1833/34, see later). Finally, reference to the table originally published in 1821 by the assay master at the Bombay mint (see p. xxx), reveals that the *'Chandore'* rupee was coined at Chandor and that the *'Jeereeputka'* rupee was coined at Nasik[647], although the table does not give the dates when the rupees were struck. None of this provides conclusive evidence, but it does seem to point to the existence of a mint at Nasik from about 1818 to about 1834 (see catalogue) and another at Chandore sometime early in this period, at least.

This conclusion is confirmed by a letter from the Collector of Ahmadnagar to Bombay, dated

---

[645] Bombay Mint Proceedings, IOR P/411/41 p. 13, 19th March 1823. Extract of a report from the Commissioner in the Deccan 25th August 1823? Transferred from the Revenue Department.

[646] Bombay Gazetteer, vol. XII, Khandesh. Government Press Bombay, 1880, p. 195.

[647] See introductory section to transitional and local mints of the Bombay Presidency. Also Stevens JONS No. 180 p. 29.

4th November 1833[648]:

With reference to your letter dated 4th May last regarding the custom of stamping coins in subordinate treasuries and directing me to prohibit such a practice in all the treasuries in this zillah, I have the honor to annex, to be laid before Government, copy of a letter from Mr Andrews, 1st Assistant Collector at Nassick, detailing his proceedings in consequence of these instructions.

I apprehend Mr Andrews has misunderstood the instructions of Government by stopping the mints at Chandore and Nassick, but I beg to solicit the instructions of Government on this point.

The Chandore rupee is coined at Chandore and the Jerryputka at Nassick, and both are in circulation in this zillah, as well as in other parts of the Deccan, and some inconvenience will, I imagine, be experienced by the deficiency in the circulation which will be created by these mints being stopped.

The Chandore mint coined last year 183,928 and the Nassick mint 69,383 and yielded a revenue to Government of 1358.2.66.

There is also a mint for coining copper at Chandore which coined 27,050 rupees and yielded a revenue to Government of 103.-.64 last year.

Rupee of Nasik, AH 1236
Obverse: sikka mubārak bādshāh ghazi shāh alām (= the auspicious coin of the victorious Emperor Shah Alam).
Reverse: (ẓarb gulshanābād) sanah [RY] julūs maimanat mānūs (= struck at Gulshanabad in the [RY] year of tranquil prosperity)

The Bombay Government replied (in 1833)[649]:

The mints at Nassick and Chandore, I am directed by His Lordship in Council to state, should be reopened, as otherwise inconvenience may arise from the want of Chandore and Jurreeputtee rupees in Candeish and Gungthurree.

The same entry in the records shows that both mints appear to have been working in 1820, because the author refers back to an event when W. Wilkins wrote to Captain H. Pottinger (Collector of Ahmednuggur)[650]:

---

[648] Bombay Consultations, IOR P/409/28, No. 651, 27th November 1833.
[649] Bombay Consultations, IOR P/409/28, No. 651, 27th November 1833.
[650] Bombay Consultations, IOR P/409/28, No. 651, 27th November 1833.

I have the honor to acknowledge the receipt of your letter of the 1ˢᵗ instant with an enclosure from the Commissioners calling upon me to report whether the mints of Nassick and Chandore were under our immediate control or farmed out for a stated period.

In reply I beg leave to state that the mints of both places are not farmed out, but the business of coinage is entrusted to natives who pay a percentage to Government upon the number of rupees coined, and consequently the operations at both these mints can be suspended whenever it is the pleasure of Government to have recourse to that measure, and I should conceive that there could not be any inconvenience whatever in placing the mints under the control of the Committee in Bombay provided any benefit is contemplated by that arrangement.

The only control exercised at present by Government over the mint master is that whenever the operation of coining takes place, one of the Carcoons of the Kumavisdar's establishment with a peon or two is present to take an account of the number of coins which are struck during the day and who, when the day's work is over, locks up the dies and the keys are deposited with the Kumavisdar.

Thus, despite some inconsistencies, the records provide good evidence that two mints were operating, one at Nasik and one at Chandore, throughout the 1820s and into the early 1830s. The mint at Nasik produced the Jaripataka rupees, which were identified by Maheshwari and Wiggins[651].

The design of any coins issued from the Chandore mint is not known but may have been of the standard Chandori type of rupee. The quote above also indicates that there was a significant output of copper coins from the Chandore mint in 1832 at least. Again, the identity of these coins is not certain (but see Lingen ONS Newsletter 152 for a copper coin with mint name Gulshanabad).

A possible example of the Chandore rupee

Other mints may have been operational after 1823, because there is an entry in the records that shows the number of coins struck on average, annually, in various places during the period 1823 to 1833[652].

Mint	Number	Comments
Candeish	*80,000*	
Ahmednuggur & Nassick	*205,000*	*Chandore rupee*

Average annual coinage for 10 years prior to 1833/34 at the Presidency and subordinates.

---

[651] Maheshwari & Wiggens, Maratha Mints and Coinage (1989).
[652] Bombay Consultations, 1835. IOR P/411/54, No. 5 & 6. 21ˢᵗ January 1835.

Khandesh

Khandesh (or Candeish) was a district to the north of Nasik but exactly where in this district a mint might have existed is not clear. The assay master's report of 1821 states that the Chandor rupee was the standard coin of Khandesh (see p. 318) so it seems likely that any mint in Khandesh would have produced the Chandor rupee. Indeed, the table above might even be referring to the mint at Chandor, which is not far from Khandesh. Alternatively, the table may refer to the number of coins shipped to the treasuries at Khandesh rather than the number produced there. If coins were produced at a mint in Khandesh, there is currently no information known about the design of the coins.

Poona Mint

Rupees were first struck at Poona during the Moghul occupation at the end of the seventeenth and the beginning of the eighteenth centuries. They bear the name of the emperor Aurangzeb and the mint name of Muhiabad *urf* Pune. The Marathas had a firm hold in Poona by the middle of the eighteenth century and coins were struck there in the name of Muhammad Shah, the Moghul emperor. Regular and systematic minting of coins by the Maratha government started about 1760 at Poona and several different types were issued there, namely the *Hali sikka*, the *Ankusi* and the *Pharasi sikka*. These coins were struck until 1818 when, during the third Maratha war, Poona was taken by the British following the battle of Kirkee. On the annexation of the Peshwa's territory, the EIC took over the mint at Poona and continued to issue the *Hali sicca* and the *Ankusi* in much the same form, but they were properly dated in the Fasli era on the reverse[653]. That the mint was kept in operation is confirmed in a record of the receipts and expenditure for the territories conquered from and ceded by the Peshwa in 1818/1819, wherein are found the costs of running the Poona Mint (Rs 2569-3-89) for 1818/19 and an estimate of the costs for 1820 (Rs 2500-0-0)[654].

The coins were issued by the Tanksale or mint master family of Deshasth Brahmans under the supervision of British officers and they were apparently allowed to add ten percent copper alloy to the silver coins as their profit[655].

---

[653] Wiggins K.W., (1996). Acquisition of Indian Mints by E.I.CO. Numismatic Panorama, New Delhi.
[654] Boards Collections F/4/697, p. 708.
[655] Bombay Gazetteer (1885). Vol. XVIII, Part II, Poona, p. 104. Government Central Press, Bombay.

In 1820 the mint establishment at Poona was cited by Captain Gibbon as[656]:

	Rs
2 Hammermen	*12*
1 Stamp Holder	*9*
2 Billow Boys	*30*
3 Coolies	*18*
1 Smith	*9*
1 Bhistee	*10*
1 Engraver of Stamps	*22*
5 Peons	*30*
2 Carkoons	*35*
Sundries	*25*
Rs	*200*

Establishment of the Poona mint in 1820

Silver Coins

Prior to 1820 the EIC records contain references to coining of copper coins at the Poona mint, but little on the coinage of silver.

Shortly before August 1822 the Poona mint was closed for some time owing to the discovery of frauds. The reason for the closure was outlined by the Commissioner for the Deccan in a letter to Government in 1823[657]:

…The mint farm was knocked down to him for the year [for 1821/22] at a public auction as the highest bidder and he entered into security for the payment, and the faithful performance of his engagement. The weight and assay of the coin to be struck were particularly specified, and for every deviation from the standard he was to be fined 500 rupees. The contractor adhered to the conditions of his agreement until the month of May 1822 when he was found out mixing up more than the prescribed quantity of alloy in the coins. The extent to which this deterioration had been caused not being known, some decisive measures became necessary to check the evil and the mint was accordingly shut up and the Farmer placed in jail to stand his trial for the fraudulent breach of contract. In the examination which followed, it was discovered that he had sent a considerable quantity of depreciated money into circulation, and being found guilty of the charge brought against him was sentenced to pay a fine of 3700 rupees, double the amount which he gained by debasing the coin and indemnifying Government for the loss sustained by the closure of the mint – which was 3637 rupees.

The closure of the mint caused great inconvenience due to the shortage of circulating coin and it was reopened, although, exactly when this happened is not clear[658].

In 1823 the assay master at Bombay reported on the outcome of tests he had conducted on

---

[656] Bombay Consultations, IOR P/408/45, p. 323, 26th April 1820.
[657] Bombay Consultations, IOR P/408/55, p. 77, 22nd October 1823.
[658] Bombay Gazetteer (1885). Vol. XVIII, Part II, Poona, p. 104 footnote. Government Central Press, Bombay.

Hali Sicca rupees lately coined at Poona[659]:

	Weight Grs Decls	Touch Pct	Pure Silver Grs Decls	Value of 100 In B'bay Rupees
No 1	175	97.75	171 – 06	103 – 87
No 2	175	97.75	171 – 06	103 – 87
No 3	175.25	97.50	170 – 86	103 – 75
Av. of 17	175	97.75	171 – 06	103 – 87

Assay of Hali Sicca Rupees by the Bombay assay master (Decls = Deciles)

These coins were presumably sent to Bombay for assay after the mint had been reopened, implying that the mint must have been open by March 1823[660]. The contractor who had been responsible for the mint prior to its closure was Appajee Muckajeesett who, in 1824, sent a petition soliciting the remission of an indemnification to Government for the loss sustained from the mint at Poona having been closed on account of his breach of agreement. The Bombay Government rejected his petition, as they did a second petition from him[661].

Ankusi rupee with the ankus mark on the reverse

  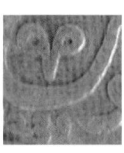

Hali sicca rupee with the head of a cobra (scissors) on the reverse
The rupees can be distinguished by the presence of the Fasli date and either the 'Scissors' (head of the cobra) or the Ankus mark on the obverse.

In 1826 the Collector at Poona asked for advice on whether or not he was allowed to accept

---

[659] Bombay Consultations, IOR P/411/41, 5th February 1823.

[660] Bombay Mint Proceedings IOR P/411/41 p. 13, 19th March 1823. Extract of a report from the Commissioner in the Deccan 25th August 1823? Transferred from the Revenue Department.

[661] Bombay Consultations, IOR P/411/42 p. 13, 25th February 1824.
  Bombay Consultations, IOR P/411/42 p. 69, 11th August 1824.

an offer for the mint contract that was not the highest in cash terms but was made by a person who had been responsible for keeping the mint in operation for the previous two years. This letter states that[662]:

During the last two years the farmer (who is the person that has offered the least sum this year) has sustained considerable loss from the small number of rupees that have fallen from the mint…

From this it is apparent that not many rupees were struck during the years 1824 and 1825 (Fasli 1234 and 1235). Government confirmed that the Collector could choose whomsoever he considered most suitable for the contract and this he duly did at the rate of 3,200 rupees for *'the current Faslee'*.

By 1831 the new mint at Bombay had begun operation and the Collector at Poona wondered if he should issue a contract for the mint for that year[663]. He was informed that he should issue a contract for silver only and that the new Bombay mint would provide copper coins[664].

The Poona mint was still producing rupees in January 1834 because the Collector informed Bombay that[665]:

…two silver coins continue to fall from the mint of Poona both having the Fusly year "1243" stamped upon them. These are called the one "Hallee Sicca" and the other "Ankoosee". The Poona mint not having been ordered to be stopped…

However, by September 1834 the mint appears to have been closed[666].

The EIC records confirm the dates observed on the coins themselves. These range from Fasli 1230 to 1244 (AD 1820 to 1834).

Copper Coins

Poona/Satara pice

In 1819 the Commissioner of the Deccan asked for copper coins to be supplied to Poona from the Bombay Mint. However, the mint committee replied that they had never had any intention of supplying copper coins to the Deccan from Bombay, but that they did have a supply of copper

---

[662] Bombay Consultations, IOR P/408/65, 19th July 1826.

[663] Bombay Consultations, IOR P/411/50, 7th June 1831.

[664] Bombay Consultations, IOR P/411/50, 29th June 1831.

[665] Bombay Consultations, IOR P/411/53, 22nd January 1834.

[666] Bombay Consultations, IOR P/411/53, No 277, 22nd October 1834.

that could be sent to Poona for coining locally[667]. Initially the price of copper was too high for the authorities at Poona[668], but as the price fell they asked for a sample to be sent and half a ton was duly dispatched[669]. The trial showed that to produce pice at the rate of 64 to the rupee, given the cost of the copper, would result in a loss to Government. By 1820 the cost of the copper had fallen, and the mint committee at Bombay was insistent that any pice produced at Poona should be exchanged at 64 to the rupee even if this meant a slightly lower weight[670]. This rate was consistent with the rate that the mint committee had asked both Broach and the Southern Concan to achieve and they were obviously trying to establish a standard throughout the Presidency. This did not pose a problem for the authorities at Poona[671], and presumably minting of the coins started in that year, since specimens exist dated Fasli 1230. As has been stated above, the Collector at Poona was instructed not to renew the contract for copper coins in 1831 and thus pice dated Fasli 1240 (1830) are the last to be issued by the Poona mint.

The copper pice bear a Nagari inscription and can be identified by the presence of the Fasli date on the obverse. However, a contemporary quote reveals that pice struck at Poona were identical to those struck at Satara so these two cannot be differentiated (see chapter 8)

Rahimatpur Mint

Rahimatpur pice

The only coins identified as having been issued from the Rahimatpur mint are those rather crude copies of the 1820/21 copper coins issued by the British for use in the Southern Concan. These copies are dated 1828 and 1829. A letter to the Bombay Government dated 1830, reveals the source of these copper coins[672]:

The profit on a coinage of this weight is so great that a spurious pice very nearly resembling the original has been brought down in considerable quantities from the distant town of Ruhimutpoor in the Putwurdhun's territory. These counterfeit pice are not quite so well executed as the Bankote coinage. The copper is of a little inferior quantity [quality?] and there is a very slight difference of weight.

---

[667] Bombay Consultations, IOR P/411/39, p. 30, 7th April 1819.
[668] Bombay Consultations, IOR P/411/39, p. 32, 21st April 1819.
[669] Bombay Consultations, IOR P/411/39, p. 130, 1st September 1819.
[670] Bombay Consultations, IOR P/411/40., 29th March 1820.
[671] Bombay Consultations, IOR P/411/40, 26th April 1820.
[672] Bombay Consultations, IOR P/411/49, 1st September 1830. Petition from Nathooset bin Abaset to Bombay Government.

This quote, written in 1830, appears to establish that the coins dated 1828 and 1829, were not a second official issue of pice for the Southern Concan, but were, in fact, imitative pieces produced outside of the collectorate and sold for a profit. Usually copies of this nature would closely follow the design of the original coin, but these 1828/29 pieces have a slightly different design, and obviously bear different dates. This fact misled Pridmore into believing that they were a later official issue, albeit rather more crudely struck.

Surat Mint

When the British first arrived at Surat in 1612 there was no mint operating in the town. EIC commerce was conducted in foreign gold and silver coins for the first few years that the Company resided there[673]. In fact, their first factory was established in what had previously been the local Moghul mint and which had been closed before the British arrived. However, in August 1618 the Company was obliged to move from this site because the mint was to be re-opened[674]. Henceforth, commerce had to be conducted using local mohurs and rupees and imported coin had to be converted in the Moghul's (and later the Nawab's) mint. In 1759, the British captured Surat and for the next forty years occupied the fort leaving the Nawab in nominal charge of the city. However, increasingly, the Britsh took more and more control of the town as well as the fort until, in 1800 they took complete control of the place[675, 676].

Treaty with the Nawab of SuratArticles of Agreement between the Hounourable East India Company and their successors and the Nawab Nuseer-ood-Deen Khan, etc. etc., and his heirs and successors, for the better administration of the Government of the City of Surat and its dependencies, concluded on the 13th May 1800, or the 19th of Zilhuj 1214 of the Hegira.

Whereas the Hounarable the English East India Company have been subjected to a heavy expenses for the protection of the city of Surat, and whereas the existing system of internal government in the said city has been found inadequate to the protection of the persons and property of the inhabitants; and whereas the Right Honourable the Earl of Mornington, Governor-General of the British possessions in India, and the Nawab Naserooddeen, etc., are mutually desirous of providing more effectually for the external defense of the city of Surat, and for the security, ease, and happiness of the inhabitants, the following Articles of Agreement are concluded on behalf of the Honourable English Company and their successors, by the Honourable Jonathan Duncan, Governor of Bombay, vested with full powers for that purpose by the said

---

[673] Forrest GW (Ed) (1887). Selections from the Letters, Despatches and Other State Papers Preserved in the Bombay Secretariat. Home Series Vol 1, Printed at the Government Central Press Bombay. P. 9.
   Letter from Surat to Agra? Dated 6th October 1630.
[674] Foster W., (1906). The English Factories in India 1618-1621. Clarendon Press, Oxford.
   p. 36 – reference to the English being moved from the old mint house to a new one on July 13th 1618.
   pp. 38-40 Sir Thomas Roe's negotiations with Prince Khurram in August 1618.
[675] Bombay Gazetteer (1877), Gujarat, Surat and Broach. Vol. II. Government Central Press, Bombay. pp. 128-134.
[676] From Jan Lingen C.U. Aitchison: A collection of Treaties, Engagements and Sanads relating to India and Neighbouring Countries, vol 8. p.385-387:

Governor-General on the one part, and by the Nawab Nuseerooddeen, and his heirs and successors on the other part: - …….

Article 2: The Nawab Naseerooddeen agrees that the management and collection of revenues of the city of Surat, and of the territories, places, and other dependencies thereof, the administration of civil and criminal justice, and generally the whole civil and military government of the said city and its dependencies, shall be vested for ever entirely and exclusively in the Honourable English Company.

Article 3: It is agreed that the Nawab shall be treated on all occasions with the same respect and distinction as his predecessors.

Article 4: The English Company agree to pay to the Nawab Naseerooddeen and his heirs, out of the revenues of Surat and his dependencies, in four equal quarterly payments, one lakh of Rupees annually, which shall be considered to be the first charge payable from the said revenues. The Company also engage to pay to the said Nawab and his heirs, in addition to the above mentioned lakh of Rupees, a proportion of one-fifth of the annual revenues now arising, or which may hereafter arise, from the said city and its dependencies, after deducting the said lakh of Rupees, the sum payable to the Mahrattas, and the charges of collection. The residue of the revenues, after the forgoing reductions, shall be at the disposal of the said Company.

Article 5: In order that the Nawab may at all times have full satisfaction in respect to the revenues of Surat and its dependencies, he, the said Nawab, shall be at liberty to inspect all the accounts thereof from time to time, or to station a vakeel or accountant, at his own expense, in all or in any of the offices of collection, for the purpose of taking and transmitting to His Excellency copies of all or any of the accounts of the said revenue.

Based on this it would seem that the EIC took control of the Surat mint in May 1800[677]. However, several entries in the records seem to show that there was a British mint master much earlier than this. In 1800 JohnJohn Church wrote[678]:

…I observe in the year 1789 on my receiving charge of the mint I found the proportions of standard silver to be 508 rice of pure silver with 44 of alloy agreeably whereto the rupee weighing 548½ rice contains 43.72 rice of alloy or 7.97 per cent of its weight, at which rate I have sedulously endeavoured and I hope successfully to maintain it…

and even before that the EIC appears to have been able to issue orders concerning the mint (see chapter 2, pp.55-56).

Regnal Years

As previously discussed (see chapter 4) the coins issued from the Bombay and Surat mints are dated RY 46. However, KM records Surat rupees dated RY 49, 51, 52, 53, 54 and 6x (KM 76) under French India. This seems an unlikely attribution and whilst these rupees might have been produced somewhere other than Surat itself (for instance at Bhaunagar, which has been

---

[677] Pridmore p. 126, although the original source for this has not yet been traced.

[678] Bombay Public Consultations. IOR P/342/44. p. 2352. Letter from the Surat mint master (JohnJohn Church), dated 8th November 1800.

suggested by Jan Lingen as a place that forged Surat rupees[679]), it is also possible that they might have been produced in a local mint, perhaps controlled by the Nawab, in defiance of the British. Assuming the coin dated RY 6x represents the postumous year 60 of Shah Alam, this equates to 1815 when the Surat mint proper was closed by the British (see below).

There nevertheless are strong arguments against the Nawab being responsible for the issue of these coins, not least the treaty signed in 1800 (shown above). However, there can be no doubt that the Nawab was receiving an income from a mint, whether his own or that of the EIC, between 1808 and 1815, because an entry in the records dated 1816 shows the amount of revenue derived from the mint of Surat by the Nawab as about 1193 rupees p.a.[680]

Gold and Silver Coins

Surat mohur. RY 46

Silver rupee. RY 4[6]
Obverse of both coins: sikka mubārak bādshāh ghazi shāh alām (= The auspicious coin of the victorious Emperor Shāh Alām).
Reverse of both coins: ẓarb surat sanah 46 julūs maimanat mānūs (= Struck at Surat in the 46th year of tranquil prosperity).

Minting of silver coins had started by June 1800 because an entry in the records shows the number of coins struck from from 100,000 dollars during June and July[681]:

---

[679] Lingen J, (2009), JONS 200, pp. 52-54.
[680] Bombay Mint Procedimgs. IOR p/411/37 (1816), pp. 47-49.
[681] Bombay Public Consultations. IOR P/342/43. p. 1724. Letter from the Collector at Surat (Edward Galley), dated 25th August 1800.

June 26ᵗʰ	*22,996.2*
June 27ᵗʰ	*10,999*
July 1ˢᵗ	*17000*
July 3ʳᵈ	*10000*
July 7ᵗʰ	*17000*
July 9ᵗʰ	*22000*

These produced at 216.3.24 per […] dollars: 216801.1.31 rupees. Exactly when the minting of gold began is not known.

Management of the Mint

The usual method of managing the provincial mints in the Bombay Presidency was for the Collector to contract the mint work for an annual fee to a local person. At the Surat Mint, however, a full-time mint master was appointed. The first of these was JohnJohn Church[682], who by 1806 had been replaced by C. Wren[683]. Wren was followed, in 1807, by Thomas White[684], who was, in turn, replaced by John Morison[685].

Date	Mint Master
1800 to ~1806	JohnJohn Church (George Brown was acting mint master in July 1800)[686]
~1806 to July 1807	C. Wren
August 1807 to December 1809	Thomas White
January 1810 to 1815	JohnJohn Morison

In order to ensure the quality of the coins, on the 9ᵗʰ December 1801, the Judge & Magistrate at Surat was instructed to go to the mint and select a few coins randomly to send to Bombay for Assay. This he duly did on the 29ᵗʰ September 1802, the next time that a coinage took place[687]. Obviously the mint was not very active during the first 9 months of 1802. The coins were found to be satisfactory[688].

Having produced his report, but before sending it, he obtained copies of the mint records of Surat and added a postscript to his report. This reviewed the entries relating to the standard of

---

[682] Bombay Consultations, IOR P/342/46, p. 371, 20ᵗʰ February 1801. Letter from mint master (JohnJohn Church) to Government, dated 12ᵗʰ February 1801.

[683] Bombay Consultations, IOR P/343/34, p. 3631, 22ⁿᵈ July 1806. Letter from the mint master at Surat (Mr Wren) to Government, dated 15ᵗʰ July 1806.

[684] Bombay Consultations, IOR P/343/48, p. 6473, 21ˢᵗ August 1807. Letter from Government to mint master at Surat (now White) 21ˢᵗ August 1807.

[685] Bombay Consultations, IOR P/344/19, p. 7808, 8ᵗʰ December 1809. Minute

[686] Bombay Public Consultations. IOR P/342/43. p. 1520. Letter from the acting mint master at Surat (George Brown), dated 21ˢᵗ July 1800

[687] Bombay Consultations, IOR P/342/57, p. 3242, 8ᵗʰ October 1802. Letter from the Judge and Magistrate at Surat to Government dated 30ᵗʰ September 1802.

[688] Bombay Consultations, IOR P/342/57, p. ?, 15ᵗʰ October 1802. Letter from the assay master (Mr Scott) to Government, 13ᵗʰ October 1802.

the Surat rupee over the preceding twenty years or so. He found that the Surat rupee had contained less silver then that of Bombay in 1765. When the Surat rupee had first been issued it was meant to contain 2.18% alloy but this had gradually increased until by 1772 it was supposed to contain about 5%. Even then, this standard was not adhered to and the coins contained even more alloy and this continued throughout the years 1780 to 1784:[689]

PS Since writing the above I have received and read over the Surat diary of the mintage. It commences in 1762 and concludes in 1790 but several parts of it have been lost. From the diary it appears that in 1765 the Surat rupee was worse than that of Bombay by 5.5 per cent.

In November 1771 the Chief and Council write to the Court of Directors "that they had with the Nabob fixed the standard of the rupee at an alloy of 22 rice which makes it 2⅓ per cent superior to the Bombay mint". Hence the Surat rupee contained 4 per cent of alloy & the Bombay rupee only 1⅔.

In 1784 they write to the Bombay Government "that on the establishment of the Surat mint the standard was 538 rice pure silver and 12 rice of alloy", that is the alloy was 2.18 per cent. Only the same was continued during Hyder [Konle] Khan's time. In the time of [Jikhbeghkan] it contained, they say, 526 rice pure silver & 24 rice of alloy. This amounts to 4.36 per cent alloy.

In 1772 I see a further change was made on the fineness of the rupee for the standard was now fixed at 514.5 rice of pure silver 35.5 rice of alloy. This is an alloy of 4.956 or 5 per cent nearly. But the Surat mint in its actual coinage never kept even to this standard, for by assays of its rupees for 7 years viz: 1773, 80, 81, 82, 83 and 84 (sic) the alloy had increased above the standard from 1569 to 3364 [I'm not sure what this means].

In 1775 the Court of Directors tried to intervene to re-establish the standard and in 1789, someone called "the chief" tried to fix the amount of alloy at about 6.5% but all these efforts were in vain:

In 1775 the Court of Directors recommended the rupee to be of the same fineness that it had been in 1767. That is to say that it should be of the same fineness that it had been in the time of Hyther Coolie Khan, or that it should contain no more than 2.18 per cent of alloy (see regulation by the Surat Committee in August 1767). This, like all other repetitions for the standard of the Surat mint seems never [to have] taken place. I do not observe that such rupees were ever coined either in 1767 or after the Company orders in 1775.

Last of all I observe that in February 1789 the chief fixes that standard of fineness for the Surat rupee at 35.5 rice of alloy or 6.454 per cent. This is the latest regulation for standard that this diary contains. Like the rest it appears not to have been put in execution.

What the present [regulation] is for fineness I do not know but it is very necessary to get this information from Surat when no rupee that shall in future be coined either there or here should exceed it by the smallest fraction. With regard to the weight of the rupee the diary contains no information but I imagine it is the rupee of the Mogul of 178.314 grains.

---

[689] Bombay Public Consultations. IOR P/342/44. p. 2282. Letter from Bombay Assay Master (Scott) to Government, dated 12th November 1800.

The judge and magistrate went on to speculate about why control of the fineness of the Surat rupee had been so difficult concluding that it was largely political for monetary gain. The fineness should finally be fixed at the then standard, whatever that was:

The diary of the mint of Surat might furnish abundant materials for reflection and shows in many respects the danger of speculating in a political matter of so great difficulty & delicacy. A good state of the coinage is at once the interest of the sovereign & the people, nor does it appear to me to be possible consistently with the welfare of either to make [...]. The mintage was at once a source of revenue to the King of Dilhi, the Company, the Nabob & the Mahrattas. Under those circumstances we constantly kept pressing the Nabob to make his coinage very pure but still insisting on our portion of the profits of it. It surely was forgotten during a period of 30 years that it is only from the alloy of a coinage that any profit whatever can arise. We tried to get the advantage undiminished from him while at the same time we endeavoured to take away the very means that produced it.

I think it would be advisable to keep at present to the standard now fixed for the Surat rupee whatever that may be, for all changes are attended with loss or inconvenience. The complaints of the shroffs and merchants on this subject are often short sighted or interested. They are fearful at one time (surely without reason) that a pure coinage would be bought up by the neighbouring mints, at another time they complain that the coin is not sufficiently good for the purposes of commerce or exchange. I image it is not difficult to see on which side of the question the real cause for apprehension lies.

I have had but a few hours to consider this Surat diary which I hope will plead my excuse if any error should afterwards appear in what I have said.

Change of Management, 1806-1807

The cost of producing coins at Surat began to come under scrutiny in 1806 when the mint master at Surat wrote to Bombay about the matter[690] and the mint and assay masters at Bombay wrote a joint letter to Government in July of 1806[691]:

In reply to your secretary's letter of the 4th ultimo, accompanying copy of a letter from Messrs Bruce Fawcett & Co to Government of the 27th of January on the subject of the returns of silver from the Surat mint for bullion sent to it for coinage, we have to observe that there is no kind of doubt but that the Surat mint does not deliver the number of rupees to the holder of bullion which it ought to do and that it is, and long has been, the practice of that mint to keep back a greater sum than the expense of coinage, together with the Company's duties [amount to].

It is evident (for example) that 100 dollars contain silver enough to make very nearly 227 Surat rupees. Something is lost by the melting and refining. The expense of coining is 2 per cent and the Company's duty ½ per cent. Our mint contractor here has delivered for 100 dollars, as far as 220 Surat rupees, but he complains that he suffered a little loss and we may perhaps be obliged to be satisfied with a fraction of one

---

[690] Bombay Consultations, IOR P/343/34, p. 3631, 22nd July 1806. Letter from the mint master at Surat (Mr Wren) to Government, dated 15th July 1806.

[691] Bombay Public Consultations. IOR P/343/31. p. 1469. Letter from Charles Watkins (mint master) and Helenus Scott (assay Master) to Government, dated 2nd April 1806

rupee less on 100 dollars. With this however, he will be quite satisfied. Nor can we see any reason why such conditions should not be very satisfactory to any fair minter, either here or at Surat.

We have had repeated conversations with the mint contractor with regard to his coining the Surat rupees, at Surat, on the above mentioned conditions. With the conditions he is perfectly satisfied, but he tells us that he foresees that at Surat he will meet with great opposition from the shroffs and others who have an interest to keep the Surat mint on its present footing. He further says that his absence would materially interfere with his engagements at Bombay. These difficulties however, may be got over by Government assuring the contractor at Surat of their full support against the combinations of individuals. On such terms we have no doubt but our mint contractor will get one of his own family to carry on the Surat coinage at Surat, or men will be easily found there to do so, when they are sure of receiving the protection of Government. The resistance from interested individuals is the only difficulty that can arise in such a case.

Resolution

Ordered that copy of the preceding report be referred to the mint master at Surat with intimation that Government expect he will reduce the expense of coinage at Surat to the same standard as at Bombay or to report the obstructions he may experience in carrying the same into effect, being authorized for this purpose to correspond with the mint master at Bombay, who is to be directed to communicate with Mr Wren the expense of coinage in the Bombay mint.

In November they sent a more detailed letter:[692]

According to the order conveyed to us by you we have attentively considered the mint master of Surat's letter of the 15th ultimo and the following reflections have occurred to us:

It is, we conceive, the intention of Government that a percentage be levied on the coinage at Surat by which the expenses of the coinage shall be fully paid in the first place, the remainder going to Government. After the payment of this percentage the bullion holder is to receive back all that remains of his silver, not a grain of which is to remain unaccounted for.

On this principle we are not yet satisfied with the offer [of] the Surat mint master of 220 rupees for 100 dollars as expressed in his letter, for a good deal of the silver he receives would remain entirely unaccounted for.

To make this perfectly evident let us examine his proposals.

The expenses of making the coins at Surat are no more than 1½ per cent but the Surat mint master states in his letter of 15th July that the use of a lead instead of a copper alloy creates an expense of ½ per cent. If therefore a copper alloy be adopted at Surat the expenses of minting will be but one per cent

100 dollars gross produce	*Rs 266*
The Surat mint master returns	*Rs 220*
Leaving rupees	*6*
Now, 6 rupees equals to per cent	*2.2.60*
Deduct Government customs as	

---

[692] Bombay Public Consultations. IOR P/343/38. p. 6302. Letter from Charles Watkins (mint master) and Helenus Scott (assay master) to Government, dated 28th November 1806

Stated by the mint master   -.2.-
Leaving   2.-.60

If the mintage costs 1½ per cent, the
usual rate he would have to pay for it   1.2.-
             -.2.60

or nearly ¾ per cent which seems to be entirely unaccounted for

If however the adoption of a copper alloy saves him on the mintage ½ per cent as he states then there remains in his hands no less then Rs 1.-.60 or nearly 1¼ per cent of which he gives no account. This is above twice as much as he proposes paying to Government.

We now beg leave to recommend that the Surat mint master be called upon solumnly and upon honor to declare at what rate per cent he can conduct his coinage, 1 with a lead alloy and, 2 with a copper alloy. When we know this we know as well as they can do at Surat what return they ought to make to the bullion holder & what should go to Government. In Bombay the deduction from the bullion holder is 3 per cent. If Government choose to make the same deduction at Surat it is evident that the Honble Company ought to receive 2 per cent clear, instead of half a per cent as stated by the Surat mint master, The bullion holder will get in that case the same return from both mints.

The Surat mint master offers to return 220 rupees for 100 dollars, observing that the Bombay mint returns only 219.80 (he should have said 219.88). That is to say he offers to return a little more than 1/3 of one per cent above the return of the Bombay mint. The reason is evident.

We pay our mint contractor per cent   2.2
He pays for his mintage at the most   1.2
Hence he gains per cent on
Making of the coin   1

His is at one the secret of an offer that has the superficial appearance of advantage. It may be asked why the Surat coins can be made so much cheaper than those of Bombay. We answer that it chiefly arises from the great difference of expense of labour and also in part from the constitution of their mint which as we shall presently see is defective in this very respect. Our mint contractor positively refuses even with a copper alloy to abate more than a few reas of this percentage. It may be seen that not a grain of silver is left unaccounted for here if anyone should choose to make the inquiry.

Themint an assay masters considered that the Surat mint had been badly run for the previous 30 years and, in particular, noticed that in order for people to get their silver minted they had to negotiate with people called 'Bhurteahs' and there was no direct access to the mint. These Bhurteahs somehow made money out of this process but it was very opaque. They considered that this practice should be stopped although they wanted to make sure that the Bhurteahs did not starve so they proposed that the mint contractor should support them:

We have long considered the constitution of the Surat mint and we think it is radically wrong. No mint master there however great his knowledge or however just his intention can protect the public at all times from fraud. Accordingly for 30 years past with an exception of a few years of late, it has exhibited, as the records of Government abundantly show, a scene of disorder. It has given rise to a most disordered state of the coinage both here and there. The cause of the evil still remains altho' it has ceased for a time to operate so extensively. This great cause, of which we so much complain is the employment of men called Bhurteahs, who exclusively are authorized to bring the silver of individuals to the mint. They have no acknowledged profit but it cannot be believed that they labour without profit. They are permitted against all the ordinary practices of Government to bargain with individuals who have bullion for return in rupees, which they will agree to make. Thus the bullion holder is left (as the former returns from the Surat mint will prove) to their mercy. We anxiously recommend that the office of Bhurteah [must] cease forever & that individuals may be allowed to carry their silver to the Surat mint whenever it suits their conveniency.

Instead of Bhurteahs we advise that a mint contractor may be employed to make the coin at Surat. He should be a man of character & give security in a large sum for his honestly both with regard to the public and individuals. Such a man would certainly not make the coins for 1 or perhaps even 1½ per cent. He ought to have a reasonable & an open profit for his office is most important. From such an office we should have a great degree of security & his avowed and honorable allowances would support some of the Bhurteahs whom we wish not (so far as is possible) to deprive of their bread. Until this regulation is adopted we confess that we do not expect to see the Surat mint on that footing which is so desirable unless those who make the coins are bound by penalties and held by heavy responsibility. It is impossible that any mint master can protect the public or Government in the coinage of Surat.

We conceive that 3 per cent collected on the coinage of Surat would in this way amply reward a mint contractor besides paying a mint master & affording a certain revenue to Government.

We do not say that this last proposal from Surat keeps back much more of the silver from the bullion holder than may be absolutely necessary to pay the contractor & the other demands in a well regulated mint, but we complain that this silver is kept back there from the bullion holder secretly without an avowed object & (as we conclude) that it must be absorbed by the Bhurteahs without answering any good purpose. Men will never labour without reward in any situation, but to employ men in a mint without any open and avowed means of living is of all systems the most ruinous.

Should Government be pleased to adopt our suggestion with regard to placing a mint contractor in the Surat mint, we should think it proper that this person should pay a visit to the Presidency that he may be made fully to comprehend our systems and that an agreement in all respects may be established between the two mints intimately connected as they are. Until this is done we recommend that the Surat mint may be stopped altogether.

We shall at a future time take the liberty of recommending a further system of check on the Surat coinage for it cannot go materially wrong without damaging both our gold and silver and producing as it did for many years both loss & inconveniency to Government & the public.

The specimens sent us of the Surat coinage with a copper alloy is unexceptionable. No objection would be made to it here but before it is adopted by Government (and it would be very desirable to have it adopted) it should be ascertained at Surat if it would be willingly received there. We still think that such objections would be unreasonable and ill-founded.

Resolution

Ordered that a copy of the preceding report be forwarded to the mint master at Surat for such remarks as occur to him repecting more especially the manner in which the Bhurteahs derive their emolument and the *expediency of dispensing with their services as above proposed. Another copy to be sent to the chief at Surat for his final opinion in the question suggested in the last paragraph as to the currency of the Surat rupee if coined with copper alloy*

Accordingly, in 1807 the mint master was directed to change the management of the mint. Up until then five Bhurtiahs had overseen the operation of the mint. Three very young ones were descended from those who had served in the mint for half a century, and two who had recently transacted the business of the mint by themselves, and whose ancestors had been doing it for upwards of 75 years[693]. Henceforth, the Bhurtiahs were to be replaced by a Superintendent reporting directly to the mint master and paid by the Company as a salaried employee. The then current Bhurtiahs were allowed to become contractors if they chose, and would receive half a percent for the contract. If they refused then the mint master was to consult the Chief and Collector of Surat as to the next steps to be taken[694]. The Bhurtiahs were not happy with this and would only agree to continue to operate the mint on a three-month trial[695]. These problems appear to have been resolved and the mint continued in operation. However, by the time that JohnJohn Morison took over in 1810, the mint buildings had fallen into a state of dilapidation because the mint contractors could not afford to maintain the buildings, as they had done in the past, with their lower income[696].

In 1813 the capability of the mint at Surat was again being questioned and the mint master was asked to show how many coins had been produced during the previous year. He replied that between 1st May 1812 and the 28th February 1813 the mint had produced just over 40,000 rupees-worth of silver coins and a mere 272 mohurs-worth of gold coin.

The ability of the Surat mint to produce rupees of the same standard as those produced at Bombay continued to be questioned, with the Surat mint master claiming that he did not have the necessary equipment to conduct assays as accurately as those performed in the Bombay mint[697].

Eventually the Bombay Government deemed it necessary to issue a proclamation declaring that the Bombay and Surat coinages were of the same standard[698]:

Proclamation issued 1st July 1813.
Notice is hereby given that the coinage of the Bombay and Surat mints being in all respects of the same standard and purity, and received as such in all the public treasuries at the Presidency and subordinates, the payments from those treasuries will be regulated on the same principle'

However, the criticism continued throughout 1814 with an ex employee of the mint claiming that the standard achieved was not high enough[699] even though these were clearly refuted by the mint

---

693 Bombay Consultations, IOR P/343/42, p. 742, 13th February 1807.
694 Bombay Consultations, IOR P/343/48, p. 6473, 21st August 1807.
695 Bombay Consultations, IOR P/343/49, p. 7456, 22nd September 1807.
696 Bombay Consultations, IOR P/344/23, 4th April 1810.
697 Bombay Consultations, IOR P/408/17, p. 502, 19th May 1813.
698 Bombay Consultations, IOR P/408/18, p. 716, 7th July 1813.
699 Bombay Consultations, IOR P/411/35, p. 92, 4th May 1814.

master[700].

Finally, in 1815 the Bombay Government discussed the subject of the Surat mint and came to a decision to close it. The Bombay mint master saw three benefits in this[701]:

1. *That it is under no efficient control from the want of an European gentleman on the spot duly qualified to conduct the department of assay.*
2. *That it enables the Surat shroffs to establish a fraudulent exchange by making a distinction between the Bombay & Surat rupee to the disadvantage of the former.*
3. *That it deprives this mint* [i.e. Bombay] *of profit that would otherwise accrue to it, and which would enable Government without incurring a greater expense, to put the mint here on a more respectable and efficient footing.*

The Governor in Council agreed with this and ordered that the Surat Mint should be abolished from the 1st November 1815. The following advertisement was therefore issued:

The Right Honorable the Governor in Council is pleased to announce for general information that the mint at Surat will be abolished from the 1st of the ensuing month of November and that the whole of the coinage under this Presidency will in future be conducted at the mint at Bombay.

There were petitions from the local traders[702] and from the Nawab of Surat[703] but all to no avail[704] and the Surat mint was duly closed for the production of gold and silver coins.

Copper Coins

For some reason, Pridmore excluded the copper coins of Surat from his catalogue but events surrounding various coinages of copper pice at Surat are recorded in the EIC archives.

Possible copper pice of Surat. Wt = 10.47g. Diameter = 25.3mm. (From Ashmolean museum, Oxford).
Obverse: falūs bādshāh shāh alām (= falūs of the Emperor Shāh Alām).
Reverse: (ẓarb) surat sanah [RY] julūs (= struck at surat in [RY]).

At the end of 1802 and the beginning of 1803 a copper coinage amounting to 18,000 rupees-worth was undertaken, but this was insufficient to meet demand and more copper was requested

---

[700] Bombay Consultations, IOR P/411/35, 29th June 1814.
[701] Bombay Consultations, IOR P/411/36, 11th October 1815.
[702] Bombay Consultations, IOR P/411/36, 20th December 1815.
[703] Bombay Consultations, IOR P/411/36, 31st December 1815.
[704] Bombay Consultations, IOR P/411/37 p. 1, 1st January 1816.
   Bombay Consultations, IOR P/411/37, 23rd January.

and sent from Bombay[705]. The size of any coinage undertaken, as the result of this copper being sent, has not been identified.

Another coinage took place when the Surat mint master asked Bombay to send him enough copper and lead to strike 20,000 rupees-worth of pice[706]. Although he made the request in 1812, the delivery took some time and the coinage actually took place in 1813[707].

A further copper coinage probably took place in 1815 when the Surat mint master asked for lead to be sent to him to enable him to coin copper that remainded in the mint[708]:

I beg the favor of your obtaining permission from the Right Honble the Governor in Council to direct the Warehousekeeper at the Presidency to send me up by the first [Cnuzir] 110 Surat maunds of lead for the purpose of coining the copper now remaining in this mint into pice.

The warehousekeeper was ordered to comply with the request.

On the 9th June 1818[709] the Surat shroffs sent a petition to Bombay asking for more copper coins to be produced. Bombay reluctantly agreed to Surat producing more copper pice, but believed that copper coins were being hoarded by the shroffs, and that, after a small number of new pice had been produced, the shroffs would release their coins onto the market[710]. However, this coinage appears to have gone ahead without the adverse consequences that the Bombay Government predicted.

The Surat mint had been closed for gold and silver coinage in 1815 but obviously the capability to produce copper coins continued. Whether this activity was undertaken in a mint directly supervised by a British official, or was farmed out to local native manufacturers, is not clear. The latter seems most likely.

In 1824, when Surat found, again, that there was a shortage of pice locally, some of the excess pice produced in the Southern Concan were shipped to Surat to meet this need[711]. However, the local inhabitants did not like the coins and in 1826 asked for permission to strike pice locally as they had in 1818[712]. This petition was rejected and more pice were shipped from the Southern Concan[713]. However, in 1828 another request to produce the coins locally was accepted because there were no further pice available from the Southern Concan[714]. In 1831 a further offer to produce a copper coinage was made by Vrizbhookhundass Nagurdass[715], but by then the new Bombay mint was in operation and all future coins for Surat were supplied from there.

The type of copper coins issued from the Surat mint is not known. Copper coins issued before

---

[705] Bombay Consultations, IOR P/343/3. p. 155, 7th January 1803.

[706] Bombay Consultations, IOR P/408/16, p. 881, 23rd September 1812.

[707] Bombay Consultations, IOR P/408/17, p. 226, 24th March 1813.

[708] Bombay Mint Proceedings. IOR P/411/36. p. 60. Letter from the sub-Treasurer to Government, dated 16th January 1815.

[709] Bombay Consultations, IOR P/411/38, p. 135, 24th June 1818.

[710] Bombay Consultations, IOR P/411/38, p. 169, 22nd July 1818.

[711] See section on the Bankot mint. Also, Stevens P.J.E., ONS Newsletter 179.

[712] Bombay Consultations, IOR P/408/64, 15th March 1826.

[713] Bombay Consultations IOR P/408/65, 12th April 1826.

[714] Bombay Consultations, IOR p/409/5, 20th February 1828.

[715] Bombay Consultations, IOR P/411/50, 30th November 1831.

1800 (i.e. before the British took control) are known (specimen in the Ashmolean Museum, shown on p.316) and perhaps this was the style adopted by the British as they had adopted the earlier style of gold and silver coins.

Appendix to Chapter 9

Coins in circulation in the Bombay Presidency in 1820[716].

Assay Report shewing the mint standards of Bombay, Calcutta, Madras and England, and the weight, purity and intrinsic value, by assay, of all the coins, either current in the Hon'ble Company's territories under the Presidency of Bombay, or imported as bullion.

Gold Coins

Type	Weight grains, decimal	Touch % decimal	Pure Metal grains, decimal	Value of 100 in Bombay Rupees (Rupees, quarters, reas)	Comments	
Bombay Mohur	179	92	164.68	1500	In the coins of these mints, 1 part of gold represents 15 of silver	
Calcutta Mohur	204.71	91.66	187.65	1709.2233		
Madras Mohur	180	91.66	165	1502.914		
English Guinea	129.5	91.66	118.70	1081.187	1 part of gold represents 14.281 of silver	
Venetian or sequin	53	99.25	52.60	479.011	Full weight 54 grains	
Gubber or Dutch Ducat	53.25	98.25	52.31	476.500	Full weight 53¼ grains	Imported as bullion
Joaneese or PortuguesePortuguese Dollar	220.75	91.50	201.98	1839.805	Full weight 222½ grains	
Persian Toman	73.50	97.25	71.47	651.06		

Table continued on next page

---

[716] Bombay Consultations, IOR P/411/40 p. 32. Letter from the assay master to Government, dated 13th August 1821.

Gold Coins (cont)

Type	Weight grains, decimal	Touch % decimal	Pure Metal grains, decimal	Value of 100 in Bombay Rupees (Rupees, quarters, reas)	Comments
New Ekairee Pagoda	52.85	84	44.39	404.390	This coin was struck by Kishun Raj Wadder, Rajah of Mysore in the mint at Mysore. It is chiefly current in the Mysore and Southern districts of the Carnatic
Old Ekairee Pagoda	52.62	84.38	44.40	404.452	This coin was struck by Rajah Boodee Bussapa at Biddanoor
Bhol Ekairee Pagoda	52.69	84.50	44.52	405.50	Current in the Southern Mahratta country
Bhoolpuddee Pagoda	52.77	85	44.85	408.585	This coin denominated Bhoolpuddee or head of the idol is of the same coinage with the stamp a little different.
Bahandry Pagoda	52.72	84.50	44.54	405.768	This coin was struck by Hyder ally about 50 or 60 years ago at Seringapatam
Funokee Pagoda	52.80	84.63	44.68	407.037	This coin was struck by the Sultan about 30 years ago
The above six coins are usually received into the Poona treasury from the districts of Rannee Biddanoor, Koda Bunkapore, Savanoo Gudduck, Dummull Kanghulla, Andoor Kanigull & Nowlagund etc					
Guddapuddee Pagoda	50.97	76.38	38.93	354.625	These coins were struck by Esajee Ram, Mumleeder of the Paishwa, about 60 years ago at Darivar and Nargoond, but the coinage has been discontinued for at least 25 years.
Fudduck Pagoda	50.77	76.38	38.77	353.234	
Kudvanajee Pagoda	50.75	76.38	38.76	353.095	
Hallee Sicca Pagoda	50.90	76.38	38.87	354.139	
Modapuddee Pagoda	50.55	75.25	38.038	346.500	
Rajaram Ekaire Pagoda	52.80	84.13	44.42	404.632	These coins have little or no currency in this province, but as they are circulated in the camp bazaar to a small extent, they are inserted in the list
Bhatoree Pagoda	50.50	75	37.87	345.003	
Tomancien ½ Pagoda	26.12	84.63	22.105	201.359	

Table continued on next page

Gold Coins (cont)

Type	Weight (grains, decimal)	Touch (% decimal)	Pure Metal (grains, decimal)	Value of 100 in Bombay Rupees (Rupees, quarters, reas)	Comments
Bangalore pagoda	52.82	84.25	44.50	405.363	This coin was struck during the government of Hyder, in the mint at Bangalore. It has no very general circulation, but is occasionally received from individuals in payment of revenue.
Mahomed Shaie Pagoda	51.50	78.75	40.55	369.431	These coins have little currency in these provinces. Their exchange has now been fixed with reference to the rates of the Ballaree treasury and to their estimated value by the shroffs
Ventrataputkee Pagoda	51.50	76.38	39.33	358.313	
Herponbillee Pagoda	50.75	77.50	39.33	358.272	
Pavan Tharokee Pagoda	52.89	84.38	44.62	406.496	
Nagar Tharokee Pagoda	52.90	85.13	45.03	410.186	Received for assay from the Collector in the Doab. Current in the Southern Mahratta country
Gharava Tharokee Pagoda	53.85	85.25	45.18	411.543	
Bhut Padee Pagoda	52.90	84.75	44.83	408.355	
Baha Tapee Pagoda	54	84.75	45.76	416.853	
Joona Elaye Pagoda	52.50	84.38	44.29	403.500	
Navee Ekee pagoda	53	84.50	44.78	407.92	
Centeroy Fanams	5.82	59	3.43	31.278	
Sultana Fanams	5.87	58	3.40	31.012	

Silver Coins

Type	Weight grains, decimal	Touch % decimal	Pure Metal grains, decimal	Value of 100 in Bombay Rupees (Rupees, quarters, reas)	Comments
Bombay Rupee	179	92	164.68	100	
Calcutta Rupee	191.916	91.66	175.923	106.827	
Madras Rupee	180	91.66	165	100.194	
English Crown	436.36	92.5	403.63	245.101	
Spanish Dollar	415.02	89.38	370.95	225.25	Full weight 416 grains
German Crown	430.25	83.38	358.74	217.84	Full weight 433 grains
Ankoos or Chinsoree Rupee	172.50	91.75	158.26	96.105	Standard coin at Poona. Current throughout the Deccan & the Northern and Southern Concan.
Chandore rupee	172.25	91.50	157.608	95.705	Coined at Chandore, and is the standard coin of Candeish; passes equivalent with the Ankoosee Rs. Current also in the Northern Concan.
Thoora rupee	170	91.50	155.55	94.425	Current at Candeish
Jeereeputka Rupee	171.6	91.25	156.58	95.083	Coined at Nassuck; bears a discount of 8 & 12 annas per cent; current in the Northern Concan and Candeish
Belapooree rupee	171.82	85	146.04	88.685	Coined at Bellapore; current at Poona, Ahmadnuggur, the Concan etc.
Batoree Rupee	171.3	87	149.03	90.495	Coined at Bhatoor near Ahmednuggur; current in the Deccan; is inferior to the Ankoosee one per cent.
Shree Sicca Rupee	172	91.50	157.38	95.567	Coined formerly at Poona, and is esteemed better then the Ankoosee rupees by one per cent
Hallee Sicca Rupee	174.75	96.25	168.19	102.128	Coined at Poona for mercantile purposes
Waubgaum Rupee	172.55	91.50	157.88	95.872	Coined at Waubgaum, bears a discount with the Ankoosee of 8 annas per cent
Purkee Rupee	178.88	94.25	168.59	102.376	Current at Candeish. Coined by Scindia and is perhaps the same coin as assayed under the name of Berhanpoor sicca

Table continued on next page

Silver Coins (cont)

Type	Weight grains, decimal	Touch % decimal	Pure Metal grains, decimal	Value of 100 in Bombay Rupees (Rupees, quarters, reas)	Comments
Chambagoondee Rupee	171	84.75	144.92	88	Coined at Chambagoondee and bears a discount with the established Ankoosee of two per cent
Mullarshie or Bagulcota rupee	172.3	89	153.34	93.118	Coined at Bagulcota; current in the Doab, Malwan etc
Shapooree rupee	174	87	151.38	91.924	Coined at Shapoor and produces 102 Ankoosee per cent at Poona
Kittoor Shapooree rupee	174	86.25	150.07	91.013	This coin was struck originally at Kittoor; this mint has continued the coinage during the last 25 years; it is current in the district of Bettikerra, Belgaum and Padshapoor
Ongien Rupee	173	90.25	156.13	94	Coined at Ongein and Chullemaishwar. Passes in Poona at a premium of two per cent for Ankoosee rupees. Current throughout Malwa
Indore Rupee	174.50	92.50	161.41	98	Coined at Indore; current throughout Malwa
Govind Buksh Rupee	171.16	78	133.50	81.066	Coined at Aurangabad; is issued in payment to the troops at 120 for 100 Company's rupees
Nagpore Rupee	166.73	86.5	144.22	87.575	Coined at Nagpore, and is inferior at Poona to the Ankoosee rupee by four per cent
Broach rupee	177.5	87.62	155.52	94.440	The only currency at Broach. Current also at Kaira, Surat etc.
Old Broach Rupee	177.06	94.25	166.88	101.335	Coined formerly at Broach. Now disappearing
Cambay rupee	179.50	81.88	146.97	89.247	Current in the Nabob's districts, Kaira etc.
Babasye Rupee	177	84.88	150.75	91.540	Coined at Baroda, also current at Kaira etc
Walkersye Rupee	177.39	87.75	155.65	94.532	
Ashasye Rupee	176.50	86.5	152.68	92.705	

Table continued on next page

Silver Coins (cont)

Type	Weight grains, decimal	Touch % decimal	Pure Metal grains, decimal	Value of 100 in Bombay Rupees (Rupees, quarters, reas)	Comments
Mukunsye Rupee	176.62	87.5	154.54	93.842	
Wullubsye Rupee	175.56	85	150.07	91.217	
Ahmadabad sicca rupee	179.92	84	151.13	91.772	Coined formerly at Ahmadabad
New Ahmadabad Sicca Rupee	180.75	85	153.63	93.292	Present currency there, current also at Anjar and throughout Cutch
Hallee Ahmadabad Sicca Rupee	174.77	96.25	168.21	102.147	Coined at Ahmadabad, current within the walls of the city
Cutch Kowrie rupee	72.15	60.75	43.83	26.615	Coined at Anjar, current throughout Cutch
Porebunder Kowrie Rupee	74.50	69.75	51.96	31.553	Coined at Porebunder
Persian Rupee	159.12	94.50	150.36	91.309	Imported as bullion; current in the Persian Gulf
New Persian Rupee	141.3	94.50	133.52	81.083	*ditto*
Goa Rupee	168.50	86	144.91	87.995	Imported as bullion
Mysore or New Holker Rupee	173.56	94.25	163.58	99.390	Coined formerly at Mysore, now disappearing
Mulkapore rupee	173.2	71.75	124.27	75.461	Coined at Mulkapore and bears a discount of 12 per cent with the Ankusi
Meritch Hookaree Rupee	172.6	84	144.98	88.039	Coined at Meritch, bears a discount at Poona of 5 per cent
Narrainpet Rupee	172.5	80.50	138.86	84.321	A species of Hyderabad rupee coined at Narrainpet, but little known at Poona. Rate uncertain, from 9 to 12 per cent discount
Timbourne Rupee	171.3	85.50	146.46	88.936	*ditto*, coined at Timbourne by the late Sadaser Monkaiser. Is inferior to the proper Ankoosee rupee
Waye Sicca Rupee	171.8	89.50	153.76	92.760	*ditto*. Coined at Waye, & bears a discount in Poona of 1 per cent

Table continued on next page

Silver Coins (cont)

Type	Weight grains, decimal	Touch % decimal	Pure Metal grains, decimal	Value of 100 in Bombay Rupees (Rupees, quarters, reas)	Comments
Jumkundee Rupee	175	92	161	97.765	Coined at Jumkundee and passes at a discount of 2 per cent
Berhanpoore Rupee	178.8	94.75	169.41	102.87	Coined by Scindeah in Candeish
Phoolsheree Rupee	171.7	91.50	157.10	95.397	A species of Ankoosee rupee, coined at Phoolsherh, but inferior to the regular Ankoosee by 8 annas per cent
Pertabghur Rupee	170.40	87.25	148.67	90.278	Coined at Pertabghur, a species of Ankoosee rupee but 19 per cent inferior to it
Emaumee Rupee	175	95.50	167.12	101.484	The Emaumee coin was struck by the Sultan, but is not current in this province, and is seldom received by the shroffs or sabookars
Rajah Pondicherry Rupee	176.16	94.75	166.91	101.354	This coin was struck at Mysore during Poornya's administration. It is current, but not generally, in the Ranee Biddanoor district
Punlee Old Rupee	170.60	63	107.47	65.264	This coin was struck by Karweekur Maharaj at Panallee about 50 or 60 years ago. The mint still continues. The coin has very little currency in these districts.
Nepanee Perkanee Rupee	173	75.75	131	79.548	This coin was by Sidowjee Row Naik Nembalkur at Nepanee about 15 years ago. It is current in the districts of Padshapoor and that vicinity
Semboo Perkanee Rupee	172.75	79.75	137.76	83.658	Current in the Southern Mahratta Country
Moodholee Perkanee Rupee	173	57.50	99.47	60.405	This coin was struck by Malajee Row Modholkur about 30 years ago. It has very limited circulation.

Table continued on next page

Silver Coins (cont)

Type	Weight grains, decimal	Touch % decimal	Pure Metal grains, decimal	Value of 100 in Bombay Rupees (Rupees, quarters, reas)	Comments
Old Semboo Perkanee Rupee	174	89.75	156.16	94.829	This coin was struck by the Bhosla family of Sawartawdt about 200 years ago. It is but little current
Toragull Nelkantee Rupee	170	62	105.4	64	This coin was struck by Bhalasaheb of Toregull Synakhurga (about 50 years ago). It is but little current, not very generally.
Tokoshaie Rupee	173.16	94	162.77	98.84	Current in Ahmednuggur districts
Jyenuggree Rupee	172.68	90	155.41	94.37	
Mannashie Rupee	169.50	90	152.55	92.634	
Delhi Rupee	174.50	97.65	170.57	103.578	
1820 Perkanee Newest Rupee	177.9	88.75	157.88	95.875	Coined in Sawant state; received for assay from the political agent there
Spanish Independent Dollars	420.5	89.50	376.34	228.532	Coined at Chili in 1817, by the Independents

Chapter 10 – Malabar Coast[717]

As the trading horizons of the East India Company were broadened, factories were opened at other places in India and some of these were located on the Western coast. The traditional spice producing area of Kerala was one such target market for the Company's trading activities. To the British tradesmen the term 'Malabar' meant the entire coast of Kerala - from Mount Dilla (South of Mangalore) to Cape Comorin (Kanniyakumari). Traditionally, however only the northern part of the Keralan coast bears the geopolitical designation 'Malabar'. The history of the region centres on the coastal towns of Tellicherry, Mahé, Calicut and Cannanore. The former two lay very close to each other midway between the latter two, which are located to the south and north, respectively.

The British established a factory at Tellicherry (now called Thalasserry) in 1683. The grant for establishing this trading outpost was obtained from the local ruling family, the Kurungot Nairs, who held the area from their overlords, the Kolathiri Rajahs of

---

[717] This introduction is a revised version of a paper originally published by Bhandare and Stevens as a supplement to the ONSNL, 2003, No. 273.

Chirakkal. The company intended to trade in cardamom and pepper, both of which were local produce. In 1708, a fort was built at Tellicherry. Relations between the British and the local rulers were very cordial, and indeed none other than a prince of the Kolathiri household laid the corner stone of the fort. Between 1708 and 1761, the Company actively pursued its interests in the region and gradually increased its sway to adjoining areas with more privileges such as civil and judicial indemnities and the right to collect custom duties.

Meanwhile, the trading ambitions of the French East India Company were not far behind in seeking benefits from the spice trade. They sent a representative named Mollandin to another local family, the Vazhunnavars of Badagara, and established their trading enclave at Mayyazhi, about 5 miles to the North of Tellicherry. Contrary to the English, relations between the local rulers and the French were not cordial and soon a conflict broke out. The French, under a general named de Pallardin, were successful in wresting Mayyazhi from the local rulers. The victory, however, was attributed to the efforts of a French captain named Bertrand François Mahé de la Bourdonnais and in his honour the town was renamed Mahé, which is uncannily close in pronunciation, at least in part, to the original Mayyazhi. The French remained in possession of Mahé until 1954.

Calicut (now called Kozhikode) enjoys a pre-eminent position in the history of Malabar as compared to both Tellicherry and Mahé. It was here that Vasco da Gama landed in 1498 with an intention of *buscar Cristaos e Especeria* ("seeking Christians and Spices"). It had been a town of great commercial importance, frequently visited by the Arabs and the Chinese to trade in spices and 'Calico' cloth that derives its name from the town. A local dynasty ruled here, entitled 'Samuthiri' and known in European annals by the name 'Zamorin'. The PortuguesePortuguese, ever since the landing of da Gama, had tried to assert themselves politically and religiously in Malabar and that brought them into conflict with the Zamorins. This conflict lasted for several decades and resulted in the Zamorin seeking alliances with other European powers like the British and the Dutch. Although the influence of the Portuguese waned during the course of the 16th century, that of the other powers grew steadily – the British first visited Calicut in 1615 and a factory was set up in 1664. However, unlike the Portuguese, their involvement was confined to trade only. Dutch presence in Calicut lasted until 1721, when they withdrew from Malabar completely following a treaty signed between them and the British.

A Muslim family known as the 'Ali Rajahs' ruled Cannanore (now called Kannur), located north of Calicut, Tellicherry and Mahé. Originally belonging to Kolathiri stock, they were converted to Islam sometime in the 12-13th centuries. Their capital seat was the town of Arakkal. A unique feature of the household's dynastic practice was a general agreement on female primogeniture and so we see many Queens ruling Cannanore under the title of 'Beebi'. Although the words 'Ali Rajah' were commonly used to address the household, their title accommodates a more sanskritised 'Aadi Raja', literally meaning 'First King' and it was carried irrespective of the gender of the ruler. The 'Ali Rajahs carried out a spice trade of their own through ports such as Dharmapattanam that belonged to them and, as such, were viewed as competitors by the advancing European mercantile companies. In 1664, the Dutch attacked and defeated the ruler of Arakkal and imposed trading restrictions on him. The animosity between the European companies meant that the 'Ali Rajahs were friendly towards the British during the early years of British presence in Malabar. Indeed, during an internal strife with the Kolathiri family in 1720-22, the ruling 'Ali Rajah, Muhammad 'Ali, sought the help of Robert Adams, the chief of the Tellicherry factory, as a mediator. As the political equations changed in the region, however, the 'Ali Rajahs became gradually hostile to the British. The ascendancy of Hyder Ali in Mysore gave pre-eminence to the religious connections between the Mysore and Cannanore families, which were strengthened by matrimonial ties. When Hyder and later his son, Tipu, chose to subdue Malabar's local Hindu ruling families, the Cannanore family under the Beebi Junnammabi sympathised with Mysore.

In 1778, Tipu conquered the areas of Calicut and Cannanore. His intentions of waging war against the Travancore Kingdom further south brought him into direct conflict with the British, who had granted security to the ruler of Travancore under the terms of a subsidiary alliance. Mysore domination lasted sporadically in the north of the region (Cannanore) and almost continually in the south of the region. Tipu was hostile to the Zamorins of Calicut but amicably disposed towards the 'Ali Rajah family of Cannanore, presumably because of his religious affinities. As a consequence, Cannanore witnessed British depredations during the long Anglo-Mysore struggle and finally the British occupied the town in 1790. The 'Ali Raja family was nominally re-instated but actual political control remained in British hands ever after. In 1792, a treaty imposed on Tipu by the British, as a result of their success in the Anglo-Mysore war, forced him to relinquish the territory permanently.

Coinage in 18th and 19th century Malabar – a circulatory context

Indigenous coinage in Kerala may be termed sparse in a general historical sense. During the 14th-17th centuries, the chief currency of the region seems to have been gold fanams, commonly called 'Viraraya' Fanams. These were struck initially by the Hoysalas and subsequently copied by the rulers of Coorg (Kodagu). They seem to have reached the coastal region of Malabar from upland Coorg through the trade across the southernmost part of the mountain chain, the Western Ghats. The abundant variation in their design and precious metal content indicate that a few varieties may also have been struck locally. The Venad kingdom located to the south of Malabar produced a profuse copper coinage during these years and, in all probability, this was the lower metal equivalent of the gold coins, namely the fanams.

These local coinages may seem inadequate given the large volume of trade in spices that was being conducted in the region – but, in fact, this trade brought in foreign coins in quantities sufficient to satiate any exigent currency demands. The most popular of these coins was the Venetian gold sequin.

At the beginning of the 18th century, silver made its appearance in the currency regime of Malabar. Although it is widely believed that the Venad kingdom (Travancore of a later period) struck silver chukrams as early as the 1600's, Beena Sarasan has shown recently that the issue of silver chukrams was not facilitated until c.1750[718]. The earliest silver coins struck indigenously in Malabar during this period are called 'Velli Fanams'. The metallic term 'Velli', meaning silver, must have been included in the nomenclature to distinguish them from the gold fanams. The first coins of this kind seem to have been struck by the 'Ali Rajahs of Cannanore. They are mintless, bear on the obverse the inscription *al-malik al-wali 'ali raja* and on the reverse *b'al-hijarat sanah* followed by the date. They weigh around 2g and the earliest date seen on them is AH 1122 (= AD 1710). In view of the other recorded dates it is just possible that this date is a misengraving for AH 1132, and that would put the earliest date of issue c. 1720. Alexander Hamilton, who visited Cannanore in 1703, makes no mention of a silver currency. He mentions "all coins circulating being of gold" and remarks on their small size, thereby indicating a preponderance of the gold fanams[719]. On the other hand, the British are known to have collected and dispatched a sample of silver fanams of Cannanore from Tellicherry to Bombay to get them assayed, *vide* a letter dated 26th November 1729[720]. It is, therefore, evident that the issue of silver fanams at Cannanore must have begun sometime between 1703 and 1729. The probability of the date being 1720 is more likely because that was the year of accession of the 'Ali Rajah named Muhammad 'Ali. From the chronological details on these coins, they seem to have had a sporadic, yet long-lasting issue.

The reason for introducing a silver denomination weighing two grams is not known, particularly when nothing of that kind had been in circulation before. Pridmore, while discussing the British issues for Malabar, comments that the East India Company introduced their silver fanams to replace gold fanams circulating in the region because they were "tiny debased pieces subject to fluctuation and easily lost". However, to be equivalent in terms of metallic content given the contemporary rate of exchange between gold and silver, a gold fanam weighing 0.35g would have had to correspond to 4g in silver, rather than the 2g actually found. The observed specimens of 'Vira raya' Fanams do not appear debased to that extent. So reasons for the introduction of the 2g denomination still remain to be determined.

Once the denomination was introduced by the 'Ali Rajahs, it gained wide acceptance in trade. This is ostensibly because, being of silver, it was directly convertible into the predominant rupee system of currency – it was equivalent in

---

[718] Coins of the Venad Cheras', Calicut, 2000, p. 85

[719] Krump K.K.N., The Ali Rajas of Cannanore, Trivandrum, 1975, p. 12

[720] Letters from Tellicherry, vols. 1-4, 1729-1736, printed by the Superintendent, Government Press, Madras, 1934. This letter is reproduced in vol. 1 1729-31, p.17

weight to one fifth of a rupee. Perhaps this was one of the reasons that silver was chosen as a principal metal of circulation. The British followed suit and introduced their 'Velli Fanams' sometime after 1719-20, and these are the chief subject of discussion of this chapter. In British correspondence the coins are referred to by the sobriquet 'Billy' fanams, which is ostensibly an anglicised form of 'Velli'.

The French, too, struck coins of the same denomination at their factory at Mahé. It is also reported that, alongside the silver fanams, coins in the 'rupee' system were also struck there but none have survived. The French struck silver coins named 'Royalins' or 'Fanons' at their chief outpost Pondicherry, situated on the Eastern coast, and it is possible that the same name was given to the silver coins issued from Mahé. Whilst a good deal of information is available regarding the operation of the mint at Pondicherry, that for the Mahé mint is scanty. One point to note, however, is that coins with a Persian inscription seem to have been struck at Mahé at least a few years before they were at Pondicherry. This is interesting as far as adopting a native-style coinage was concerned. Although the issues struck at Mahé do not refer to a Mughal ruler, they have legends in native script mentioning a pseudo-mintname 'Puducheri' (or Purchery or Pourchréy[721]), the native name for Pondicherry. The earliest date these coins are known to bear is 1731. In c. 1738, the French silver issues of Mahé are seen to have undergone a radical change in their design. Along with a distinctly superior calligraphy, the coins now bear the letter 'P' prominently on their reverse, in all probability standing for 'Pondicherry'. The mintname on coins in this second series appears as a more Persianised 'Phulcheri' than the previous 'Puducheri'. It is believed that the coins were struck until the 1820's.

French fanam, 1750

As regards the coins of metals other than silver, both the British and the French struck copper coins. Not much research has been done about them – Pridmore refers to the British issues as 'Paisas' while the French issues are called 'Biche', presumably a corruption of 'Paisa'. When the weights of both these series of copper coins are compared, it becomes apparent that they actually complement each other and their denominational structure corresponds to the local 'Cash' system (see further under

---

[721] See Herrli H. (2003), ONSNL 177 p. 3

appropriate section p. 351). As for gold, no issue is known for the French mint at Mahé. The British are not known to have struck any gold in Malabar, apart from a pagoda issued in 1809 that Pridmore identifies as the 'Nishini' or 'Revenue' Pagoda (Hoan). However, this view has been challenged (see paper by Bhandare & Stevens[722]). That paper also discusses a gold pagoda struck by the 'Ali Rajahs of Cannanore.

During the Mysore occupation, currency in Calicut is seen to have undergone a drastic change. Initially, Tipu ordered a variant of the gold 'Vira Raya' fanams to be struck there. This variety is inscribed with a Persian letter *he* and called the 'Bahaduri Vira Raya' fanam. In tune with Tipu's currency reforms after he ascended the Mysore throne in 1782, he introduced a Paisa-Rupee-Pagoda system in Calicut. He also opened a new mint in the region at Feroke (Farrukhi), located near Calicut, which, during the later part of his reign, became the principal mint for copper and gold. While gold and copper issues of both Calicut and Feroke under Tipu (namely fanams and paisas) are fairly numerous, silver is exceedingly rare for these mints. This phenomenon was probably an outcome of the large issue of French and British silver fanams in the preceding years.

The brief description presented about the circulatory context of British coinage in Malabar enables it to be put into a wider perspective, as part of a flourishing and localised monetary economy. Pridmore failed to take this context into account while presenting his analysis of the Malabar coinage and this led him to some possibly erroneous conclusions.

The Coinage – Fifth Rupees (Fanams) – c1792 to c1798

Pridmore's assessment of the coinage of Malabar has been critically examined before[723] and that critique will not be repeated here.

In summary, the earliest of issue of the fith rupees bears a peculiar inscription on the obverse, which is derived from a Mughal legend but which incorporates the English numeral '5' in a conspicuous position. These coins have a fine calligraphy, a Hijri date of 1131, a regnal year *Ahd* (= first) and the mint name of 'Munbai'. The prototype for the design of these issues is a rupee of Shah Jahan II (see p. 337 for photo of fifth rupee, labelled 'type 1'), struck at Bombay and the coins continued in a similar style, with some changes, , throughout most of the eighteenth century and will be discussed later. In the aftermath of the 1792 treaty with Mysore that gave the Company complete control of the regions of Calicut and Cannanore, The British chose to re-instate the respective ruling families, namely the Zamorins and the 'Ali Rajahs, at both these places but only in a nominal manner. The most important implication of the Company assuming control of coinage was that it tried consciously to substitute the gold fanams with silver coins – this was in accordance with the company's efforts to drive the gold fanams out of circulation because of the economic

---

[722] Bhandare and Stevens as a supplement to the ONSNL, 2003, No. 273.
[723] Bhandare and Stevens as a supplement to the ONSNL, 2003, No. 273.

impracticality that was involved in their use following a change in the gold-silver price ratio. Although initially the Malabar Commission rejected the proposal when it was referred to it, it was decided in 1799 to strike the silver Billys. A mint was set up in Calicut and a completely new design was adopted for the Billys.

In May 1800, the Malabar province was transferred to the Government of the Madras Presidency. The issue of Billys under the Madras government, dated 1805, had a different design. These coins had the name of the Mughal Emperor, Shah Alam II, and the mint name 'Mumbai' on the reverse, while the obverse depicted a pair of scales, the letter 'T' and the AD date. The 'T99' and 'T1805' are the last issues of Billys – ostensibly struck in Malabar and they are datable due to the obvious chronological details they bear.

Reassessing the Malabar Coinage

In re-examining the coinage of Malabar, nearly 300 Billys were examined and gaps in Pridmore's classification became evident. Firstly, contrary to Pridmore's contention, many of these coins showed discernible chronological details. Many coins showed regnal years and the large number gave an opportunity for them to be studied in such detail as would be useful to arrive at a much finer classification than that attempted by Pridmore. The basis of Pridmore's grouping had to be discarded, because what he identified as a 'Malayalim' numeral 5 was in fact the English numeral turned upside down. A set of 'full die depictions' was made of each obverse and reverse, and a mix-and-match exercise was carried out to yield the most comprehensive picture of the known varieties of Billys. The task of classifying the Billys was limited to all those issues that predate the last two – the 'T99' and 'T1805' issues.

Type	Obverse	Reverse	RY
1	A	1	1
1a	A1	2.1	1, 22
1b	A1	2.2	12?, 25, 30?
2	B (B1, B2, B3)	2	2, 3, 5, 6?, 9
3	C	3	9
4	D1	2	9
5	D1	4	9
6	D2	4	9
7	D3	4A	9
8	E	5	9
9	F	6	9

Table 1. Obverse and Reverse Combinations

As Pridmore correctly noted, the Billys have 'distinct styles of execution'. This feature has been used extensively in the classification and this, combined with the regnal year details within each group served as a basis for arriving at a chronological sequence for the coins.

It was noticed that there exist nine varieties of obverses and several more varieties of reverse dies for Billys that predate the 'T99' issue. Each of them has distinct features. Some overlap occurs between these obverses and reverses and this helps to determine the chronology. For instance, reverse 2 occurs with both obverse B and D1. This overlap is shown in table 1 above.

Before proceeding to the arguments supporting the proposed chronological sequence, it is necessary to describe the different attributes of the various obverse and reverse varieties.

Matching these obverse and reverse designs with the actual specimens available, both from reported sources and the large group of 300 examined, the combinations shown in table 1 can be worked out to delineate the varieties of Billys. The observations can be tabulated with reference to some of the obverse and reverse characteristics as shown in table 2 below:

	Obverse					
Reverse	Normal '5'	Inverted '5'	Top word 'Ghazi'	Top word 'Alamgir'	Top word 'Manoos'	Top word 'Shah Alam'
RY 1	Type 1	-	Type 1	-	-	-
RYs 2,3,5 & 9	Type 2	-	Type 2	Type 3	Type 4	-
RY9 (Frozen)	Type 3	Type 8, 9	-	Type 3?	Type 5,6,7,8	Type 9
Cluster of dots, or 'flower'	Type 2, 3	Type 8, 9	Type 2	—	Type 4	Type 9
Flower with stalk	Type 1	Type 7	-	Type 3	Type 7	-
Flower with stalks and curves	Type 5	Type 6	-	-	Type 5, 6	-

Table 2. Relationship of Obverse and Reverse Varieties

Interpreting the observations: a dating sequence for the Billys

Having described the different obverse and reverse types, we will now turn to the chronological sequence in which they were issued.

The form and execution of *julūs* on reverse 6 is worth noting because it provides a direct link with the same characters on the reverse of the 'T99' issue – which has a fixed chronological placement due to the date it bears. This shows that coins of Type 9 (obverse F and reverse 6 combination) cannot be far removed from the 'T99' issues.

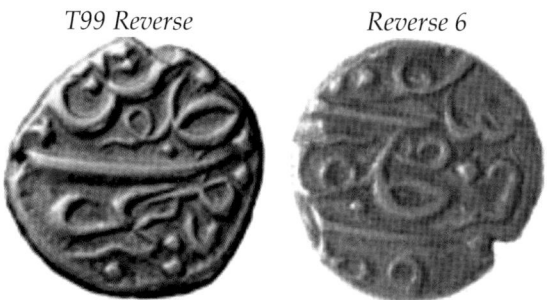

T99 Reverse   *Reverse 6*

Comparison of Reverses of T99 and Reverse 6

The differences that they show in execution from all other Billys would suggest their chronological distance from the rest of the group. Both these inferences (i.e. Type 9 is close to T99 and far from the other Billys) go well with the historical facts known about the region. We have seen that the region came under British control after 1792 and that an agreement was effected between the British and the Zamorin of Calicut, whom the British had restored to nominal power and allowed to 'continue coinage'. We have no clue what coinage was 'continued', but Pridmore mentioned the name of the mint master who was in charge of the Calicut mint in 1795 (Mr. Rickards) and assumed it was the gold fanams that were struck and gradually replaced by the 'T99' issues about seven years later. However, going by the important link in type characteristics that we have just described, it is reasonable to ascribe the Billys of Type 9 to this period. The 'continuation' of coinage mentioned in the documentary sources more likely refers to continuing striking the Billys, as they must have been struck by the British in the region before the Mysore conquest.

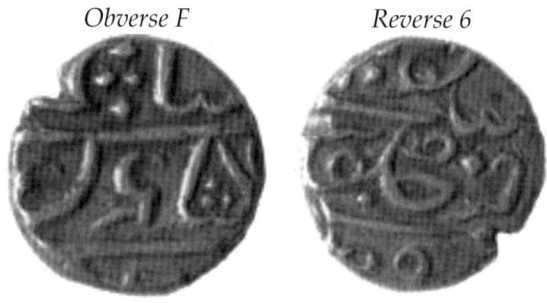

Obverse F   *Reverse 6*

Type 9

One would assume that coinage of Billys, and indeed other coinage like that of copper, must have stopped during the period of Mysore domination of Malabar. There is no historical account of how exactly the establishment of Mysore rule at Calicut and the cordial relationship that Tipu shared with the Ali Rajah family of Cannanore, affected the British at Tellicherry. But, given the extremely hostile attitude of Tipu towards the British, it is conceivable that the situation at Tellicherry would have been anything but conducive to trade, since the establishment was virtually surrounded by Tipu's forces. As a result of the treaty of Mangalore, signed in 1784 between Tipu and the British and often regarded as a document of Tipu's political virtuosity, he allowed the British to 're-establish their factory at Calicut'. It is interesting to note that the issue of French fanons in Mahé also virtually ceased during this period, and the only dates known for French copper issues are 1787 and 1790. Given the friendship between the French and Tipu the striking of a minor coinage could well have been ignored by him. However, a British coinage at Calicut during this period should be regarded an unlikely occurrence given the important theocratic implications coinage would have had in the Islamic state that was established under Tipu. That there was no British coinage during the years of Mysore domination is well reflected in the design of the Billys, which show a remarkable shift in type characteristics between issues of Type 9 and the rest of the group.

So, what about coins issued immediately before the Mysore occupation? An obvious break in the series occurs with the figure 5 being rotated from its normal position through 180°. There are three obverse designs where this is seen to have occurred – obverse D2, D3 and E. The relative chronological placement of these three designs can be judged from the fact that obverse E couples with reverse 5 on coins (Type 8), where the chronological detail seen is RY 9. It has a markedly superior degree of execution in its details over obverse D2. Obverse D3 may be placed between obverse D2 and obverse E because, although it has a degree of refinement in execution, it is not as fine as that seen in obverse E. Thus Obverse D2 links up with obverse D1 in terms of the style of execution whereas obverse D3 does so with obverse E. Both obverse D2 and D1 share a common reverse - reverse 4 – to yield types 6 and 5, respectively. Obverse D3 however shares its reverse with reverse 4a (to yield type 7), which is the same as reverse 4 but differs only in the execution of the flower motif. All these types have the chronological detail as RY 9. Stylistic comparison would suggest that this detail has been derived from the series of coins immediately preceding those with reverse 4, namely that with reverse 2 – where the RY occurs in stages as 2, 3, 5 and 9 before it is frozen on the last. It is therefore clear that coins of Type 8 (obverse E and reverse 5 combination) come last in the sequence. They are preceded by coins of Types 5, 6 and 7 (obverse D1- reverse 4, obverse D2- reverse 4 and obverse D3- reverse 4a combinations), which in turn are preceded by those of Type 4 (obverse D1 and reverse 2 combination).

Obverse E   *Reverse 5*

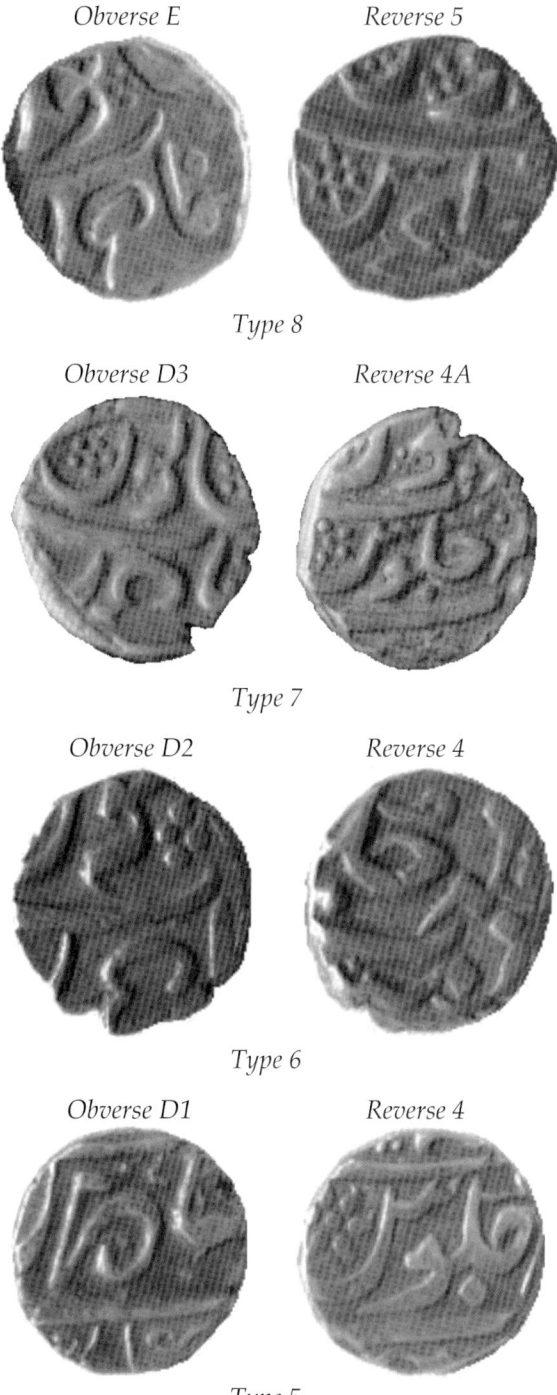

Type 8

Obverse D3   *Reverse 4A*

Type 7

Obverse D2   *Reverse 4*

Type 6

Obverse D1   *Reverse 4*

Type 5

Obverse D1   *Reverse 2*

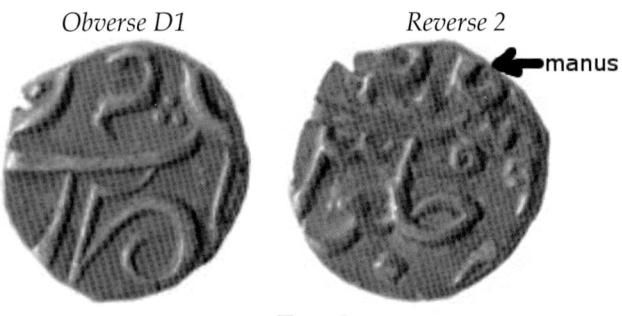

←manus

Type 4

It is also worth noting at this juncture that all coins with the said obverse and reverse types also have one common link, which also indicates their chronological proximity – they all have the word 'Manoos' in the top line on the obverse. Thus a series can be worked out depending on stylistic similarities and the occurrence of the chronological detail. If we assume that the series with regnal year 9 was indeed issued for the first time in that year, even though it is a posthumous regnal year, we see that none of the coins with that detail could have been struck prior to 1762-63. This date and a year in the early 1780's - when British coinage in Malabar must have temporarily ceased in the aftermath of the establishment of Mysore supremacy in the region after c.1780 - offers us a time bracket to accommodate the Billys with an inverted '5' (of which the first appears very rare) and some of those types that bear the frozen regnal year 9, but have the normal '5'. Judging by the preponderance of the issues of types 7 and 8 with inverted '5', it seems likely that they must have dominated in circulation for most of this time bracket. Billys with the normal '5' and having the regnal year detail frozen at 9 (namely those of Types 4 and 5, comprising combinations of obverse D1 with reverse 2 & 4) may be placed earlier than those with an inverted '5' and having the same regnal year detail. Therefore it may be concluded that coins of Types 4, 5 and 6 should be placed at this crucial juncture in working out a sequence for the Billys, their evolution and placement denoted by the numerical order.

This leaves the Billys of Type 2 (obverse B and reverse 2 combination) - those that have the word *ghazi* in the top line of the obverse inscription and also a normal form of 5. Here the sequencing becomes somewhat complicated because, although these issues bear RYs 2, 3, 5 and 9, the name of the king whose reign corresponds to them is not visible on the coins. Moreover, three distinct varieties in execution of the figure '5' are noticed. To arrange these coins in a sequence, some external help needs to be sought. This comes again from the standpoint of executional style, but in this case we have to concentrate on the reverse, rather than the obverse. If one compares the style of the engraving of legends on the reverse to the known rupees of Bombay that Pridmore lists, it becomes apparent that Billys of Type 2 match the reverse of those struck in the name of Alamgir II. The Billys and rupees with RYs 5 and 9 are remarkably similar in execution, while those with RYs 2 and 3 are similar, albeit not quite so close.

Rupee Ry 5   *Billy Ry 5*

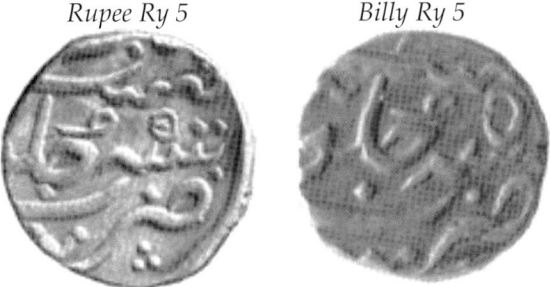

Comparison of Rupee and Billy of Alamgir RY 5

The obvious conclusion is that the RYs that these Billys bear represent the reign of Alamgir II and as such they can be placed in the period of his reign leading up to the fictitious RY 9, i.e. 1754 – 1763. Judging by the numbers, it is clear that the issue of Billys was quite profuse in this period.

Obverse B   *Reverse 2*

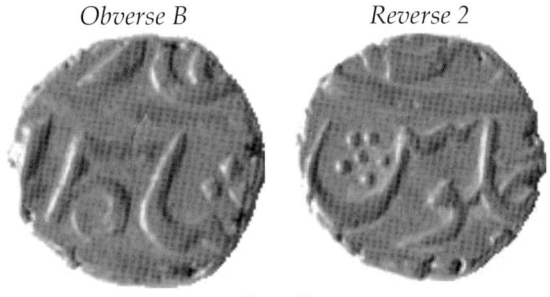

Type 2

Coins with reverse 2 designs link up with those having reverses 2.1 and 2.2, on the basis of a stylistic and executional similarity. Since coins with reverse 2.1 and 2.2 bear regnal years which are essentially from a different set (22, 25 and possibly 12 and 21, although the rendering of the last two figures is not entirely free from doubt), it would be logical to conclude that they precede those of type 2. The most likely contender to whom this set of RYs would belong is Muhammad Shah, although his name itself is not mentioned on coins, their obverses being derived from obverse A1, where the word in the top line is *ghazi*. These may be termed types 1a and 1b. Between these two, those with reverse 2.1 (type 1a) show a greater similarity to reverse 1 and therefore should precede those with reverse 2.2 (type 1b). RYs 22 and 25 of Muhammad Shah would indicate a date of issue of 1741-42 and 1744-45. Indeed, the solitary coin bearing the AH 1154 offers a concordance with the RY 22 seen on its reverse, and therefore serves as a conclusive chronological benchmark for Billys of these types. There are two entries in the records of coins being struck for Tellicherry at Bombay in 1741[724,725]:

…they request to be supplied with two lacks of rupees at the opening of the fair season, and the amount of two thousand rupees in copper pice, with the like sum in fanams…

The Gentlemen (of Tellicherry) desiring a supply of small change for the currency of the settlement, directed that the mint master prepared to the amount of two thousand rupees in fifths to be sent thither by the first good conveyance…

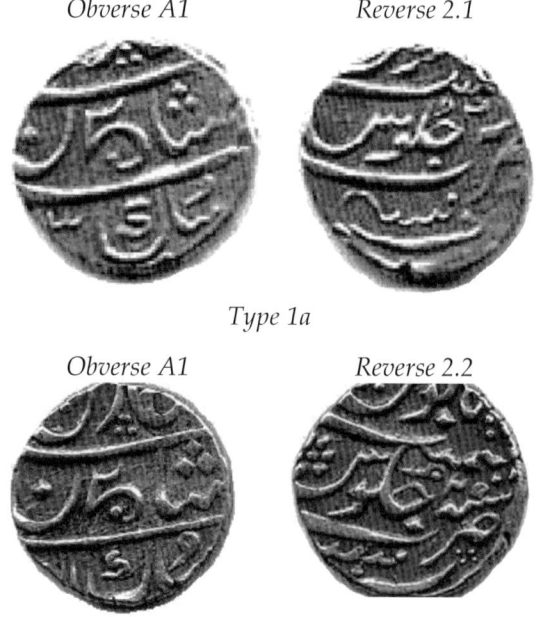

Obverse A1   *Reverse 2.1*

Type 1a

Obverse A1   *Reverse 2.2*

Type 1b

The issue of Billys began sometime between 1719 and 1727 with coins of Type 1 (obverse A and reverse 1 combination). An important archival source supports the fact that the issue of Billys was under way in December 1727 at the Bombay mint and that it was specifically being carried out for the Tellicherry factory[726].

'….and fifths of rupees now coining for Tellicherry three per cent worse …..'

All of them have the RY 1 and most have AH 1131. As such it can be inferred that their issue continued bearing these chronological details as a 'frozen' instance for some time. An archival reference in Letters from Tellicherry, mentions the coining of

---

[724] Bombay Public Consultations, 9th August 1741. India Office Collections P/341/12:

[725] Bombay Public Consultations, Friday 14th August 1741. India Office Collections P/341/12:

[726] Bombay Public Consultations, Friday 22nd December 1727. India Office Collections P/341/6:
  For rest of quote refer to Twelfth Rupees struck at Bombay for Anjengo.

Billys in Bombay to be transported to Tellicherry in 1730[727], 1733[728] and 1734[729]. One specimen in the BM collection actually bears the date AH 1143 (although the RY is still *Ahd*) quite clearly, thereby substantiating the archival reference that the issue continued at least until 1730-31.

Obverse A   *Reverse 1*

Type 1

This dating and sequential scheme leaves out the Billys in the name of 'Alamgir (Type 3 - combining obverse C and reverse 3).

Obverse C   *Reverse 3*

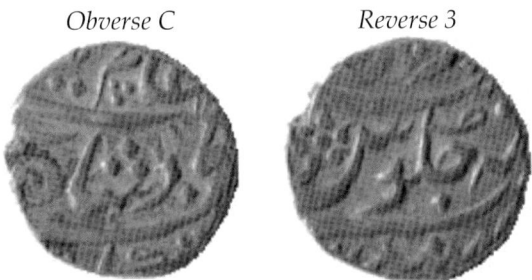

Type 3

This is quite a distinct issue judging by the fact that type characteristics such as the finesse in the execution of the legend and the differentiating mark on the reverse are different from any other designs we have discussed so far. Only one of these is known to show a chronological detail and that is RY 9, and for that we have no clue whether

---

[727] Letters from Tellicherry, vols. 1-4, 1729-1736" vol. 1, pp. 24, 29 (printed by the Superintendent, Government Press, Madras, 1934):

February 19th 1730, ...*The treasure Yo Hon. &c have been pleas'd to assign us ammog to 60000 rupees, 5981 of which being fanams or fifths...*

June 5th 1730, ...*The fifth rupees you promised to send us after the rains will be absolutely necessary......*

[728] Letters from Tellicherry, vols. 1-4, 1729-1736" vol. 2, p. 57 (printed by the Superintendent, Government Press, Madras, 1934):

May 29th 1733, ...*introduction of our fifths...*

[729] Letters from Tellicherry, vols. 1-4, 1729-1736" vol. 3, p. 63 (printed by the Superintendent, Government Press, Madras, 1934). Letter from Tellicherry to Anjengo:

November 9th 1734, ...*PS. The Honble Presidt & Col are pleased to advise us of their having directed you to send hither ten thousand rupees and a quantity of fanams as the latter cannot be put off with you but for loss; if they are fifths of rupees they will be very acceptable but if fanams [presumably tiny gold fanams] it will be entirely out of our power to disburse them*

it was put as a current year or a frozen year. Since the name of the issuing king, however, is quite certainly 'Alamgir, one would presume that the issue of these Billys was not begun before 1754, the date of his accession. It, therefore, seems that these coins were current with those discussed in the preceding paragraphs, especially those of type 2, and should this be the case, their issue adds to the volume of Billys that can be ascribed to this period. Their execution and other characteristics, however, are so markedly different from their contemporaries in circulation (Types 2, 4, 5 and 6) that it is likely that they were struck at a different mint. This would mean that, at least for the period under discussion, there could have been two mints striking Billys.

This brings us to an important question – where were the Billys actually struck? The 'T99' issues bear the mintname 'Talcheri', but conceivably were struck at Calicut. Documentary evidence makes it clear that in the years when Billys were first introduced, they were struck in Bombay and then transported to Malabar, to be put in circulation at Tellicherry (*vide supra* – "Letters from Tellicherry"). All the Billys, excepting the 'T99', bear the mint name 'Mumbai'. This would pose a question as to why the mint name on the 'T99' issue was inscribed as 'Talcheri'. A plausible answer to this is that in the immediately previous instance when the coins were being struck (i.e. before the Mysore conquest), the coins actually were struck at Tellicherry (Talcheri) even though they had the mint name on them inscribed as 'Mumbai'.

This observation may fail to convince if seen in the wake of what Pridmore describes, "Records have been traced in the Bombay mint accounts of silver Fanam coinages extending to the year 1796". But he does not give any reference to these 'accounts' and their contents. Further, Pridmore's mention itself is not free from doubt. In addition to his statement above, on p. 115 he states that "an entry in the records show that as late as the year 1796, the Bombay mint coined a quantity of silver Fanams for the west coast". When these two statements are compared it becomes clear that they do not suggest in any way that the Bombay mint was *solely* responsible for the production of Billys, or that there was a continuous production of the said specie at Bombay in the period c.1720-1796. Indeed, Pridmore appears to interpret the evidence in this way, and contends that other 'crude' varieties "appear to be locally minted imitations". Moreover, a situation wherein a supply of Billys was sent from Bombay to Tellicherry at sporadic intervals even though a mint was in operation at Tellicherry – especially to augment exigent currency demands – is not entirely unimaginable. The documentary evidence that Pridmore puts in print and that has subsequently been found, is unequivocal inasmuch as, for the early years, the minting of Billys was indeed carried out in Bombay[730,731,732], and by 1728 they were accepted in circulation by the local people[733]:

Since you say you are sufficiently supplied with fifths of rupees, we send you none of that specie, we are pleased however to find they are become current & that the country people prefer them to gold fanams, but we now send you for a tryall some of our new double copper pice to prevent the grievance you say your soldiers complain of by so considerable a loss in the exchange as three in sixteen tarrs the true value of a fanam, & are coining some single ones to send you by the next conveyance if by your advices we find they will be acceptable with you

Records also indicate that Billys were struck in 1730[734], 1733[735], 1734[736], 1738[737] as well as 1746[738]:

we shall supply you with a chest of fifths, & another of quarters, when they can be coined. By means of which we judge you will be able to keep the French, and other base Fanhams out of your treasury.

The fact that there exist two broadly different varieties of Billys in circulation for the period 1754-1763 (Type 3 and Types 2, 4, 5 & 6 – the first with the 'Alamgir' legend and the latter with *ghazi* or *manoos* legends) may indicate that while some of the Billys were struck at Bombay, others may actually have been struck at Tellicherry. This then raises the question of how to divide them into the product of 'local' and 'main' (Bombay) mints. Assuming that the supply from Bombay was sporadic, it would be reasonable to conclude that the rarer of the two types should be attributed to Bombay, while the rest were minted locally. Thus, it is likely that Billys of Type 3 were Bombay imports and those of Types 2, 4, 5 and 6 may have been struck locally.

---

[730] Letters to Tellicherry 1726-28, Vol. 1 p11 (1934). Government Press, Madras. Letter from Bombay to Tellicherry dated January 13th 1727:

We have likewise loaded on her six thousand sixty two Venetians & Gubbens, & forty eight thousand fifths of rupees…

[731] Letters to Tellicherry 1726-28, Vol. 1 p29 (1934). Government Press, Madras. Letter from Bombay to Tellicherry dated 1st December 1727:

We shall by the first secure conveyance send you twelve thousand rupees in fifths as you desire for defraying your charges over and above what we have already provided for your settlement.

[732] Letters from Tellicherry, vols. 1-4, 1729-1736 vol. 1, p. 14 (printed by the Superintendent, Government Press, Madras, 1934). Letter from Tellicherry to Bombay dated November 26th 1729:

The method we observe here in receiving the fifths of rupees when your Hon. &c. are pleased to supply us therewith, is to count and weigh then twice over, and by this means we do not make any mistakes in issuing them out

[733] Letters to Tellicherry 1726-28, Vol. 1 pp. 49-50 (1934). Government Press, Madras. Letter from Bombay to Tellicherry dated 20th September 1728.

[734] Letters from Tellicherry, vols. 1-4, 1729-1736 vol. 1, pp. 24, 19. Government Press, Madras.

[735] Letters from Tellicherry, vols. 1-4, 1729-1736 vol. 2, p. 57. Government Press, Madras.

[736] Letters from Tellicherry, vols. 1-4, 1729-1736 vol. 3, p. 63. Government Press, Madras.

[737] Letters from Tellicherry, vols. 1-4, 1729-1736 vol. 3, p. 4. Government Press, Madras.

[738] Letters to Tellicherry 1746-47, Vol. 1X p. 2 (1934). Government Press, Madras. Letter from Bombay to Tellicherry 21st August 1746.

Indeed, there seems to be more evidence to support this observation. There exists a 'crescent-marked' coinage of rupees in the name of Alamgir II bearing the mint name, Mumbai. It is likely that these Alamgir Rupees with the crescent mark were struck for circulation on the Malabar Coast. Even more interesting are the stylistic parallels that one can draw between the execution of these Rupees and Billys with the same RYs – from the standpoint of execution it is evident that the same 'hand' is responsible for cutting the dies of crescent-marked rupees as those of the Billys. The 'different' mint at this particular juncture could only have been Tellicherry and it would be reasonable to assume that the coinage at Tellicherry went under the pseudonym of Mumbai.

It is, therefore, likely that, for some time, the striking of Billys was carried out at two mints, Bombay and Tellicherry. However, there is reason to believe that, at some point, this dual coinage ceased. Judging purely from the coinage, one would hazard a guess that the turning point may be marked by the figure of a '5' being engraved upside down. Since the issues post-1763 predominantly exhibit this characteristic, it might be concluded that they were struck locally at Tellicherry (Obviously, the Billys of Type 9 must be excluded because it has been seen that they were struck at Calicut, p. 331). Since we have concluded that the T99 Billys followed type 9, the above argument provides a logical reason for the later occurrence of 'Talcheri' as the mint-name on the 'T99' issues.

The weight and diameter distribution of Billys

The following graphs show the weight and diameter distributions of the batch of Billys examined. The weight varies around 2.5g and the diameter around 12.7 to 12.8mm.

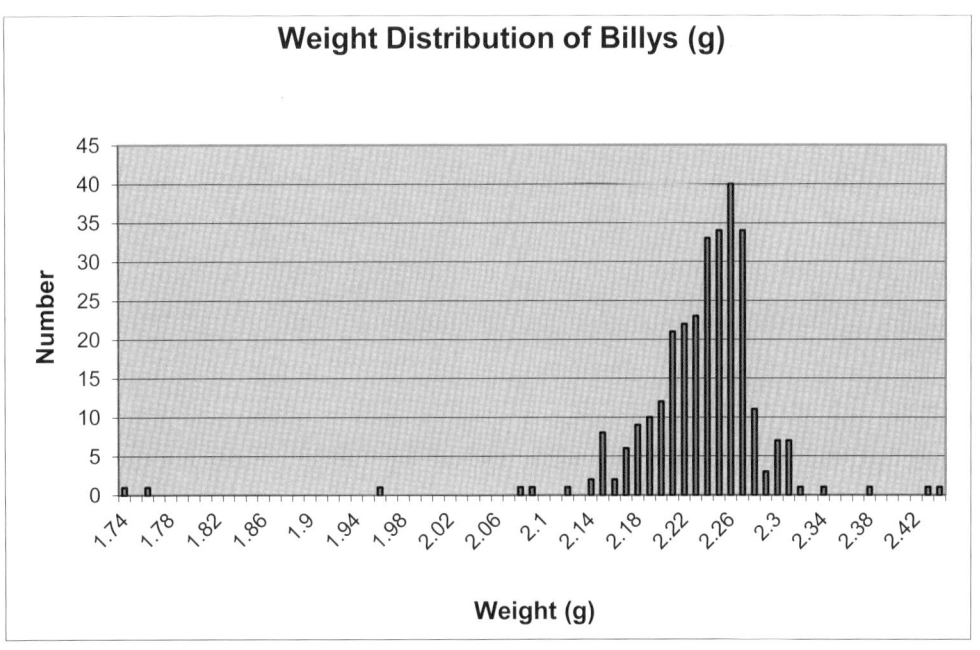

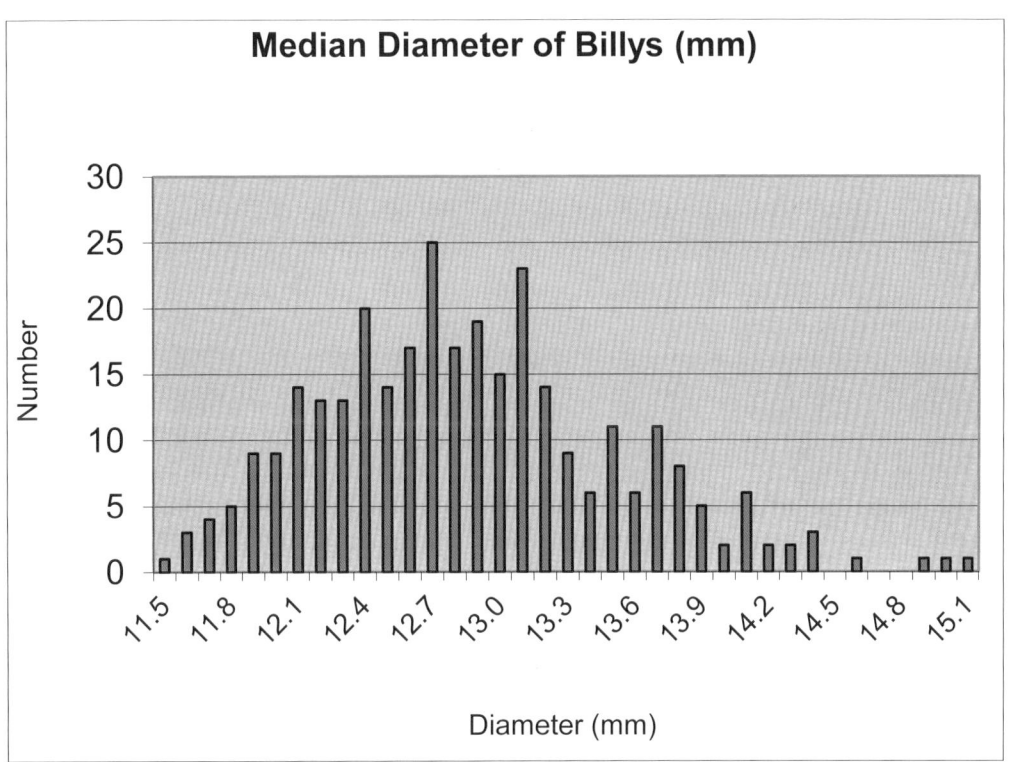

Eighth Rupee – Malabar Coast

Eighth Rupee

In marked contrast to all other silver coins, those bearing the figure 8 may be square or round, although the square coin may be a cut-down round coin. The legends and traces of the mintname (Mumbai) seen on these coins leave no doubt that they were struck for circulation in Malabar. Most striking is the fact that, instead of the usual numeral '5' in the centre of the obverse legend, these coins have '8'. The square coin weighs 1.42g, which is equal to an eighth of a rupee (two annas), but the round coins all seem to weigh around 2.5g, the weight of the fifth rupees. It is possible that the '8' was intentionally added to indicate an eighth of a rupee but why most have the weight of a fifth is not clear. Perhaps the round coins were meant to be cut down to the weight of an eighth?

These are an enigmatic coins – it is uncertain when they were struck because they lack any chronological detail. Stylistically, they comes very close to Billys of Type 2, because, as the obverse details reveal, the top word on them seems to be *ghazi*. This would mean that they probably were struck in the early 1750's. There is no documentary information available regarding the issue of an eighth rupee in Malabar but many sources mentioned by Pridmore indicate that the actual value of the Billys fluctuated, depending upon debasement and wear, anywhere between their face value, which was a fifth of a rupee, downwards to an eighth of a rupee. These fluctuations may have hampered one of the chief utilities of Billys – their direct convertibility from a regional standard to a much more widely accepted and 'national' rupee standard. The eighth rupee probably indicates an experiment whereby such a denomination was struck to counteract this fluctuation and thereby keep the advantage of the Billy-rupee conversion. However, the rarity of the coin is proof enough that this experiment, if experiment it was, failed to get off the ground.

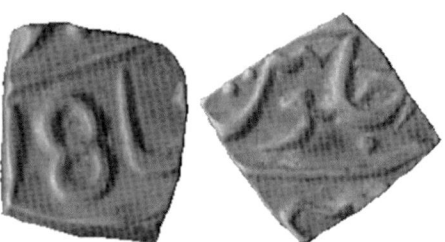

Square eighth rupee

Twelfth Rupee – For use at Anjengo

Twelfth rupee

An entry in the Consultations of the 22nd December 1727, refers to a twelfth rupee manufactured for use of the Anjengo factory[739]:

…..The President lays before the Board the mintmasters acco *of the Honble Companys bullion coin'd in the mint this present year ending the 18th instant amounting to rupees six hundred and eighty six thousand one hundred and twenty three, two quarters, fifty one Raes which is received into the Treasury and on examination found to balance the accot of silver consigned this Presidency.*

In said Acco *it is observed that Rupees one thousand nine hundred Seventy three made into Twelfths for Anjengo Settlement and sent thither in March Last are two p. Cent worse than Rupee Matt and Fifths of Rupees now Coining for Tellicherry three p. Cent worse which is thus Explained by the President – That he had Directed the former to be made two p. Cent worse. One p. Cent to provide for the Extra Charge of Coinage of that small money & one p. Cent is Gain'd to the Honble Company. The other he directed to be three p. Cent worse. Half p. Cent to defray the Extra Charge of the Workmanship & two & half P.C* *for an Equivalent to the Honble Company for their Passing at Tellicherry as fanams when Rupees are Exchanged at five or Eight fan* *& sometimes more.*
Which the Board Approve of.

Bhandare has published more information about this coin in the ONS newsletter[740]

Moghul-style – Gold

The only gold issue listed by Pridmore for use on the Malabar Coast is a pagoda (discussed below). Neither hoans nor mohurs nor their fractions were discussed by him, so, presumably, he did not know of the existence of any before 1809. Whether there was a gold coinage for Malabar during these years is therefore a question worth asking. After all, gold had been reaching the Malabar Coast in the form of Venetian sequins and when viewed in the wake of the Company's efforts in achieving convertibility between the Pagoda-Fanam and Mohur-Rupee systems, it would be

---

[739] Bombay Public Consultations, Friday 22nd December 1727. India Office Collections P/341/6:
[740] Bhandare 2005, ONSNL 182, p. 32

logical to presume there was room for some of this gold to be converted into coinages befitting one or both these systems. While reviewing his treatise in the course of facilitating the analysis of the Malabar coinage, it became evident that there are some coins that would fill this apparent gap. These are listed on p. 147 and numbered 8-11 in Pridmore's work. They are struck in the name of Alamgir II in denominations of 1, ½, ¼ and $\frac{1}{15}$th mohur. The half mohur (or half rupee in gold as Pridmore calls them) is not actually known to exist, but other coins are illustrated by Pridmore. They all reside in the British Museum collection. The most striking feature of these coins is their similarity in execution with some of the obverse and reverse die varieties of the Bombay Billys. The reverse of the mohur comes very close to reverse 4 of the Billys (see photos below), while its obverse resembles one of the rupees with a reverse similar to reverse 4 designs.

Reverse of Mohur   *Reverse 4 of Billy*

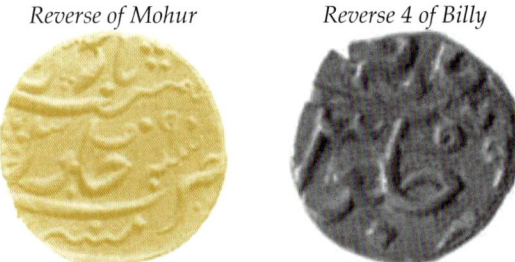

Comparison of reverse designs – Mohur/Billy, RY 9 (not to scale)

The reverse of the so-called ¼ mohur is almost identical to reverse 4 of the Billys in all its characteristics, while the obverse is again close to the rupees just mentioned.

Reverse of ¼ Mohur   *Billy Rev. 4*

Comparison of reverse designs – ¼ Mohur/Billy (not to scale)

In the case of the $\frac{1}{15}$th mohur (small 'rupee' of gold in Pridmore parlance), the illustration (in Pridmore) is not clear enough to reveal the reverse details but the obverse again shows similarity with the obverses of the mohur and the ¼ mohur. Two characteristics common to these coins are noteworthy - they all have the frozen RY 9 and also the 'lotus' mark (The RY detail is truncated on the ¼ Mohur). As is shown in succeeding sections, both these are peculiar aspects of silver issues of Malabar in the period 1763 to c.1778. It is, therefore, very likely that the gold coins, too, are issues intended for the Malabar region, although this is not so apparent for the $\frac{1}{15}$th mohur. It seems certain that the tiny gold rupees were intended for use in Bombay because there is an entry in the records referring to the counterfeiting of these coins[741] (12th December 1775):

There being several counterfeit gold rupees now circulating on the island, it is agreed to offer a reward of one thousand rupees to any person or persons who will make discovery of the persons concerned in coining them so that the offenders may be brought to justice.

There is more evidence to support this idea. The weight of the ¼ mohur that Pridmore lists is not equal to that denomination. A ¼ mohur should weigh in the range of 2.7 to 2.9g depending upon whether it was struck to a 10.8g or 11.6g standard. The specimen that Pridmore lists weighs 3.84g and is, therefore, considerably heavier than the normal weight for a quarter mohur. The only gold denomination that corresponds to that weight in the period we are talking about (1760-1780) is a pagoda (hoan). It is, therefore, evident that what has been listed by Pridmore is not a ¼ mohur at all – but a pagoda. As pagodas were not a preferred denomination in the Bombay region, it would mean that this particular issue was destined to be circulated elsewhere. The most likely area where it could have done so was south India. The resemblance in execution that the obverse of this coin has with the 'lotus'-marked rupees and the reverse with type 4 of the Billy reverses (see below) indicates that this coin is a pagoda struck for circulation on the Malabar Coast. This is also supported by the observation that its weight is not far removed from the only other gold coin from the same region and roughly proximate with it in chronological terms - the Cannanore Pagoda.

This attribution would give strength to the contention that some of the other denominations should be ascribed to Malabar as well, although it must be admitted that this inference is subjective in the absence of unequivocal evidence. The only other explanation that would account for the weight of 3.8g is that the coin may be a third of a mohur or 'Panchia'. Such coins were struck at a later date in the Bombay mint to encourage the convertibility of gold coins along the western coast, because coinage systems changed along a north-south axis, with the pagoda-fanam system gaining precedence over the mohur-rupee system. As the weight of the third mohur corresponded to that of a pagoda, the denomination had definite convertibility value. However, the history of such attempts as well as the launch of the denomination is a phenomenon that can be dated to the 1800's rather than the time period to which this particular coin can be attributed. So the probability of it being a pagoda is greater than that of it being a 'Panchia'.

---

[741] Bombay Consultations, 12th December 1775. IOR P/341/41 p619.

Pagoda – 1809

1809 pagoda

According to Pridmore[742], the gold issues of Malabar were limited to a solitary instance apart from the nondescript 'Vira Raya' Fanams. This was the 'Revenue Hoan' struck at the Calicut mint in 1809. Some thought should be given to this term and Pridmore's interpretation of it to make sense of certain features of the coin itself, like the obverse legend. His conclusion in identifying the coin, as such, stems from a draft recommendation made to the Bombay Government in 1793, wherein intentions to strike such a coin were mentioned. The main reason for this was to have a gold coin that would facilitate conversion with the 'Mohur-Rupee' system – it was intended to have the "Bombay Muhr divided into 5 parts, each part to be of the value of three rupees and the coin to be called a 'Revenue Hun'. By regulating the fanam and hun in this way, the Bombay rupee and muhr would become convenient multiples of the existing currency system". It is clear from this description that the term 'Revenue Hun' was employed with an emphasis on the convertibility aspects in mind, and not the actual collection of the revenue. It is evident that it denoted a coin that was readily acceptable in revenue transactions because of its easily convertible nature and, therefore, it was to be a 'preferred' coin for revenue payments. Designating a particular coin for revenue payments had been a practice of many 18th-19th century indigenous governments like the Marathas or the Nizam and there are enough documentary sources available to support its existence. The British in Malabar evidently resorted to it and therefore termed their gold coin a 'Revenue Hun'.

Pridmore, however, interprets the reference in a different manner. His interpretation is based on a revenue survey conducted after the Madras Government took charge of the province, in which it is indicated that the revenue of the province was tendered in "debased *Vira Raya* gold fanams, of which ten were termed a *Hoon*." References to 'Tellicherry' fanams and "debased silver coins called Billy fanams" were also made in the survey. In addition, a suggestion was made that the *Vira Raya* fanams should be recalled and the silver currency should be confined to the Bombay

---

[742] Pridmore p173

or Arcot rupee, and Madras fanams should replace the two smaller silver coins (i.e. the Tellicherry fanam and the Billys). Based on these references, and for reasons best known to him, Pridmore says, "from this it seems that the Tellicherry hun dated 1809 was struck at Calicut as a temporary measure for the revenue collections of that year.... with its issue, the recommendations made in 1793 for a *revenue hun* were completed".

Pridmore's inference defies logic. Nowhere in the sources is there an indication that this gold issue was indeed called a 'revenue hun', or for that matter that any other coin known by that term was ever struck. The recommendations were made in 1793 and the issue is dated 1809, and one would wonder why it took nearly sixteen years for them to be completed, when the mint at Calicut was up and running soon after 1793. Furthermore, the area of Malabar had been transferred from the Bombay Presidency, where the 1793 recommendation had been made, to Madras in 1800. The obvious indication seems to be that Pridmore has misconstrued the term as denoting a specific coin, as opposed to the documents, which point to it being employed as a generic term.

Pridmore's contention that the Persian legend on the obverse of these gold coins and also on the 'T99' type of Billys reads 'Nishini Sikka' may have something to do with his inference that the 1809 pagoda was a specially struck issue – because he takes the legend to mean 'government coin'. But there is nothing to suggest that 'Nishini' means 'Government' and Pridmore is silent on the source of this idea. 'Nishani' Hoan, as a generic term is found in several Maratha and other Deccani documents, but of a much earlier period and its exact connotation has been difficult to ascertain. In any case, if it had anything to do with the 'government' or revenue collection, its occurrence on the 'T99' Billys is rendered inexplicable, because there is no indication that those coins were struck under any such compliance factors as Pridmore attributes to the issue of the gold hoans. We, therefore, have to conclude that both Pridmore's reading of the legend and the meaning that he tends to derive from it, are incorrect. The word looks more like a corrupted form of 'Kampani Sikka' – especially when the nasal compound after 'K' is spelled in Persian with 'Noon' rather than 'Mim', similar to 'Mu-n-bai' instead of the phonetically closer 'Mu-m-bai' – and that would make better sense in the context of the coinage, than 'Nishini Sikka'.

Vir Raya Fanam – 1790-1809?

Calicut was captured by the British in 1790 and began to produce a new gold fanam, based on a style of fanam produced prior to 1773 and widely used throughout southern India. These tiny gold coins were called *Vir raya* fanams from one of the titles of the local Zamorin's family[743].

---

[743] Pridmore pp. 140-141, 173

Vir Raya fanam

Single, Half & Quarter Rupees – Alamgir II (1754 to 1759) [744]

Crescent-marked rupee, RY 9

The issue of 'crescent-marked' rupee coins starts with RY 5 of Alamgir II. The crescent appears to be a privy mark for the Malabar Coast. It was evidently added to distinguish the rupees intended for the Malabar Coast from the rupees circulating in Bombay, especially when both of them had the same mint name. In fact the 'machine-made Calcutta rupees' that Pridmore draws a comparison to while describing these coins, are a direct continuation of the coin type when it was reintroduced in 1810-1813. Even though struck at a much later date [745], they retain all the features of the Alamgir II issue in a rudimentary form – the Emperor's name, the privy mark itself, albeit inverted, the mint name 'Mumbai' and a flower as a differentiating mark. The crescent does not appear on the fifth rupees presumably because their circulation was limited to Malabar and as such there was no overlap with other similar-looking coins. Consequently there was no need to add a privy mark. However, a remnant of the crescent may be seen in the form of a 'circle' that appears on the obverse of fifth rupees of Type 8 – the issue that immediately preceded the 'T99' coinage and the first to be struck after the territory was wrested back from Mysore domination.

---

[744] Pridmore p. 155

[745] From Pr. – A mint statement showing coinages undertaken therein during the period 1801/2 to 1832/33, includes coinages of Bombay rupees in the financial years 1810-11 and 1812-13. The quantity struck amounted to 2,037,289. Pridmore also refers to an investigation made at Madras in 1808 which concluded that the Arcot Rupee and the Bombay rupee should remain the principal coins for the Malabar Coast. Where is this ref?

Other varieties of Malabar rupees bear a striking resemblance to fifth rupees of Types 5 and 6 in terms of execution. They are also in the name of Alamgir II and retain the RY 9, presumably as a frozen detail, but are much cruder in execution than other rupees bearing the same date.

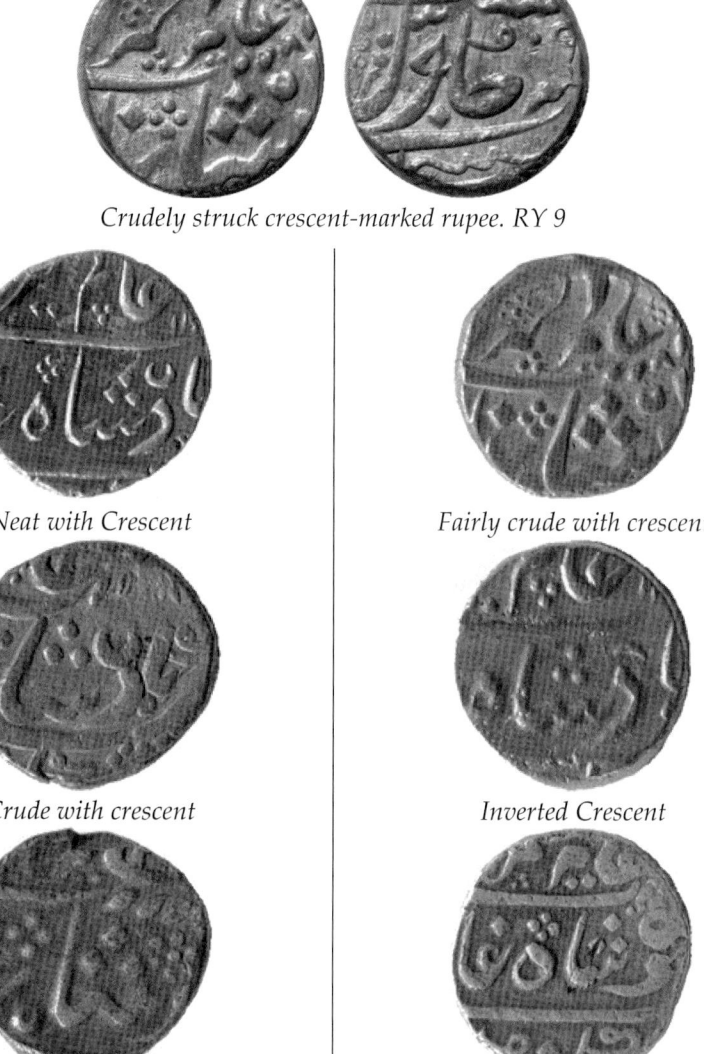

Crudely struck crescent-marked rupee. RY 9

Neat with Crescent

Fairly crude with crescent

Crude with crescent

Inverted Crescent

Dots forming a rosette

Circle

Obverses of types of rupee associated with the Malabar area, showing different symbols

The noteworthy difference (which is reflected in the fifth rupee design as well - see reverse 4 below for details) is the differentiating mark on the reverse. This is characteristically a flower with a stalk and two curves next to it. The mint name is apparently 'Munbai' but all the other traits of these coins conclusively point to the fact that they were not struck at Bombay. These coins can be further grouped into two series, which are linked with close stylistic similarities in their execution. The first retains the crescent mark whilst on the second this is replaced by another privy mark, a lotus-like symbol. It seems that the 'crescent-marked' rupees in this variety may have been struck locally at Tellicherry in the aftermath of the 'crescent'-marked rupees imported from Bombay. This is a phenomenon similar to that noted for fifth rupees. It is evident that the issue and circulation patterns for these derivative 'crescent-marked' rupees and their fractions match with those of the fifth rupees. It can, therefore, be inferred that the issue and circulation of these coins spanned the same period i.e. post-1763. In all likelihood the 'lotus' marked coins succeeded them, and probably continued being issued sporadically until 1778 when the Mysore occupation destabilised trade equations in the region.

There is a reference to coins being struck at the Bombay mint for use at Tellicherry but what denomination these might have been is not stated[746]:

...Ordered also that two lacks of Patna rupees be issued from the Treasury to the mint for being re-coined as soon as possible for the use of the Tellicherry factory

Calcutta Mint. Rupees for Use on the Malabar Coast – 1810 to 1813

Rupee struck at Calcutta

Early in the nineteenth century, rupees bearing a crescent were struck at Calcutta for use on the Malabar coast. Distinguishing features are the upside-down crescent and the neat appearance of the coins.

Copper Pattern Possibly for the Malabar Coast 1798

There is one enigmatic coin that Pridmore describes as a 'pattern' under his Madras listing (No. 341), which exhibits similarities to the Malabar issues in terms of execution and weight and is dated 1798. This date is very close to the introduction of the 'T99' silver fanam issue, which marked the introduction of a 'new coinage', struck at the Calicut mint. Pridmore's study of the coin suggests that it was partially machine-struck and the only place where this could have happened at that time was the Madras or Calcutta mints.

---

[746] Bombay Public Consultations, IOR P/341/41, 1775. p. 240. 28th March 1774.

Copper pattern for coin to be used in the Malabar area

Although full-scale coining machinery was not available at the Madras mint until 1806-07, it is possible that some experiments may have been carried out on machine punching of the blanks. Hence he attributes the piece to Madras. It seems likely that the piece was intended to be put into circulation in Malabar, judging by the weight standard and the style of execution, even though it may have been produced semi-mechanically in Madras. If this was, indeed, the case, it reveals an unknown experiment in Malabar coinage – an attempt at introducing machine-struck coins in the region. However, no evidence has been found in the EIC records to support this proposal. The rarity of the coin suggests that it was not put into circulation very widely, if at all - the reasons for which are beyond the evidence currently available. Apart from this solitary specimen, no other copper coin can be attributed conclusively to Malabar in the years after the territory was retrieved from Mysore rule.

Pice – c1700 to c1800

Pice 1729

The copper coins that Pridmore lists under his 'Malabar' section are characterised by certain features – all of them have a 'bale mark' on the obverse and an AD date on the reverse. The execution of the bale mark is typical – it is heart-shaped with the curves showing a depression on the sides just before they join to form the bottom end of the 'heart'. Also noteworthy is the fact that the obverse and reverse devices are enclosed in circular borders. The weights indicate that the coins are based on a 6 gm standard, with fractions weighing around 3 and 1.5 gm following in succession. They have been widely identified as 'Pice' from documentary evidence, but their denominational structure may have been based on a local standard in vogue on the coast further south, where a 6 gm copper coin equalled a 4-Cash denomination.

There are earlier references to copper coins in the records[747,748], but Pridmore's attribution of these coins to the Malabar Coast is based on two archival references[749,750] from 1742, from which he was able to determine that coins of approximately the weight referred to, and with the date 1742, were probably the coins destined for Tellicherry. Since these coins had a distinctive style it was possible to infer that other coins of this style but with different dates were also for use at Tellicherry.

The attribution of these pieces by Pridmore to the Malabar Coast is correct, but some of their aspects that he only hints at are worth discussing here. It is important to note that, like the Billys, the copper coins also fitted into a wider currency picture for the region. Although no indigenous authorities like the 'Ali Rajahs of Cannanore or the Zamorins of Calicut are known to have struck any copper coins, the French mint at Mahé produced a series of copper coins (see above, p. 327-328). As noted, these were called 'Biches' and there are important comparisons to be drawn between the French and British copper issues in Malabar to highlight their complimentary nature. Firstly, there exists a similarity in design for both these issues – the French issues bear a group of fleurs-de-lis, a symbol of the house of Bourbon and, therefore, an indication of French sovereignty, quite similar to the 'bale mark' that became associated with the British East India Company and its sovereign rights. The reverse designs of these coinages are the same: they both prominently show the AD date; the design element of enclosing both the obverse and reverse motifs in a circular border features in both these coinages; and lastly, the weights of the French biches and their denominational structure closely match those of the British issues.

---

[747] Bombay Public Consultations, 9th August 1741. India Office Collections P/341/12:
…they request to be supplied……the amount two thousand rupees in copper pice….

[748] Bombay Public Consultations, 14th August 1741. India Office Collections P/341/12:
…But in regard to the article of copper pice as they will only yield about rupees twenty three, one quarter and eighty seven raes per maund, and copper being now at a higher rate as was experienced in the sale of a parcel the 7th Instant, which went off at twenty four rupees, two quarters and twenty five raes the maund, a loss would arise to our Honble Masters were we to comply with that request. And we have been obliged to fall on the coining of tutenague [zinc] pice thro' the scarcity and dearness of copper, agreed to give the above reasons to Tellicherry, and at the same forward a muster of pice [presumably this means zinc pice] that provided they will answer, we will on receiving their answer send them a sufficient supply.

[749] Bombay Public Consultations, 4th February 1742. India Office Collections (taken from Pridmore):
As the gentlemen at Tellicherry have requested a supply of copper pice, the Board esteem it proper to reserve about 300 Surat mans to comply with the Tellicherry requests well as to meet the other services at this place.

[750] Bombay Public Consultations, 22nd February 1742. India Office Collections (taken from Pridmore):
In our Consultation of the 4th instant a quantity of copper was reserved for coining into pice for the service of this place and Tellicherry. The mint people have coined a pice of the size and weight of pennyweights 4 and grains 2 3/16 each pice.

Chapter 11 – Soho Mint

Copper Pice – 1791 to 1794

Up until very late in the eighteenth century, the copper coins of the Bombay Presidency were poorly manufactured and very crude although they do appear to have circulated quite widely in India (see earlier chapters). Plans to send copper coins manufactured in England, to India, started as early as 1786[751]:

We transmit you by this dispatch a small box containing some copper money which has been coined for the use of our settlement of Fort Marlbo'. A description of their weights and value as proportioned to a Dollar is also transmitted under No… in the packet. Eighteen tons thereof will be transmitted them as a supply for 1786 and a further 30 tons is intended them for 1787.

As we are desirous of extending the export of copper coin from this country, we renew our directions of the 30 November last, para 15, that you send us specimens of every species of copper money current on the Coast adding thereto your opinion how far it may be expedient to send you over a quantity and to what extent. Particular care will be taken here in execution of them and we conceive it may prove equally beneficial to us and useful to you to be furnished with regular supplies. Drawings for the reverse sides of the coins, a description of their proper weights calculated in avoirdupois grains, as also the number of each sized piece that will be given in exchange for rupees or pagodas, describing of what specie, must accompany your information.

Of the specimens now sent, the small size weighing 50 grains avoirdupois are rated to pass at 400 to the dollar, the middle size of 100 grains at 200 ditto and the large size of 150 grains at 133 ditto, which will serve for your guidance in calculating the proportions the coin shall bear to the rupee or pagoda, which we would have ascertained as near as possible by the same ratio.

In 1790, the Bombay authorities were informed that the existing circulating copper coins were to be replaced by a new coinage sent out from England. The Court of Directors in London considered that replacing all of the copper coin in one go would be too expensive and so they determined to do it gradually[752]:

We can by no means think of superseding the copper coinage current upon your coast by subjecting ourselves to the heavy loss that would attend the calling in that at present in circulation, as stated in these paragraphs, but as we have it much at heart to effect an improvement of this article, & are of opinion it may be effected gradually without any loss whatever, we propose by the ships of the next season to consign you a few tons by way of a trial & shall also hereafter keep you from time to time supplied therewith in about the same proportions that you shall conceive the old coinage may annually diminish. You will therefore

---

[751] Dispatches to Bombay. IOR E/4/1004 (1786-1786), p. 277. Dispatch dated 31st July 1787
[752] Dispatches to Bombay. IOR E/4/1006 (1789-90), p. 393-394 Dispatch dated 21st April 1790

after receipt of these advices desist from any further coinage of copper whatever & keep us regularly informed of the progress and success of the present undertaking.

However, by 1791 a decision had been taken to replace all circulating copper coins in one go with 100 tons of new coins. Accordingly, 35 tons of coins were sent from England to Bombay aboard the "Essex" with instructions not to open the casks until the rest of the shipment arrived[753]:

In the advices of the last season the Governor and Council were informed of the Court's intention in regard to the establishment of a new copper coinage for the use of Bombay and its subordinate settlements. I have now the Court's orders to desire you will communicate to the Governor and Council that instead of accomplishing the measure in the gradual manner therein pointed out, it has been resolved at once to abolish the old circulation & replace it by new issues. In pursuance of this determination, the Court gave directions for striking a quantity of copper to the extent of 100 tons which is equal to what you represent to be at present in use, & they were in hopes of being able to consign the whole by the last ship of this season, but having experienced a disappointment in this particular, not more than about 35 tons being yet executed, that quantity only is now forwarded upon the Essex, & the remainder will follow by the first ships of the succeeding season. In carrying this measure into effect, the Court have adopted the inscriptional devices recommended by the Bombay Provisional Mint Master but have made a material alteration in the proportions of the weight, as one of the [guiding] principles that weighed with the Court in adopting the measure was to give the public a coin not only surpassing the old in elegance of workmanship, but also in intrinsic value, whereby they are better secured from impositions in respect to its being counterfeited.

With the subsequent consignments, the Governor and Council will receive the needful instructions respecting the points to be attended to in calling in the old circulation & issuing the new, & until these shall be received, the Court direct that the parcels now sent may on their landing be housed and carefully secured 'till the period of their issue.

A further 65 tons was duly received aboard the "Rockingham" with instructions on how to issue them[754].

By the ship Essex of the last season we forwarded you 34 tons 15 cwt? 2lb Of copper coinage, part of the quantity of 100 tons intended for the use of Bombay and its subordinates which we hope has come duly to hand. The ships Rockingham and Sulivan now under dispatch will convey the remaining quantity.

Agreeable to the intimation conveyed in our secretary's letter of the 3rd May last we now proceed to communicate our instructions in respect to their disposition:

The coins were designed to be issued at a weight that would deter counterfeiting:

---

[753] Dispatches to Bombay. IOR E/4/1007 (1790-91), p. 549-551. Dispatch dated 3rd May 1791
[754] Dispatches to Bombay. IOR E/4/1008 (1791-93), p. 59. Dispatch dated 8th February 1792

As counterfeiting the circulating specie is an evil found to exist in most countries where the coin passes at a rate far exceeding its intrinsic value (all charges of workmanship included) we have for the purpose of checking a fraud of this nature resolved that the large pieces weighing 200 grains each shall be issued to exchange at the rate of 50 to a rupee. The second size weighing 150 grains, at 66⅔ to a rupee. The third size weighing 100 grains each, at 100 to a rupee. The smallest size weighing 50 grains, at 200 to a rupee.

At these rates of currency the public will receive for each rupee a quantity of pure copper equal in weight to 10,000 avoirdupois grains. By the coin now in circulation they receive only 7,314. The difference in this respect alone is nearly 50 per cent in their favour which, combined with the elegance of their appearance will we conceive not only secure them an early circulation in the Company's districts but be the means also of their finding their way into the more interior parts of the country.

Bombay was directed to issue a proclamation calling in the old coins in exchange for the new:

Upon the next of these advices, we direct that you forthwith issue a proclamation at the Presidency and the various subordinates signifying that all persons in possession of copper pice of the Company's former issues on or before the (naming such period as shall allow reasonable time both for the Presidency and subordinates) bring them in to the Company's Treasury or such other place as may be convenient for the purpose of receiving in lieu thereof an equivalent in the coinage now sent. Notice must also be given that from and after such date the old pice will be considered as no longer current. In the execution of this order you must be attentive to being imposed upon in the receipt of any other pice than those actually issued from the Company's mint. We apprehend if there are any counterfeits in circulation they may be easily distinguished from the true ones. As the measures pursued by former Government on a similar occasion (vide cons…) appear to be well calculated to secure our interests in this respect we refer you thereto, and direct that they be adopted in the present instance with any others that your experience and local knowledge may suggest necessary on the occasion.

The total quantity shipped was 660 casks weighing 100 tons 14 cwts 2 qtrs 13½ lbs[755], broken down as follows:

Casks	Tons	Hundred weight	Quarters	Pounds
99	15	1	3	22
159	25	11		9 ½
234	34	18		6
168	25	3	2	4

[755] Dispatches to Bombay. IOR. Dispatches to Bombay. E/4/1006, pp. 393-394.
  Ibid. E/4/1007, pp. 549-551.
  Ibid. E/4/1008, pp. 60-64.

From these numbers, together with the known weight of each piece, the approximate number of each denomination delivered to India can be calculated and compared to the number known to have been produced[756]. These numbers match extremely closely.

Weight of each piece (grains)	Calculated number delivered	Number given by Doty[757]
200	1,183,630	1,174,630
150	2,671,270	2,690,351
100	5,472,740	5,472,740
50	7,895,440	7,903,280

The coins were to be issued at the rate of:

200s @ 50 to a rupee

150s @ 66⅔ to a rupee

100s @ 100 to a rupee

50s @ 200 to a rupee

As recorded above, the intention of this rate was to make one rupee worth 10,000 grains avoirdupois weight of copper (e.g. 200 times 50) compared to the then existing rate of 7314 grains i.e. the coins contained less than their intrinsic value of copper. This, combined with the greatly increased quality of the design, would reduce the amount of forgery that was obviously worrying the authorities at the time.

Pice 1791. Wt = approx. 6.5g

Major Pridmore makes a rather ambiguous comment about the fact that the Company had established a mint at French Ordinary Court in London, and that this may have played a part in the decision to manufacture the coins in England, rather than locally in Bombay. This might imply that the coins were struck at a mint in

---

[756] Doty R. (1998). The Soho Mint and the Industrialization of Money, Spink & BNS, London, pp. 305-306, & p. 310.

[757] *ibid*

London. Doty has examined the records of the Soho mint in some detail, and his work confirms that these coins were indeed struck at Soho and not in London. This is also supported by the minutes of the meetings of the Court of Directors, who, on 13th January 1791, agreed that Boulton would be employed to undertake the coinage. On 2nd February a Mr. Williams was instructed to deliver 100 tons of copper to Mr. Boulton at Soho, Nr. Birmingham. In fact, Mr. Williams didn't think that he could deliver the copper before the middle of March, and it presumably took some time to complete the coinage, because on 24th August the Court agreed to advance Boulton £6000 for the work that he was then carrying out[758].

The coins were issued to the public by a resolution dated 7th August 1792[759]:

The Board now proceed to take into consideration the 7th, 8th, 9th, 10th, and 11th paragraphs of the Honble Company's commands of the 8th February last respecting the copper coinage sent out by the ships of the season. Agreed that a publication be issued as soon as possible signifying that all persons in possession of copper pice of the Company's former issues do, on or before the 30th September next, bring them into the Company's Treasury for the purpose of receiving in lieu thereof an equivalent in the new coinage now sent out and for which the public will receive for each rupee a quantity of pure copper equal in weight to 10,000 avoirdupois grains, and by the coin now in circulation they only receive 7314, the difference in this respect alone is nearly equal to 50 per cent. As it is hereby declared that from and after the 1st September next the old pice shall not pass current in this town or Island of Bombay nor shall any person or persons be obliged to receive or accept the same in payment and that any coin of a counterfeit kind shall immediately be cut in two and forfeited to the Company for which purpose the necessary minters and shroffs must attend at the Treasury, who shall be answerable for the receipt of any pice not coined by the Company, and the Assistant to the Treasurer must always be at the Treasury at the usual office hours that no favour or affection may be shown to anyone.

Agreed also that the Assistant to the Treasurer be directed to issue the new coinage after the 15th of the month in all payments to be made in pice.

Resolved also that copy of these paragraphs from the Company's commands and our proceedings thereon be sent to Tannah and Tellicherry and they be directed to acquaint us what quantity of pice they have in circulation in order that we may send a sufficient quantity of the new coinage to replace them.

Pridmore records that further deliveries occurred in 1792, 1793 and 1794. The 1792 delivery was probably the second load of 1791 coins and perhaps more of these were delivered in 1793 although this has not been confirmed. However, a second coinage

---

[758] Minutes of the Meetings of the Board of Directors. IOR B/112, p. 764.

Ibid. B/112, p. 825.

Ibid. B/112, p. 877.

Ibid. B113, p. 374.

[759] Bombay Public Consultations, IOR P/342/14, 1792. p. 507. Resolution 7th August 1792

was undertaken in 1793 and shipped to India in 1794 (Doty). The coinage consisted of double pice, pice and half pice. The coins were dated 1794[760].

We approve the several measures you have taken for issuing the copper coinage and have given the needful directions for putting in hand the additional quantity you have indented for. Attention will also be paid to your observation respecting the different sizes and you will in all probability receive the whole quantity by some of the later ships of the season.

We shall also communicate to the person employed in manufacture your remarks in respect to the difference in outturn by weight and tale and desire that the like if possible may be avoided in any future consignment.

Pice 1794

The 1½ pice denomination was discontinued, presumably because it caused confusion with the double pice. It would appear from the records that 50 tons of copper coins were delivered this time[761]:

The Accomptant General lays before the Board a statement of the difference in produce between delivering the copper coin by weight and by tale.

This showed that approximately 50 tons of coins had been delivered by three ships: The Raymond, the Woodford and Sir Edward Hughes

Privy Marks 1791-1794

Dot below V

No dot below V

---

[760] Dispatches to Bombay. IOR E/4/1009 (1793-94), p. 53. Dispatch dated 19th February 1794
[761] Bombay Public Consultations, IOR P/342/19, 1795. p. 126. 20th January 1795

On some coins, dots appear in the centre of the flan on either obverse or reverse or both. These may have been privy marks deliberately added in the mint but more likely they reflect the way in which the matrix dies were produced (i.e. some kind of compass device use to mark out the circle). If this assumption is correct then these dots are mistakes and should have been removed before dies were produced.

Varieties 1791-1794

Some parts of the design vary more than others, e.g. particularly the pivot on the reverse. This observation reveals something about the way that the dies were produced. It seems likely that the majority of the design was put onto some master punch and other features, such as the pivot, were added later in the multiplication process

| Long Pivot | Medium Pivot | Short Pivot | Fat Pivot | No Pivot |

Variation in pivots on pice coins

Copper Pice 1804

Double pice, 1804

In December 1802, the mint and assay masters wrote to the Bombay Government suggesting that more copper coins should be sent from England and that a good profit could be made from this[762]:

…It is not only very expensive to coin copper in this country but it is impossible with the present machinery to do it well. It is harder than silver or gold & the natives work it with less

---

[762] Bombay Public Consultations. IOR P/343/1. p. 4198. Letter from Le Messurier & Scott to Bombay board, dated 12th December 1802

perfection. On this account it is certainly desirable to have the copper money sent hither from England.

Should the present price of copper in England permit it, we would recommend that the copper be sent of the same weight that they were in 1792, for any [change] in the coinage should be avoided unless very necessary. If however it should not be advantageous to the Honble Company of such a weight, we do not see any material objection to reduce it to the rate that we proposed in our letter of the 15th November. We refer to that letter regarding the copper coins of 6 reas which weigh 150 grains. We are still of opinion that they are unnecessary or inconvenient & that the other three pieces of 200, 100 & 50 grains each are quite sufficient for the purposes of this place.

By the accounts of copper coins in the Accountant General's office, it appears that the Honble Company in the years 1791, 2, 3 & 4 sent them from England to the amount of rupees 70,592 . 2 . 57 by which there was a clear profit of rupees 38,194 . 2 . 75. This is a considerable advantage & it is one that will continue, for our copper coins are in demand not only in the countries subject to the Company's authority but in a certain degree also in the Mahratta Territories. Whither they are gradually carried & never return to us.

It would be very desirable to be able to determine the amount of copper coin required for this side of India but after all our inquiries we are not as convinced that it can be done with much accuracy. If this Government should judge it proper to give them currency at Surat & its neighbourhood, which has hitherto not been the case, a much greater number could be disposed of than has yet been practicable.

Mr Galley, the Mint Master in 1788 stated that the amount of copper money in circulation under this Presidency was about the following values:

In Bombay	*Rupees 100,000*
Salsette & [Carabjah]	*Rupees 25,000*
Tellichery	*Rupees 10,000*
Total	*Rupees 135,000*

Since that time the whole provinces of Malabar & Canara have come under the Company's authority & our money will be received in every part of them, for altho' they are placed at present under the Madras [Presidency] yet the commercial connection & natural intercourse remain with Bombay.

Upon the whole we are of opinion that the Company may now send out from England a quantity of copper coin equal to a lac of rupees, a certain proportion in each ship. This may probably be disposed of without much delay, when an estimate may be formed with more certainty then at present of the annual quantity that is required for this Presidency.

This was passed to London with a recommendation that it be accepted:

Ordered that the subject of the above letter be brought to the notice of the Honble the Court of Directors by the ships under dispatch with a recommendation that the quantity of copper coin suggested in the concluding paragraph may be consigned to this Presidency.

Appendix

1. AH/AD/RY Concordance

Alamgir II	AH	Date year commenced	RY	Date RY Commenced
	1167	29-10-1753	1	03-06-1754
	1168	18-10-1754	2	23-05-1755
	1169	07-10-1755	3	11-05-1756
	1170	26-09-1756	4	01-05-1757
	1171	15-09-1757	5	20-04-1758
	1172	04-09-1758	6	09-04-1759
	1173	25-08-1759		Died 29th Nov 1759

Shah 'Alam II	AH	Date year commenced	RY	Date RY Commenced
	1173	25-08-1759	1	30-11-1759
	1174	13-08-1760	2	18-11-1760
	1175	02-08-1761	3	07-11-1761
	1176	23-07-1762	4	28-10-1762
	1177	12-07-1763	5	17-10-1763
	1178	01-07-1764	6	06-10-1764
	1179	20-06-1765	7	25-09-1765
	1180	09-06-1766	8	14-09-1766
	1181	30-05-1767	9	04-09-1767
	1182	18-05-1768	10	23-08-1768
	1183	07-05-1769	11	12-08-1769
	1184	27-04-1770	12	02-08-1770
	1185	16-04-1771	13	22-07-1771
	1186	04-04-1772	14	10-07-1772
	1187	25-03-1773	15	30-06-1773
	1188	14-03-1774	16	19-06-1774
	1189	04-03-1775	17	09-06-1775
	1190	21-02-1776	18	28-05-1776
	1191	09-02-1777	19	17-05-1777
	1192	30-01-1778	20	07-05-1778
	1193	19-01-1779	21	26-04-1779
	1194	08-01-1780	22	14-04-1780
	1195	28-12-1780	23	04-04-1781
	1196	17-12-1781	24	24-03-1782
	1197	07-12-1782	25	14-03-1783
	1198	26-11-1783	26	03-03-1784
	1199	14-11-1784	27	19-02-1785
	1200	04-11-1785	28	09-02-1786
	1201	24-10-1786	29	29-01-1787
	1202	13-10-1787	30	18-01-1788
	1203	02-10-1788	31	07-01-1789
	1204	21-09-1789	32	27-12-1789
	1205	10-09-1790	33	16-12-1790
	1206	31-09-1791	34	06-12-1791
	1207	19-08-1792	35	24-11-1792
	1208	09-08-1793	36	14-11-1793
	1209	29-07-1794	37	03-11-1794

Appendix

Shah 'Alam II (cont)	AH	Date year commenced	RY	Date RY Commenced
	1210	18-07-1795	38	23-10-1795
	1211	07-07-1796	39	12-10-1796
	1212	26-06-1797	40	01-10-1797
	1213	15-06-1798	41	20-09-1798
	1214	05-06-1799	42	10-09-1799
	1215	25-05-1800	43	30-08-1800
	1216	14-05-1801	44	19-08-1801
	1217	04-05-1802	45	09-08-1802
	1218	23-04-1803	46	29-07-1803
	1219	12-04-1804	47	18-07-1804
	1220	01-04-1805	48	07-07-1805
	1221	21-03-1806	49	26-06-1806
				Shah Alam died on 18th Nov 1806

Muhammad Akbar II	AH	Date year commenced	RY	Date RY Commenced
	1221	21-03-1806	1	18-11-1806
	1222	11-03-1807	2	08-11-1807
	1223	28-02-1808	3	27-10-1808
	1224	16-02-1809	4	16-10-1809
	1225	06-02-1810	5	06-10-1810
	1226	26-01-1811	6	25-09-1811
	1227	16-01-1812	7	14-09-1812
	1228	04-01-1813	8	03-09-1813
	1229	24-12-1813	9	23-08-1814
	1230	14-12-1814	10	13-08-1815
	1231	03-12-1815	11	01-08-1816
	1232	21-11-1816	12	21-07-1817
	1233	11-11-1817	13	11-07-1818
	1234	31-10-1818	14	30-06-1819
	1235	20-10-1819	15	18-06-1820
	1236	09-10-1820	16	08-06-1821
	1237	28-09-1821	17	28-05-1822
	1238	18-09-1822	18	18-05-1823
	1239	07-09-1823	19	06-05-1824
	1240	26-08-1824	20	25-04-1825
	1241	16-08-1825	21	15-04-1826
	1242	05-08-1826	22	04-04-1827
	1243	25-07-1827	23	23-03-1828
	1244	14-07-1828	24	13-03-1829
	1245	03-07-1829	25	02-03-1830
	1246	22-06-1830	26	19-02-1831
	1247	12-06-1831	27	09-02-1832
	1248	31-05-1832	28	28-01-1833
	1249	21-05-1833	29	18-01-1834
	1250	10-05-1834	30	07-01-1835
	1251	29-04-1835	31	27-12-1835
	1252	18-04-1836	32	16-12-1836
	1253	07-04-1837		Died 28th Sep 1837

Bahadur Shah II	AH	Date year commenced	RY	Date RY Commenced
	1253	07-04-1837	1	28-09-1837
	1254	27-03-1838	2	18-09-1838
	1255	17-03-1839	3	08-09-1839
	1256	05-03-1840	4	27-08-1840
	1257	23-02-1841	5	17-08-1841
	1258	12-02-1842	6	06-08-1842
	1259	01-02-1843	7	26-07-1843
	1260	22-01-1844	8	15-07-1844
	1261	10-01-1845	9	04-07-1845
	1262	30-12-1845	10	23-06-1846
	1263	20-12-1846	11	13-06-1847
	1264	09-12-1847	12	01-06-1848
	1265	27-11-1848	13	20-05-1849
	1266	17-11-1849	14	11-05-1850
	1267	06-11-1850	15	30-04-1851
	1268	27-10-1851	16	19-04-1852
	1269	15-10-1852	17	08-04-1853
	1270	04-10-1853	18	28-03-1854
	1271	24-09-1854	19	18-03-1855
	1272	13-09-1855	20	06-03-1856
	1273	01-09-1856	21	23-02-1857
	1274	22-08-1857	22	13-02-1858

Deposed 29th Mar 1858

Index

Index

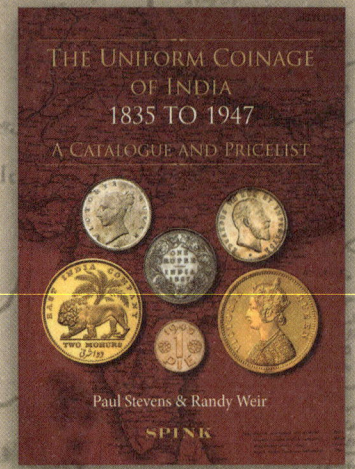